C0-FTQ-910

Jacksonian Panorama

THE AMERICAN HERITAGE SERIES

The American Heritage Series

under the general editorship of

ALFRED F. YOUNG *and* LEONARD W. LEVY

Jacksonian Panorama

edited by

Edward Pessen
City University of New York

THE BOBBS-MERRILL COMPANY, INC.
INDIANAPOLIS

in memory of
Dorothy and Harry Barlin

Copyright © 1976 by the Bobbs-Merrill Company, Inc.
Printed in the United States of America
All rights reserved. No part of this book shall be reproduced or transmitted in any form or by any means, electronic or mechanical, including photocopying, recording, or by any information or retrieval system, without written permission from the Publisher:

The Bobbs-Merrill Company, Inc.
4300 West 62nd Street
Indianapolis, Indiana 46268

First Edition
First Printing 1976

Library of Congress Cataloging in Publication Data

Pessen, Edward
Jacksonian panorama

(American heritage series, AHS-85)
Bibliography: p. xvii
United States—Social conditions, politics, and government—second quarter of nineteenth century—Journals, diaries, addresses, reports, correspondence, editorials, circulars.
HN54.J3 309.1'73'081 75-20140
ISBN 0-672-60142-7 (pbk.)

Contents

Foreword

We Americans love to put labels on the "periods" of our history, and no matter how much the historians tell us that newer scholarship suggests the names should be changed, the tags stick. Most historians don't want us to call the period from the mid-1820s to the mid-1840s "The Age of Jackson." Jackson, they say, was not that dominant; political life was not that crucial; and so many important things were happening that had no relationship to Jackson or the Jacksonians. They especially don't want it called the "Age of Jacksonian Democracy" or the "Era of the Common Man," because they have grave doubts as to whether it was either.

Our editor Edward Pessen has done as much as any scholar to give a newer, more hardheaded view of the period. But the title *Jacksonian Panorama* is a compromise. *Jacksonian* seems to be inevitable—otherwise how would anyone know what historical time this book covers? *Panorama* is meant to suggest that the selections encompass not Jackson alone, not politics alone, not national affairs alone, but the whole sweep of American life, especially its society and culture. The editor is avowedly skeptical of the conventional pieties about "equality," "democracy," and Jackson. This might be expected of someone whose books include *Riches, Class, and Power Before the Civil War*, which deals with the inequality of American society, and *Most Uncommon Jacksonians*, which deals with the radical leaders of the early labor movement who also do not fit the Jacksonian stereotype.

In 1954 the American Heritage Series brought out *Social Theories of Jacksonian Democracy*, edited by Joseph Blau, a pioneering volume still happily in print, which directed attention to a group of thinkers then almost lost to historians. Professor

Pessen's anthology of original sources is interestingly different, reflecting the points of focus of recent scholarship. It deals not so much with thinkers as with doers, not so much with thought in the formal, systematic sense as with values and traits of the people at large. It deals not only with the democratic side but with the diverse, often raw, currents jostling each other which could be antidemocratic, inequalitarian, and racist. It is a collection, therefore, much like the period itself: big, multifaceted, fascinating, and bursting with vitality.

This book is one of a series created to provide the essential primary sources of the American experience, especially of American thought. The American Heritage Series constitutes a documentary library of United States history, filling a need long felt among scholars, students, libraries, and general readers for authoritative collections of original materials. Some volumes illuminate the thought of significant individuals, such as James Madison or John Marshall; some deal with movements, such as the Antifederalist or the Populist; others are organized around special themes, such as Puritan political thought or American Catholic thought on social questions. Many volumes take up the large number of subjects traditionally studied in American history for which surprisingly there are no documentary anthologies; others pioneer in introducing new subjects of increasing importance to scholars and to the contemporary world. The series aspires to maintain the high standards demanded of contemporary editing, providing authentic texts, intelligently and unobtrusively edited. It also has the distinction of presenting pieces of substantial length which give the full character and flavor of the original. The American Heritage Series is, we believe, the most comprehensive and authoritative of its kind.

Alfred F. Young
Leonard W. Levy

Selected Bibliography

No short bibliographical comment could possibly do justice to the vast literature on the topics treated in this book. Fortunately a number of essays have been published in recent years on different facets of the antebellum decades. Valuable bibliographical studies include those of Alfred A. Cave, *Jacksonian Democracy and the Historians* (Gainesville: University of Florida Press, 1964); Edward Pessen, *Jacksonian America: Society, Personality, and Politics* (Homewood: Dorsey, 1969), 352–394; Louis Filler, *The Crusade Against Slavery*, 1830–1860 (New York: Harper and Row, 1960), 281–304; C. S. Griffin, *The Ferment of Reform, 1830–1860* (New York: Thomas Y. Crowell, 1967) which is essentially an extended bibliographical essay; and Pessen, *Riches, Class, and Power Before the Civil War* (Lexington, Mass.: D. C. Heath, 1973), Bibliography. In view of the availability of these comprehensive essays, this bibliography can be brief, citing only publications that have strongly influenced my thinking.

Useful recent discussions of antebellum society are by Oscar Handlin, *Boston's Immigrants, 1790–1880: A Study in Acculturation* (New York: Atheneum, 1968, revised and enlarged edition); Stephan Thernstrom and Richard Sennett, eds., *Nineteenth-Century Cities: Essays in the New Urban History* (New Haven: Yale University Press, 1969); Peter R. Knights, *The Plain People of Boston, 1830–1860: A Study in City Growth* (New York: Oxford University Press, 1971); D. Clayton James, *Antebellum Natchez* (Baton Rouge: Louisiana State University Press, 1968); Sam Bass Warner, *The Private City: Philadelphia in Three Phases of Its Growth* (Philadelphia: University of Pennsylvania Press, 1968); Kenneth W. Wheeler, *To Wear a City's Crown: The Beginnings of Urban Growth in Texas, 1836–1865* (Cambridge: Harvard University Press, 1968); Gerald N. Grob, *The State and the Mentally Ill: A History of Worcester State Hospital in Massachusetts, 1830–1920* (Chapel Hill: University of North Carolina Press, 1966); Pessen, "A Social and Economic Portrait of Jacksonian Brooklyn: Inequality, Social Immobility, and Class Distinction in the Nation's Seventh City," *New-York Historical Society Quarterly*, LV (October 1971), 318–353; Benjamin J. Klebaner, "The Home Relief Controversy in Philadelphia, 1782–1861," *Pennsylvania Magazine of History and Biography*, LXXVIII (October 1954), 413–423; Pessen, "The Egalitarian Myth and the American Social Reality: Wealth, Mobility, and Equality in the 'Era of the Common Man,' " *American Historical Review*, 76 (October 1971), 989–1034; and Tamara K. Hareven, ed., *Anonymous Americans: Explorations in Nineteenth-Century Social History* (Engelwood Cliffs: Prentice-Hall, 1971).

There has been a particularly great outpouring of publications on politics and political issues. Significant studies that have appeared in the past five years include John M. McFaul, *The Politics of Jacksonian Finance* (Ithaca: Cornell University Press, 1972); Pessen, "*Should* Labor Have Supported Jackson? or Questions the Quantitative Studies Do Not Answer," *Labor History*, XIII (Summer 1972), 427–437; Donald B. Cole, *Jacksonian Democracy in New Hampshire, 1800–1851* (Cambridge: Harvard University Press, 1970); Ronald P. Formisano, *The Birth of Mass Political Parties, Michigan, 1827–1861* (Princeton: Princeton University Press, 1971); James Rogers Sharp, *The Jacksonians versus the Banks: Politics in the States After the Panic of 1837* (New York: Columbia University Press, 1970); Herbert Ershkowitz and William G. Shade, "Consensus or Conflict? Political Behavior in the State Legislatures during the Jacksonian Era," *Journal of American History*, LVIII (December 1971), 591–621; Joseph C. Burke, "The Cherokee Cases: A Study in Law, Politics, and Morality," *Stanford Law Review*, 21 (February 1969), 500–531; Gerald S. Henig, "The Jacksonian Attitude toward Abolitionism in the 1830's," *Tennessee Historical Quarterly*, XXVII (spring 1969), 42–56; Wayne W. Smith, "Jacksonian Democracy on the Chesapeake: Class, Kinship and Politics," *Maryland Historical Magazine*, LXIII (March 1968), 55–67; Robert E. Shalhope, "Jacksonian Politics in Missouri: A Comment on the McCormick Thesis," *Civil War History*, XV (September 1969), 210–225; Michael Wallace, "Changing Concepts of Party in the United States: New York, 1815–1828," *American Historical Review*, LXXIV (December 1968), 453–491; Edward Pessen, "Who Governed the Nation's Cities in the Era of the Common Man?" *Political Science Quarterly*, LXXXVII (December 1972), 591–614; and Pessen, ed., *New Perspectives on Jacksonian Parties and Politics* (Boston: Allyn and Bacon, 1969).

Antebellum reform is treated in David Brion Davis, ed., *Ante-Bellum Reform* (New York: Harper and Row, 1967); Walter Hugins, ed., *The*

Reform Impulse, 1825–1850 (New York: Harper and Row, 1972); Michael B. Katz, *The Irony of Early School Reform: Educational Innovation in Mid-Nineteenth Century Massachusetts* (Cambridge: Harvard University Press, 1968); Bertram Wyatt-Brown, *Lewis Tappan and the Evangelical War Against Slavery* (Cleveland: Press of Case Western Reserve University, 1969); Pessen, *Most Uncommon Jacksonians: The Radical Leaders of the Early Labor Movement* (Albany: State University of New York Press, 1967); Philip J. Staudenraus, *The African Colonization Movement 1816–1865* (New York: Columbia University Press, 1961); Pessen, "Perfectionist Social Thought in the Jacksonian Era," in Michael McGiffert and Robert Allen Skotheim, eds., *American Social Thought: Colonial Beginnings to the Civil War* (Reading: Addison-Wesley, 1972), 277–336; Robert S. Pickett, *House of Refuge: Origins of Juvenile Reform in New York State, 1815–1857* (Syracuse: Syracuse University Press, 1969); William W. Cutler III, "Status, Values and the Education of the Poor: The Trustees of the New York Public School Society, 1805–1853," *American Quarterly*, XXIV (March 1972), 69–85; and Raymond A. Mohl, *Poverty in New York, 1783–1825* (New York: Oxford University Press, 1971); and David J. Rothman, *The Discovery of the Asylum: Social Order and Disorder in the New Republic* (Boston: Little, Brown, 1971).

Introduction

The second quarter of the nineteenth century has long been described by American historians as the "Jacksonian era" or the "era of the common man." These interchangeable labels provide a strong clue to the interpretations or historical appraisals of scholars using them. Reference to an age of Jackson suggests a belief not only that Andrew Jackson was the dominant figure of the period but that he and his party waged political battles of decisive importance in behalf of democracy and the plebeian orders against the forces of aristocracy and large property. The companion rubric, "era of the common man," indicates that the masses came into their own, and not only politically. It suggests that while in the political arena Jackson was championing the cause of ordinary folk, the entire society was being democratized. Supposedly, poverty largely disappeared, wealth became more equally distributed, class lines more fluid, ascension up the social ladder a commonplace, and opportunity to achieve success came within the grasp of almost all persons. The flourishing of many reform movements in the latter part of the period has been widely regarded as yet one more testimony to the expansion both of social democracy and the influence of the common folk who most benefited from it.[1]

1. Influential works that contain some of these interpretations are: Arthur M. Schlesinger, Jr., *The Age of Jackson* (Boston: Little, Brown, 1945); Dixon Ryan Fox, *The Decline of Aristocracy in the Politics of New York 1801–1840* (New York: Columbia University Press, 1919); Claude G. Bowers, *Party Battles of the Jackson Period* (Boston: Houghton Mifflin, 1922); Carl R. Fish, *The Rise of the Common Man, 1830–1850* (New York: Macmillan, 1927); John William Ward, "The Age of the Common Man," in John Higham, ed., *The Reconstruction of American History* (New York: Harper and Brothers, 1962), 82–97; Alice Felt Tyler, *Freedom's*

While this roseate version of antebellum American civilization is a most comforting one, it appears to fly in the face of a great deal of evidence. Modern researchers, particularly those who have used statistical or quantitative approaches, have brought to light a great weight of data that sharply challenges, if it does not totally refute, the notions of Jacksonian egalitarianism and the dominance of the common man.[2] Of course much of the recently disclosed evidence was either unknown or unavailable to persons living one hundred and forty years ago. And yet, as the documents that follow make clear, many respected contemporaries reported a wide variety of American practices that were alien to the egalitarian interpretation. This is not to say that misery reigned supreme during the era or that the civilization developing in the New World was a mere mirror image of the society of the Old. As European visitors were quick to discern, American civilization was unlike theirs in myriad ways, tangible and intangible. Where an American institution was similar to a European, it typically had a distinctive character that set it apart from the latter. But the differences were not so clear-cut as we have been taught to believe. We have liked to think that the United States was unique in being freer, happier—simply better than other countries. The evidence suggests rather that the United States was different. The complex actuality of life here fell far short of the idealized portrait drawn by yea-saying contemporaries and later scholars.

Perhaps the most original feature of the American scene was its people. A heterogeneous mixture of nations and races, Americans over the course of time had evolved a distinctive blend of traits and values that fascinated—and often repelled—most foreign

---

Ferment, Phases of American Social History (Minneapolis: University of Minnesota Press, 1944); and Joseph L. Blau, ed., *Social Theories of Jacksonian Democracy* (Indianapolis: Bobbs-Merrill, 1954).

2. Stuart Blumin, "Mobility and Change in Ante-Bellum Philadelphia," in Stephan Thernstrom and Richard Sennett, eds., *Nineteenth-Century Cities: Essays in the New Urban History* (New Haven: Yale University Press, 1969), 165–208; Sidney H. Aronson, *Status and Kinship in the Higher Civil Service* (Cambridge: Harvard University Press, 1964); and Edward Pessen, "The Egalitarian Myth and the American Social Reality: Wealth, Mobility, and Equality in the 'Era of the Common Man,'" *American Historical Review*, 76 (October 1971), 989–1034.

visitors as well as their own more sensitive and reflective countrymen.[3] Many scholars continue to be wary of the concept of national character, suspicious of the chauvinistic uses to which it has sometimes been put, and unconvinced that territorial boundaries separate the human family by personality as well as by nationality. It is hard to disagree, however, with David Potter that "to deny that the inhabitants of one country may, as a group, evince a given trait in higher degree than the inhabitants of some other country amounts almost to a denial that the culture of one people can be different from the culture of another people." [4] National cultures *do* differ and so do the ways of the people who shape and are in turn shaped by these cultures. Certainly articulate Americans and foreign travelers were convinced that the inhabitants of the United States were a breed apart. The detailed report they left depicts a people markedly unlike Europeans of the time.

One of the most widely noted facets of the Americans' personality was their unwillingness to accept or believe anything but the best about themselves. The trait is displayed in our own time not least in the insistence that most of the Europeans who visited our country in the decades before 1850—particularly the best and most discerning of them—found Americans to be an attractive people whose very faults were charming.[5] The documents in Part One, a representative sampling of contemporary observations on American traits and values, do not substantiate this happy judgment. Most visitors, whether dull or bright, put together the same mournful catalog of American characteristics. Alexis de

3. Edward Pessen, *Jacksonian America: Society, Personality, and Politics* (Homewood: Dorsey, 1969), chap. 2, "The Jacksonian Character: A Contemporary Portrait of American Personality, Traits, and Values," 5–38.

4. David M. Potter, "The Quest for the National Character," in John Higham, ed., *The Reconstruction of American History*, 209. See also Michael McGiffert, ed., *The Character of Americans: A Book of Readings* (Homewood: Dorsey, 1964).

5. Henry Steele Commager, *The American Mind* (New Haven: Yale University Press, 1950); and Commager, ed., *America in Perspective: The United States through Foreign Eyes* (New York: Random House, 1947), introduction, xvi, xx. In the latter, Commager writes that the version of European visitors "added up to a flattering picture," while "jaundiced criticism came from the second-rate commentators rather than from the magisterial ones."

Tocqueville, widely regarded as the most brilliant of them all, was perhaps the most unsparing. If, as Henry Steele Commager has observed, Tocqueville indeed wrote "the most penetrating interpretation of American character ever penned," Americans can derive little comfort from the fact. For as I have noted elsewhere, Tocqueville took "a very dim view of that character. Like so many other observers, he marveled at American *achievements* in politics, technology, construction, transportation. When his work is examined closely for its views on character and personality, however, it discloses an American who is paltry, anti-intellectual, unattractively materialistic, boring, insecure, vulgar, boastful, snobbish, pompous, conformist, cold and humorless, whose optimism concerns low goals, whose egalitarianism is disquieting, whose gregariousness derives from his own smallness as an individual." [6]

The unlovely ways of Americans as individuals may help better to explain some of the measures taken by American government, whether toward Indian tribes, Negro slaves, free blacks, or uncompromising dissenters, and the more unattractive features of American society. The surest thing about these traits is that they were not genetic in origin, but rather were molded by the unique temporal history and cultural circumstances of the United States. The boastfulness alluded to above, as well as the insecurity and extreme sensitivity about the opinions of others, for example, seem obviously to have been related to the youthfulness of the nation and the crudeness or pristine quality of much of its civilization.

The rawness of Jacksonian society manifested itself in various ways. In contrast to most of the great European nations, whose essential boundaries had been reached several centuries earlier and had subsequently remained static, the United States was a nation in constant growth. Throughout the period, new states were being carved out of the huge, largely uncolonized territory west of the Mississippi that had been purchased at the beginning of the century. Life in the more isolated areas of this domain was primitive, lonely, often dangerous (documents 18–22). Cities that

6. Pessen, *Jacksonian America*, 35, n. 2.

sprang up in the more settled districts of the new West were surprisingly similar to their eastern seaboard counterparts, not least because their leaders went to great pains to make them so.[7] And yet their limited cultural resources and their crude techniques for dealing with the problems that inevitably confront crowded urban populations betokened their recent origins. As for the cities on the Atlantic, although they had been created during the seventeenth century, they were old only in an American sense, not comparing in antiquity with the great urban centers of Europe, some of which went back almost a millennium. In the United States of the 1820s and 1830s older cities, as well as the newer, relied on methods of street cleaning, fire fighting, police protection, conveying water to residents, and safeguarding health that had changed little since colonial times (documents 26–29). One of the significant developments of the second quarter of the nineteenth century was precisely the movement of urban taxpayers to increase drastically the quantity of public expenditures for these and related problems, and in so doing to accomplish marked qualitative improvement in the techniques for dealing with them.[8]

The "transportation revolution" that charmed the army of foreign travelers, lured European capital, intruded itself into national politics as the issue of "internal improvements," and bound this sprawling, constantly expanding nation into a single market, was in a sense an outgrowth of the growing pains of a youthful nation that had as yet populated only a small portion of its territory. The profusion of turnpikes, canals, steamboats, and railroads that traversed the American landscape during the era enabled newer settlements to flourish by shipping their products to older ones.

7. Richard C. Wade, *The Urban Frontier: The Rise of Western Cities, 1790–1830* (Cambridge: Harvard University Press, 1959).

8. James F. Richardson, "The Struggle to Establish a London-Style Police Force for New York City," *New-York Historical Society Quarterly*, XLIX (April 1965), 175–198; Roger Lane, *Policing the City: Boston 1822–1885* (Cambridge: Harvard University Press, 1967); Jacob Judd, "Policing the City of Brooklyn in the 1840s and 1850s," *Journal of Long Island History*, VI (Spring 1966), 13–22; and Judd, "Brooklyn's Health and Sanitation, 1834–1855," *Journal of Long Island History*, VII (Winter-Spring, 1967), 40–52.

Frederick Jackson Turner's portrait of the American's mental characteristics was inferred from the circumstances of frontier life and has been criticized accordingly by modern scholars.[9] The traits that a primitive social environment *should* have produced were not necessarily the traits that did emerge: history is seldom a perfectly logical exercise. And yet there seems little doubt that the rude manners, the openness and hospitality, the simplicity whether of the fare or the discourse, and the proneness to violence observed in the West were products of the region's circumstances.

The sale of human beings in a nation that had come into being proclaiming that all men are created equal can be and has been construed in many ways, not least as a source of the psychic tension that is invariably produced when the contradiction between the ideals and the practice of a people is too flagrant. The subject is of course too vast and too complex to be dealt with satisfactorily in a brief passage. Whatever else they were, slave sales were a sign too of the rawness of antebellum society.

The United States of the era was the closest thing to a democracy in the western world, under the definition of the term that relates it to the extent of the suffrage. Certainly that was the definition that was most popular in this country. In the first three decades of the nineteenth century, freehold and property requirements for voting were discarded, at least for adult white males, in most elections in most of the states. It needs to be kept in mind that the situation was a complicated one in which typically the qualifications for voting within a state differed, depending on whether the elections were national, state, or local, varying too according to the level of office. In many cities during the 1830s, for example, the qualifications for voting for the mayor were greater or more demanding than were those for aldermanic elections. Even such astute visitors as Tocqueville and Michael

9. Frederick Jackson Turner, "The Significance of the Frontier in American History," American Historical Association, *Annual Report for 1893* (Washington, 1894), 199–227; George W. Pierson, "The M-Factor in American History," *American Quarterly*, XIV (Summer Supplement, 1962), 275–289; and David M. Potter, *People of Plenty: Economic Abundance and the American Character* (Chicago: University of Chicago Press, 1954), 142–160.

Chevalier believed that propertyless "commoners" truly ruled the United States, because they possessed the vote.

Actually, small cliques or entrenched machines appear to have exercised control in the days of popular suffrage as they had done before. One of the features of the period was the replacement of the caucus system for choosing candidates by the nominating convention. This seemed a most significant democratic change, for by it the people's elected representatives met in open session to select candidates, in contrast to the earlier system under which small groups of legislators made the nominations at closed meetings. Modern studies reveal, however, that under the new system as under the old, small "juntos" and "regencies" continued to handpick candidates and run the parties in most states.[10] Formal political platforms were eschewed by the major parties, while the actual policies their officeholders followed were determined not by the electorate who ostensibly ruled but by party managers and leaders. That such policies were invariably promoted as according with the popular will and conducive to the popular interest proved only the astuteness of the propagandists who said these things, not the truthfulness of what they said. In the cities of the nation the expansion of suffrage had very little effect on the relatively patrician character of mayors, the inordinate wealth and status of councils and boards of aldermen, or the kind of legislation they characteristically enacted. Then, as earlier, municipal laws appear to have benefited large property owners above all.[11]

Political campaigns were bitterly, often violently, waged in antebellum America, doubtless suggesting to some observers that contests of such intensity necessarily concerned issues of great moment. DeWitt Clinton, himself a victim of the near incessant scheming and vituperation of the Tammany and Regency ma-

10. Richard P. McCormick, *The Second American Party System: Party Formation in the Jacksonian Era* (Chapel Hill: University of North Carolina Press, 1966); and Edward Pessen, *Jacksonian America: Society, Personality, and Politics*, 154–179, 211–247, 308–346.

11. Edward Pessen, "Who Governed the Nation's Cities in the 'Era of the Common Man?' " *Political Science Quarterly*, LXXXVII (December 1972), 591–614.

chines in New York State, had shrewdly noted that in many cases the pettier or smaller the issues in an election the greater the hostility of the men and factions engaging in it. Democracy affected the flavor, the tone, the techniques or the form rather than the substance of politics in Jacksonian America (documents in Part Three). "The spirit of the times," in Martin Van Buren's phrase, required ambitious politicians to adopt new devices and to speak a new language, and the more resourceful of them proved capable of doing so. The result was a lively politics marked by demagogy, bombast, mudslinging, scurrilous propaganda. The "new men of politics," many of them self-made opportunists of humble background, had no compunctions about resorting to demagogic practices that might have given pause to some of their more patrician predecessors. (Too much should not be made of this point, however, in view of the low tone of Federalist-Republican party battles in the 1790s and early 1800s.)

Perhaps the most characteristic feature of the politics of the period was the frank adoption by the major parties of the "spoils system." The displacement of talented political officeholders by members of the party faithful was not an unknown practice of the "first party system" in the era of Washington, Jefferson, and Hamilton. What was new in the removals of the national administrations that followed John Quincy Adams's was the frankness with which party loyalty superseded competence as the chief criterion for appointment, the extent of the removals (granting that Jackson's alleged "wholesale turnover" was not nearly so great as had been believed), the adoption of the policy by both major parties, and the increasing reliance of these parties on the financial contributions of those they favored with office. The spoils system was of decisive importance in turning the second party system into the modern party system. In the modern party system, major parties are essentially pragmatic coalitions that concentrate on winning and holding office rather than achieving an ideological program, basing themselves on broad constituencies of diverse persuasion, enforcing loyalty not by appeals to a philosophical program but rather by promises of practical rewards or punishments. Favors in the form of appointments to office and, on the other hand, finances contributed by the beneficiaries of favors, were the cement binding the major parties together.

The intense interest of the major parties in success at the polls did not mean that they were totally devoid of principle or solely preoccupied with electoral victory. Democrats and Whigs differed on a number of interesting and important issues. But these issues were not ideological in the usual meaning of that term. They were not concerned with the distribution of wealth, let alone the capitalistic system, and had little connection either with the needs of the common man or the furthering of egalitarianism that ostensibly characterized the era.

Equality was more apparent than real. Charmed by the absence of formal class distinctions or of an official aristocracy in the United States, Tocqueville and most other travelers concluded that this was therefore an egalitarian society whose choicest spots were available to all but a few pariahs.[12] The visitors were struck by the relative absence of paupers or beggars on the streets, the seeming prosperity (for most of the period) of the working class, the wide extent of landownership and the happy lot of farmers, the great number of "self-made men"—or men who claimed they were—and the constant flux that appeared to mark the competition for worldly goods. Surface differences between American and European society thus blinded observers to underlying similarities.

Keen-eyed travelers who reported American manners and public behavior accurately were unable to describe or analyze the society with similar sureness, since the social situation was not as readily discernible as were the traits and habits of the people. Accurate *appraisals* of society, in contrast to accurate *reporting* either of personal traits or social incidents, required a knowledge of under-the-surface social evidence that no contemporary visitor possessed. That visitors could not possibly have been aware that subsequent research would refute the chief assumptions of the

12. For a fuller statement of the "egalitarian" thesis see Pessen, "The Egalitarian Myth and the American Social Reality", 989–991. Also see Pessen, *Jacksonian America*, 39–46, for a discussion of the role played by European visitors in winning acceptance for the egalitarian view.

egalitarian thesis, better explains their acceptance of false notions; it does not make the latter any the less erroneous. In fact, paupers existed in great numbers here, if great pains were indeed taken to keep them off the streets.[13] Workers and most farmers in America led precarious, economically marginal existences. Their real wages were low, the quality of their lives was bleak, the proportion of the community's wealth they owned was minuscule.[14] Far from being self-made, almost all rich men were relatively well born. They had not only inherited much of their wealth but had typically held on to it stubbornly through all manner of vicissitudes that befell the economy.[15] Flux characterized not "vertical" movement up and down the social ladder but rather the "horizontal" movement of great numbers of poor people into and out of the nation's villages and cities, a migration that only further reduced an influence in the community that had been slight to begin with.[16]

A number of contemporaries somehow managed to penetrate the fog of yea-saying propaganda that permeated the intellectual atmosphere of the time. The most glaring inequities in this society affected "minorities." (The term requires quotation marks because

13. Raymond A. Mohl, *Poverty in New York 1783–1825* (New York: Oxford University Press, 1971); and Benjamin J. Klebaner, "Public Poor Relief in America, 1790–1860" (Columbia University doctoral dissertation, 1952).

14. Gavin Wright, " 'Economic Democracy' and the Concentration of Agricultural Wealth in the Cotton South, 1850–1860," *Agricultural History*, XLIV (January 1970), 63–94; Hugh Hill Wooten, "A Fourth Creek Farm from 1800 to 1830," *North Carolina Historical Review*, XXX (April 1953), 167–175; Robert H. George, "Life on a New Hampshire Farm, 1825–1835," *Historical New Hampshire*, XXII (Winter 1967), 3–16; Stuart Mack Blumin, "Mobility in a Nineteenth-Century American City: Philadelphia, 1820–1860," (University of Pennsylvania doctoral dissertation, 1968), 46–48; and Pessen, "The Egalitarian Myth and the American Social Reality", 1020–1027.

15. Pessen, "Did Fortunes Rise and Fall Mercurially in Antebellum America? The Tale of Two Cities: Boston and New York," *Journal of Social History*, 4 (Summer 1971), 339–357; and Pessen, "The Egalitarian Myth and the American Social Reality," 1004–1015.

16. Stephan Thernstrom and Peter R. Knights, "Men in Motion: Some Data and Speculations about Urban Population Mobility in Nineteenth-Century America," *Journal of Interdisciplinary History*, I (Autumn 1970), 7–35; and Peter R. Knights, *The Plain People of Boston, 1830–1860: A Study in City Growth* (New York: Oxford University Press, 1971).

these groups when combined constituted most of the nation's population.) Blacks when slaves were treated as subhuman, whether patronizingly so as in the case of house slaves, or more brutally so as in the case of southwestern field slaves. Blacks when free were humiliated in countless ways (documents 61 and 62); discrimination continuing from the cradle to the grave affected their economic circumstances, their living conditions, their status, and their educational and other opportunities. The leading modern scholar of free northern Negroes concludes that their situation was superior to that of their enslaved brothers only in that they could manage to protest against it—unfortunately, however, to no avail.[17]

Women were as a matter of course treated as subordinate creatures. When of the working class, they typically got a fraction of the wage paid men for doing the same work, while often relegated to "woman's work" for wages that were ludicrously low (document 65). When of the middle and upper classes, they lived confined lives that were sterile and more humiliating than those experienced by European women of roughly similar status (documents 63 and 64). Urged by contemporary publicists to serve as pure, pious, acquiescent adornments to men, with marriage—preferably well before age twenty—as their sufficient goal in life,[18] there is some question as to the extent to which such ideals were realized. A recent examination of the lives of Southern women discloses that practice often differed sharply and unpleasantly from a theory that stressed the genteel and toil-free lives led by ladies.[19] Most women did not align themselves with Abby Kelley, Frances Wright, Margaret Fuller, the Grimké sisters, and those other champions of women's rights, who both by advocacy and by example urged their sisters on to lives of real meaning and achievement. For while the quality of life available to the

17. Leon Litwack, *North of Slavery, The Negro in the Free States, 1790–1860* (Chicago: University of Chicago Press, 1961).

18. Barbara Welter, "The Cult of True Womanhood: 1820–1860," *American Quarterly*, XVIII (Summer 1966), 151–174.

19. Ann Firor Scott, *The Southern Lady: From Pedestal to Politics 1830–1930* (Chicago: University of Chicago Press, 1970).

American white woman was found wanting when measured against an absolute standard of justice and equality, it nevertheless compared favorably with the lot of women elsewhere. Opportunities for work outside the home, property rights in marriage, the availability of divorce, relative freedom from chaperoning, a deference from men that for all the derision it evoked from feminists was doubtless preferable to the coldness and near brutality that were shown women in other places, represented in fact a superior situation. Probably more important in inducing American women to accept their lot than were their actual conditions of life, was a persistent indoctrination that undeviatingly over the generations had suggested that femininity and all it connoted in the way of subordination flowed inevitably from femaleness. The fact remains that during the "era of the common man," in the United States as in Europe women were denied political rights as well as economic, social, intellectual, and moral equality.

Precise evidence on the real income and standard of living for the white male working population is lacking for the second quarter of the nineteenth century. Inadequate census data leave the industrial worker's lot a mystery, while the "life-style" of farmers, devoid as it was in so many cases of measurable income, forecloses the possibility of accurately recording their level of consumption. Contemporary accounts that probed beneath the surface of the American manual worker's "healthful looks," "cheerful demeanor," and "attractive clothing," disclosed an unattractive existence that was poor, precarious, unhealthful, and culturally meager (documents 56–60). This was the picture drawn not alone by the numerous labor journals and smaller agricultural press of the time[20] but by sensitive middle-class observers as well. When these reports are supplemented by the recent disclosures of the glaring maldistribution of wealth that characterized both

20. Richard H. Abbott, "The Agricultural Press Views the Yeoman: 1819–1859," *Agricultural History*, XLII (January 1968), pp. 35–48; and Pessen, "*La Première Presse du Travail: Origine, Role, Idéologie,*" in Jacques Godechot, ed., *La Presse Ouvrière, 1819–1850* (Paris: *Centre National de La Recherche Scientifique*, 1966), 43–67.

urban and rural communities in all sections of the nation, it becomes clear that the great mass of Americans who labored for a living derived very little from the cornucopia that allegedly rained plenty over the land.

In the face of these and other inequities, the nation had an abundance of issues crying out for consideration if not resolution. But the "genius of American politics" then as later appears to have consisted in the disposition by the major parties either to avoid dealing with these issues or to attempt to give the electorate the impression that they were being met head on, when in fact matters that were at best tangential to the electorate were under discussion in Washington or in state capitals.

A nice example of this pattern is afforded by the "bank war" (documents 72 and 73). President Andrew Jackson in the summer of 1832 vetoed the bill passed by Congress that called for the re-charter of the second Bank of the United States when its charter would lapse in 1836. Following his reelection in the fall of 1832, Jackson the next year moved to "remove the deposits" of federal funds from the bank (actually to cease storing *future* deposits with it). Despite congressional opposition and the refusal of two secretaries of the treasury to go along with his policy, Jackson, with the approval of a complaisant third secretary of the treasury, Roger Brooke Taney—appointed after one predecessor had been kicked upstairs and the other fired outright—"removed" the deposits, which commencing October 1, 1833, were to be stored with selected state banks. Contemporaries in and out of Jackson's party, like later scholars some of whom were otherwise sympathetic to his policies and critical of Nicholas Biddle, the imperious president of the second bank, assailed Jackson's policy. They have claimed that the bank had exercised a constructive, stabilizing role in its relations with private and state banks throughout the nation, that its own notes were relatively sound, that its policies had promoted economic growth of the West and South and were popular in all sections of the country, and that the state banks which replaced it as repository of federal funds were typically less ably led and inclined to follow a more erratic banking policy than had "Biddle's Bank."[21] The new depositories were quite rightly dubbed "pet banks" by the nation at large, in view of the fact that Jackson's chief interest in selecting the first local banks was the Democratic politics rather than the banking experience or ability of their directors.[22]

In the veto message, as in the Democratic propaganda that followed, the president's policies were referred to as antiaristocratic, even anticapitalistic, in the interests of honest labor while opposed to those of monopolistic property. It is true that Jackson appears to have been motivated in part by a suspicion of all banks and that some Democrats came to be increasingly hostile toward the "paper profits" that banks earned for their directors and stockholders. The struggle over banking policy, however, represented no attack either on capitalism or the profit system, for all the rhetoric portraying the issue in such terms.

On the state as well as the national level Democrats and Whigs took opposing positions on interesting issues that riveted the attention of the American people.[23] Divisions over the tariff, distribution of land revenues to the states, reapportionment of congressional seats, territorial expansion, the power of the executive, currency policy, or internal improvements were by no means insignificant. Yet a form of political alchemy would be required to transform these matters into issues affecting the distribution of wealth, influence, status, or opportunity within the country. In a number of cases distinctively unlike types of men were attracted

21. Jean Alexander Wilburn, *Biddle's Bank: The Crucial Years* (New York: Columbia University Press, 1967); Bray Hammond, *Banks and Politics in America from the Revolution to the Civil War* (Princeton: Princeton University Press, 1957); Walter B. Smith, *Economic Aspects of the Second Bank of the United States* (Cambridge: Harvard University Press, 1953); Thomas P. Govan, *Nicholas Biddle, Nationalist and Public Banker* (Chicago: University of Chicago Press, 1959); and Robert V. Remini, *Andrew Jackson and the Bank War* (New York: W.W. Norton, 1967).

22. Frank Otto Gatell, "Spoils of the Bank War: Political Bias in the Selection of Pet Banks," *American Historical Review*, LXX (October 1964), 35–58.

23. Joel H. Silbey, *The Shrine of Party: Congressional Voting Behavior, 1841–1852* (Pittsburgh: University of Pittsburgh Press, 1967) and Herbert Ershkowitz and William G. Shade, "Consensus or Conflict? Political Behavior in the State Legislatures during the Jacksonian Era," *Journal of American History*, LVIII (December 1971), 591–621.

to the one party or the other, divided by life-style, religious denomination, ethnic or national identification, race, occupation, and the general character of the communities in which they lived.[24] But the differences were not between social radicals and conservatives. The contests between the major parties were not issueless affairs, waged by men whose only interest was the spoils of office. Many of the participants did care about the points in dispute. The fact remains, however, that these controversies were typically peripheral to the issue of egalitarianism.

The avoidance of the great issues by the major parties led to the formation of new parties. The Working Men's parties of the 1820s and 1830s arose in many of the large cities and were critical of the nation's social and political institutions. The Working Men had a small following and failed to make a significant impact during their brief time in the sun.[25] The failure of the major parties to confront the slavery issue led in 1840 to the creation of the Liberty Party. While the new party did not make clear precisely what measures it would take against the South's "peculiar institution," its failure to attract more than a handful of voters that year probably testified more to the indifference and the racial feelings of most white voters than to the party's own ineptness.

Not all the great national issues were avoided. The southern Indian tribes, whose lands were coveted by white settlers and speculators, and who were ordered to remove by state governments responsive to the clamor of these interest groups, were in fact driven across the Mississippi by the federal government. Andrew Jackson brushed aside federal treaties, Supreme Court decisions, and Whig opposition, expelling the most civilized

24. John Vollmer Mering, *The Whig Party in Missouri* (Columbia: University of Missouri Press, 1967); Donald B. Cole, "The Presidential Election of 1832 in New Hampshire," *Historical New Hampshire*, XXI (Winter 1966), 32–50; Lee Benson, *The Concept of Jacksonian Democracy: New York As a Test Case* (Princeton: Princeton University Press, 1961); and Ronald P. Formisano, *The Birth of Mass Political Parties: Michigan, 1827–1861* (Princeton: Princeton University Press, 1971).

25. Pessen, "The Workingmen's Movement of the Jacksonian Era," *Mississippi Valley Historical Review*, XLIII (December 1956), 428–443; and Pessen, "The Working Men's Party Revisited," *Labor History*, IV (Fall 1963), 203–226.

Cherokee on the ground, among others, that they were not civilized (documents 82–84). In supporting the contentions of Georgia against the tribes, Jackson took a position that helped bring on the nullification crisis later in 1832. Some nullifiers appear to have believed that a president of such strong state rights views would sympathize with their assertion that states had the right to nullify or refuse to honor federal policy they held unconstitutional. They did not count on the president's inconsistency, his hatred of John C. Calhoun, and his strong nationalism (document 75). The president's nationalism also accounted for the belligerence of his policy toward the French government during his second term, although his own notorious temper appears to have played an important part in aggravating that particular crisis (document 76).

Several other national issues or nonissues of the era appear to have arisen largely because of personality conflicts. Such was the "Eaton affair," which split Jackson's cabinet and titillated the capital early in Old Hickory's first administration. Democratic propagandists and some later scholars interpreted the snubbing of the wife of Jackson's secretary of war as a disguised Calhounist plot to take control of the administration.[26] Whether the uproar in fact masked a struggle for power or represented merely a president's overweening ego, as some Jackson supporters thought it did, it clearly had nothing to do either with the interests of havenots or with any other great national theme. The same can be said about the "corrupt bargain," which the Jacksonians utilized brilliantly to help win the 1828 election for The Hero on the ground that he had been corruptly denied the highest office four years earlier when Henry Clay allegedly sold his soul to install John Quincy Adams in the presidency in return for the secretaryship of state (document 68). That a great mass of voters appear to have taken such trivia seriously while giving little hearing to calls for social change, abolition, or protection of Indian rights should

26. Richard H. Brown, "The Missouri Crisis, Slavery, and the Politics of Jacksonianism," *South Atlantic Quarterly*, LXV (Winter 1966), 55–72; Robert V. Remini, *Andrew Jackson* (New York: Harper and Row, 1969), 112–116; and Arthur M. Schlesinger, Jr., *The Age of Jackson*, 54.

dispel romantic notions about the idealism of the common man. Pragmatic or opportunistic politics that dealt with the great issues primarily through rhetorical flourishes, while in fact avoiding them or brushing them only lightly, did indeed accord well with the "genius" of the American people.

Local political issues were typically concerned with mundane matters (documents 85 and 86), their contestants not purporting to deal with grandiose principles. City governments more readily than larger units took on down-to-earth problems of direct concern to people of all classes, such as public education, the welfare of the indigent, the treatment of criminals, the removal of refuse, or the regulation of local commerce. The niggardly expenditures set aside for some of these responsibilities pointed toward the power that great property owners and taxpayers wielded over municipal affairs.

One explanation of the many reform movements that flourished during the era is precisely the indifference of government and the failure of the great men of politics to deal or even to try to deal with the new problems plaguing the nation. "Voluntary associations" were created nationally and locally to help cope with the consequences of a vast influx of poor Irish and other European immigrants, urban overcrowding and inequality, the business cycle, not to mention the continuation of such earlier evils as slavery, insufficient and stigmatized education for the poor that required pauper's oaths, and the neglect of the congenitally enfeebled (documents in Part Six).

Tocqueville wrote that Americans "of all conditions" joined these organizations. From the rosters of leaders and members of hundreds of these associations in the northeastern cities, it appears rather that the minority of Americans who were of prosperous condition predominated in and determined the policies of these groups.[27] The motives of men engaged in social benevolence were most varied and often defied detection. Altruism, religious zeal, noblesse oblige, humanitarianism, social guilt, self-interest broadly

27. Pessen, *Riches, Class, and Power Before the Civil War* (Lexington, Mass.: D.C.Heath, 1973), chap. 12.

construed, civic mindedness, and in some cases a desire to achieve "social control," played varying parts in the socially purposive activities undertaken by relatively well-to-do men.[28] Scholars have been extremely interested in fathoming the hidden inner springs of social involvement. Perhaps an even more fruitful line of inquiry would be to analyze the policies and actions of the reform associations and the consequences of their behavior. For ultimately the historical effect and significance of these groups will be determined by what they did rather than by what their leaders may have felt.

Not that the behavior of reform organizations was simple or uncomplicated. Most of them would work within the system, trying to ameliorate the condition of some disadvantaged or aggrieved group. While means of amelioration they advocated might vary (documents 91–94, 97–98), they typically had one thing in common: society's fundamental institutions were not to be tampered with (document 99). This was so because in the operative philosophy of most reform groups, the blame for social disharmony, as for the failure of individuals or of classes of men, lay not with society or its institutions but with individuals. Failure was said to result from weaknesses that were supposedly within the power of the individual to reject or overcome. Regeneration required reeducation of the individual in the broadest sense, including inculcation of the central truth that he had been responsible for his own downfall. Where the causes of misery were clearly congenital, as with the crippled and enfeebled, the path to be followed was of course a different one, modified by the impossibility of achieving success in the ordinary sense and by society's interest in treating such unfortunates in a manner both rational and ethical.

28. There are interesting discussions of motives in Robert S. Pickett, *House of Refuge: Origins of Juvenile Reform in New York State, 1815–1857* (Syracuse: Syracuse University Press, 1969); Raymond A. Mohl, *Poverty in New York 1783–1825*; M.J. Heale, "The New York Society for the Prevention of Pauperism, 1817–1823," *New-York Historical Society Quarterly*, LV (April 1971), 153–176; Martin B. Duberman, ed., *The Antislavery Vanguard: New Essays in the History of Abolitionism* (Princeton: Princeton University Press, 1965); and David J. Rothman, *The Discovery of the Asylum: Social Order and Disorder in the New Republic* (Boston: Little, Brown, 1971).

A small segment of the reform movement was sharply critical of, or sought to replace, the capitalistic economy and society of the United States. This radical wing of American reform reflected the heterogeneity of the larger movement. Some of its members confined themselves to caustic criticism of the private property system and its works, while others offered elaborate blueprints for the good society (documents 100 and 101). Some believed the brave new world could be created by men as they were, while others agreed with Fanny Wright that until equality was first "planted in the mind, in the habits, in the manners, in the feelings" of men, it could never be planted in their condition. Some would have a new socialist order created in the nation at large, to be achieved by a people who had been educated to appreciate its advantages (document 102). Others, like the "Associationists" at Brook Farm and elsewhere, would proselytize for what Arthur Bestor has called "communitarianism" by the power of their own example, creating "backwoods utopias" that it was hoped would induce the mass of men to imitate (documents 103–105). In one sense, the "utopians" were divided between those who regarded planned communities essentially as milieus conducive to the spiritual regeneration of men, stressing Christian prayer and worship in their designs, and those whose approach was essentially secular.[29] The common feature of these radical movements that were hostile to capitalism was the small following and influence attained.

If American society was unlovely, falling far short of the portrait drawn by Pollyannish word painters, it was so largely because of the limitations of the people inhabiting it. Ignorance, fear, greed, hostility toward alleged inferiors of another race or

29. For modern discussions of these matters see Arthur C. Bestor, *Backwoods Utopias: The Sectarian and Owenite Phases of Communitarian Socialism in America: 1663–1829* (Philadelphia: University of Pennsylvania Press, 1950); Pessen, "Perfectionist Social Thought in the Jacksonian Era," in Michael McGiffert and Robert Allen Skotheim, eds., *American Social Thought: Colonial Beginnings to the Civil War* (Reading, Mass.: Addison-Wesley, 1972), I, 277–336; Pessen, *Most Uncommon Jacksonians: The Radical Leaders of the Early Labor Movement* (Albany: State University of New York Press, 1967); and John L. Thomas, ed., *Ante-Bellum Reform* (New York: Harper and Row, 1967).

condition, unrealistic cockiness, combined perhaps with a realistic awareness that American life would not be kind to perfectionist doctrines, appear to have turned most people away from radical social change.

The central moral and social problem of the era, to Americans and outsiders alike, was slavery. "Reform" in this field was at first preempted by colonizationists, typically white men of standing and substance, whose idea of a solution to the problem was to ship freed Negroes out of the country to a colony in Africa. The charge was well made that colonizationists sought to get rid of a people they considered inferior (documents 88–89). If colonization aroused little enthusiasm, neither did it evoke great hostility. Abolitionism was another matter (document 90). Abolitionists like other reformers were torn by controversy. The antislavery movement was divided over politics, the meaning of "immediatism" and gradualism, the proper form to be taken by propaganda, the roles to be played by women and by Negroes, and many other issues.[30] But if leading abolitionists such as William Lloyd Garrison, Arthur Tappan, Theodore Weld, or William Goodell might harbor intense dislike for each other, their feelings of animosity paled when measured against the bitter hatred many whites felt toward all abolitionists. White champions of the slave's humanity and his right to freedom were loathed by most of their white American contemporaries and appear to have inspired many scholars generations later to search for the mental quirks and psychic aberrations that were believed to have accounted for behavior so "abnormal."

The United States of the second quarter of the nineteenth century was neither an age of egalitarianism nor of great popular power and influence. American civilization was uniquely diverse, turbulent, dynamic, its style crude and vigorous. Surface manners that appeared to reflect the character and wishes of the common

30. The literature on abolitionism is vast. Two useful general works are Louis Filler, *The Crusade Against Slavery, 1830–1860* (New York: Harper and Row, 1960); and Martin B. Duberman, ed., *The Antislavery Vanguard: New Essays in the History of Abolitionism.*

man evidently misled many contemporaries and later scholars alike into thinking that a totally new kind of democratic social and economic order had been created here. The actual gulf between the institutions of the Old World and the New appears to have been not nearly so great as persons on both sides of the Atlantic assumed it to be.

[To preserve the tone of the period, documents herein are reproduced with their archaic spelling, punctuation, and some variations of style.]

PART ONE

American Traits

Materialism

1. Michael Chevalier

At the bottom of all an American does is money

Love of money was the dominant value of Americans. This was the judgment not alone of the army of European travelers who visited the United States during the second quarter of the nineteenth century but of many sensitive Americans as well. "Things are in the saddle riding mankind," Emerson admonished his countrymen. Philip Hone attributed the shoddy construction that caused building accidents and steamboat explosions to a warped scale of values in which lust for profit rated higher than pride in workmanship or respect for life. In a short essay, carefully worded to avoid giving direct offense, the brilliant Alexis de Tocqueville warned that the preoccupation with worldly acquisition might in time make Americans so gross and insensitive that they would lose even the ability to satisfy their material needs. Michael Chevalier, a young Frenchman who visited the United States a few years after Tocqueville departed in 1832, like his better known predecessor came on an official mission for the French government. Chevalier was fascinated by the dynamism of the youthful American society. As the following passages indicate, he attributed positive as well as negative consequences to American money-lust. But he had no doubt that dollar worship was the operative religion of this country.

If accidents of so serious a nature succeeded each other with such frequency in Europe, there would be a general outcry. The police and the legislative power would vie with each other in their efforts to put a stop to them. Steamboats would become the terror of travellers, the public would abandon them, and they would be left

From Michael Chevalier, *Society, Manners and Politics in the United States* (Boston: Weeks, Jordan, 1839), 223, 224, 277, 298, 299.

deserted on the rivers. The effect would be the same, in a degree, around the large eastern cities, because society there is beginning to be regularly organised, and a man's life counts for something. In the West, the flood of emigrants, descending from the Alleghanies, rolls swelling and eddying over the plains, sweeping before it the Indian, the buffalo, and the bear. At its approach the gigantic forests bow themselves before it, as the dry grass of the prairies disappears before the flames. It is for civilisation, what the hosts of Ghengis Khan and Attila were for barbarism; it is an invading army, and its law is the law of armies. The mass is everything, the individual nothing. Wo to him who trips and falls! he is trampled down and crushed under foot. Wo to him who finds himself on the edge of a precipice! The impatient crowd, eager to push forward, throngs him, forces him over, and he is at once forgotten, without even a half-suppressed sigh for his funeral oration. *Help yourself!* is the watchword. The life of the genuine American is the soldier's life; like the soldier he is encamped, and that, in a flying camp, here to-day, fifteen hundred miles off in a month. It is a life of vigilance and strong excitement; as in a camp, quarrels are settled in the west, summarily and on the spot, by a duel fought with rifles, or knives, or with pistols at arm's length. It is a life of sudden vicissitudes, of successes and reverses; destitute to-day, rich to-morrow, and poor the day after, the individual is blown about with every wind of speculation, but the country goes on increasing in wealth and resources. Like the soldier, the American of the West takes for his motto, *Victory or death!* But to him, victory is to make money, to get the dollars, to make a fortune out of nothing, to buy *lots* at Chicago, Cleveland, or St. Louis, and sell them a year afterward at an advance of 1000 per cent.; to carry cotton to New Orleans when it is worth 20 cents a pound. So much the worse for the conquered; so much the worse for those who perish in the steamboats! The essential point is not to save some individuals or even some hundreds; but, in respect to steamers, that they should be numerous; staunch or not, well commanded or not, it matters little, if they move at a rapid rate, and are navigated at little expense. The circulation of steamboats is as necessary to the West, as that of the blood is to the human system. The West will beware of checking and fettering it by regulations and restrictions of any sort. The time is not yet come, but it will come hereafter. . . .

In general, the American is little disposed to be contented; his idea of equality is to be inferior to none, but he endeavours to rise only in one direction. His only means, and the object of his whole thought, is to subdue the material world, or, in other words, it is industry in its various branches, business, speculation, work, action. To this sole object every thing is made subordinate, education, politics, private and public life. Every thing in American society, from religion and morals to domestic usages and daily habits of life, is bent in the direction of this common aim of each and all. If there are some exceptions to this general rule, they are few, and may be referred to two causes; first, American society, exclusive as it is, is not destined to remain forever imprisoned in this narrow circle, and it already contains the germs of its future condition ages hence, whatever that may be; and secondly, human nature, although bounded, is not exclusive, and no force in the world can stifle its eternal protest against exclusiveness in taste, institutions, and manners. Speculation and business, work and action, these, then, under various forms, make the exclusive object to which the Americans have devoted themselves, with a zeal that amounts to fanaticism; this was marked out for them by the finger of Providence, in order that a continent should be brought under the dominion of civilisation with the least possible delay. . . .

It is certain that the Americans are an exaggeration of the English, whom Napoleon used to call a nation of shop-keepers. The American is always bargaining; he always has one bargain afoot, another just finished, and several more in meditation. All that he has, all that he sees, is merchandise in his eyes. The poetical associations which invest particular spots or objects with a character of sanctity, have no place in his mind. The spire of his village church is no more than any other spire to him, and the finest in his view, is the newest, the most freshly painted. To him a cataract is a motive power for his machinery, *a mill privilege;* an old building is a quarry of bricks and stones, which he works without the least remorse. The Yankee will sell his father's house, like old clothes or rags. In his character of pioneer, it is his destiny to attach himself to nothing, to no place, edifice, object, or person, except his wife, to whom he is indissolubly bound night and day, from the moment of marriage till death parts them.

At the bottom, then, of all that an American does, is money; beneath every word, money. But it would be a mistake to suppose that he is not capable of making pecuniary sacrifices; he is in the habit of subscribing to all useful objects, and he does so without reluctance or regret, oftener than we are accustomed to do, and more liberally also; but his munificence and his donations are systematic and calculated. It is neither enthusiasm nor passion that unties his purse strings, but motives of policy or considerations of propriety, views of utility and regard for the public good, in which he feels his own private interests to be involved. The American, therefore, admits some exceptions to his general commercial rule of conduct. He gives money, he attends committee-meetings, he draws up in haste a report or an opinion; he even goes in person, at high speed, to Washington, in order to present a set of resolutions to the President, or he hastens to a neighbouring city to attend a public dinner, and returns in equal haste; but he requires in this case that the exception to the general rule should be sharply defined and the cause strongly marked, that the public interest should be at stake. And he particularly insists that the sacrifice should be of money only, once for all, and that his time should be respected. To everything of a private nature, to everything that takes up his time and demands his attention, he applies the mercantile principle, nothing for nothing. He pays the services of others with dollars, and he expects others to do the same by him, because he looks upon compliments as too hollow and light to be put in the scale against labour, and because distinctions, such for instance as precedence, are unknown and incomprehensible to him. With him it is an indisputable maxim, that the labourer is worthy of his hire. The ideas of service and salary are so inseparably connected in his mind, that in American almanacs it is common to see the rate of pay annexed to the lists of public officers. He is of opinion that nobody can live on a dry crust and glory; he thinks of the welfare of his wife and children, of a provision for his old age, and if he were told that there is a country in which these considerations are disregarded, for the purpose of obliging a neighbour or paying a courtesy to a magistrate, such a thing would appear absurd to him.

Mania for Speculation

2. Frederick Marryat

The ruling passion—the spirit of barter

Speculation is as old as commercial capitalism. Traces of it can be found in Greek and Roman antiquity. No people, however, seem to have speculated as did the Americans. Golden prospects lured natives and foreigners alike. Nor was the shortage of valuable metals a problem to a people capable of substituting paper currency for coin and of manufacturing quantities of the flimsy stuff. Many contemporaries attributed the era's "flush times" as much to the innate traits of the people as to the opportunities afforded by the growth in population, territory, and transportation facilities. The following selection is from the account written by one of the most widely-read English visitors, Captain Frederick Marryat. Marryat was a lively writer, not above exaggeration, with a predilection for getting into embarrassing scrapes as he toured the country. But he was a good reporter, whose findings were corroborated by other contemporaries of more sedate character.

Progressing in the stage, I had a very amusing specimen of the ruling passion of the country—the spirit of barter, which is communicated to the females, as well as to the boys. I will stop for a moment, however, to say, that I heard of an American, who had two sons, and he declared that they were so clever at barter, that he locked them both up together in a room, without a cent in their pockets, and that before they had *swopped* for an hour, they had each gained two dollars a piece. But now for my

From Frederick Marryat, *A Diary in America* (Philadelphia: Carey and Hart, 1839), 65–67.

fellow-passengers—both young, both good-looking, and both ladies, and evidently were total strangers to each other. One had a pretty pink silk bonnet, very fine for travelling; the other, an indifferent plush one. The young lady in the plush, eyed the pink bonnet for some time; at last *Plush* observed in a drawling half-indifferent way:

"That's rather a pretty bonnet of your's, miss."

"Why, yes, I calculate it's rather smart," replied Pink.

After a pause and closer survey.—"You wouldn't have any objection to part with it, miss?"

"Well now, I don't know but I might; I have worn it but three days, I reckon."

"Oh, my? I should have reckoned that you carried it longer—perhaps it rained on them three days."

"I've a notion it didn't rain, not one.—It's not the only bonnet I have, miss."

"Well now, I should not mind an exchange, and paying you the *balance.*"

"That's an awful thing that you have on, miss."

"I rather think not, but that's as may be—Come, miss, what will you take?"

"Why I don't know,—what will you give?"

"I reckon you'll know best when you answer my question."

"Well, then, I shouldn't like less than five dollars."

"Five dollars and my bonnet! I reckon two would be nearer the mark—but it's of no consequence."

"None in the least, miss, only I know the value of my bonnet.—We'll say no more about it."

"Just so, miss."

A pause and silence for half a minute, when Miss Plush, looks out of the window, and says, as if talking to herself, "I shouldn't mind giving four dollars, but no more." She then fell back in her seat, when Miss Pink, put her head out of the window, and said:—"I shouldn't refuse four dollars after all, if it was offered," and then she fell back to her former position.

"Did you think of taking four dollars, miss?"

"Well! I don't care, I've plenty of bonnets at home."

"Well," replied Plush, taking out her purse, and offering her the money.

"What bank is this, miss?"

"Oh, all's right there, Safety Fund, I calculate."

The two ladies exchange bonnets, and Pink pockets the balance.

I may here just as well mention the custom of *whittling,* which is so common in the Eastern states. It is a habit, arising from the natural restlessness of the American when he is not employed, of cutting a piece of stick, or anything else, with his knife. Some are so wedded to it from long custom, that if they have not a piece of stick to cut, they will whittle the backs of the chairs, or anything within their reach. A Yankee shown into a room to await the arrival of another, has been known to whittle away nearly the whole of the mantel-piece. Lawyers in court whittle away at the table before them; and judges will cut through their own bench. In some courts, they put sticks before noted whittlers to save the furniture. The Down Easters, as the Yankees are termed generally, whittle when they are making a bargain, as it fills up the pauses, gives them time for reflection, and moreover, prevents any examination of the countenance—for in bargaining, like in the game of brag, the countenance is carefully watched, as an index to the wishes. I was once witness to a bargain made between two respectable Yankees, who wished to agree about a farm, and in which whittling was resorted to.

They sat down on a log of wood, about three or four feet apart from each other, with their faces turned opposite ways—that is, one had his legs on one side of the log with his face to the east, and the other his legs on the other side with his face to the west. One had a piece of soft wood, and was sawing it with his penknife; the other had an unbark-of hickory stick which he was peeling for a walking-stick. The reader will perceive a strong analogy between this bargain and that in the stage between the two ladies.

"Well, good morning—and about this farm?"

"I don't know; what will you take?"

"What will you give?"

Silence, and whittle away.

"Well, I should think two thousand dollars, a heap of money for this farm."

"I've a notion it will never go for three thousand, any how."

"There's a fine farm, and cheaper, on the north side."

"But where's the sun to ripen the corn?"

"Sun shines on all alike."

"Not exactly through a Vermont hill, I reckon. The driver offered me as much as I say, if I recollect right."

"Money not always to be depended upon. Money not always forthcoming."

"I reckon, I shall make an elegant 'backy stopper of this piece of sycamore."

Silence for a few moments. Knives hard at work.

"I've a notion this is as pretty a hickory stick as ever came out of a wood."

"I shouldn't mind two thousand five hundred dollars, and time given."

"It couldn't be more than six months, then, if it goes at that price."

(Pause.)

"Well, that might suit me."

"What do you say, then?"

"Suppose it must be so."

"It's a bargain then *(rising up,)* come let's liquor on it."

3. Michael Chevalier

The ever-moving sea of speculation

Like other contemporaries, Chevalier was convinced that instability was the norm in America. In the following selection he suggests that Americans thrived on flux, ever ready either to gamble again what they

From Michael Chevalier, *Society, Manners and Politics in the United States*, pp. 309–311. Footnotes are in the original.

had recently gained, or to leap to their feet to try to regain what they had recently lost, in either case urged on by a mania for speculation. That this allegedly ceaseless ebb and flow actually was not borne out by detailed evidence appears to have bothered contemporaries little. Such evidence was unknown to them; their judgments were formed by vivid if random impressions.

The American concerns himself little about that; violent sensations are necessary to stir his vigorous nerves. Public opinion and the pulpit forbid sensual gratifications, wine, women, and the display of a princely luxury; cards and dice are equally prohibited; the American, therefore, has recourse to business for the strong emotions which he requires to make him feel life. He launches with delight into the ever-moving sea of speculation. One day, the wave raises him to the clouds; he enjoys in haste the moment of triumph. The next day he disappears between the crests of the billows; he is little troubled by the reverse, he bides his time coolly, and consoles himself with the hope of better fortune. In the midst of all this speculation, whilst some enrich and some ruin themselves, banks spring up and diffuse credit, railroads and canals extend themselves over the country, steamboats are launched into the rivers, the lakes, and the sea; the career of the speculators is ever enlarging, the field for railroads, canals, steamers, and banks goes on expanding. Some individuals lose, but the country is a gainer; the country is peopled, cleared, cultivated; its resources are unfolded, its wealth increased. *Go ahead!*

If movement and the quick succession of sensations and ideas constitute life, here one lives a hundred fold more than elsewhere; all is here circulation, motion, and boiling agitation. Experiment follows experiment; enterprise succeeds to enterprise. Riches and poverty follow on each other's traces, and each in turn occupies the place of the other. Whilst the great men of one day dethrone those of the past, they are already half overturned themselves by those of the morrow. Fortunes last for a season; reputations, during the twinkling of an eye. An irresistible current sweeps away everything, grinds everything to powder, and deposits it again under new forms. Men change their houses, their climate, their trade, their condition, their party, their sect;[1] the States change their laws, their officers, their constitutions. The soil itself, or at least the houses, partake in the universal instability.[2] The existence of social order, in the bosom of this whirlpool seems a miracle, an inexplicable anomaly. One is tempted to think, that such a society, formed of heterogeneous elements, brought together by chance, and following each its own orbit according to the impulse of its own caprice or interest,—one would think, that after rising for one moment to the heavens, like a water-spout, such a society would inevitably fall flat in ruins the next; such is not, however, its destiny. In the midst of this general change, there is one fixed point; it is the domestic fire-side, or, to speak more correctly, the conjugal bed. An austere watchman, sometimes harsh even to fanaticism, wards off from this sacred spot everything that can disturb its stability; that guardian is the religious sentiment. Whilst that fixed point shall continue invariable, whilst that sentinel shall persist in his vigilant watch over it, the social system may make new somersets, and undergo new changes without serious risk; it may be pelted by the storm, but while it is made fast to that hold, it will neither split nor sink. It may even be divided into separate and independent masses, but it will still grow in energy, in resources, in extent.

The influence of the democracy is so universal in this country, that it was quite natural for it to raise its head amidst the

1. The causes of religious changes are various. It is not rare to see Americans, on becoming rich, abandon their former sect for Episcopalianism, for instance, which is the most fashionable. The change, however, from one sect to another is less considerable than is supposed in Catholic countries; for the different Protestant sects differ less from each other, than a Jansenist from a Molinist, or a Jesuit from a Gallican. But we must except from this remark the Anglican church, which has a peculiar character, discipline, and liturgy, and the two not very numerous sects of Unitarians, who deny the divinity of Christ, and Universalists, who reject the doctrine of reprobation.

2. The American houses are low and slight; the walls are generally only a brick and a half, sometimes only one in thickness; when, therefore, the course of the street is changed, as is often the case in New York, they are set forward or back with little difficulty, and they are often even raised bodily. In the country, the houses are mostly of wood, and are often transported a considerable distance on wheels. Between Albany and Troy, I was stopped on the road by a house of more than forty feet front, which was travelling in this manner.

speculators. There have, therefore, been strikes on the part of the workmen, who wish to have a share in the profits of speculation, and who have demanded higher wages and less work. The former demand was just, for all provisions, all articles of consumption have risen in price. These coalitions are by no means timid in this country; for the English practice of haranguing in public and getting up processions prevails here, and the working class here feels its strength, is conscious of its power, and knows how to make use of it. The different traders have held their meetings in Philadelphia, New York, and other places, discussed their affairs publicly, and set forth their demands. The women have had their meeting as well as the men. That of the seamstresses of Philadelphia attracted notice; Matthew Carey, known as a political writer, presided, assisted by two clergymen. Among the demands of the trades, that of the journeymen bakers, who, by virtue of the rights of man and the sanctity of the seventh day, would not make bread Sundays, is worthy of attention. The principal trades have decided that all work shall be suspended until the masters, if this name can be applied here except in derision, have acceded to their *ultimatum*. That every one may know this, they have caused their resolutions to be published in the newspapers, signed by the president and secretaries of the meeting.

Shrewdness

4. Charles Dickens

Love of "smart" dealing

Closely related to the American's love of money was his admiration of likely-to-succeed behavior. Charles Dickens was amazed and somewhat appalled that shrewdness and cleverness appeared to rate so high in the American scheme of things. Although the great English novelist was

From Charles Dickens, *American Notes* (New York: Macmillan, 1893 [originally published in London, 1842]), 215.

enthusiastically received when he visited the United States at the beginning of the 1840s, the subsequent account of his travels infuriated many Americans, unwilling to accept its biting judgments.

Another prominent feature is the love of "smart" dealing, which gilds over many a swindle and gross breach of trust; many a defalcation, public and private; and enables many a knave to hold his head up with the best, who well deserves a halter—though it has not been without its retributive operation, for this smartness has done more in a few years to impair the public credit, and to cripple the public resources, than dull honesty, however rash, could have effected in a century. The merits of a broken speculation, or a bankruptcy, or of a successful scoundrel, are not gauged by its or his observance of the golden rule, "Do as you would be done by," but are considered with reference to their smartness. I recollect, on both occasions of our passing that ill-fated Cairo on the Mississippi, remarking on the bad effects such gross deceits must have when they exploded, in generating a want of confidence abroad, and discouraging foreign investment: but I was given to understand that this was a very smart scheme by which a deal of money had been made: and that its smartest feature was, that they forgot these things abroad, in a very short time, and speculated again, as freely as ever. The following dialogue I have held a hundred times:—"Is it not a very disgraceful circumstance that such a man as So and So should be acquiring a large property by the most infamous and odious means, and notwithstanding all the crimes of which he has been guilty, should be tolerated and abetted by your Citizens? He is a public nuisance, is he not?" "Yes, Sir." "A convicted liar?" "Yes, Sir." "He has been kicked, and cuffed, and caned?" "Yes, Sir." "And he is utterly dishonourable, debased, and profligate?" "Yes, Sir." "In the name of wonder, then, what is his merit?" "Well, Sir, he is a smart man."

Evasiveness

5. Frances Trollope

Nothing can equal their skill in evading a question

Akin to shrewdness was an evasiveness designed to mask one's objectives. The following sample of Yankee evasiveness was gathered by one of the most intelligent of the visitors, Mrs. Frances Trollope, mother of the Victorian novelist Anthony Trollope. Mrs. Trollope's detailed reporting of some of the unlovelier public habits of Americans did not endear her to citizens of this country, many of whom branded her a carping critic. She appears however to have been an honest, conscientious observer.

The Quakers have been celebrated for the pertinacity with which they avoid giving a direct answer, but what Quaker could ever vie with a Yankee in this sort of fencing? Nothing in fact, can equal their skill in evading a question, excepting that with which they set about asking one. I am afraid that in repeating a conversation which I overheard on board the Erie canal boat, I shall spoil it, by forgetting some of the little delicate doublings which delighted me—yet I wrote it down immediately. Both parties were Yankees, but strangers to each other; one of them having, by gentle degrees, made himself pretty well acquainted with the point from which every one on board had started, and that for which he was bound, at last attacked his brother Reynard thus:—

"Well, now, which way may you be traveling?"

"I expect this canal runs pretty nearly west."

"Are you going far with it?"

"Well, now, I don't rightly know how many miles it may be."

"I expect you'll be from New York?"

"Sure enough I have been at New York, often and often."

"I calculate, then, 'tis not there as you stop?"

"Business must be minded, in stopping and in stirring."

From Frances Trollope, *Domestic Manners of the Americans* (London: Whittaker, Treacher, 1832), 2 vols., II, pp. 209–212.

"You may say that. Well, I look then you'll be making for the Springs?"

"Folks say as all the world is making for the Springs, and I expect a good sight of them is."

"Do you calculate upon stopping long when you get to your journey's end?"

" 'Tis my business must settle that, I expect."

"I guess that's true, too; but you'll be for making pleasure a business for once, I calculate?"

"My business don't often lie in that line."

"Then, may be, it is not the Springs as takes you this line?"

"The Springs is a right elegant place, I reckon."

"It is your health, I calculate, as makes you break your good rules?"

"My health don't trouble me much, I guess."

"No? Why that's well. How is the markets, sir? Are bread stuffs up?"

"I a'nt just capable to say."

"A deal of money's made by just looking after the article at the fountain's head."

"You may say that."

"Do you look to be making great dealings in produce up the country?"

"Why that, I expect, is difficult to know."

"I calculate you'll find the markets changeable these times?"

"No markets ben't very often without changing."

"Why, that's right down true. What may be your biggest article of produce?"

"I calculate, generally, that's the biggest, as I makes most by."

"You may say that. But what do you chiefly call your most particular branch?"

"Why, that's what I can't justly say."

And so they went on, without advancing or giving an inch, 'till I was weary of listening; but I left them still at it, when I stepped out to resume my station on a trunk at the bow of the boat, where I scribbled in my note-book, this specimen of Yankee conversation.

Anti-Intellectualism

6. Francis J. Grund
We consider professors secondary men

Tocqueville had found "the spirit of Americans averse to general ideas; it does not seek theoretical discoveries." Americans were said to value neither the life of the mind nor the men who pursued it. In the following selection Francis Grund, a German visitor, offers a ringside seat at a discussion in which a number of Boston's leading men express their scorn for abstract learning and those who engage in it. Grund could hardly have been accused of an anti-American bias, since he was so enamored of the United States that he had decided to transform what was originally a visit into lifelong residence and American citizenship. As the passage attests, Grund had a remarkable ear for American conversation.

"We are a common sense, matter-of-fact people," added he exultingly; "we leave genius and enthusiasm to Europeans."

"Thank Heaven!" exclaimed his neighbour on the left, "I have no genius in *my* family; my children are all brought up to be industrious."

"You may thank the Lord for that," replied our entertainer; "I never saw a genius yet who was either himself happy or capable of making others so. I have brought up my sons to become merchants and manufacturers; only Sam, the poor boy who is a little hard of hearing, and rather slow of comprehension, shall go to college. Our merchants, sir, are the most respectable part of the community."

"What college do you mean to send him to?" demanded I, in order to ascertain whether he had been serious.

"I shall send him to Harvard University," he replied; "the oldest literary institution in the country. Have you not yet been to see it?"

I told him that I had been but a few days in Boston, but that I should certainly take an early opportunity of visiting the institution.

From Francis J. Grund, *Aristocracy in America* (London: Richard Bentley, 1839), 2 vols., II, pp. 33–39.

"Do so," he said; "you will find it well worth your while; it will convince you that, while we have been making money, we have not altogether neglected arts and sciences."

"Which are your cleverest men in the various departments of science?" demanded I.

"Why, they are none of them very clever in *our* sense of the word. We consider professors as secondary men. Our practice is to give the different professorships away to young men, in order to induce them to devote themselves to the branch they are to teach. Our country is as yet too young for old professors; and, besides, they are too poorly paid to induce first-rate men to devote themselves to the business of lecturing."

"In this manner," rejoined I, "you will never have eminent men in the higher departments of philosophy."

"We have as yet no time to devote to abstract learning," he observed; "we are too young for that. Our principal acquirement consists in common sense; all the rest we consider as moonshine. You must know," he said, with a countenance in which superiority of knowledge was mingled with condenscension of manners, "that a young man learns as much in six months in a counting-room as in four years at college. My friends do not entirely agree with me; but I often told them that our colleges only made poor gentlemen, and spoiled clever tradesmen."

He then counted over the names of most of the rich men in Boston, who, he said, were all self-taught country boys, possessed of no other learning than the art of making dollars in a neat, handsome, clean manner. "This," he added, "has given them a higher standing in society than they could have acquired by all the philosophy in the world, and enabled them to marry into the oldest and most aristocratic families of the place.

"Take, for instance, the case of our friend. . . . What does he know except making money? What has he ever learned except negociating, or rather *shaving* notes? What college did he ever go to, except that of our brokers in State-street? And has he not married the daughter of one of our richest men? Has he not got one of the largest fortunes with her? And is he not now connected with some of our first people—with the real back-bone of our

Boston aristocracy? And do you know the answer his father-in-law gave to one of his old friends, who remonstrated with him for giving his daughter away to a *parvenu* from the country? 'I give my daughter to any man,' said he, 'who will come to Boston and have wit enough to make a hundred thousand dollars in six years.' There's common sense for you, I trust: that's what we call practical philosophy."

"It is certainly a melancholy fact," sighed the gentleman next to me, who now for the first time opened his lips, "that a great number of our young men, who have gone to college, have afterwards been unsuccessful in business. I think our education is not sufficiently practical;—we are still attached to the European system."

"Not only that," replied our entertainer, "but most of our students contract habits of idleness, which will never answer in this country. They want to imitate your English gentleman, when their patrimony—I mean their *share* in their father's fortune—is scarcely sufficient to keep them alive. Do you remember Mr. . . .'s reply to a young gentleman who had asked him his advice as to what he ought to do in order to succeed in business? 'Take off your kid gloves,' said he, 'and go to work.' There's philosophy for you, equal to your Kants and Leibnitz! Mr. . . . , you know, is a plain-spoken man, who came to Boston without a cent in his pocket, and is now one of our most respectable citizens."

"But if this be the prevailing taste of your townsmen," said I, "why do you call Boston the Athens of the United States?"

"That appellation," replied he, "refers to our women, not to our gentlemen. Our ladies read a great deal. And why should they not? What else have they to do? And we have, besides, a lot of literary twaddles, manufactured by the wholesale at Cambridge, who attempt to turn the heads of our young girls with the nonsense they call 'poetry,' which fills nearly all our papers, instead of clever editorials. If we have one poet among us, we have at least fifty, the joint earnings of whom would not be sufficient to keep a dog. But then poets don't turn *our* heads, you see; we are too much occupied with business."

"But how do your literary men manage to get on?" demanded I: "I know several of them quite in easy circumstances."

"They marry rich women, who can afford paying for being entertained. They show their common sense in that. It's quite the fashion for our rich girls to *buy themselves a professor,* previous to taking a trip to Europe."

"And then," added my neighbour on the right, "literary reputations are in this city not acquired, as in other places, through the medium of public opinion; but by the aid of a small coterie, composed of a few 'leading citizens,' who have the power of setting a man up, or putting him down, just as they please; the process being this: Mr. A. or Mr. B., wealthy gentlemen in Beacon-street, declare Mr. Smith a fine scholar; and immediately half a dozen of their clique will repeat the same assertion. The individual in question is thus made fashionable, so that any one speaking against him is considered unacquainted with the usages of society. Those, therefore, whose opinion—if they dare to have one—is different from Mr. A.'s and Mr. B.'s, are most likely to keep it to themselves; while every person aspiring to rank and fashion publicity swears to his scholarship: for our people, you must know, are accustomed to do everything from fear; nothing from love. If you want to succeed in anything,—if you want to carry any particular measure,—enlist half a dozen influential citizens in your behalf, and the rest will not dare *to back out.* That's the way things are done in this city.

Conformity

7. Alexis de Tocqueville

Freedom of opinion does not exist

Americans liked to think that they were above all an independent people. In their belief the American acted in accord with his own private concept

From Alexis de Tocqueville, *Democracy in America* (New York: Henry G. Langley, 1845), 2 vols., I, chap. XV, pp. 284–287, 288, 289.

of right and wrong. The sociologist David Riesman has called this rugged individualist "inner directed." Reflective contemporaries saw a very different fellow, whose behavior was motivated largely by the desire to please others. In James Fenimore Cooper's striking phrase, " 'They say,' was the monarch of this country." Characteristically, Americans did not what they wished to do but what they believed would be well received.

In his famous discussion of the "tyranny of the majority" over public opinion, Alexis de Tocqueville tried to explain the causes and nature of conformity in America. He spent nine months here in 1831–1832 with his companion Gustave Beaumont preparing a report on American penitentiaries for the French government. Fortunately Tocqueville observed much more than prisons. His two-part *Democracy in America*, published in 1835 and 1840, is above all a classic for its insights into the character and values of Americans and its dazzling theoretical speculations. Its chief fault was the thin factual basis of some of its social theorizing. But if Tocqueville is suspect as reporter of American society, he remains a marvelous analyst of its psyche.

POWER EXERCISED BY THE MAJORITY IN AMERICA UPON OPINION.

In America, when the majority has once irrevocably decided a question, all discussion ceases—Reason for this—Moral power exercised by the majority upon opinion—Democratic republics have applied despotism to the minds of men.

It is in the examination of the exercise of thought in the United States that we clearly perceive how far the power of the majority surpasses all the powers with which we are acquainted in Europe. Thought is an invisible and subtle power that mocks all the efforts of tyranny. At the present time the most absolute monarchs in Europe cannot prevent certain opinions hostile to their authority from circulating in secret through their dominions and even in their courts. It is not so in America; as long as the majority is still undecided, discussion is carried on; but as soon as its decision is irrevocably pronounced, everyone is silent, and the friends as well as the opponents of the measure unite in assenting to its propriety. The reason for this is perfectly clear: no monarch is so absolute as to combine all the powers of society in his own hands and to conquer all opposition, as a majority is able to do, which has the right both of making and of executing the laws.

The authority of a king is physical and controls the actions of men without subduing their will. But the majority possesses a power that is physical and moral at the same time, which acts upon the will as much as upon the actions and represses not only all contest, but all controversy.

I know of no country in which there is so little independence of mind and real freedom of discussion as in America. In any constitutional state in Europe every sort of religious and political theory may be freely preached and disseminated; for there is no country in Europe so subdued by any single authority as not to protect the man who raises his voice in the cause of truth from the consequences of his hardihood. If he is unfortunate enough to live under an absolute government, the people are often on his side; if he inhabits a free country, he can, if necessary, find a shelter behind the throne. The aristocratic part of society supports him in some countries, and the democracy in others. But in a nation where democratic institutions exist, organized like those of the United States, there is but one authority, one element of strength and success, with nothing beyond it.

In America the majority raises formidable barriers around the liberty of opinion; within these barriers an author may write what he pleases, but woe to him if he goes beyond them. Not that he is in danger of an auto-da-fé, but he is exposed to continued obloquy and persecution. His political career is closed forever, since he has offended the only authority that is able to open it. Every sort of compensation, even that of celebrity, is refused to him. Before making public his opinions he thought he had sympathizers; now it seems to him that he has none any more since he has revealed himself to everyone; then those who blame him criticize loudly and those who think as he does keep quiet and move away without courage. He yields at length, overcome by the daily effort which he has to make, and subsides into silence, as if he felt remorse for having spoken the truth.

Fetters and headsmen were the coarse instruments that tyranny formerly employed; but the civilization of our age has perfected despotism itself, though it seemed to have nothing to learn. Monarchs had, so to speak, materialized oppression; the democratic republics of the present day have rendered it as entirely an affair of the mind as the will which it is intended to coerce. Under the absolute sway of one man the body was attacked in order to subdue the soul; but the soul escaped the blows which were directed against it and rose proudly superior. Such is not the course adopted by tyranny in democratic republics; there the body is left free, and the soul is enslaved. The master no longer says: "You shall think as I do or you shall die"; but he says: "You are free to think differently from me and to retain your life, your property, and all that you possess; but you are henceforth a stranger among your people. You may retain your civil rights, but they will be useless to you, for you will never be chosen by your fellow citizens if you solicit their votes; and they will affect to scorn you if you ask for their esteem. You will remain among men, but you will be deprived of the rights of mankind. Your fellow creatures will shun you like an impure being; and even those who believe in your innocence will abandon you, lest they should be shunned in their turn. Go in peace! I have given you your life, but it is an existence worse than death."

Absolute monarchies had dishonored despotism; let us beware lest democratic republics should reinstate it and render it less odious and degrading in the eyes of the many by making it still more onerous to the few.

Works have been published in the proudest nations of the Old World expressly intended to censure the vices and the follies of the times: Labruyère inhabited the palace of Louis XIV when he composed his chapter upon the Great, and Molière criticized the courtiers in the plays that were acted before the court. But the ruling power in the United States is not to be made game of. The smallest reproach irritates its sensibility, and the slightest joke that has any foundation in truth renders it indignant; from the forms of its language up to the solid virtues of its character, everything must be made the subject of encomium. No writer, whatever be his eminence, can escape paying this tribute of adulation to his fellow citizens. The majority lives in the perpetual utterance of self-applause, and there are certain truths which the Americans can learn only from strangers or from experience.

If America has not as yet had any great writers, the reason is given in these facts; there can be no literary genius without freedom of opinion, and freedom of opinion does not exist in America. The Inquisition has never been able to prevent a vast number of anti-religious books from circulating in Spain. The empire of the majority succeeds much better in the United States, since it actually removes any wish to publish them. Unbelievers are to be met with in America, but there is no public organ of infidelity. Attempts have been made by some governments to protect morality by prohibiting licentious books. In the United States no one is punished for this sort of books, but no one is induced to write them; not because all the citizens are immaculate in conduct, but because the majority of the community is decent and orderly. . . .

In that immense crowd which throngs the avenues to power in the United States, I found very few men who displayed that manly candor and masculine independence of opinion which frequently distinguished the Americans in former times, and which constitutes the leading feature in distinguished characters wherever they may be found. It seems at first sight as if all the minds of the Americans were formed upon one model, so accurately do they follow the same route. A stranger does, indeed, sometimes meet with Americans who dissent from the rigor of these formulas, with men who deplore the defects of the laws, the mutability and the ignorance of democracy, who even go so far as to observe the evil tendencies that impair the national character, and to point out such remedies as it might be possible to apply; but no one is there to hear them except yourself, and you, to whom these secret reflections are confided, are a stranger and a bird of passage. They are very ready to communicate truths which are useless to you, but they hold a different language in public.

Restless Temper

8. Alexis de Tocqueville
He is goaded onward by a passion stronger than life

Almost all contemporaries were struck by the vitality and energy of the American people. Mrs. Trollope found a "vast continent" here, with "a busy, bustling, industrious population, hacking and hewing their way through it." Many believed that Americans were inspired to thrust outward, geographically, and upward, socially, largely by a love of gain. The American farmer, remarked a shrewd English visitor, would give up one piece of land for another if he could sell for ten dollars what he bought for eight. As always Tocqueville had an explanation for the observed behavior. According to him, materialistic motives were complemented by others in accounting for American wanderlust: Americans constantly moved from one place to another "for the emotions it excites as much as for the gain it procures."

It would be difficult to describe the avidity with which the American rushes forward to secure this immense booty that fortune offers. In the pursuit he fearlessly braves the arrow of the Indian and the diseases of the forest; he is unimpressed by the silence of the woods; the approach of beasts of prey does not disturb him, for he is goaded onwards by a passion stronger than the love of life. Before him lies a boundless continent, and he urges onward as if time pressed and he was afraid of finding no room for his exertions. I have spoken of the emigration from the older states, but how shall I describe that which takes place from the more recent ones? Fifty years have scarcely elapsed since Ohio was founded; the greater part of its inhabitants were not born within its confines; its capital has been built only thirty years, and its territory is still covered by an immense extent of uncultivated fields; yet already the population of Ohio is proceeding westward, and most of the settlers who descend to the fertile prairies of Illinois are citizens of Ohio. These men left their

From Alexis de Tocqueville, *Democracy in America*, I, chap. XVII, p. 322.

first country to improve their condition; they quit their second to ameliorate it still more; fortune awaits them everywhere, but not happiness. The desire of prosperity has become an ardent and restless passion in their minds, which grows by what it feeds on. They early broke the ties that bound them to their natal earth, and they have contracted no fresh ones on their way. Emigration was at first necessary to them; and it soon becomes a sort of game of chance, which they pursue for the emotions it excites as much as for the gain it procures.

Insecurity

9. Harriet Martineau

How do you like this country

Most people like praise, but Americans appeared to be desperate for it. In Tocqueville's devastating words, Americans "unceasingly harass you to extort praise, and if you reject their entreaties, they fall to praising themselves. It would seem as if, doubting their own merit, they wished to have it constantly exhibited before their eyes. Their vanity is not only greedy, but restless and jealous; it will grant nothing, while it demands everything, but is ready to beg and quarrel at the same time." Even Harriet Martineau, an indefatigable and fair-minded traveler whose sympathy for this people was matched by few visitors, was appalled by the obsequious craving for praise displayed by Americans.

When I was on my voyage out, the Americans on board amused themselves with describing to me how incessantly I should be met by the question how I liked America. When we arrived within a few miles of New York, a steam-boat met us, bringing the friends of some of the passengers. On board this steam-boat, the passengers went up to the city. It happened to be the smallest, dirtiest, and most clumsy steamer belonging to the port. A splashing rain drove us down into the cabin, where there was barely standing room for our company. We saw each other's faces

From Harriet Martineau, *Society in America* (New York: Saunders and Otley, 1837), 2 vols., II, pp. 166, 167.

by the dim light of a single shabby lamp. "Now, Miss M." said some of the American passengers, "how do you like America?" This was the first time of my being asked the question which I have had to answer almost daily since. Yet I do not believe that many of my interrogators seriously cared any more for my answer than those who first put the question in the dirty cabin; or than my little friend Charley, who soon caught the joke, and with grave face, asked me, every now and then, "How do you like this country?" I learned to regard it as a method of beginning conversation, like our meteorological observations in England; which are equally amusing to foreigners. My own impression is, that while the Americans have too exalted a notion of England, and too little self-respect as a nation, they are far less anxious about foreign opinions of themselves than the behaviour of American travellers in England would lead the English to suppose. The anxiety arises on English ground. At home, the generality of Americans seem to see clearly enough that it is yet truer with regard to nations than individuals that, though it is very pleasant to have the favourable opinion of one's neighbours, yet, if one is good and happy within oneself, the rest does not much matter. I met with a few who spoke with a disgusting affectation of candour, (some, as if they expected to please me thereby, and others under the influence of sectional prejudice,) of what they called the fairness of the gross slanders with which they have been insulted through the English press: but I was thankful to meet with more who did not acknowledge the jurisdiction of observers disqualified by prejudice, or by something worse, for passing judgment on a nation. The irritability of their vanity has been much exaggerated, partly to serve paltry purposes of authorship; and yet more from the ridiculous exhibitions of some Americans in England, who are no more to be taken as specimens of the nation to which they belong than a young Englishman who, when I was at New York, went up the Hudson in a drizzling rain, pronounced that West Point was not so pretty as Richmond; descended the river in the dark, and declared on his return that the Americans were wonderfully proud of scenery that was nothing particular in any way.

It will be well for the Americans, particularly those of the east and south, when their idea of honour becomes as exalted as that which inspired their revolutionary ancestors. Whenever they possess themselves of the idea of their democracy, as it was possessed by their statesmen of 1801, they will moderate their homage of human opinion, and enhance their worship of humanity.

Boastfulness

10. Basil Hall

The constant habit of praising themselves

Closely related to the emotional insecurity which drove Americans to entreat praise from strangers was a boastfulness that manifested itself in a variety of ways. Americans insisted on praising their rivers, their government, their literature, their manners, to skeptical if not disbelieving visitors. Francis Lieber, an admiring German visitor, fell to gnashing his teeth at the information proffered him by a friendly American, apropos of nothing in particular, that the Hudson was as fine as the Rhine. Captain Basil Hall, who visited the United States in the late 1820s, created a sensation here by calling attention to the American penchant for self-praise and other unattractive traits.

We were . . . introduced with much kindness to many persons, most of whom, the instant we were presented, began to exact our admiration of their country, their people, their institutions, all the while praising every thing so highly themselves, that there was hardly room left for us to slip in a word edgewise. The praise of one's own country, its manners and customs, in conversation with a foreigner, comes so near to praising one's self, that the person to whom it is addressed feels a sort of awkwardness either in joining, or in declining to join, in such commendations.

Persons of sense and information were, of course, above descending to such arts to extort praise, and many Americans

From Basil Hall, *Travels in North America in 1827 and 1828* (Edinburgh: Cadell, 1829), 3 vols., II, pp. 41–43, I, pp. 109–111.

whom I met with at Albany, and elsewhere, were fully of my opinion as to the impolicy of making such demands upon the admiration of their guests—but I speak of the general, average mass of society in America, the current of whose thoughts, whether flowing at the surface or beneath it, appears always to set in one direction, and prompts such expressions as the following:—

"Don't you think this a wonderful country? Don't you allow that we deserve great credit for what we are doing? Do not we resemble the Old Country much more than you expected? Had you any idea of finding us so far advanced? Are not the western parts of our State improving very rapidly? Is not our canal the finest work in the world? Don't you admit that we are becoming a great nation? What do you think of us, upon the whole?"

It was really not easy, "upon the whole," to devise civil answers to these and a hundred other similar questions—and yet to keep decently within the truth. It often grieved me very much, when driven into a corner and obliged to say something which fell short of their expectations;—for nothing could be more kind, or hospitable, or more obliging in all respects, than the Americans were to us, from end to end of the country. One of the chief sources of pain, therefore, arising out of these direct, but often unanswerable interrogations, was the necessity of appearing to make inadequate returns for so much friendly attention. I have frequently entered a room feeling every way grateful for kindnesses shown to my family and to myself; and, from being in perfect good-humour with what I had seen during the day, was not only willing but anxious to commend every thing in moderation, or with certain obvious, but not strained or uncivil qualifications. But, before I had been half an hour in company, I had the mortifying conviction forced upon me, that so far from giving satisfaction, I was grievously disappointing the very persons it was essentially my wish, as it certainly was my duty, to please; but who would not receive at my hands any thing in the way of commendation, short of such raptures as I really could not bring myself to express. . . .

At this early stage of the journey, I find from my notes that the most striking circumstance in the American character, which had come under our notice, was the constant habit of praising themselves, their institutions, and their country, either in downright terms, or by some would-be indirect allusions, which were still more tormenting. I make use of this sharp-edged word, because it really was exceedingly teasing, when we were quite willing and ready to praise all that was good, and also to see every thing, whether good or bad, in the fairest light, to be called upon so frequently to admit the justice of such exaggerations. It is considered, I believe, all over the world, as bad manners for a man to praise himself or his family. Now, to praise one's country appears, to say the least of it, in the next degree of bad taste.

It was curious to see with what vigilant adroitness the Americans availed themselves of every little circumstance to give effect to this self-laudatory practice. I happened one day to mention to a lady, that I had been amused by observing how much more the drivers of the stages managed their horses by word of mouth, than by touch of the whip. Upon which she replied, "Oh yes sir, the circumstance you relate is very interesting, as it shows both intelligence in the men, and sagacity in the animals." This was pretty well; but I merely smiled and said nothing, being somewhat tickled by this amiable interchange of human wisdom and brute sagacity. The lady's suspicions however instantly took fire on seeing the expression of my countenance, and she answered my smile by saying, "Nay, sir, do you not think the people in America, upon the whole, particularly intelligent?"

Thus it ever was, in great things as well as in small, on grave or ludicrous occasions; they were eternally on the defensive, and gave us to understand that they suspected us of a design to find fault, at times when nothing on earth was farther from our thoughts. Whenever any thing favourable happened, by chance or otherwise, to be stated with respect to England, there was straightway a fidget, till the said circumstance was counterbalanced by something equally good, or much better, in America. To such an extent was this jealous fever carried, that I hardly recollect above half-a-dozen occasions during the whole journey, when England was mentioned, that the slightest interest of an agreeable kind was manifested on the part of the audience; or that a brisk cross fire was not instantly opened on all hands, to depreciate what had been said; or which was still more frequent, to build up something finer, or taller, or larger, in America to overmatch it. It always occurred to me, that they paid themselves and their institutions the very poorest description of compliment by this course of proceeding; and it would be quite easy to show why.

Thin Skin

11. Frances Trollope

They wince if a breeze blows over them

Allied to their addiction to self-praise was the Americans' intolerance of criticism. According to Tocqueville it was connected to insensitivity toward criticism. "In the United States," he wrote, "it is not easy to make a man understand that his presence may be dispensed with; hints will not always suffice to shake him off. I contradict an American at every word he says, to show him that his conversation bores me, he instantly labors with fresh persistency to convince me: I preserve a dogged silence, and he thinks I am meditating deeply on the truths that he is uttering; at last I rush from his company, and he supposes that some urgent business hurries me elsewhere. This man will never understand that he wearies me to death unless I tell him so, and the only way to get rid of him is to make him my enemy for life." As Mrs. Trollope noted, many Americans did not simply dislike criticism of themselves and their country: they acted as though there could be no justification for it.

Having now arrived nearly at the end of our travels, I am induced, ere I conclude, again to mention what I consider as one of the most remarkable traits in the national character of the Americans; namely, their exquisite sensitiveness and soreness respecting every thing said or written concerning them. Of this, perhaps, the most remarkable example I can give, is the effect produced on nearly every class of readers by the appearance of Captain Basil Hall's

From Frances Trollope, *Domestic Manners of the Americans*, II, pp. 184–187.

"Travels in North America." In fact, it was a sort of moral earthquake, and the vibration it occasioned through the nerves of the Republic, from one corner of the Union to the other, was by no means over when I left the country in July, 1831, a couple of years after the shock.

I was in Cincinnati when these volumes came out, but it was not till July, 1830, that I procured a copy of them. One bookseller to whom I applied, told me that he had had a few copies before he understood the nature of the work, but that after becoming acquainted with it, nothing should induce him to sell another. Other persons of his profession must, however, have been less scrupulous, for the book was read in city, town, village, and hamlet, steam-boat, and stagecoach, and a sort of war-whoop was sent forth perfectly unprecedented in my recollection upon any occasion whatever.

It was fortunate for me that I did not procure these volumes till I had heard them very generally spoken of, for the curiosity I felt to know the contents of a work so violently anathematised, led me to make enquiries which elicited a great deal of curious feeling.

An ardent desire for approbation, and a delicate sensitiveness under censure, have always, I believe, been considered as amiable traits of character; but the condition into which the appearance of Capt. Hall's work threw the Republic, shews plainly that these feelings, if carried to excess, produce a weakness which amounts to imbecility.

It was perfectly astonishing to hear men, who, on other subjects, were of some judgement, utter their opinions upon this. I never heard of any instance in which the common sense generally found in national criticism, was so overthrown by passion. I do not speak of the want of justice, and of fair and liberal interpretation: these, perhaps, were hardly to be expected. Other nations have been called thin-skinned, but the citizens of the Union have, apparently, no skins at all; they wince if a breeze blows over them, unless it be tempered with adulation. It was not, therefore, very surprising that the acute and forcible observations of a traveller they knew would be listened to, should be received testily. The extraordinary features of the business were, first, the excess of the rage into which they lashed themselves; and, secondly, the puerility of the inventions by which they attempted to account for the severity with which they fancied they had been treated.

Not content with declaring that the volumes contained no word of truth from beginning to end, (which is an assertion I heard made very nearly as often as they were mentioned,) the whole country set to work to discover the causes why Capt. Hall had visited the United States, and why he had published his book.

I have heard it said with as much precision and gravity as if the statement had been conveyed by an official report, that Capt. Hall had been sent out by the British government expressly for the purpose of checking the growing admiration of England for the government of the United States,—that it was by a commission from the Treasury he had come, and that it was only in obedience to orders that he had found any thing to object to.

I do not give this as the gossip of a coterie; I am persuaded that it is the belief of a very considerable portion of the country. So deep is the conviction of this singular people that they cannot be seen without being admired, that they will not admit the possibility that any one should honestly and sincerely find aught to disapprove in them, or their country.

Prudishness

12. Frederick Marryat

There are certain words never used in America

If contemporary visitors can be believed, Americans outdid their English cousins in "Victorianism," that is in those aspects of the term connoting great shame in the presence of the unclothed human body, in art portraying it, or in language too clearly describing it. Americans were found to be unhappy with *The Rape of the Lock* as too salacious a title.

From Frederick Marryat, *A Diary in America*, p. 154.

Nude sculptures were shown to the sexes separately, with the advice that the female nude was thinking spiritual thoughts. Marryat's report captures attitudes discerned by many travelers.

They object to everything nude in statuary. When I was at the house of Governor Everett, at Boston, I observed a fine cast of the Apollo Belvidere; but in compliance with general opinion, it was hung with drapery, although Governor Everett himself is a gentleman of refined mind and high classical attainments, and quite above such ridiculous sensitiveness. In language it is the same thing. There are certain words which are never used in America, but an absurd substitute is employed. I cannot particularize them after this preface, lest I should be accused of indelicacy myself. I may, however, state one little circumstance which will fully prove the correctness of what I say.

When at Niagara Falls I was escorting a young lady with whom I was on friendly terms. She had been standing on a piece of rock, the better to view the scene, when she slipped down, and was evidently hurt by the fall: she had, in fact, grazed her shin. As she limped a little in walking home, I said, "Did you hurt your leg much?" She turned from me, evidently much shocked, or much offended,—and not being aware that I had committed any very heinous offence, I begged to know what was the reason of her displeasure. After some hesitation, she said that as she knew me well, she would tell me that the word *leg* was never mentioned before ladies. I apologized for my want of refinement, which was attributable to having been accustomed only to *English* society; and added, that as such articles must occasionally be referred to, even in the most polite circles in America, perhaps she would inform me by what name I might mention them without shocking the company. Her reply was, that the word *limb* was used; "nay," continued she, "I am not so particular as some people are, for I know those who always say limb of a table, or limb of a piano-forte."

There the conversation dropped; but a few months afterwards I was obliged to acknowledge that the young lady was correct when she asserted that some people were more particular than even she was.

I was requested by a lady to escort her to a seminary for young ladies, and on being ushered into the reception-room, conceive my astonishment at beholding a square piano-forte with four *limbs*. However, that the ladies who visited their daughters might feel in its full force the extreme delicacy of the mistress of the establishment, and her care to preserve in their utmost purity the ideas of the young ladies under her charge, she had dressed all these four limbs in modest little trousers, with frills at the bottom of them!

Rudeness

13. Frances Trollope

The dislike which gentlemanly feeling is sure to create

If contemporary observers could be believed, the rules of ordinary civility were regularly violated by Americans. Evidently fearful that politeness might be construed by visitors as acquiescence in "aristocratic" behavior demeaning to the spirit of equality, some Americans identified discourtesy with democratic manliness. The following selection, drawn from a southern newspaper, describes the injuries inflicted on the Duke of Saxe-Weimar, himself one of the more sympathetic foreign observers of the American scene.

A short time before we arrived in America, the Duke of Saxe-Weimar made a tour of the United States. I heard many persons speak of his unaffected and amiable manners, yet he could not escape the dislike which every trace of gentlemanly feeling is sure to create among the ordinary class of Americans. As an amusing instance of this, I made the following extract from a newspaper.

> A correspondent of the Charlestown Gazette tells an anecdote connected with the Duke of Saxe-Weimar's recent journey through

From Frances Trollope, *Domestic Manners of the Americans*, I, pp. 307–309.

our country, which we do not recollect to have heard before, although some such story is told of the veritable Capt. Basil Hall. The scene occurred on the route between Augusta and Milledgeville; it seems that the sagacious Duke engaged three or four, or more seats, in the regular stage, for the accommodation of himself and suite, and thought by this that he had secured the monopoly of the vehicle. Not so, however; a traveller came along, and entered his name upon the book, and secured his seat by payment of the customary charges. To the Duke's great surprise on entering the stage, he found our traveller comfortably housed in one of the most eligible seats, wrapped up in his fearnought, and snoring like a buffalo. The Duke, greatly irritated, called for the question of consideration. He demanded, in broken English, the cause of the gross intrusion, and insisted in a very princely manner, though not, it seems, in very princely language, upon the incumbent vacating the seat in which he had made himself so impudently at home. But the Duke had yet to learn his first lesson of republicanism. The driver was one of those sturdy southrons, who can always, and at a moment's warning, whip his weight in wild cats: and he as resolutely told the Duke, that the traveller was as good, if not a better man, than himself; and that no alteration of the existing arrangement could be permitted. Saxe-Weimar became violent at this opposition, so unlike any to which his education hitherto had ever subjected him, and threatened John with the application of the bamboo. This was one of those threats which in Georgia dialect would subject a man to "a rowing up salt river;" and, accordingly, down leaped our driver from his box, and peeling himself for the combat, he leaped about the vehicle in the most wild-boar style, calling upon the prince of a five acre patch to put his threat in execution. But he of the star refused to make up issue in the way suggested, contenting himself with assuring the enraged southron of a complaint to his excellency the Governor, on arrival at the seat of government. This threat was almost as unlucky as the former, for it wrought the individual for whom it was intended into that species of fury, which, though discriminating in its madness, is nevertheless without much limit in its violence, and he swore that the Governor might go to ——, and for his part he would just as leave lick the Governor as the Duke; he'd like no better fun than to give both Duke and Governor a dressing in the same breath; could do it, he had little doubt, &c. &c.; and instigating one fist to diverge into the face of the marvelling and panic-stricken nobleman, with the other he thrust him down into a seat alongside the traveller, whose presence had been originally of such sore discomfort to his excellency, and bidding the attendants jump in with their discomfited master, he mounted his box in triumph, and went on his journey.

Unattractive Table Manners

14. James Fenimore Cooper

Americans are the grossest feeders of any civilized nation

After returning from several years' travel in Europe, James Fenimore Cooper in 1838 published two novels, *Homeward Bound*, and *Home As Found*, deploring the inroads made by mediocrity, conformity, and crass materialism among his countrymen. In a series of essays he published that same year under the title, *The American Democrat*, Cooper assessed—somewhat gloomily—the chief features of his country's new civilization. In the following passage he relates the unattractive fare and table manners of Americans to their disinterest in the amenities and finer points of civilization.

The Americans are deficient on many points of civilization, solely for the want of physical force in given places, the practice of covering large surfaces unavoidably retarding the improvements of the nation. This is rather the subject of regret, than a matter of reproach. They are almost ignorant of the art of music, one of the most elevating, innocent and refining of human tastes, whose influence on the habits and morals of a people is of the most beneficial tendency. This taste and knowledge are not only wanting to the people, but an appreciation of their importance. They are also wanting in most of the high tastes, and consequently in the high enjoyments, that accompany a knowledge of all the

From James Fenimore Cooper, *The American Democrat* (Cooperstown: H. and E. Phinney, 1838), 155–157.

fine arts in general, and in much that depends on learning, research, and familiarity with the world.

The Americans excel in humanity, in the ordinary comforts, though inferior to the English in this respect, in general civility, in the means of motion while confined to great routes, in shipping and most of the facilities of trade, in common instruction and an aptitude to ordinary pursuits, and in an absence of the sophisms that beset older and more artificial systems. It is, however, to be regretted, that as the nation recedes from the struggle that created the present system, the truths that came uppermost in the collision, are gradually yielding to a new set of sophisms, more peculiar to the present order of things.

There is a familiar and too much despised branch of civilization, of which the population of this country is singularly and unhappily ignorant; that of cookery. The art of eating and drinking, is one of those on which more depends, perhaps, than on any other, since health, activity of mind, constitutional enjoyments, even learning, refinement, and, to a certain degree, morals, are all, more or less, connected with our diet. The Americans are the grossest feeders of any civilized nation known. As a nation, their food is heavy, coarse, ill prepared and indigestible, while it is taken in the least artificial forms that cookery will allow. The predominance of grease in the American kitchen, coupled with the habits of hasty eating and of constant expectoration, are the causes of the diseases of the stomach so common in America. The science of the table extends far beyond the indulgence of our appetites, as the school of manners includes health and morals, as well as that which is agreeable. Vegetable diet is almost converted into an injury in America, from an ignorance of the best modes of preparation, while even animal food is much abused, and loses half its nutriment.

The same is true as respects liquors. The heating and exciting wines, the brandies, and the coarser drinks of the laboring classes, all conspire to injure the physical and the moral man, while they defeat their own ends.

These are points of civilization on which this country has yet much to learn, for while the tables of the polished and cultivated partake of the abundance of the country, and wealth has even found means to introduce some knowledge of the kitchen, there is not perhaps on the face of the globe, the same number of people among whom the good things of the earth are so much abused, or ignorantly wasted, as among the people of the United States. National character is, in some measure, affected by a knowledge of the art of preparing food, there being as good reason to suppose that man is as much affected by diet as any other animal, and it is certain that the connection between our moral and physical qualities is so intimate as to cause them to react on each other.

Dullness

15. Charles Dickens

Undertakers on duty would be sprightly beside them

"There is little of what is called *fun* in America," wrote the friendly critic Francis Lieber. Mrs. Trollope thought "Jonathan . . . a very dull boy." She believed Englishmen were not particularly lively, but compared with Americans they were "whirligigs" to whom "every day is a holy day and every night a festival." Others mourned the "funeral solemnity" and the "oppressive atmosphere" of American social occasions. In the following excerpt from the notes of the great English novelist, Americans at public meals were found a disquietingly silent and dull people.

We are to be on board the Messenger three days: arriving at Cincinnati (barring accidents) on Monday morning. There are three meals a day. Breakfast at seven, dinner at half-past twelve, supper about six. At each, there are a great many small dishes and plates upon the table, with very little in them; so that although there is every appearance of a mighty "spread," there is seldom really more than a joint: except for those who fancy slices of beetroot, shreds of dried beef, complicated entanglements of yellow pickle; maize, Indian corn, apple-sauce, and pumpkin.

From Charles Dickens, *American Notes*, p. 137.

Some people fancy all these little dainties together (and sweet preserves beside), by way of relish to their roast pig. They are generally those dyspeptic ladies and gentlemen who eat unheard-of quantities of hot corn-bread (almost as good for the digestion as a kneaded pincushion), for breakfast, and for supper. Those who do not observe this custom, and who help themselves several times instead, usually suck their knives and forks meditatively, until they have decided what to take next: then pull them out of their mouths; put them in the dish; help themselves; and fall to work again. At dinner, there is nothing to drink upon the table, but great jugs full of cold water. Nobody says anything, at any meal, to anybody. All the passengers are very dismal, and seem to have tremendous secrets weighing on their minds. There is no conversation, no laughter, no cheerfulness, no sociality, except in spitting; and that is done in silent fellowship round the stove, when the meal is over. Every man sits down, dull and languid; swallows his fare as if breakfasts, dinners, and suppers, were necessities of nature never to be coupled with recreation or enjoyment; and having bolted his food in a gloomy silence, bolts himself, in the same state. But for these animal observances, you might suppose the whole male portion of the company to be the melancholy ghosts of departed book-keepers, who had fallen dead at the desk: such is their weary air of business and calculation. Undertakers on duty would be sprightly beside them; and a collation of funeral baked-meats, in comparison with these meals, would be a sparkling festivity.

Strange Conversationalists

16. Charles Dickens

You will hear one phrase repeated over and over

The American way of discourse disconcerted thoughtful people. James Fenimore Cooper winced at the preciosity and pretentiousness of persons

From Charles Dickens, *American Notes*, pp. 164, 165.

who considered themselves fashionable. As for ordinary Americans, the repetitiveness of their speech was maddening to some visitors, as the following passage from Dickens indicates.

Whenever the coach stops, and you can hear the voices of the inside passengers; or whenever any bystander addresses them, or any one among them; or they address each other; you will hear one phrase repeated over and over and over again to the most extraordinary extent. It is an ordinary and unpromising phrase enough, being neither more nor less than "Yes, Sir;" but it is adapted to every variety of circumstance, and fills up every pause in the conversation. Thus:—

The time is one o'clock at noon. The scene, a place where we are to stay to dine, on this journey. The coach drives up to the door of an inn. The day is warm, and there are several idlers lingering about the tavern, and waiting for the public dinner. Among them, is a stout gentleman in a brown hat, swinging himself to and fro in a rocking-chair on the pavement.

As the coach stops, a gentleman in a straw hat looks out of the window:

STRAW HAT. (To the stout gentleman in the rocking-chair.) I reckon that's Judge Jefferson, an't it?

BROWN HAT. (Still swinging; speaking very slowly; and without any emotion whatever.) Yes, Sir.

STRAW HAT. Warm weather, Judge.

BROWN HAT. Yes, Sir.

STRAW HAT. There was a snap of cold, last week.

BROWN HAT. Yes, Sir.

STRAW HAT. Yes, Sir.

A pause. They look at each other very seriously.

STRAW HAT. I calculate you'll have got through that case of the corporation, Judge, by this time, now?

BROWN HAT. Yes, Sir.

STRAW HAT. How did the verdict go, Sir?

BROWN HAT. For the defendant, Sir.

STRAW HAT. (Interrogatively.) Yes, Sir?

BROWN HAT. (Affirmatively.) Yes, Sir.

BOTH. (Musingly, as each gazes down the street.) Yes, Sir.

Another pause. They look at each other again, still more seriously than before.

BROWN HAT. This coach is rather behind its time to-day, I guess.

STRAW HAT. (Doubtingly.) Yes, Sir.

BROWN HAT. (Looking at his watch.) Yes, Sir; nigh upon two hours.

STRAW HAT. (Raising his eyebrows in very great surprise.) Yes, Sir!

BROWN HAT. (Decisively, as he puts up his watch.) Yes, Sir.

ALL THE OTHER INSIDE PASSENGERS (among themselves). Yes, Sir.

COACHMAN (in a very surly tone). No it an't.

STRAW HAT. (To the coachman.) Well, I don't know, Sir. We were a pretty tall time coming that last fifteen mile. That's a fact.

The coachman making no reply, and plainly declining to enter into any controversy on a subject so far removed from his sympathies and feelings, another passenger says, "Yes, Sir;" and the gentleman in the straw hat in acknowledgment of his courtesy, says "Yes, Sir," to him, in return. The straw hat then inquires of the brown hat, whether that coach in which he (the straw hat) then sits, is not a new one? To which the brown hat again makes answer, "Yes, Sir."

STRAW HAT. I thought so. Pretty loud smell of varnish, Sir?

BROWN HAT. Yes, Sir.

ALL THE OTHER INSIDE PASSENGERS. Yes, Sir.

BROWN HAT (to the company in general). Yes, Sir.

The conversational powers of the company having been by this time pretty heavily taxed, the straw hat opens the door and gets out; and all the rest alight also.

Catalog of Unlovely Traits

17. James Fenimore Cooper

The defects in American deportment are numerous and palpable

In the following selection Cooper sums up the flaws in American behavior. In his explanation, American incivility and boorishness were unfortunate consequences of a civilization peculiarly sensitive about its youthfulness, its alleged equality, its few achievements.

The American people are superior in deportment, in several particulars, to the people of Europe, and inferior in others. The gentlemen have less finesse, but more frankness of manner, while the other classes have less vulgarity and servility, relieved by an agreeable attention to each other's rights, and to the laws of humanity in general. On the whole, the national deportment is good, without being polished, supplying the deficiency in this last essential, by great kindness and civility. In that part of deportment which affects the rights of all, such as the admission of general and common laws of civility, the absence of social selfishness, and a strict regard to the wants and feebleness of woman, all other nations might be benefitted by imitating this.

The defects in American deportment are, notwithstanding, numerous and palpable. Among the first, may be ranked insubordination in children, and a general want of respect for age. The former vice may be ascribed to the business habits of the country, which leave so little time for parental instruction, and perhaps, in some degree, to the arts of political agents, who, with their own advantage in view, among the other expedients of their cunning, have resorted to the artifice of separating children from the natural advisers, by calling meetings of the young, to decide on the fortunes and policy of the country. Every advertisement calling assemblies of the young, to deliberate on national concerns, ought to be deemed an insult to the good sense, the

From James Fenimore Cooper, *The American Democrat*, pp. 144–148.

modesty, and the filial piety of the class to which it is addressed.

The Americans are reproached, also, with the want of a proper deference for social station; the lower classes manifesting their indifference by an unnecessary insolence. As a rule, this charge is unmerited, civility being an inherent quality of the American character; still, there are some who mistake a vulgar audacity for independence. Men and women of this disposition, require to be told that, in thus betraying their propensities, they are giving the strongest possible proofs that they are not what their idle vanity would give reason to suppose they fancy themselves, the equals of those whom they insult by their coarseness.

More of this class err from ignorance, want of reflection, or a loose habit of regulating their conduct in their intercourse with others, than from design. The following anecdote will give an instance of what is meant, and, as the circumstance related is true, the reader will perceive the ludicrous impression that is left, by these gross improprieties of behaviour. A gentleman, who shall be called Winfield, perceiving a girl of eight or ten years of age, endeavoring to find an entrance to his house, enquired her errand. "I have some hats for *Winfield's girls*," was the answer. Although shocked at this rudeness, Mr. Winfield told the child, that by going to a certain door, she would find a servant to receive her. "Oh!" replied the girl, "I have already seen the *Irish lady*, in the kitchen." This Irish *lady*, was the cook, a very good woman in her way, but one who had no pretensions to be so termed!

Such a confusion in the ideas of this child, is a certain proof of a want of training, for the young ladies who were treated so disrespectfully, were not the less ladies, nor did the cook become more than a cook, for the vulgarity. Facts are not to be changed by words, and all they obtain, who fancy their language and deportment can alter the relations of society, is an exposure of their own ignorance.

The entire complexion, and in many respects, the well being of society, depends on the deportment of its different members, to each other. It behoves the master to be kind to the servant, the servant to be respectful and obedient to his master; the young and inexperienced to defer to the aged and experienced; the ignorant to attend to the admonitions of the wise, and the unpolished to respect the tastes and habits of the refined.

In other countries, where positive ordinances create social distinctions in furtherance of these ends, it is believed they cannot be obtained in any other manner; but it is to be hoped that America is destined to prove, that common sense and the convictions of propriety and fitness, are as powerful agents as force. The servility and arrogance of a highly artificial social scale are not to be desired, but, having positive social facts, also, which cannot be dispensed with, it is vain to resist them. Civility and respect are the sure accompaniments of a high civilization, and the admission of obvious facts is an indispensable requisite of common sense, as their denial is evidence of infatuation and folly.

There is a moral obligation in every man to conduct himself with civility to all around him. Neither are his particular notions of what is proper, to be taken as an excuse for his rudeness and insults. Refinement and the finesse of breeding are not expected from the majority, but none are so ignorant, in this country, as not to distinguish between what is proper and what is improper in deportment.

Some men imagine they have a right to ridicule what are termed "airs," in others. If it could be clearly established what are "airs," and what not, a corrective of this sort might not be misapplied. But the term is conventional, one man experiencing disgust at what enters into the daily habits of another. It is exceedingly hazardous, therefore, for any but those who are familiar with the best usages of the world, to pronounce any thing "airs," because it is new to them, since what has this appearance to such persons may be no more than a proof of cultivation and of a good tone of manners.

On the other hand, many who have been thrown accidentally and for short periods, into the society of the more refined classes, adopt their usages without feeling or understanding their reasons and advantages, caricaturing delicacy and sentiment, and laying stress on habits, which, though possibly convenient in themselves, are not deemed at all essential by men and women of the world. These affectations of breeding are laughed at, as the "silverforkisms" of pretenders. To the man of the world it is unnecessary to point out the want of taste in placing such undue stress on these immaterial things, but it may not be unnecessary to the novice in the usages of the better circles, to warn him that his ignorance will be more easily seen by his exaggerations, than by his deficiencies of manner. The Duc de Richlieu is said to have detected an imposter by his *not* taking olives with his fingers.

But these are points of little interest with the mass, while civility and decency lie at the root of civilization. There is no doubt that, in general, America has retrograded in manners within the last thirty years. Boys, and even men, wear their hats in the houses of all classes, and before persons of all ages and conditions. This is not independence, but vulgarity, for nothing sooner distinguishes a gentleman from a blackguard, than the habitual attention of the former to the minor civilities established by custom. It has been truly said, that the man who is well dressed respects himself more, and behaves himself better, than the man that is ill dressed; but it is still more true that the man who commences with a strict observance of the commoner civilities, will be the most apt to admit of the influence of refinement on his whole character.

PART TWO

A Raw Society

Mountain Men

18. Osborne Russell

Christmas dinner a l'Indian

Among the most picturesque figures in American life in the first half of the nineteenth century were the "mountain men." The economic role of these men was to trap furbearing animals for the great fur trading companies. Their chief interest derives, however, from the lonely, primitive lives forced on them by their total separation from civilization. The following selection is from what has been described as the most accurate of the journals kept by a mountain man. It captures the dangers, the occasional conviviality, and the simplicity of the circumstances of these men.

BACK AGAIN TO THE HUNTING GROUNDS—SOLITARY REFLECTIONS ON A PEAK OF THE ROCKIES

On the 20th of July [1837] we left the rendezvous and traveled up Green River about ten miles. 21st—We traveled up Green River until noon, when we discovered a trail of eight or ten Blackfeet and a buffalo fresh killed and butchered, with the meat tied up in small bundles on the ground, which they had left on seeing us approach, and ran into the bushes. We, supposing them to be a small scouting party, tied their bundles of meat on to our saddles and still kept on our route but had not gone far before we discovered them secreted among some willows growing along a branch which crossed our trail. I was ahead leading the party when I discovered them. We stopped and one of my comrades, whose name was Allen, began to arrange the load on his pack mule. In the meantime I reined my horse to the left and rode onto

From Osborne Russell, *Journal of a Trapper 1834–1843* (Boise: Syms-York, 1921), 65–67, 113–116. Reprinted by courtesy of the publisher.

a small hillock nearby and casting a glance towards the bushes, which were about 150 yards distant, I saw two guns pointed at me. I instantly wheeled my horse, but to no purpose. The two balls struck him, one in the loins and the other in the shoulder, which dropped him under me. The Indians at the same time jumped out of the bushes, sixty or seventy in number, and ran toward us, shooting and yelling. I jumped on a horse behind one of my comrades and we scampered away toward the rendezvous, where we arrived at dark. 25th—The parties started and all traveled with Mr. Fontanelle's party up Green River ten miles, intending to keep in their company five or six days and then branch off to our first intended route. 26th—We traveled twenty miles northwest across a low range of hills and encamped in a valley lying on a branch of Lewis Fork called "Jackson's Little Hole." 27th—We traveled down this stream 18 miles northwest. This stream ran through a tremendous mountain in a deep, narrow canyon of rocks. The trail ran along the cliffs from 50 to 200 feet above its bed and was so narrow in many places that only one horse could pass at a time for several hundred yards, and one false step would precipitate one into the chasm below. After leaving the canyon we encamped at a small spring in "Jackson's Big Hole," near the southern extremity. 28th—Traveled up the valley north fifteen miles and encamped. Killed some buffalo and staid next day. 30th—Left the camp in company with two trappers and one camp keeper. We received instructions from Mr. Fontanelle to meet the camp at the mouth of Clark's Fork of the Yellowstone on the 15th of the ensuing October, where they expected to pass the winter, but he said if he should conclude to change his winter quarters he would cause a tree to be marked at Howell's grave and bury a letter in the ground at the foot of it containing directions for finding the camp.

We traveled north till near sunset and encamped about forty miles from the main party. 31st—We traveled to the fork five miles below Jackson's Lake and ascended it in the same direction I had done the season before and encamped about fifteen miles from the valley. August 1st—We reached the dividing spring about four o'clock p. m. and stopped for the night. 2d—We encamped at the inlet of the Yellowstone Lake. 3d—Traveled down the east shore of the lake and stopped for the night near the outlet at the steam springs. 4th—We took our course east northeast and after traveling all day over rugged mountains, thickly covered with pines and underbrush, we encamped at night about ten miles north of the secluded valley, on the stream which runs through it. After we had encamped we killed a deer, which came in good time, as we had eaten the last of our provisions the night previous at the Yellowstone Lake and the flies and mosquitoes were so bad and the underbrush so thick that we had not killed anything during the day. 5th—We traveled up a left hand branch of this stream northeast fifteen miles through the thick pines and brush until near the head, where we encamped in a beautiful valley about two miles in circumference, almost encircled with huge mountains whose tops were covered with snow, from which small rivulets were issuing clear as crystal, and, uniting in the smooth, grassy vale, formed the stream which we had ascended. We concluded to spend the next day at this place, as there were no flies or mosquitoes, for though warm and pleasant in the day, the nights were too cold for them to survive. The next day, after eating a light breakfast of roasted venison, I shouldered my rifle and ascended the highest mountain on foot. I reached the snow in about an hour, when, seating myself upon a huge fragment of granite and having full view of the country around me in a few moments was almost lost in contemplation. This, said I, is not a place where heroes' deeds of chivalry have been achieved in days of yore, neither is it a place of which bards have sung until the world knows the precise posture of every rock and tree or the winding turn of every streamlet. But on the contrary those stupendous rocks whose surface is formed into irregular benches rising one above another from the vale to the snow, dotted here and there with low pines and covered with green herbage intermingled with flowers, with the scattered flocks of sheep and elk carelessly feeding or thoughtlessly reposing beneath the shade, having Providence for their founder and Nature for shepherd, gardener and historian. In viewing scenes like this the imagination of one unskilled in science wanders to the days of the Patriarchs and after numerous conjecturing returns without any fixed decision. Wonder is put to the test, but having no proof for its argument, a doubt still remains, but supposition steps forward and taking the place of knowledge, in a few words solves the mysteries of ages, centuries and eras. After indulging in such a train of reflections for about two hours, I descended to the camp, where I found my companions had killed a fat buck elk during my absence and some of the choicest parts of it were supported on sticks around the fire. My ramble had sharpened my appetite and the delicious flavor of roasted meat soon rid my brain of romantic ideas. My companions were men who never troubled themselves about vain and frivolous notions, as they called them. With them every country was pretty when there was weather, and as to beauty of nature or arts it was all a "humbug," as one of them, an Englishman, often expressed it. "Talk of a fine country," said he, "and beautiful places in these mountains. If you want to see a beautiful place, go to Highland and see the Duke of Rutland's place." "Aye" says a son of Erin, who sat opposite with an elk rib in one hand and a butcher knife in the other, while the sweat rolling from his face mingled in the channels of grease which ran from the corners of his mouth, "Aye, an' ye would see a pretty place, go to old Ireland and take a walk in Lord Farnham's domain. That is the place where ye can see plisure. Arrah, an' if I were upon that same ground this day I'd fill my body with good ould whisky." "Yes," says the backwoods hunter on my left, as he cast away his bone and smoothed down his long auburn hair with his greasy hand, "Yes, you English and Irish are always talking about your fine countries, but if they are so mighty fine," said he with an oath, "why do so many of you run off and leave them and come to America to get a living?" From this the conversation turned into an argument in which the hunter came off victorious, driving his opponents from the field.

A WINTER WITH THE INDIANS NEAR GREAT SALT LAKE—CHRISTMAS DINNER A L'INDIAN

On the 1st of October [1840] I again left the fort with a Frenchman who had an Indian wife and two children, and was going on to Green River to pass the winter with them. We traveled up Portneuf about fifteen miles, where we stopped the next day and hunted antelope, and the day following we traveled up the stream about twenty miles, when, after staying ten days, we went to the Soda Springs on Bear River. Here we concluded to spend a month on Bear River, traveling slowly, hunting beaver and antelope, as the latter is the only game in this part of the country. Beaver also were getting very scarce. On the 15th of November the snow began to fall and my comrade started, with his family, across the mountains to Green River and I returned towards the fort. On my way down Bear River I met thousands of antelope traveling towards their winter quarters, which is generally Green River valley. I followed Bear River down to Cache valley, where I found twenty lodges of Snake Indians and staid with them several days. They had a considerable number of beaver skins, but I had nothing to trade for them. They told me if I would go to the fort and get some goods, return and spend the winter with them, they would trade their furs with me. I started for the fort with one of them whom I engaged to assist me with my horses. I arrived at the fort on the 23rd of November, when, after getting such articles for trade as I wished, and my personal supplies for the winter, I returned to Cache valley, accompanied by a halfbreed. On arriving at the village I found several Frenchmen and halfbreed trappers encamped with the Snakes. One Frenchman, having an Indian wife and child, invited me to pass the winter in his lodge, and as he had a small family and large lodge, I accepted the invitation and had my baggage taken into his lodge and neatly arranged by his wife, who was a Flathead. The neat manner in which her lodge and furniture was kept would have done honor to a large portion of the "pale faced" fair sex in the civilized world.

We staid in this valley until the 15th of December, when it was unanimously agreed to go to the Salt Lake and there spend the remainder of the winter. The next day we traveled across the valley in a southwest direction, then took into a narrow defile which led us through the mountain into the valley on the eastern borders of the lake. The day following we moved along the valley in a southerly direction and encamped on a small branch close to the foot of the mountain. The ground was still bare and the autumnal growth of grass was the best I ever saw at this season of the year.

18th—I arose about an hour before daylight, took my rifle and ascended the mountain on foot to hunt sheep. The weather was clear and cold but the mountain being steep and rugged and my rifle heavy, the exercise soon put me in a perspiration. After climbing about half a mile I sat down on a rock to wait for daylight, and when it came I discovered a band of about 100 rams within about eighty yards of me. I shot and killed one. The others ran about fifty yards further and stopped. While I was reloading my rifle one of them ascended a high pinnancle of rock which jutted over a precipice. There were others nearer me, but I wished to fetch this proud animal from his elevated position. I brought my rifle to my face, the ball whistled through his heart, and he fell headlong over the precipice. I followed the band at some distance among the crags and killed two more, butchered them, then returned and butchered the two I had first killed, and returned to camp and sent some men with horses to get the meat.

Dec. 20th—We moved along the borders of the lake about ten miles and encamped on a considerable stream running into it called Weaver's River. At this place the valley is about ten miles wide, intersected with numerous springs of salt and fresh, hot and cold water, which rise at the foot of the mountain and run through the valley into the river and lake. Weaver's River is well timbered along its banks, principally with cottonwood and box elder. There are also large groves of sugar maple, pine and some oak growing in the ravines about the mountains. We also found large numbers of elk which had left the mountains to winter among the thickets of wood and brush along the river.

CHRISTMAS

December 25th—It was agreed on by the party to prepare a Christmas dinner, but I shall first endeavor to describe the party and then the dinner. I have already said the man who was the proprietor of the lodge in which I staid was a Frenchman with a

Flathead wife and one child. The inmates of the next lodge were a halfbreed Iowa, a Nez Perce wife and two children, his wife's brother and another halfbreed; next lodge was a halfbreed Cree, his wife (a Nez Perce) two children and a Snake Indian. The inmates of the third lodge was a halfbreed Snake, his wife (a Nez Perce) and two children. The remainder were fifteen lodges of Snake Indians. Three of the party spoke English but very broken, therefore that language was made but little use of, as I was familiar with the Canadian French and Indian tongue.

About ten o'clock we sat down to dinner in the lodge where I staid, which was the most spacious, being about thirty-six feet in circumference at the base, with a fire built in the center. Around this sat on clean epishemores all who claimed kin to the white man (or to use their own expression, all who were gens d'esprit), with their legs crossed in true Turkish style, and now for the dinner.

The first dish that came on was a large tin pan eighteen inches in diameter, rounding full of stewed elk meat. The next dish was similar to the first, heaped up with boiled deer meat (or as the whites would call it, venison, a term not used in the mountains). The third and fourth dishes were equal in size to the first, containing a boiled flour pudding, prepared with dried fruit, accompanied by four quarts of sauce made of the juice of sour berries and sugar. Then came the cakes, followed by about six gallons of strong coffee ready sweetened, with tin cups and pans to drink out of, large chips or pieces of bark supplying the places of plates. On being ready, the butcher knives were drawn and the eating commenced at the word given by the landlady. As all dinners are accompanied by conversation, this was not deficient in that respect. The principal topic which was discussed was the political affairs of the Rocky Mountains, the state of governments among the different tribes, the personal characters of the most distinguished warrior chiefs, etc. One remarked that the Snake chief, Pahda-hewakunda, was becoming very unpopular and it was the opinion of the Snakes in general that Mohwoom-hah, his brother, would be at the head of affairs before twelve months, as his village already amounted to more than three hundred lodges, and, moreover, he was supported by the bravest men in the nation, among whom were Ink-a-tosh-a-pop, Fibe-bo-un-to-wat-see and Who-sha-kik, who were the pillars of the nation and at whose names the Blackfeet quaked with fear. In like manner were the characters of the principal chiefs of the Bannock, Nez Perce, Flathead and Crow nations and the policy of their respective nations commented upon by the descendants of Shem and Japhet with as much affected dignity as if they could have read their own names when written, or distinguish the letter B from bull's foot.

Dinner being over, the tobacco pipes were filled and lighted, while the squaws and children cleared away the remains of the feast to one side of the lodge, where they held a sociable tete-à-tete over the fragments. After the pipes were extinguished all agreed to have a frolic shooting at a mark, which occupied the remainder of the day.

Violence

19. Thomas Ford

Mob violence must be put down

The following document reflects a reaction against both violence and intolerance. The governor of Illinois warns citizens of his state against resumption of violence toward the Mormons, a group feared and loathed by many rural folk on moral and religious grounds.

I am continually informed of your preparations and threats to renew the war, and exterminate the Mormons. One would suppose that you ought to rest satisfied with what you have already done. The Mormon leaders, if they ever resisted the law, have submitted to its authority. They have surrendered the public arms; and appeared to be ready to do any thing required, to make atonement for whatever wrong may have been done. Since the

Thomas Ford, *Address to the People of Warsaw, in Hancock County* (Springfield, Illinois, July 25, 1844).

assassination of their two principal leaders, under circumstances well calculated to inflame their passions, and drive them to excesses for the purposes of revenge, they have been entirely peaceful and submissive; and have patiently awaited the slow operation of the laws to redress the wrongs of which they complained. There has been no retaliation; no revenge; and for any thing I can ascertain, there will be none. Those of your people, who are charged with being the most hostile to them, have lived, if they knew it, in perfect security from illegal violence. I am anxious for a pacification of your difficulties. You cannot drive out, or exterminate the Mormons. Such an effort would be madness, and would not be permitted by the people of the State. You cannot be sustained in it either by force or law. You are blinding yourselves to your weakness, and keeping up an agitation which must fail of the purpose intended, and recoil with terrible energy upon your own heads. I exhort you to reconsider your infatuated resolutions. Try your Mormon neighbors again, and if you cannot dwell together in amity, you may at least refrain from injuring each other. From the moderation of the Mormons, under what they conceive to be the deepest injury, you might well hope that if they ever entertained designs inconsistant with your liberty and happiness, that those designs have been abandoned. They are also interested in preserving the peace.—It is not natural to suppose that they, any more than yourselves, wish to live in continual alarm. They hope for quiet, and will be peaceful and submissive in order to enjoy it. But you are continually driving them to desperation by an insane course of threatening and hostility, and depriving yourselves of peace by the same means used to disquiet them.

If I have said any thing severe in this address, I pray you, attribute it to my deep conviction that your course is improper and unwarrantable. Such is the opinion of the people at large in the State, and all over the country. From being right in the first instance, you have put yourselves in the wrong, and there are none who sustain you. As men of sense you are bound to see, if you will open your eyes, that you cannot effect your purposes. Nevertheless you are still training and drilling, and keeping together, and threatening a renewal of the war.—I have said to you often that you cannot succeed; by this time you ought to see it yourselves. What can your small force do against two thousand armed men, entrenched in a city, and defending themselves, their wives and their children?—Besides, if you are the aggressors, I am determined that all the power of the State shall be used to prevent your success. I can never agree that a set of infatuated and infuriated men shall barbarously attack a peaceful people, who have submitted to all the demands of the law; and when they had full power to do so, refrained from inflicting vengeance upon their enemies.—You may count on my most determined opposition—upon the opposition of the law and upon that of every peaceful law abiding citizen of the country. This is not spoken in anger. God knows, I would do you no injury unless compelled to do so to sustain the laws. But mob violence must be put down. It is threatening the whole country with anarchy and ruin. It is menacing our fair form of government, and destroying the confidence of the patriot in the institutions of his country.

I have been informed that the Mormons about Lima and Macedonia, have been warned to leave the settlements.—They have a right to remain and enjoy their property. As long as they are good citizens, they shall not be molested; and the sooner those misguided persons withdraw their warning and retrace their steps, the better it will be for them.

20. James A. Thome

A violent mob attacked the house

The activities of abolition societies were often greeted by furious mob violence, particularly in strongholds of the American Colonization

From James A. Thome, letter to Theodore Weld, May 12, 1836, in Gilbert H. Barnes and Dwight L. Dumond, eds., *Letters of Theodore Dwight Weld, Angelina Grimké Weld, and Sarah Grimké, 1822–1844* (New York: D. Appleton-Century, 1934), I, pp. 298–301. (Reprint edition, New York: Da Capo Press, 1970). Copyright 1934 by the American Historical Association; copyright renewed 1962 by Dwight L. Dumond and Elizabeth B. Pumphrey. Reprinted by permission of the copyright owners.

Society. The following letter, written by one of the abolition movement's little known activists to the celebrated Theodore Weld, illustrates the physical dangers faced by members of the antislavery movement.

Newark, Licking Co. [Ohio] May 2, 1836.

Dear Bro. Weld

I am here waiting a few hours for the stage to take me home to Ky. It is exceedingly warm, and my mind and body are both too much relaxed to permit me to entertain you. But I know you are impatient to hear from our Anniversary, and I trust therefore that your *eagerness* will supply my want of *sprightliness.*

Previous—a week or two—to the meeting, 60 or 70 of the Granville citizens signed and published a *remonstrance* against the proposed meeting. Great efforts were made to prevent the Delegates from attending. Instructions were left, as it would seem, with every tavern keeper within 20 miles around to urge the Delegates, who might stop with them, to turn back. The report was currently circulated that there was to be a dreadful mob, that blood would be shed and perhaps some lives lost, and the Delegates were entreated not to proceed another step toward Granville. Others gave out word that the place of meeting was changed from G. to Putnam.

I reached G. (in company with Bros. Streeter and Wattles) on Tuesday eve. Found a large no. assembled. Learned that the Anniversary was to be held in Mr. A. Bancroft's Barn where you lectured once. Had a meeting there on Tuesday eve. I lectured. Fine state of feeling. Quakers on the one hand and infidels on the other shouted *amen* as I proceeded. No disturbance.

On Wednesday the meeting opened ½ after 10 o'cl. Guthrie read an excellent Report. Birney spoke on the right of Discussion. A large congregation out—"Women not a few." In the afternoon I read an address to the Ladies of Ohio. The girls from the schools and other Ladies to the number of 70 or 80 were present. It took hold of the women mightily. Resolutions were offered and remarks made by John Rankin, Jas. H. Dick[e]y, Prof. H. Cowles, Foote of Cleveland and others.

Rankin and Foote did nobly. A wakeful attention all the time. Not a whisper of a mob. Had no meeting in Barn at night. Several of the brethren went into the neighborhoods around and Lectured. Jno. Alvord went south 2 miles to a school house. A violent mob attacked the house, broke in the windows—sash and all—throwing in stones of several pounds weight. Astonishing to tell, no one was injured. Several (John among them) were *egged* from head to foot. The audience sallied out and drove off the mob, cudgelling them after the *right manner* (my *peace principles* are giving way you perceive). The same night a gang of fellows were prowling about Dr. Bancrofts House, where I was staying, threatening to break the windows before morning. We went to bed, fully expecting to be waked up by the shattering of the windows. *Not an egg was thrown.* The next morning (Thursday) we heard that the most *respectable citizens* had held a meeting late at night and voted to send Expresses to St. Albans, Mount Vernon, Newark, etc., for mobs. The Expresses started off between 10 and 12 o'cl. at night. We were told we should have *trouble* before night. We convened at the Barn by 9 o'cl. Many provided themselves with *clubs* to give the mob a *suitable* reception. The number present was *greater* by far than at any previous meeting. Twice as many *Ladies.* Proceeded to the most *important* business first. A Resolution was passed to raise $5,000 within the year. $4,500 were pledged on the spot. The sum was then unanimously raised from 5 to $10,000. The officers for the year were then chosen. King remains President. He was not present, but sent a *strong Letter.* The Exec. Comm. was located in Hamilton Co., and is composed of the *officers* living in that county. Aug. Wattles is Cor. Sec. Intends to help Birney, instead of going on his Negro Expedition. This he will defer for some time. Rankin gave us a strong Report on the duties of the church. Speeches were made by Mahan, Bushnel[l], Wattles, etc. About 11 o'cl. an express came in stating that the mob, amounting to 200 had just left the village, on their way to the Barn, with a *fiddler* at their head. It caused a little consternation. Some of the Ladies were very much frightened. But the announcement was treated with so much scorn by the principal men, that the House was soon restored to order. When it was told that they were coming, with a *fiddler* at their head, Prof. John Cowles cried out "let them come". Judson of Milan said "let 'em fiddle—" Said another "we are ready for 'em". We went right on with our business until we got through, then adjourned, *sine die,* between 1 and 2 o'cl. The mob didn't come. It was proposed that we walk up to the village in one body—double file. We did so. Our procession extended half way to the village, from the Barn. It looked grand and imposing. The mobites were on the tops of the hills looking down upon us and they seemed to be abashed. Their vision was like that of Balaam, Numb[ers] 23: 9, 10, "For from the top of the rocks I saw him and from the hills I behold him, etc."

We moved on to the village. A part of the procession halted at Dr. Bancroft's. Another part, composed chiefly of students of the college and female seminaries, went on right by the tavern where the mob had made their head quarters. There they were assaulted and several severe scuffles ensued. Two or three abolitionists were knocked down with clubs. One was a student (Lewis) from Oberlin. Another a student of Granville. The mobites fared the worst however, for they were paid in their own coin, with *bloody interest.*

After dinner the Delegates began to disperse. They presented a ludicrous spectacle riding out of town, in every direction, on their *shaved-tailed horses* (A great no. of the horses had their tails and manes cut close off). When Bro. Birney was about leaving Dr. Bancrofts, on his *shaved-tailed horse,* the mob gathered about the door, abusing him most vilely. When he rode off they followed him with a shower of eggs and with curses. Not an egg touched him.

When I saw *Birney* egged out of town, by a mob, and no man or christian or minister or *magistrate,* to punish the indignity, I could stand no more. I wept.

Before night the mob dispersed and went to their homes, growling with disappointment. They were enraged at the Granville people because they would neither aid them, nor treat them, nor feed them. Some of the citizens anti-abolitionists were absolutely obliged to conceal themselves to escape the violence of the mob. On Thursday night, there was all the stillness of the sabbath day. No one's house was touched. There has been no disorder since. On the contrary there has been a powerful reaction. On yesterday (sabbath) evening Bro. Alvord lectured to a full audience in the Pres[byterian] Conference Room on the Bible Arg't. The most absorbed attention. Not a stone, nor an egg, nor a whisper of disorder. He has another appointment to lecture tomorrow afternoon in the same place. Probably will lecture there all week. Wouldn't wonder if he got 50 names to the constitution. In a word, dear Bro. everything has redounded to the good of the cause. 1. The weather. Very fair. 2. The *confusion* in the councils of the mob. They supposed that the meeting would continue until Friday Eve. and they had layed their plans to attack us on Thursday night and drive us out of town. Thus we had time to do all our business and peaceably disperse, before they got the steam up. 3. The division in the ranks of the mob. This weakened their forces and turned their attention from us to themselves. They had several hard fights among their own company.

We had a glorious meeting. Nearly 200.—30 or 40 *female* Delegates. All noble souls. The cause in this state has received a *mighty impulse,* depend upon it. We are beginning to talk of abolitionizing the state in a year or two, and of having our next anniversary in Cincinnati, with 2000 Delegates. The society has taken the Philan'pist under its wing. Prof. Drury is very much stirred up. I think there will be a blow up in the college shortly. Little didn't attend—afraid. Carr didn't attend. We were refreshed by the attendance of the *three sisters* from Cin.—Fact. Among those who sent out to Mount Vernon, etc., for mobs, there were members of Mr. Little's church! One of his members gave a *barrel of cider* to the mob. Don't this *freeze your blood?* I am going home to spend a week or two. Then will return to Oberlin. Allan goes to New York. I *did* think of going, but gave it out.

Your brother James [Thome]

21. Report of Committee

The spirit of violence reigned triumphant

Anti-Catholicism flourished in the 1830s and 1840s, fed by the sharp increase in Irish immigration to cities along the Atlantic coast. Anti-Catholic demagogues and fanatics concocted lurid tales of alleged Catholic plots to dismember the country and commit atrocities against its citizens. In actuality, Catholics were victims, rather than perpetrators, of atrocious behavior. The most notorious example of the spilling over of religious bigotry into mob violence occurred on August 11, 1834, when a working-class mob stormed and burned the Ursuline Convent in Charlestown, outside of Boston. This atrocity was triggered by rumors that a nun was being held in the convent against her wishes. The following passage is from a report prepared by some of Boston's leading citizens, men representative of both major parties and above all of the city's social, economic, and intellectual leadership.

. . . The rioters began to assemble in considerable numbers, arriving on foot and in wagons from different quarters; and a party of about forty or fifty proceeded to the front of the building, using violent and threatening language. They were addressed by the lady at the head of the establishment, who, desiring to know their wishes, was replied to that they wanted to enter and see the person alleged to be secreted. She answered, that their selectmen had that day visited the house, and could give them satisfactory information, and that any of them on calling the next day at a suitable hour, might see for themselves; at the same time remonstrating against such violation of the peace and of the repose of so many children of their most reputable citizens.

Shortly afterwards, the same, or another party, with increased numbers, approached the convent, using still more threatening and much gross and indecent language. The lady above referred to again addressed them in terms of remonstrance and reproach,

From *Report of the Committee*, Relating to the Destruction of the Ursuline Convent, August 11, 1834 (Boston: Samuel N. Dickinson, 1842), 13–16.

and desired to know whether none of their selectmen were present. Some of them replied that one was there, mentioning his name. He then came forward and announced his presence, stating that he was there for the purpose of defending her. She inquired whether he had procured the attendance of any others of the Board; and upon being answered in the negative, replied that she would not trust the establishment to his protection, and that if he came there to protect them, he should show it by taking measures to disperse the mob.

It appears from various testimony that he did attempt to dissuade the rioters from their design, by assurances that the selectmen had seen the nun who was supposed to have been secreted, and that the stories reported concerning her were untrue. But his assertions drew forth only expressions of distrust and insult. The mob continued upon the ground with much noise and tumult, and were in that state left by this magistrate, who returned home and retired to bed.

At about eleven o'clock, a bonfire was kindled on the land of Alvah Kelly, adjoining that of the eastern boundary of the convent, and distant about two hundred and seventy yards from the building, the fences of which were taken for the purpose. This is believed to have been a concerted signal for the assembling of all concerned in the plot. . . .

At the time of this attack upon the convent, there were within its walls, about sixty female children and ten adults; one of whom was in the last stages of pulmonary consumption, another suffering under convulsion fits, and the unhappy female, who had been the immediate cause of the excitement, was by the agitations of the night in raving delirium.

No warning was given of the intended assault, nor could the miscreants, by whom it was made, have known whether their missiles might not kill or wound the helpless inmates of this devoted dwelling. Fortunately for them, cowardice prompted what mercy and manhood denied: after the first attack, the assailants paused awhile from the fear that some secret force was concealed in the convent or in ambush to surprise them; and in this interval the governess was enabled to secure the retreat of her little flock and terrified sisters into the garden. But before this was fully effected, the rioters, finding they had nothing but women and children to contend against, regained their courage, and ere all the inmates could escape, entered the building. . . .

Three or four torches which were, or precisely resembled, engine torches were then brought up from the road; and immediately upon their arrival, the rioters proceeded into every room in the building, rifling every drawer, desk and trunk which they found, and breaking up and destroying all the furniture, and casting much of it from the windows; sacrificing in their brutal fury, costly piano fortes and harps, and other valuable instruments; the little treasures of children, abandoned in their hasty flight; and even the vessels and symbols of christian worship.

After having thus ransacked every room in the building, they proceeded with great deliberation, about one o'clock, to make preparation for setting fire to it. For this purpose, broken furniture, books, curtains and other combustible materials, were placed in the centre of several of the rooms; and, as if in mockery of God as well as of man, the Bible was cast, with shouts of exultation, upon the pile first kindled; and as upon this were subsequently thrown the vestments used in religious service, and the ornaments of the altar, these shouts and yells were repeated. Nor did they cease until the Cross was wrenched from its place, and cast into the flames, as the final triumph of this fiend-like enterprise.

But the work of destruction did not end here. Soon after the convent was in flames, the rioters passed to the library, or bishop's lodge, which stood near, and after throwing the books and pictures from the windows, a prey to those without, fired that also.

Some time afterwards they proceeded to the farm-house, formerly occupied as the convent, and first making a similar assault with stones and clubs upon the doors and windows, in order to ascertain whether they had any thing to fear from persons within, the torches were deliberately applied to that building; and, unwilling to leave one object connected with the establishment to escape their fury, although the day had broken, and three buildings were then in flames or reduced to ashes, the extensive barn, with its contents, was in like manner devoted to destruction. And not content with all this, they burst open the tomb of the establishment, rifled it of the sacred vessels there deposited, wrested the plates from the coffins, and exposed to view the mouldering remains of their tenants.

Nor is it the least humiliating feature in this scene of cowardly and audacious violation of all that man ought to hold sacred and dear, that it was perpetrated in the presence of men vested with authority, and of the multitudes of our fellow citizens, while not one arm was lifted in the defence of helpless women and children, or in vindication of the violated laws of God and man. The spirit of violence, sacrilege, and plunder, reigned triumphant. Crime alone seemed to confer courage; while humanity, manhood, and patriotism, quailed, or stood irresolute and confounded in its presence.

Primitive Conditions in the Rural West

22. Patrick Shirreff

I began to feel uneasy about the sleeping accommodation

Conditions on the Illinois prairie in the 1830s would not have appealed to the finicky. The amenities were either lacking or minimal, with the level of social relations often primitive, as is disclosed in the following observations by one of the more intrepid of the foreign visitors.

The hotel at which our party was set down, was so disagreeably crowded, that the landlord could not positively promise beds, although he would do every thing in his power to accommodate us. The house was dirty in the extreme, and confusion reigned throughout, which the extraordinary circumstances of the village went far to extenuate. I contrived, however, to get on pretty well,

From Patrick Shirreff, *A Tour Through North America* (Edinburgh: Oliver and Boyd, 1835), 228, 229, 235–237.

having by this time learned to serve myself in many things, carrying water for washing, drying my shirt, wetted by the rain of the preceding evening, and brushing my shoes. The table was amply stored with substantial provisions, to which justice was done by the guests, although indifferently cooked, and still more so served up.

When bed-time arrived, the landlord showed me to an apartment about ten feet square, in which there were two small beds already occupied, assigning me in a corner a dirty pallet, which had evidently been recently used, and was lying in a state of confusion. Undressing for the night had become a simple proceeding, and consisted in throwing off shoes, neckcloth, coat, and vest, the two latter being invariably used to aid the pillow, and I had long dispensed with a nightcap. I was awoke from a sound sleep towards morning, by an angry voice uttering horrid imprecations, accompanied by a demand for the bed I occupied. A lighted candle, which the individual held in his hand, showed him to be a French trader, accompanied by a friend, and as I looked on them for some time in silence, their audacity and brutality of speech increased. At length I lifted my head from the pillow, leant on my elbow, and with a steady gaze, and the calmest tone of voice, said,—"Who are you that address me in such language?" The countenance of the angry individual fell, and he subduedly asked to share my bed. Wishing to put him to a farther trial, I again replied, "If you will ask the favour in a proper manner, I shall give you an answer." He was now either ashamed of himself, or felt his pride hurt, and both left the room without uttering a word. Next morning, the individuals who slept in the apartment with me, discovered that the intruders had acted most improperly towards them, and the most noisy of the two entered familiarly into conversation with me during breakfast, without alluding to the occurrence of the preceeding evening. . . .

Next day I applied for dinner at a house where a poor man was suffering much from sickness, and medical assistance had been called in. The family were about to sit down to a good dinner, of which I partook, paying $6\frac{1}{4}$d. sterling. Night closed on me while in the middle of a prairie, and I felt some apprehension of passing the cottages, which are not easily discovered in a faint light, being almost invariably situated a few yards in the forest, and of the same dark shade. A breeze, highly tainted with the scent of fried pork, led me to expect a house, and to which a light, proceeding from a half-opened door, served to guide me. I found four travellers, the landlord, and his wife, assembled in a poor habitation, lighted by what they termed a string, or piece of twine, dipt in tallow, and which gave a glimmering light, so that we could scarcely distinguish objects. There seemed to be only three tea-cups in the house; the party had, consequently, to feed by turns, and, being a stranger, I was requested by all to seat myself at the first table, an honour to which my appetite led me to make no serious objection.

One of the travellers was descended from the original French, a little merry fellow, speaking indifferent English, and two others consisted of an old man and his son, originally from Kentucky. Both of these individuals differed in their language and manners from most of the people I had come in contact with since leaving Canada. The old man spoke a good many words according to negro pronunciation, and both were addicted to swearing. The son, about thirty-five years of age, was one of the best-looking and finest formed men I met in America. I soon discovered he was slightly intoxicated, and a most profligate character. Being anxious to shun conversation with him, I was annoyed at his placing his chair beside mine; and as there was neither another house nor apartment to retire to, I endeavoured to make the most of my situation. Having replied to his enquiry what countryman I was, by asking him to guess, he successively said, Dutchman, German, Englishman, and Irishman, and fearing he might lose patience, I at last told him a Scotchman. He had never heard of Scotchmen before, and insisted I must be one of the Scotch-Irish, which I afterwards learnt means, in this part of the world, the inhabitants of the north of Ireland. The discussion about Scotch-Irish suggested the proudest feat of his life. He said Jim Partridge was an Irishman, able to whip any man in America, and who must have been heard of in my country. He had a whipping-match with Jim, who fell, and was in act of being gouged, when the bystanders lifted him off Jim, who, seizing a stick, cut his head with it in a dreadful manner. Gouging is performed by twisting the fingers into the hair of the victim, and with the thumb forcing the eye out of its socket. This savage act has long been known in Kentucky and some of the western states, and was often resorted to when parties quarrelled. It is now, however, confined to the lowest blackguards, and of rare occurrence. The eyes of the wretch sparkled with delight when relating the prostrate situation of Jim, and the prospect of gouging him, and he explained his brutal attempt by placing his fingers in my hair and on my face, when I could scarcely trust his intentions. He also insisted that I should feel the indention made by Jim's stick, and I thought his skull must have been as hard as his heart to have withstood such a blow.

The house was in all respects a mean one, containing little furniture, and two beds, from one of which rose an emanciated person, labouring under aberration of mind, and to whom the house and lands adjoining belonged. I began to feel uneasy about the sleeping accommodation, as both beds would be required for the family, and there was no garret apartment. The landlord at length drew forth from the corner of the room a dirty tick and covering, which were placed in the middle of the floor, and formed the sleeping place of five individuals, who arranged themselves latitudinally on the pallet. I was anxious for an outside berth, in order to have sea-room in case of accident, but the complaisance of the gouger deprived me of this position, and I found myself placed for the night between the old man and his son. None of the travellers thought of unrobing; and after putting off my shoes, I laid my head on my knapsack, which was the only thing in shape of a pillow to be had. My situation was far from enviable; fumes of whisky and squirts of tobacco juice assailing me on every side, and I considered the partner of my bed more savage than the wolf of the forest. Speedily falling into a profound sleep, from which I was awoke at daybreak by the Frenchman searching for his saddle, the horrors of my situation flashed on my mind, and I stealthily crawled from the bed, my movements being accelerated by the gouger muttering an ugly oath.

On gaining the outside of the door, the freshness of the air was delightful. The sky was cloudless, and in walking through the trees, the paroquets fluttered from their resting-places with a shrill cry. On reaching the opposite side of the wood, herds of cattle were seen streaming from the forest, and the smoke of the morning fires ascending in graceful columns, undisturbed by the serene atmosphere. The prairie-hen rose from the pathway with a purring noise, and the little gophers stood on end, and seemed to regard me as an intruder. The sun peered above the prairie, as if rising from the ocean, and gilded the nodding sunflower, whose brilliancy was heightened by dewdrops sparkling on the blossom leaves, and with which I washed my face. Nature was decked in a winning garb, and the events of the previous evening were forgotten in wooing her beauties.

New Cities

23. Harriet Martineau

Chicago looks raw and bare

Harriet Martineau was perhaps the most indefatigable of the foreign visitors, traversing the length and breadth of the United States during her stay in the mid-1830s. The following selection gives her reaction to the vigorous young city growing on the shores of Lake Michigan.

Chicago looks raw and bare, standing on the high prairie above the lake-shore. The houses appeared all insignificant, and run up in various directions, without any principle at all. A friend of mine who resides there had told me that we should find the inns intolerable, at the period of the great land sales, which bring a concourse of speculators to the place. It was even so. The very sight of them was intolerable; and there was not room for our party among them all. I do not know what we should have done, (unless to betake ourselves to the vessels in the harbour,) if our

From Harriet Martineau, *Society in America*, I, pp. 259–261.

coming had not been foreknown, and most kindly provided for. We were divided between three families, who had the art of removing all our scruples about intruding on perfect strangers. None of us will lose the lively and pleasant associations with the place, which were caused by the hospitalities of its inhabitants.

I never saw a busier place than Chicago was at the time of our arrival. The streets were crowded with land speculators, hurrying from one sale to another. A negro, dressed up in scarlet, bearing a scarlet flag, and riding a white horse with housings of scarlet, announced the times of sale. At every street-corner where he stopped, the crowd flocked round him; and it seemed as if some prevalent mania infected the whole people. The rage for speculation might fairly be so regarded. As the gentlemen of our party walked the streets, store-keepers hailed them from their doors, with offers of farms, and all manner of land-lots, advising them to speculate before the price of land rose higher. A young lawyer, of my acquaintance there, had realised five hundred dollars per day, the five preceding days, by merely making out titles to land. Another friend had realised, in two years, ten times as much money as he had before fixed upon as a competence for life. Of course, this rapid money-making is a merely temporary evil. A bursting of the bubble must come soon. The absurdity of the speculation is so striking, that the wonder is that the fever should have attained such a height as I witnessed. The immediate occasion of the bustle which prevailed, the week we were at Chicago, was the sale of lots, to the value of two millions of dollars, along the course of a projected canal; and of another set, immediately behind these. Persons not intending to game, and not infected with mania, would endeavour to form some reasonable conjecture as to the ultimate value of the lots, by calculating the cost of the canal, the risks from accident, from the possible competition from other places, &c., and, finally, the possible profits, under the most favourable circumstances, within so many years' purchase. Such a calculation would serve as some sort of guide as to the amount of purchase-money to be risked. Whereas, wild land on the banks of a canal, not yet even marked out, was selling at Chicago for more than rich land, well improved, in the finest part of the valley of the Mohawk, on the banks of a canal which is already the medium of an almost inestimable amount of traffic. If sharpers and gamblers were to be the sufferers by the impending crash at Chicago, no one would feel much concerned: but they, unfortunately, are the people who encourage the delusion, in order to profit by it. Many a high-spirited, but inexperienced, young man; many a simple settler, will be ruined for the advantage of knaves.

Others, besides lawyers and speculators by trade, make a fortune in such extraordinary times. A poor man at Chicago had a pre-emption right to some land, for which he paid in the morning one hundred and fifty dollars. In the afternoon, he sold it to a friend of mine for five thousand dollars. A poor Frenchman, married to a squaw, had a suit pending, when I was there, which he was likely to gain, for the right of purchasing some land by the lake for one hundred dollars, which would immediately become worth one million dollars.

There was much gaiety going on at Chicago, as well as business. On the evening of our arrival a fancy fair took place. As I was too much fatigued to go, the ladies sent me a bouquet of prairie flowers. There is some allowable pride in the place about its society. It is a remarkable thing to meet such an assemblage of educated, refined, and wealthy persons as may be found there, living in small, inconvenient houses on the edge of a wild prairie. There is a mixture, of course. I heard of a family of half-breeds setting up a carriage, and wearing fine jewellery. When the present intoxication of prosperity passes away, some of the inhabitants will go back to the eastward; there will be an accession of settlers from the mechanic classes; good houses will have been built for the richer families, and the singularity of the place will subside. It will be like all the other new and thriving lake and river ports of America.

24. Michael Chevalier

Cincinnati is more than a "mere slaughter-house"

For all their pristine quality, the growing cities of the West moved swiftly to create the refinements of traditional urban culture. Chevalier describes admiringly some of the features of the young city known to many Americans as "porkopolis."

Letter xviii

CINCINNATI

Memphis, (Tenn.), Jan. 1, 1835.

Cincinnati has been made famous by Mrs Trollope, whose aristocratic feelings were offended by the pork-trade, which is here carried on on a great scale. From her accounts many persons have thought that every body in Cincinnati was a pork merchant, and the city a mere slaughter-house. The fact is that Cincinnati is a large and beautiful town, charmingly situated in one of those bends which the Ohio makes, as if unwilling to leave the spot. The hills which border the *Belle Rivière* (Beautiful River, the French name of the Ohio) through its whole course, seem here to have receded from the river bank, in order to form a lofty plain, to which they serve as walls, whenever the Ohio does not serve as a foss, and on which man might build a town above the reach of the terrible floods of the river. Geologists, who have no faith in the favours of the fabled Oreads, will merely attribute this table-land to the washing away of the mountains, in the diluvian period, by the River Licking, now a modest little stream, which, descending from the highlands of Kentucky, empties itself into the Ohio opposite Cincinnati. However this may be, there is not, in the whole course of the river, a single spot which offers such attractions to the founders of a town.

From Michael Chevalier, *Society, Manners and Politics in the United States*, pp. 190–195. Footnotes are in the original.

The architectural appearance of Cincinnati is very nearly the same with that of the new quarters of the English towns. The houses are generally of brick, most commonly three stories high, with the windows shining with cleanliness, calculated each for a single family, and regularly placed along well paved and spacious streets, sixty feet in width. Here and there the prevailing uniformity is interrupted by some more imposing edifice, and there are some houses of hewn stone in very good taste, real palaces in miniature, with neat porticoes, inhabited by the aristocratical portion of Mrs Trollope's hog-merchants, and several very pretty mansions surrounded with gardens and terraces. Then there are the common school-houses, where girls and boys together learn reading, writing, cyphering, and geography, under the simultaneous direction of a master and mistress.[1] In another direction you see a small, plain church, without sculpture or paintings, without coloured glass or gothic arches, but snug, well carpeted, and well-warmed by stoves. In Cincinnati, as everywhere else in the United States, there is a great number of churches; each sect has its own, from Anglican Episcopalianism, which enlists under its banner the wealth of the country, to the Baptist and Methodist sects, the religion of the labourers and negroes. On another side, stands a huge hotel, which from its exterior you would take for a royal residence, but in which, as I can testify, you will not experience a princely hospitality; or a museum, which is merely a private speculation, as all American museums are, and which consists of some few crystals, some mammoth-bones, which are very abundant in the United States, an Egyptian mummy, some Indian weapons and dresses, and a half-dozen wax-figures, representing, for instance, Washington, General Jackson, and the Indian Chiefs, Black Hawk and

1. According to the official report of the Trustees and visiters of the common schools, dated July 30, 1833, there were then in Cincinnati 6,000 children between the ages of 6 and 16 years, exclusive of 230 children of colour for whom there is a separate school. About 2,300 children attended the common schools and 1,700 private schools. The number of common schools is 18, under the care of 12 masters and 5 assistants, 6 mistresses and 7 assistant mistresses. The masters receive 400 dollars a year, and the assistants 250; the school mistresses 216, and the assistants 168. These salaries are thought to be too low.

Tecumseh, a figure of Napoleon afoot or on horseback, a French cuirass from Waterloo, a collection of portraits of distinguished Americans, comprising Lafayette and some of the leading men of the town, another of stuffed birds, snakes preserved in spirits, and particularly a large living snake, a boa constrictor, or an anaconda. One of these museums in Cincinnati is remarkable for its collection of Indian antiquities, derived from the huge caves of Kentucky, or from the numerous mounds on the banks of the Ohio, of which there were several on the site of Cincinnati.[2]

As for the banks they are modestly lodged at Cincinnati, but a plan of a handsome edifice, worthy of their high fortune, and sufficient to accommodate them all, is at present under consideration. The founderies for casting steam-engines, the yards for building steamboats, the noisy, unwholesome, or unpleasant work-shops, are in the adjoining village of Fulton, in Covington or Newport on the Kentucky bank of the river, or in the country. As to the enormous slaughter of hogs, about 150,000 annually, and the preparation of the lard, which follows, the town is not in the least incommoded by it; the whole process takes place on the banks of a little stream called Deer Creek, which has received the nickname of the Bloody Run, from the colour of its waters during the season of the massacre, or near the basins of the great canal, which extends from Cincinnati towards the Maumee of Lake Erie. Cincinnati has, however, no squares planted with trees in the English taste, no parks nor walks, no fountains, although it would be very easy to have them. It is necessary to wait for the ornamental, until the taste for it prevails among the inhabitants; at present the useful occupies all thoughts. Besides, all improvements require an increase of taxes, and in the United States it is not easy to persuade the people to submit to this. . . . Cincinnati also stands in need of some public provision for lighting the streets, which this repugnance to taxes has hitherto prevented.

2. This museum has one show which I never saw anywhere else; it is a representation of the Infernal Regions, to which the young Cincinnati girls resort in quest of that excitement which a comfortable and peaceful, but cold and monotonous manner of life denies them. This strange spectacle seems to afford a delicious agitation to their nerves, and is the principal source of revenue to the museum.

Cincinnati has had water-works, for supplying the inhabitants with water, for about 20 years; for an annual rate, which amounts to about 8 or 12 dollars for a family, each has a quantity amply sufficient for all its wants. A steam-engine on the banks of the river raises the water to a reservoir on one of the hills near the city, 300 feet high, whence it is conducted in iron pipes in every direction. The height of the reservoir is such that the water rises to the top of every house, and fire-plugs are placed at intervals along the streets to supply the engines in case of fire. Several of the new towns in the United States have water-works, and Philadelphia, among the older cities, has an admirable system of works, which, owing to a series of unsuccessful experiments, have cost a large sum.[3] At this moment, a plan for supplying Boston with water is under discussion, which will cost several millions, because the water must be brought from a distance. New York is also engaged in a similar work, the expense of which will be about five millions. The Cincinnati water-works have not cost much above 150,000 dollars, although they have been several times completely reconstructed. It is generally thought in the United States, that the water-works ought to be owned by the towns, but those in Cincinnati belong to a company, and the water-rate is, therefore, higher than in Philadelphia and Pittsburg. The city has three times been in negociation for the purchase of the works, and has always declined buying on advantageous terms; the first time the establishment was offered for 35,000 dollars, and the second time for 80,000; the third time, 125,000 dollars were demanded, and 300,000 or 400,000 will finally be paid for it. In this case, as in regard to lighting the streets, the principal cause of the refusal of the city to buy was the unwillingness to lay new taxes.

The appearance of Cincinnati as it is approached from the water, is imposing, and it is still more so when it is viewed from one of the neighbouring hills. The eye takes in the windings of the

3. The water used in Philadelphia is supplied by the Schuylkill, a fall in which is made to drive the pumps, by which the reservoirs are filled. The Fairmount works are arranged and ornamented with much taste, and at very little expense; the ornamental part, strictly speaking, merely consists of some lawns, wooden balustrades, and two wretched statues; yet the effect is very elegant.

Ohio and the course of the Licking, which enters the former at right angles, the steamboats that fill the port, the basin of the Miami canal, with the warehouses that line it and the locks that connect it with the river, the white-washed spinning works of Newport and Covington with their tall chimnies, the Federal arsenal, above which floats the starry banner, and the numerous wooden spires that crown the churches. On all sides the view is terminated by ranges of hills, forming an amphitheatre yet covered with the vigorous growth of the primitive forest. This rich verdure is here and there interrupted by country houses surrounded by colonnades, which are furnished by the forest. The population which occupies this amphitheatre, lives in the midst of plenty; it is industrious, sober, frugal, thirsting after knowledge, and if, with a very few exceptions, it is entirely a stranger to the delicate pleasures and elegant manners of the refined society of our European capitals, it is equally ignorant of its vices, dissipation, and follies.

At the first glance one does not perceive any difference between the right and left bank of the river; from a distance, the prosperity of Cincinnati seems to extend to the opposite shore. This is an illusion; on the right bank, that is, in Ohio, there are none but freemen; slavery exists on the other side.

25. Basil Hall

Everything in this bustling place appeared to be in motion

Mrs. Trollope described Rochester, in northern New York State, as a city put together so hastily that tree stumps could be found in the cellars of many houses. Captain Hall's description conveys the hectic pace at which the city was built.

On the 26th of June 1827, we strolled through the village of Rochester, under the guidance of a most obliging and intelligent

From Basil Hall, *Travels in North America in 1827 and 1828*, I, pp. 160–166.

friend, a native of this part of the country. Everything in this bustling place appeared to be in motion. The very streets seemed to be starting up of their own accord, ready-made, and looking as fresh and new, as if they had been turned out of the workmen's hands but an hour before—or that a great boxful of new houses had been sent by steam from New York, and tumbled out on the half-cleared land. The canal banks were at some places still unturfed; the lime seemed hardly dry in the masonry of the aqueduct, in the bridges, and in the numberless great saw-mills and manufactories. In many of these buildings the people were at work below stairs, while at top the carpenters were busy nailing on the planks of the roof.

Some dwellings were half painted, while the foundations of others, within five yards' distance, were only beginning. I cannot say how many churches, court-houses, jails, and hotels I counted, all in motion, creeping upwards. Several streets were nearly finished, but had not as yet received their names; and many others were in the reverse predicament, being named, but not commenced,—their local habitation being merely signified by lines of stakes. Here and there we saw great warehouses, without window sashes, but half filled with goods, and furnished with hoisting cranes, ready to fish up the huge pyramids of flour barrels, bales, and boxes lying in the streets. In the centre of the town the spire of a Presbyterian church rose to a great height, and on each side of the supporting tower was to be seen the dial-plate of a clock, of which the machinery, in the hurry-skurry, had been left at New York. I need not say that these half-finished, whole-finished, and embryo streets were crowded with people, carts, stages, cattle, pigs, far beyond the reach of numbers;—and as all these were lifting up their voices together, in keeping with the clatter of hammers, the ringing of axes, and the creaking of machinery, there was a fine concert, I assure you!

But it struck us that the interest of the town, for it seems idle to call it a village, was subordinate to that of the suburbs. A few years ago the whole of that part of the country was covered with a dark silent forest, and even as it was, we could not proceed a mile in any direction except that of the high-road, without coming full-butt against the woods of time immemorial. When land is cleared for the purposes of cultivation, the stumps are left standing for many years, from its being easier, as well as more profitable in other respects, to plough round them, than to waste time and labour in rooting them out, or burning them, or blowing them up with gunpowder. But when a forest is levelled with a view to building a town in its place, a different system must of course be adopted. The trees must then be removed sooner or later, according to the means of the proprietor, or the necessities of the case. Thus one man possessed of capital will clear his lot of the wood, and erect houses, or even streets, across it; while on his neighbour's land the trees may be still growing. And it actually occurred to us, several times, within the immediate limits of the inhabited town itself, in streets, too, where shops were opened, and all sorts of business actually going on, that we had to drive first on one side, and then on the other, to avoid the stumps of an oak, or a hemlock, or a pinetree, staring us full in the face.

On driving a little beyond the streets towards the woods, we came to a space, about an acre in size roughly enclosed, on the summit of a gentle swell in the ground.

"What can this place be for?"

"Oh," said my companion, "that is the grave yard."

"Grave yard—what is that?" said I; for I was quite adrift.

"Why, surely," said he, "you know what a grave yard is? It is a burying ground. All the inhabitants of the place are buried there, whatever be their persuasion. We don't use churchyards in America."

After we had gone about a mile from town the forest thickened, we lost sight of every trace of a human dwelling, or of human interference with nature in any shape. We stood considering what we should do next, when the loud crash of a falling tree met our ears. Our friendly guide was showing off the curiosities of the place, and was quite glad, he said, to have this opportunity of exhibiting the very first step in the process of town-making. After a zig-zag scramble amongst trees, which had been allowed to grow up and decay century after century, we came to a spot where three or four men were employed in clearing out a street, as they declared, though any thing more unlike a street could not well be conceived. Nevertheless, the ground in question certainly formed part of the plan of the town. It had been chalked out by the surveyors' stakes, and some speculators having taken up the lots for immediate building, of course found it necessary to open a street through the woods, to afford a line of communication with the rest of the village. As fast as the trees were cut down, they were stripped of their branches and drawn off by oxen, sawed into planks, or otherwise fashioned to the purposes of building, without one moment's delay. There was little or no exaggeration, therefore, in supposing with our friend, that the same fir which might be waving about in full life and vigour in the morning, should be cut down, dragged into daylight, squared, framed, and before night, be hoisted up to make a beam or rafter to some tavern, or factory, or store, at the corner of a street, which twenty-four hours before had existed only on paper, and yet which might be completed, from end to end, within a week afterwards.

On our way back again to the carriage, which had been left standing in the avenue, or nick cut for the road in the forest, we fell in with a gentleman on horseback, rifle in hand, and bearing in testimony of his successful sport, a large bunch of wild pigeons and sleek-skinned black squirrels, tied to his saddle-bow. He had been gunning, he told us, for a couple of hours; in the course of which time, he had first lost his horse, and in looking for it, had missed his marks, and so of course lost himself. "And now," continued the sportsman, "that I am fairly out of the thicket, I am almost as much at a loss as I was before. For," continued he, jestingly to our companion, "you have been getting up such a heap of new work here, a man does not know the land from day to day. You have placed such a lot of taverns and houses on the skirts of the forest; so many lime-kilns, grocery stores, and what not, side by side, or jumbled altogether, amongst the trees, that, for the life of me, I don't know scarcely where I have got to, more than I did a while ago when straying amongst the trees after my horse."

After our new acquaintance had rode on, I asked who he was. My friend desired me to guess. I thought it might be the baker?

the butcher? the attorney? the bookseller? "No! no! none of these." The mason? said I, or some such indispensable personage? "No—you are still wrong." Had I guessed all night, I never should have thought of naming the dancing master! but so it was. After laughing a little, I don't know well why, I acknowledged myself well pleased to have witnessed so undeniable a symptom of refinement peeping out amongst the rugged manners of the forest.

Older Cities

26. John H. Griscom

The courts and alleys are prolific sources of disease

John Griscom was a member of a small band of highminded reformers who sought to improve conditions of urban life by making their fellow citizens aware of the repulsive situation of the mass of urban residents. The following excerpt is drawn from what the dean of American medical historians, Richard H. Shryock, has called Griscom's "one-man sanitary survey" of New York City.

The subject of *sewerage* is destined to be one, which of necessity must ere long occupy the attention of the people and the government, and upon which an intelligent and judicious officer of health may throw much light. It will, I am satisfied, be found not only the most economical, but the *only* mode, in which the immense mass of filth daily generated in this large city, can be effectually removed. In some foreign cities, underground sewerage on a regular uniform plan throughout, the sewers constructed on the most scientific and substantial plans, has been carried out in the completest manner, with the most decidedly beneficial results upon the general health and comfort. We are annually giving

From John H. Griscom, M.D., *The Sanitary Condition of the Laboring Population of New York* (New York: Harper and Brothers, 1845), 52–55.

proofs of our belief in their necessity, by the construction of single sewers in various places, as they are demanded by circumstances, but it is done without reference to any uniform plan, and it is feared that thus much confusion and great additional expense, will fall upon the treasury when ever it shall be deemed proper to project and carry out over the whole city a complete and uniform system; and I believe, "to this complexion must we come at last." One thing especially brings this conviction; since the introduction of the Croton, the rain water cisterns being useless, the bottoms of them have in many instances been taken out, and they have been converted into cispools, into which the refuse matter of the houses is thrown. Great trouble is thus saved to families and domestics, but it needs no prophetic vision to perceive, that an immense mass of offensive material, will thus be soon collected, its decomposition polluting the air, in the immediate precincts of our chambers and sitting rooms, and generating an amount of miasmatic effluvia, incalculably great and injurious. Discharge all the contents of our sinks and cispools, through sewers into the rivers, and we will avoid two of the most powerful causes of sickness and early death.

The great quantity of water from the sky, the hydrants, the unused wells, &c., now accumulating beneath the surface, must find its way into many basements and cellars, rendering them very damp and unhealthy, and for which sewers constitute the only remedy.

Another mooted sanitary question, is the influence of *grave-yards, vaults,* and other burial-places, in large cities, upon the health of the inhabitants. Some acute men are now endeavoring to maintain that no specific bad results have ever been, or can be, justly attributed to them, while others, among whom is Chadwick, regard them as highly objectionable, and on this side appears the most direct and positive evidence. In this city are some places of interment, which, whatever may be said of their effects on health, are certainly crowded and offensive to a high degree; their condition and influence, as certainly, demand an intelligent and careful investigation.

While writing this communication, there applied to me for medical advice, a young man, who had gone, in good health, into a vault of a church in a densely populated part of the city, to see the coffin containing the remains of a relative; he had been in but a few moments when the effluvia was so offensive and powerful, as almost entirely to overcome him. He immediately retired, returned home, and when I saw him, three hours after, he was laboring under a considerable degree of fever, and other disordered symptoms, which he said had all come on since his visit to the vault. He thinks the vault must have contained not less than 200 bodies. The place has before been complained of, and it is difficult to avoid the belief that more or less injury must be inflicted by it on the health of the neighborhood.

Not the least important of the results which should be obtained from the appointment of an officer to superintend the affairs of public health, is that of keeping a constant watch upon the progress of diseases, drawing the proper inferences obtainable from a careful inspection of the mortality returns, and giving them to the public in a suitable form and manner. Living as we are in constant subjection to attacks of bodily disease, induced by the circumstances of life, the lances of death held constantly "in rest," by a thousand unseen hands, waiting only the stirring of the breeze to thrust them at our unconscious frames, such an officer should be as a sentinel upon the tower, watching with an intelligent and never closing eye, the manœuvres of the wily enemy, and with a ready pen, alert to send the alarm to every quarter, and prepare the city for a defence against his approaches. The inhabitants may be, some, reckless of danger, and careless of life, others may affect to despise the warnings of the watchman, and scoff at the "Philosophy of Diseases," but it is no less the duty of the faithful magistrate and officer, to see that at all points the constituency are guarded, with whatever of science *and* virtue they can find.

There is in this city but one officer in the receipt of the certificates of death—the only source of knowledge of the diseases which prevail. He is the City Inspector. It is by law made his duty to publish every Tuesday, a list of the deaths occurring during the preceding week, and in January, "to publish the whole number of deaths which shall have occurred in the city of New York during the preceding year, with the sexes, ages and diseases of the persons so dying." This is the *letter* of the law, and any boy, who has the *quantum sufficit* of reading, writing, and arithmetic, with a fair proportion of patience, may make out the tables in the unscientifically alphabetical mode in which it has usually been done. But of what use is this? we learn by it that 9,000 or 10,000 deaths, occur annually; we are informed of the diseases which cause the *deaths,* (if the arrangement is worthy of dependence, which it is not always,) but of the *causes of the diseases* we are told nothing. To derive the proper and full advantage from the returns of mortality, we must look beyond the mere name of the diseases, and ascertain the *sources of those diseases. Now!* the reports are useful for little more than to satisfy ordinary curiosity, or to enable the preacher "to point a moral"—but if properly analyzed, and their whole bearing and influence exposed and elucidated, they would become valuable aids to the private physician, and to the public officer of health, in studying the liabilities of New York, and the influences of its climate, position, temperature, and other circumstances in producing diseases.

If I may be allowed to illustrate this point, by referring to a result of my own study of some of the Annual Reports, I will recall attention to the discovery, that in this city there is less consumption among the native residents, than in Boston or Philadelphia. This is proved by a calculation, the correctness of which may be tried at any time, which has not yet been questioned, and which turns the tables completely, as they were before set down, by those who would make New York a comparative Golgotha.

This officer should study the influences of seasons, localities, and many other circumstances, on the aspects of disease, and he should keep a record of the Barometric, Thermometric, Hygrometric, and Pluvial changes. An improvement in the certificate of death, is also much needed; a more clear designation of medical terms, inquiries into the condition and physical circumstances of the decedent, the length of his residence in this country, if a foreigner, and the influence of the change of climate upon the cause of death, and many other points, are necessary to obtain correct and specific conclusions, respecting the diseases of New

York; while a thorough knowledge of the wants of science, and of what has been done abroad, in countries where the subject has constituted the labor of the lives of the most gifted individuals, is highly desirable. All this knowledge can only be obtained, and the improvements properly urged and applied, by an individual of good medical education, and one who has a taste, and willingness for the work. A capable Health Officer would be well employed, and it should be made his interest, to devote his time and talents to the dissemination of sound precepts concerning the preservation of health and life, among the people, to whom knowledge on these subjects is now almost inaccessible. To a vast number, for whom instruction as to the best method of regulating their internal and external domiciliary, and their personal arrangements, is most desirable, it could be given in such forms as would certainly arrest attention and be productive of incalculable benefits. The circumstances of life, which have influence in producing disease, are endless in number, and yet the sufferers, in too many instances, are wholly ignorant of their power, or even of their existence. This is true to a great extent of the rich and educated, as every physician knows, but it is emphatically the case with the destitute and ignorant, to whom the laws of health and life, are a sealed book.

These labors I regard as answering to the *spirit* of the law, and, in nearly the words of an able writer on poverty and crime, "The wisest civil regulations that can be devised, will avail but little for the advancement of society, if the officers who execute them, look not beyond the letter of their commissions, and fail to communicate what they learn of the causes, the remedy, and the prevention of diseases."

To this subject the language of an inspired penman may be literally applied;—"the letter killeth, but the spirit giveth life."

A sanitary police, composed of such individuals as are herein suggested, would constitute an efficient corps of *Health Missionaries*. Their time would be principally devoted to the purpose of teaching the poor the rules which should regulate their household operations; and the value of fresh air, ventilation, cleanliness, temperance, &c., would form constant themes for them. The circulation of Tracts on Health, distributed with the same freedom as religious tracts now are, by hands equally interested in the comforts and condition of the poor, would form a powerful addition to their means of usefulness. The Dispensary Physician wields for these purposes, a power possessed by no other class of men.

To the habits of life of many of the laboring classes, to their confinement in small apartments, and to *their ignorance of the laws of life and health,* by which especially, even their contracted arrangements are unnecessarily kept in a bad condition, we are to look for no inconsiderable amount of the injury which they sustain. The moisture, filth, and confined atmosphere of the courts and alleys, are also prolific sources of disease; in the occupations of many lurks the enemy. But if we restrict our attention to them, we shall overlook a very large proportion of the causes of mortality, and with all our efforts to improve the sanitary condition of our city, we should fail in some of the most essential points. A well regulated and efficient Health Police might do much towards correcting the existing evils, but to carry the desired reform to the utmost limit, and with a greater permanency, measures which no police can carry out, are necessary. And as these evils are not confined to the laboring and destitute part of our population, but afflict also the wealthier portion, a more healthy state of public opinion is absolutely necessary, to effect the desired results.

27. Thomas Hamilton

No one can be in New York without hearing the alarm of fire

Visitors were appalled both at the commonness of fires in American cities and the disposition of Americans to put up with them. Fire fighting for most of the era was left to voluntary organizations that characteristically

From Thomas Hamilton, *Men and Manners in America*, pp. 36–38.

were unable to cope with any but the smallest conflagrations. A number of contemporaries attempted to explain this phenomenon. After the Wall Street District was gutted by the great fire of December 1835, the retired merchant Philip Hone recorded in his diary his conviction that his countrymen's excessive greed led them to shoddy construction that often resulted in loss of life, while it also made them indifferent to the consequences of their behavior. In the following passage Thomas Hamilton, modestly conceding his inability to explain the causes of the excessive fires in the United States, offered a useful description of how Americans dealt with them.

No one can be four-and-twenty hours in New York without hearing the alarm of fire. Indeed, a conflagration here is so very ordinary an occurrence, that it is attended by none of that general anxiety and excitement which follow such a calamity in cities less accustomed to combustion. The New York firemen are celebrated for resolution and activity; and as the exercise of these qualities is always pleasant to witness, I have made it a point to attend all fires since my arrival. The four first were quite insignificant, indeed, three of the number were extinguished before my arrival, and I barely got up in time to catch a glimpse of the expiring embers of the fourth. But in regard to the fifth, I was in better luck. Having reached the scene, more than half expecting it would turn out as trumpery an affair as its predecessors, I had at length the satisfaction of beholding a very respectable volume of flame bursting from the windows and roof of a brick tenement of four stories, with as large an accompaniment of smoke, bustle, clamour, and confusion as could reasonably be desired. An engine came up almost immediately after my arrival, and loud cries, and the rattle of approaching wheels from either extremity of the street, gave notice that farther assistance was at hand. Some time was lost in getting water, and I should think the municipal arrangements, in regard to this matter, might be better managed. In a few minutes, however, the difficulty was surmounted, and the two elements were brought fairly into collision.

The firemen are composed of young citizens, who by volunteering this service,—and a very severe one it is,—enjoy an exemption from military duty. Certainly nothing could exceed their boldness and activity. Ladders were soon planted; the walls were scaled; furniture was carried from the house, and thrown from the windows, without apparent concern for the effects its descent might produce on the skulls of the spectators in the street. Fresh engines were continually coming up, and were brought into instant play. But as the power of water waxed, so unfortunately did that of the adverse element; and so far as the original building was concerned, the odds soon became Pompey's pillar to a stick of sealing-wax, on fire.

Day now closed, and the scene amid the darkness became greatly increased in picturesque beauty. At intervals human figures were seen striding through flame, and then vanishing amid the smoke. In the street, confusion became worse confounded. Had the crowd been composed of stentors, the clamour could not have been louder. The inhabitants of the adjoining houses, who, till now, seemed to have taken the matter very coolly, at length became alarmed, when the engines began to play on them, and ejected a torrent of chairs, wardrobes, feather-beds, and other valuable chattels from every available opening. The house in which the fire broke out was now a mere shell; the roof gone, and all the wooden-work consumed. The flames then burst forth in the roof of the house adjoining on the right, but the concentrated play of many engines soon subdued it. All danger was then at an end. The inhabitants began to reclaim the furniture which they had tumbled out into the street, and I have no doubt went afterwards to bed as comfortably as if nothing had happened. I saw several of the inmates of the house that had been burned, and examined their countenances with some curiosity. No external mark of excitement was visible, and I gave them credit for a degree of *nonchalance*, far greater than I should have conceived possible in the circumstances.

On the whole, I have no deduction to make from the praises so frequently bestowed on the New York firemen. The chief defect that struck me, was the admission of the crowd to the scene of action. This caused, and must always cause, confusion. In England, barriers are thrown across the street at some distance, and rigorously guarded by the police and constables. On suggesting this improvement to an American friend, he agreed it would be desirable, but assured me it was not calculated for the meridian of the United States, where exclusion of any kind is always adverse to the popular feeling. On this matter, of course, I cannot judge, but it seems to me clear, that if the exclusion of an idle mob from the scene of a fire, increases the chance of saving property and life, the freedom thus pertinaciously insisted on, is merely that of doing private injury and public mischief.

With regard to the frequency of fires in New York, I confess, that after listening to all possible explanations, it does appear to me unaccountable. I am convinced, that in this single city there are annually more fires than occur in the whole Island of Great Britain. The combustible materials of which the majority of the houses are composed, is a circumstance far from sufficient to account for so enormous a disparity. Can we attribute it to crime? I think not; at least it would require much stronger evidence than has yet been discovered to warrant the hypothesis. In the negligence of servants, we have surer ground. These are generally negroes, and rarely to be depended on in any way, when exempt from rigid *surveillance*. But I am not going to concoct a theory, and so leave the matter as I find it.

28. Frances Trollope

New York appeared a lovely and noble city

As was true of the great cities in the Old World, sordid squalor was juxtaposed against elegance and beauty in America's older cities. That this was a raw society did not mean that it was lacking in refinement. The eastern seaboard culture was more than two centuries old by the 1830s. The level of life in the older cities served as the standard aspired to by newer communities, while also representing one of the intriguing facets

From Frances Trollope, *Domestic Manners of the Americans*, II, pp. 156–161.

of a varied culture. That the physical city was praised lavishly by so caustic a critic as Mrs. Trollope adds to the impressiveness of the encomiums lavished on it. As the conclusion of the following passage indicates, however, her praise was not unmixed.

I have never seen the bay of Naples, I can therefore make no comparison, but my imagination is incapable of conceiving any thing of the kind more beautiful than the harbour of New York. Various and lovely are the objects which meet the eye on every side, but the naming them would only be to give a list of words, without conveying the faintest idea of the scene. I doubt if ever the pencil of Turner could do it justice, bright and glorious as it rose upon us. We seemed to enter the harbour of New York upon waves of liquid gold, and as we darted past the green isles which rise from its bosom, like guardian centinels of the fair city, the setting sun stretched his horizontal beams farther and farther at each moment, as if to point out to us some new glory in the landscape.

New York, indeed, appeared to us, even when we saw it by a soberer light, a lovely and a noble city. To us who had been so long travelling through half-cleared forests, and sojourning among an "I'm-as-good-as-you" population, it seemed, perhaps, more beautiful, more splendid, and more refined than it might have done, had we arrived there directly from London; but making every allowance for this, I must still declare that I think New York one of the finest cities I ever saw, and as much superior to every other in the Union, (Philadelphia not excepted,) as London to Liverpool, or Paris to Rouen. Its advantages of position are, perhaps, unequalled any where. Situated on an island, which I think it will one day cover, it rises, like Venice, from the sea, and like that fairest of cities in the days of her glory, receives into its lap tribute of all the riches of the earth.

The southern point of Manhattan Island divides the waters of the harbour into the north and east rivers; on this point stands the city of New York, extending from river to river, and running northward to the extent of three or four miles. I think it covers nearly as much ground as Paris, but is much less thickly peopled.

The extreme point is fortified towards the sea by a battery, and forms an admirable point of defence; but in these piping days of peace, it is converted into a public promenade, and one more beautiful, I should suppose, no city could boast. From hence commences the splendid Broadway, as the fine avenue is called, which runs through the whole city. This noble street may vie with any I ever saw, for its length and breadth, its handsome shops, neat awnings, excellent *trottoir,* and well-dressed pedestrians. It has not the crowded glitter of Bond-street equipages, nor the gorgeous fronted palaces of Regent-street; but it is magnificent in its extent, and ornamented by several handsome buildings, some of them surrounded by grass and trees. The Park, in which stands the noble city-hall, is a very fine area. I never found that the most graphic description of a city could give me any feeling of being there; and even if others have the power, I am very sure I have not, of setting churches and squares, and long drawn streets, before the mind's eye. I will not, therefore, attempt a detailed description of this great metropolis of the new world, but will only say that during the seven weeks we stayed there, we always found something new to see and to admire; and were it not so very far from all the old-world things which cling about the heart of an European, I should say that I never saw a city more desirable as a residence.

The dwelling houses of the higher classes are extremely handsome, and very richly furnished. Silk or satin furniture is as often, or oftener, seen than chintz; the mirrors are as handsome as in London; the cheffoniers, slabs, and marble tables as elegant; and in addition, they have all the pretty tasteful decoration of French porcelaine, and or-molu in much greater abundance, because at a much cheaper rate. Every part of their houses is well carpeted, and the exterior finishing, such as steps, railings, and door-frames, are very superior. Almost every house has handsome green blinds on the outside; balconies are not very general, nor do the houses display, externally, so many flowers as those of Paris and London; but I saw many rooms decorated within, exactly like those of an European *petite maîtresse.* Little tables, looking and smelling like flower beds, portfolios, nick-nacks, bronzes, busts, cameos, and alabaster vases, illustrated copies of lady-like rhymes bound in silk, and, in short, all the pretty coxcomalities of the drawing-room scattered about with the same profuse and studied negligence as with us.

Hudson Square and its neighbourhood is, I believe, the most fashionable part of the town; the square is beautiful, excellently well planted with a great variety of trees, and only wanting our frequent and careful mowing to make it equal to any square in London. The iron railing which surrounds this enclosure is as high and as handsome as that of the Tuilleries, and it will give some idea of the care bestowed on its decoration, to know that the gravel for the walks was conveyed by barges from Boston, not as ballast, but as freight.

The great defect in the houses is their extreme uniformity—when you have seen one, you have seen all. Neither do I quite like the arrangement of the rooms. In nearly all the houses the dining and drawing-rooms are on the same floor, with ample folding doors between them; when thrown together they certainly make a very noble apartment; but no doors can be barrier sufficient between dining and drawing-rooms. Mixed dinner parties of ladies and gentlemen, however, are very rare, which is a great defect in the society; not only as depriving them of the most social and hospitable manner of meeting, but as leading to frequent dinner parties of gentlemen without ladies, which certainly does not conduce to refinement.

Disease

29. Boston Medical Association

Imagination is apt to convert attacks of disease into the epidemic

The cholera epidemic of 1832 caused a great fear to spread over the nation's cities. The following document illustrates on the one hand the

Resolutions passed by the Boston Medical Association (Boston, June 25, 1832).

alertness of the medical leaders of one of the greatest American cities and on the other the tentativeness and lack of specificity of their thinking.

At a Special Meeting of the Boston Medical Association, held June 25, 1832, it was unanimously Voted; That the following resolutions be adopted; that they be signed by the Chairman of the Meeting, and the Standing Committee and Secretary of the Association; and that a copy of the same be sent to the Commissioners of Health, and be published in the Daily papers of the City.

The Boston Medical Association, contemplating the possibility that the Cholera, which has been spread over a large portion of the Globe, may, in the course of its progress, visit our own city, deem it expedient now to adopt such measures of preparation and concert, as may enable them to afford the most efficient aid, in case of such an event, to their fellow citizens.

The Association therefore vote, That they will at all times co-operate with the City Authorities, in judicious measures for the promotion of the public security; that they will render prompt and gratuitous services to the poor, that they will endeavour to give efficacy to public and private charities; and that while they discountenance unnecessary alarms, they will, to the best of their belief, render a true and frank account of the state and progress of the disease.

To secure an efficient co-operation among the members of the Association, it is believed that no better method can be adopted, than a strict and continued adherence to the code of by-laws, which has hitherto produced so much unanimity and good understanding among the profession. And the Standing Committee of the Association are requested to act as a Committee of Vigilance, and to call meetings whenever in their opinion further measures on the part of the Association may be necessary.

To avoid multiplicity of instructions relating to this disease, this Association adopt, and recommend to their fellow citizens, the general precautionary directions given by the Consulting Physicians of the city. Since, however, no general directions can apply to a diversity of habits and constitutions, they recommend that violent and sudden changes should not be made in the habits of living of those, who have hitherto enjoyed health, any farther than to reduce such habits within the limits of caution, if they have been irregular or excessive. Those persons who are accustomed to live without stimulants should not now resort to them; and those with whom a moderate use of stimulants is habitual, should not wholly abandon them, until the apprehension of the epidemic is past. Such articles of diet as the experience of the individual has shewn to be harmless in his particular case, may in general be persevered in, in temperate quantities. Clothing must be varied, not only with reference to the weather, but also with regard to the constitution, mode of life, and previous habits of the individual.

In regard to remedial treatment, it is particularly recommended that the specific medicines which have been proposed for Cholera, should not be applied before the existence of the disease is well ascertained. In times of panic, imagination is apt to convert all attacks of disease, into those of the apprehended epidemic. The treatment recommended for Cholera, would be detrimental to persons in health, and pernicious in many of our febrile and inflammatory diseases. In general, the description given by the Consulting Physicians of the city, is sufficient to identify the disease when it appears; but where doubts exist, remedies should be delayed, until medical advice can be obtained.

The power given by law to the City Authorities, to remove persons from one place to another, the Association confidently hope will be exercised, in the case of the sick, with great forbearance and discretion. Few exigencies can be expected to arrive, requiring removals of the sick, except where the degree of destitution, filth and neglect, are such as to render it certain, that the condition of the patient himself would be improved by an exchange for more comfortable lodgings. In general, patients can be better attended and nursed in their own houses, than elsewhere; provided the necessary means are at their disposal. Should it happen that any spot, or district of the city, is more infested with the disease than other parts, the safety of the public will be more promoted by the removal of the healthy inhabitants, than of the sick.

The maratime and peninsular situation of our city, the well known salubrity of our air and soil, the generally temperate habits of our population, and their comparative exemption from malignant epidemics, which have afflicted other parts of our continent, lead us to indulge a confident hope, that even should the Cholera pervade this Hemisphere, as it has done the Eastern, our own city will not be a distinguished point in the records of its progress.

JOHN DIXWELL,
Chairman.
JOHN RANDALL,
JACOB BIGELOW,
JOHN B. BROWN,
GEORGE HAYWARD,
JOHN WARE,
Standing Committee.
JOSEPH W. MC'KEAN,
Secretary.

IN THE BOARD OF COMMISSIONERS OF HEALTH, June 26, 1832.

Slave Sales

30. BASIL HALL

I shall expose to sale, for cash, a slave for life

The sale of slaves stamped the United States a primitive as well as an amoral society. Some of the most vivid reporting of this peculiar feature of American culture was done by foreign visitors. They were less prone than Americans to take for granted an institution so shocking to persons of sensibility, and they did not share in the widespread American conviction that Negroes were fit for nothing better.

Although the debates in the National Legislature formed the chief object of interest at Washington, many other incidental matters arose, from time to time, to vary the picture.

Basil Hall, *Travels in North America in 1827 and 1828*, III, pp. 34–41.

The following advertisement caught my eye, in one of the newspapers:—

> MARSHAL'S SALE
>
> By authority of a writ of fieri facias, issued from the Clerk's Office of the Circuit Court, in this district, for the county of Washington, to me directed, I shall expose to salc, for cash, on Tuesday, the 15th instant, Negro GEORGE, a slave for life, and about sixteen years old. Seized and taken in execution of, as the goods and chattels of Zachariah Hazle, and will be sold to satisfy a debt due by him to William Smith.
>
> Sale to be at the County Court-House Door, and to commence at 12 o'clock, M.
>
> TENCH RINGGOLD,
>
> jan 10 dts Marshal District of Columbia

I had often, in the course of my life, in the British West India possessions, and elsewhere, seen slavery in full operation; but as I had never happened to be actually present at the sale of a negro, I resolved to witness it for once, and in a place where, at first sight, such an incident might least of all have been looked for.

I repaired to the County Court-House, accordingly, at noon, on the 15th of January, 1827, and having found my way along an empty passage, I reached a door, from which people were departing and others entering, like bees crowding in and out of a hive. This was the Court of Justice. But the matters under discussion were either so completely technical, or my head was so full of the black boy, that I could not follow what was going on.

I came again into the passage, and walked along to the front door, which nearly faces the Capitol, distant about one-third of a mile. The flags were just hoisted on the top of the building, which intimate that the Senate and the House of Representatives had assembled to discuss the affairs of this free nation—slavery amongst the rest.

The only man I could see in the passage, was a great heavy-looking black fellow, who appeared so much downcast and miserable, that I settled within myself that this must needs be no other than Negro George, placed there for inspection. But the

Deputy-marshal, who entered at this moment, holding in one hand the advertisement copied above, and in the other the writ of fieri facias alluded to therein, undeceived me, by saying that the man I pointed to was a slave indeed, though not for sale, but that I should see the other immediately.

It was soon buzzed about, I suspect, amongst the purchasers, that a suspicious-looking stranger was making enquiries respecting the boy; for a tall man, wrapped in a cloak, whom I had observed for some time cutting large junks of tobacco from a lump which he drew from his waistcoat pocket, and thrusting them into his mouth, evidently in a fidget, now came up to me, and said, with an air of affected carelessness, "Do you mean to buy the lad, sir?"

"I? Oh, no!" I exclaimed.

The tall man drew a satisfied breath on hearing this, and said, in a more natural tone, "I am glad of it, sir—for I do; and am very anxious to succeed, because I know the chap well, and have become interested in him, and he himself—ah! there he stands—wishes to become my property."

"How is that?"

"Why," said he, "you must know that his owner was indebted to me fifty dollars, and would not or could not pay me, so I had a lien upon this boy, and the Court allowed me to have him latterly, pending the litigations. There have been three or four law-suits about him, and he has been knocking about from hand to hand ever since March, 1822—five years—and he is now to be sold to satisfy this debt."

"What says the boy to all this?" I asked.

"Come here, George," he called, and the lad joined us. "Don't be scared, my boy," said the gentleman, "there is no one going to hurt you."

"O, I am not scared," answered the boy, though he trembled all the while. He looked very ill at ease, I thought, and I soon found out the cause, in his apprehension of being purchased by a person, of whom, I suppose, he had some previous knowledge, and whose looks certainly were as little inviting as any thing could well be. He was a short, lean man, with a face deeply wrinkled, not so much with age or care, as with the deep seams of intemperance.

His two little eyes were placed so far back in his head, that you could not see them in profile, and when viewed in front through a pair of enormous spectacles, sparkled in a very ominous manner; while his straight, scanty, and disordered hair, formed an appropriate sky-line to the picture. I began to take considerable interest in the little fellow's fate, and whispered to my tall companion, that I hoped he would get the boy.

After various delays, the slave was put up to auction, at the end of the passage, near which four or five persons had by this time collected. There was a good deal of laughing and talking amongst the buyers, and several jests were sported on the occasion, of which their little victim took no more notice, than if he had been a horse or a dog. In fact, he was not a chubby shining little negro, with a flat nose, thick lips, and woolly hair, but a slender, delicate-looking youth, more yellow than black, with an expression every way suitable, I thought, with the forlorn situation in which he was placed—for both his parents, and all his brothers and sisters, he told me, had been long ago sold into slavery, and sent to the Southern States—Florida or Alabama—he knew not where!

"Well, gentlemen," cried the Deputy-marshal, "will you give us a bid? Look at him—as smart a fellow as ever you saw—works like a tiger!"

One of the spectators called out, "Come, I'll say 25 dollars;" another said 35—another said 40—and at last 100 dollars were bid for him.

From the spot where I was standing, in the corner, behind the rest of the party, I could see all that was passing. I felt my pulse accelerating at each successive offer, and my cheek getting flushed—for the scene was so very new that I almost fancied I was dreaming.

The interest, after a time, took a different character, to which, however, I by no means wished to give utterance, or in any shape to betray; but at this moment, the Deputy-marshal, finding the price to hang at 100 dollars, looked over to me, and said, "Do give us a bid, sir—won't you?"

My indignation was just beginning to boil over at this juncture, and I cried out, in answer to this appeal, with more asperity than good sense or good breeding,—"No! no! I thank God we don't do such things in my country!"

"And I wish, with all my heart," said the auctioneer, in a tone that made me sorry for having spoken so hastily—"I wish we did not do such things here."

"Amen!" said several voices.

The sale went on.

"We can't help it, however," observed the Marshal; "we must do our duty. 100 dollars are bid, gentlemen! One—hundred—dollars!"

The ominous personage with the deep-set eyes now called out, to my horror, and that of the poor boy, "120!"

Just at this moment a farmer, who had come from the country, and seemed pleased with the looks of the youth, nodded to the auctioneer, and said, "130."

My tall friend now said, "140," which was echoed by the new comer with, "142!"

Upon which these two bidders having exchanged looks, walked apart for a couple of minutes, whispering something, which I did not hear. I observed the farmer nod several times, as if assenting to some compromise. They now returned, and the tall gentleman said, "I will give 143 dollars for him," while the other, though more than once appealed to by the auctioneer, spoke no more.

"143 dollars are bid for this lad! One hundred and forty-three dollars—once! twice!—Are you all done, gentlemen?—Thrice!—The lad is yours, sir,—a slave for life!"

I patted the boy on the head, wished his new master, my tall friend, all joy of his bargain, and ran off as fast as I could down one of the avenues, hoping, by change of place, to get rid of the entanglement of many unpleasant thoughts which crowded upon me during the sale; and perhaps willing, by a good scamper over the ground, to satisfy myself of the identity of my own freedom.

I asked a gentleman afterwards, whether such things were common in that part of the country. Instead of answering my question, he picked up a newspaper at random, and pointed out the following advertisement.

MARSHAL'S SALE

By authority of a writ of fieri facias, issued from the Clerk's Office of the Circuit Court of this district, for the county of Washington, to me directed, I shall expose to public sale, for cash, on Monday, 31st instant, the following slaves, viz.:—Charity, Fanny, Sandy, Jerry, Nace, Harry, Jem, Bill, Anne, Lucy; Nancy and her five children, George, Penn, Mary, Francis, and Henry; Flora and her seven children, Robert, Joseph, Fanny, Mary, Jane, Patty, and Betsy; Harry; and also four mules, four carts, one carriage and harness. Seized and taken in execution, as the goods and chattels of John Threlkeld, and will be sold to satisfy a debt due by him to the Bank of the United States, use of the United States, and the Bank of the United States.

Sale to be at the dwelling of Alexander Burrows, and commence at 11 o'clock A. M.

TENCH RINGGOLD,
Marshal of the district of Columbia

31. THOMAS HAMILTON

When a woman is sold, he usually gets in a few indecent jokes

Hamilton's selection illustrates both the manner of conducting a slave sale in New Orleans and a conservative Englishman's reaction to the phenomenon.

There are slave auctions almost every day in the New Orleans Exchange. I was frequently present at these, and the man who wants an excuse for misanthropy, will nowhere discover better reason for hating and despising his species. The usual process

From Thomas Hamilton, *Men and Manners in America*, pp. 317–318.

differs in nothing from that of selling a horse. The poor object of traffic is mounted on a table; intending purchasers examine his points, and put questions as to his age, health, &c. The auctioneer dilates on his value, enumerates his accomplishments, and when the hammer at length falls, protests, in the usual phrase, that poor Sambo has been absolutely thrown away. When a woman is sold, he usually puts his audience in good humour by a few indecent jokes.

One of the first human beings whom I happened to see thus sold was a poor woman, apparently dying of a consumption. She was emaciated, her voice was husky and feeble, and her proper place was, evidently, the hospital. It was with difficulty she was raised upon the table, "Now, gentlemen, here is Mary!" said the auctioneer; "a clever house-servant and an excellent cook. Bid me something for this valuable lot. She has only one fault, gentlemen, and that is shamming sick. She pretends to be ill, but there is nothing more the matter with her than there is with me at this moment. Put her up, gentlemen—shall I say a hundred dollars to begin with? Will nobody say a hundred dollars for Mary, a clever servant and excellent cook? Thank you, sir, fifty—well, fifty dollars is bid for her." Here the auctioneer stopped for a minute or two, while several men began feeling the poor woman's ribs, and putting questions as to her health.

"Are you well?" asked one man.

"Oh, no, I am very ill."

"What is the matter with you?"

"I have a bad cough and pain in my side."

"How long have you had it?"

"Three months and more."

Here the auctioneer, finding such interrogatories did not tend to enhance the value of the lot, again went on. "Never mind what she says, gentlemen, I told you she was a shammer. Her health is good enough. Damn her humbug. Give her a touch or two of the cow-hide, and I'll warrant she'll do your work. Speak, gentlemen, before I knock her down. Seventy dollars only, bid,—going, going, going, gone!" The sale concluded amid sundry jests at the expense of the purchaser. "A bloody good lot of skin and bone," said one.

"I guess that 'ere woman will soon be food for the land-crabs," said another; and amid such atrocious merriment the poor dying creature was led off.

If such scenes are acted in a Christian country, it is the duty of every traveller to take care, at least, that they shall not be done in a corner, that they shall be proclaimed loudly to the world, and that those who perpetrate the enormities shall receive their due meed of indignation and contempt.

The time is past when it was necessary to write whole volumes, in illustration of the evils and injustice of slavery. These are now admitted and confessed by every one. They are so great as to admit of no exaggeration by eloquence, nor of palliation or concealment by sophistry. Public opinion in England requires no stimulus.

I feel anxious, that writing on this subject I should be clearly understood. It may not be a crime—it, probably, ought not to be charged as one—in the American people, that slavery still exists in by far the larger portion of the territory of the Union. But now when the United States have enjoyed upwards of half a century of almost unbroken prosperity, when their people, as they themselves declare, are the most moral, the most benevolent, the most enlightened in the world, we are surely entitled to demand, what have this people done for the mitigation of slavery? what have they done to elevate the slave in the scale of moral and intellectual being, and to prepare him for the enjoyment of those privileges to which, sooner or later, the coloured population *must* be admitted?

The answer to these questions unfortunately may be comprised in one word—NOTHING.

PART THREE

The Raucous Politics of Democracy

32. Basil Hall

The spirit of party seems to enter into everything

To the amazement of foreign visitors Americans seemed to be in a perpetual "election fever." Certainly they were ready to talk politics at the slightest provocation. If the talk was typically animated, it was because political feelings were strong. Some contemporaries and later students alike have leaped to the conclusion that because Americans felt so intensely about politics, the issues evoking such emotion must have been vitally significant. In the following excerpt Captain Hall appears to have discerned the situation more shrewdly: American party spirit was "directed more exclusively to the means, than to any useful end."

During our stay at Albany, we went frequently into company, especially to dinners and to evening parties, both large and small, which afforded us the most agreeable opportunities of seeing and judging of the state of domestic society; one feature of which ought to be mentioned, as it meets a stranger's observation in every quarter of that wide country. I mean the spirit of party—not to call it politics—or rather, to define it more correctly, the spirit of electioneering, which seems to enter as an essential ingredient into the composition of every thing.

The most striking peculiarity of this spirit, in contradistinction to what we see in England, is that its efforts are directed more exclusively to the means, than to any useful end. The Americans, as it appears to me, are infinitely more occupied about bringing in a given candidate, than they are about the advancement of those measures of which he is conceived to be the supporter. They do

From Basil Hall, *Travels in North America in 1827 and 1828*, II, pp. 59–62.

occasionally advert to these prospective measures, in their canvassing arguments in defence of their own friends, or in attacks upon the other party; but always, as far as I could see, more as rhetorical flourishes, or as motives to excite the furious acrimony of party spirit, than as distinct or sound anticipations of the line of policy which their candidate, or his antagonist, was likely to follow. The intrigues, the canvassings for votes, all the machinery of newspaper abuse and praise, the speeches and manœuvres in the Legislature, at the bar, by the fireside, and in every hole and corner of the country from end to end, without intermission, form integral parts of the business—apparently far more important than the candidate's wishes—his promises—or even than his character and fitness for the office.

All these things, generally speaking, it would seem, are subordinate considerations; so completely are men's minds swallowed up in the technical details of the election. They discuss the chances of this or that State, town, or parish, or district, going with or against their friend. They overwhelm one another with that most disagreeable of all forms of argument—authorities. They analyze every sentence uttered by any man, dead or alive, who possesses, or ever did possess, influence; not, it must be observed, to come at any better knowledge of the candidate's pretensions as a public man, but merely to discover how far the weight of such testimony is likely to be thrown into their own scale, or that of the opposite party.

The election of the President, being one affecting the whole country, the respective candidates for that office were made the butts at which all political shafts were aimed, and to which every other election was rendered subservient, not indirectly, but by straight and obvious means. It was of no importance, apparently, whether the choice to be made, at any given election, were that of a governor, a member to Congress, or to the Legislature of the State—or whether it were that of a constable of the obscure ward of an obscure town—it was all the same. The candidates seldom, if ever, that I could see, even professed to take their chief ground as the fittest men for the vacant office—this was often hardly thought of—as they stood forward simply as Adams men or

Jackson men—these being the names, it is right to mention, of the two gentlemen aiming at the Presidency. Although the party principles of these candidates for any office, on the subject of the Presidential election, could not—nine cases in ten—afford any index to their capacity for filling the station to which they aspired, their chance of success was frequently made to hinge upon that matter exclusively. Thus the man who could bring most votes to that side of this grand, all-absorbing Presidential question, which happened to have the ascendency for the time being, was sure to gain the day, whether he were or were not the best suited to fill the particular vacancy.

More or less this interference of Presidential politics in all the concerns of life, obtained in every part of America which I visited. There were exceptions, it is true, but these were so rare, that the tone I have been describing was assuredly the predominant one every where. The consequence was, that the candidates for office, instead of being the principals, were generally mere puppets—men of straw—abstract beings, serving the purpose of rallying points to the voters from whence they might carry on their main attack in the pursuit of an ulterior object, which, after all, was equally immaterial in itself, but which served, for the time being, to engross the attention of the people as completely as if it were of real consequence to them. In these respects, therefore, the Presidential contests in America resemble those field sports in which the capture of the game is entirely subordinate to the pleasures of its pursuit.

Low Tone of Party Battles

33. J. S. Buckingham

American politics was at once ludicrous and disgusting

Most visitors were amazed at the strong language used by American political parties in denouncing one another as election day approached.

From J. S. Buckingham, *America* (London: Fisher, Son, 1841) 3 vols., I, pp. 68–69.

State contests that were almost issueless evoked a bitter oratory suggesting that the republic would go under if party A's candidate defeated party B's. Students of comparative politics will note with interest that the epithets Whigs and Democrats hurled at each other fall into a classic mold of political exaggeration.

Heretofore, the composition of the legislature for the State of New York, including the two houses, the Assembly and the Senate, as well as the Governor, was, like that of the Congress or legislature of the general government, democratic, or favourable to the existence of Mr. Van Buren's administration. The changes in public opinion, wrought by the commercial disasters of which I have previously spoken, had occasioned such a feeling of hostility to the present cabinet—as the supposed cause of those financial difficulties, from which all classes were more or less suffering—that the Whigs determined to avail themselves of this change, to effect a complete renovation of their two houses of State legislature, by making their own party predominant. Accordingly, the note of preparation was sounded early, by all their organs of the press; and while committees were forming in town and country, and meetings held every night in the week, by old and young, to organize and arrange their plans of operation, pass strong resolutions, print them in the newspapers, and distribute them freely through every part of the city; the editors themselves were all busily engaged in aiding these operations by their daily appeals. A stranger arriving in the country, and not knowing any thing of the state of parties beforehand, or of the mode of warfare practised on such occasions, would have imagined that the fate of the whole Union depended on the issue of this single election; that if it were carried in favour of the Whigs, the nation would instantly be restored to the highest degree of commercial prosperity; but that, if carried against them, the result would be universal bankruptcy, total annihilation of all the elements of prosperity, the dissolution of the Union, the insurrection of the slave population, and the destruction of all that was worth preserving in the country. There was no term of opprobrium too severe for them to apply to their opponents, the democratic republicans. They called them atheists, infidels, agrarians, incendiaries, men who were without religion and without honesty, who desired to pull down all that was venerable in the institutions of the country, to seize the property of the rich and divide it among the poor, to demolish the churches, to destroy the courts of justice, to let loose all the criminals from the jails, to abolish all government, and to produce only a chaos of anarchy and confusion. Some few who heard all this, seemed really to believe it; but the greater number knew it to be merely electioneering language, and disregarded it accordingly; though they had no objection whatever to its use, provided it would attain the end they had in view.

To me it was at once both ludicrous and disgusting; ludicrous, because of the gravity with which it was reiterated, day after day, in the face, not only of repeated contradictions and disavowals of any such objects or such doctrines on the other side; but in spite of challenges, again and again repeated, to produce any well-authenticated speech or writing of any of the democratic party, in which such doctrines were avowed, or from which they could even be inferred; but which challenges were no more heeded than if they had never been offered.

34. Seba Smith

Major Jack Downing ridicules state party battles

The gulf between the lofty rhetoric of major party political warriors and the sordid actual quality of the motives of many of them, as of the measures they fought over, inspired a number of satirical treatments of party warfare. "Major Jack Downing" appeared on the scene, a fictional character compounded of unlettered naïveté on the one hand and

From Seba Smith, *The Life and Writings of Major Jack Downing* (Boston: Lilly, Wait, Coleman and Holden, 1834), 121–129. Bracketed "Note by the Editor" is in the original.

realism, honesty, and mother wit on the other. (Actually, there was not one Major but two. One was the creation of Seba Smith, a Maine publisher, the other, of the distinguished New Yorker, Charles Augustus Davis. Davis's Downing, a member of the "Downingsville Militia," savaged the Jacksonians more viciously than Smith's.) A great crony of General Jackson, Smith's Major Downing was better able to flay the opportunists who claimed to act in accord with Old Hickory's "principles." In the following selection, Smith's Downing satirizes the major parties' preoccupation with scoring points at the expense of their opponents.

Letter xxviii

IN WHICH MR. DOWNING TELLS HOW THE JACKSONITES IN THE LEGISLATURE HAD A DREADFUL TUSSLE TO POUR A 'HEALING ACT' DOWN THE THROATS OF THE HUNTONITES.

> [*Note by the Editor.* The bitterness of feeling occasioned by the struggle for the ascendency between the two parties in 1830, still rankled in the breasts of the members of the Legislature in 1831. The Huntonites had acquired the ascendency the preceding session, but now the Jacksonites were in power, and they contended that the acts of the Huntonites in 1830 were unconstitutional and void. They therefore set about preparing a "healing act" to declare all the doings of the preceding Legislature *valid* in the lump. When this Bill was brought forward, it produced a storm in the Legislature, almost unparalleled. The Huntonites considered it altogether a useless provoking piece of political trickery. They contended that if the acts of the former Legislature were in fact unconstitutional, no law passed by this Legislature could make them constitutional; and considering it a wanton attempt to heap insult and odium upon them, they fought against it almost while life and breath remained. A fierce debate on the passage of this Bill was carried on for several days. But the Jacksonites had the power in their own hands, and the Bill was finally passed. The scene is somewhat minutely described in the two following letters.]

Portland, Feb. 4, 1831.

Dear Uncle Joshua—If you got my postscript to this letter that I sent you yesterday, I spose you wont sleep nor eat much till you hear something more about it. So I thought I'd try to send you a little bit of a letter to-day. O dear, uncle, there 's terrible times here again, and I'm half afraid it's agoing to be worse than it was last winter. The Legislater 's been all in the wind this two or three days, pulling and hauling and fighting like smoke. The wheels of government are all stopt; I cant say as they are *trigged,* as they used to be last winter, but they are fairly stopped, because nobody dont pull 'em along; for when the members are all pulling each other's caps, how can they pull the wheels of government? They seemed to get along very well ever since they've been here till now, and I thought they most all belonged to them are two clever parties that tried so hard to save the State last winter; I mean the democratic republicans and the national republicans. But somehow or other this week a quarrelsome gang of Jacksonites and Huntonites has got into the Legislater and kicked up such a bobbery, it seems as though they 'd tare the State all to pieces. My heart 's been up in my mouth a dozen times for fear the State would go to ruin before I could get out of it; and I 've scratched round and picked up what few bean-poles and ax-handles I had left, and got all ready to set sail to Boston, for I'me determined to be off before the state goes to rack. And I advise you and all our friends at Downingville to pack up as soon as you get this letter, and be all ready as soon as you hear a cracking down this way to fly for your lives away back into New-Hampshire or Vermont. The trouble as near as I could understand it begun in this way. The Jacksonites said the Huntonites worked so hard last winter in trying to trig the wheels of government, and tare the constitution to pieces, that they made themselves all sick, dreadful sick, and had n't got well yet; and it was time to do something to try to cure 'em; for their sickness was so catching that all the State would be taken down with it in a little while, if they want cured.

But the Huntonites said they want sick a bit; they never was better in their lives; and moreover, it was false that they had tried to trig the wheels of government last winter, or tear a single leaf out of the constitution; if any thing of that kind was done, they said the Jacksonites did it, and as for taking doctor's stuff they'd no notion of it. But the Jacksonites said 'twas no use, the

Huntonites were all sick, and they must take some doctor stuff, and if they would n't take it willingly they must be *made* to take it. So they went to work and fixed a dose that they called a *healing act,* that they said would cure all the Huntonites and any body else that had catched the sickness of 'em. The Huntonites declared 'twas no use for 'em to fix it, for they never would take it as long as they lived, that's what they wouldn't; they were as well as any body, and they'd fight it out till next June before they'd take it. Howsomever, the Jacksonites got their dose ready, and yesterday they carried it into the House of Representatives and told the Huntonites they must take it, and 'twould do 'em good. As soon as the Huntonites smelt of it, they turned up their noses, and said no, before they'd take that are plaguy dirty stuff they'd fight 'em all over the State, inch by inch. But the Jacksonites said 'twas no use, they might sniff as much as they pleased, it was the only thing that would cure 'em, and they must take it, and more than all that, they was the strongest and they *should* take it.

Some of the Huntonites looked pale as tho' they were a little grain frightened, and some of them looked red as though they were mad as a March hair. And some of 'em begun to talk to the Jacksonites and tell 'em how unreasonable it was to make 'em take doctor stuff when they want sick. They were well now, and like as not if they should take it t'would make 'em all sick.

One of 'em, that talked like a very clever man got up and coaxed 'em to ask the Judges of the great Court if they thought there was any *need* of their taking sich a dose, or if it would do 'em any good if they did take it. But the Jacksonites said no, they shouldn't ask no sich questions. They understood the business well enough, they knew the Huntonites were sick, and they knew this would cure 'em, and swallow it they should. Well, the Huntonites see how 'twas gone goose with 'em, and they thought the only chance left was to put their hands over their mouths and fight and kick and scrabble with all their might and keep it out of their throats as long as they could. Still they tried to talk and reason with the Jacksonites about it. They asked 'em to let them have time to examine the medicine carefully and see what it was made of, or that they would tell 'em what it was made of, or why they thought it would do any good to take it. But the Jacksonites said they shouldn't tell 'em any thing about it, it would be 'casting pearls before swine,' and the good book said they mustn't do so.

The men who had fixed the dose knew what they were about, they had fixed it right, and the Huntonites must open their mouths and take it, and not parley any more about it. And now the real tussle and the hard fight begun. The house seemed to be so full of Jacksonites and Huntonites that I guess there was n't but a few republicans left. And I could n't help minding that the Jacksonites took the seats of the democratic republicans, and the Huntonites took the seats of the national republicans. Well, the Jacksonites took the dose in one hand, and grab'd the Huntonites with the other, and tipped their heads back, and were jest agoing to pour it down their throats, when the Huntonites fetched a spring and kicked it away to the fourth day of April. But the Jacksonites run after it and got it back again in about half an hour, and clinched 'em again, and got all ready to pour it down; but jest as they got it almost to their lips, the Huntonites fetched another spring and kicked it away to the fourth of March. Away went the Jacksonites after it again, and brought it back, and clinched the Huntonites in the same manner as before, and they kicked it away again, but they did n't kick this time quite to the end of February.

So they kept it agoing all the forenoon, but every time the Huntonites kick'd the bitter dose away, it didn't go so far as it did the last time before. I spose they begun to grow tired and could n't kick so hard. Well, then they tried to adjourn so as to get some dinner, but the Jacksonites would n't let 'em. And they kept 'em there till four o'clock in the afternoon without any dinner, and I dont know but they thought the Huntonites would get so hungry after awhile that they would swallow it down without much fuss. But it all would n't do, the nearer it come to 'em, the tighter the Huntonites gritted their teeth together, and I guess they'd a starved before they would take it. Well after the Jacksonites had tried nearly twenty times to pour down the bitter dose, and the Huntonites had kicked it away as many times, both parties seemed to be nearly tired out, and so they finally agreed to adjourn till nine o'clock this morning. I thought the Huntonites, if they once got out, would cut and run home and get clear of the plaguy stuff. But instead of that they all come in again this morning, and they've been at it again all day, hammer and tongs, the Jacksonites trying to pour it down, and the Huntonites fighting against it, tooth and nail.

How it 'll come out I cant tell. Whether the State will be ruined if they dont take it, I cant tell; or whether it will cure them if they do take it, I can't tell. But I can assure you, dear uncle, there's a greater fuss here, than there was when the little boy said he run and jumped over a fence and tore his trowses as if the heavens and earth were coming to pieces. If we live through it, I shall let you know something more about it. Your loving neffu,

Jack Downing

Letter xxix

IN WHICH MR. DOWNING TELLS HOW THE JACKSONITES AT LAST GOT THE 'HEALING ACT' DOWN THE THROATS OF THE HUNTONITES.

Portland, Saturday, March 5, 1831.

Dear Uncle Joshua.—I aint dead, but I spose you begin to feel kind of uneasy about me, bein I have n't writ home so long. Well, I'll tell you how 'twas; I've had *this ere cold* and one thing another, so bad, I did n't feel hardly smart enough to write. And besides I got so skeer'd that night the Jacksonites poured their doctor stuff, what they call the healing plaster, down the throates of the Huntonites, that I did n't dare to go nigh 'em agin for a good while for fear they'd pour some of their pesky stuff down my throat. But I'm sorry I did n't write afore, for I've let it alone so long now, that my work has got desputly behindhand. When I writ to you before, the Jacksonites were holding the Huntonites by the hair of the head with one hand and trying to cram the healing plaster down their throats with 'tother, and the Huntonites were kicking and scrabbling, and gritting their teeth together with all their might, and doubling up their fists and stamping, and declaring up hill and down, that they would never take it. And they were so upstropulous about it for awhile, I did n't know as they ever would swallow it. But the Jacksonites were the stoutest, and held on to 'em like a dog to a root, and kept 'em there all day and all the evening till about midnight, and then the poor Huntonites seemed to be a most dragged out. I fairly pitied 'em. Along in the first of it they threatened pretty stoutly, and declared by every thing that's black and blue, if they had to take this dirty dose and should happen to be strongest next year, they'd make the Jacksonites take a dose worth two of this. But all the threatening did n't do any good; and then they fell to begging and coaxing, and that did n't do any good nother. The Jacksonites said they should not only take it, but they should take it that night before they slept. At last they got their hands and feet tied, and kept bringing it up a little nearer and little nearer to their mouths, and the Huntonites, got so they could n't do nothing but *spit.* But the Jacksonites did n't mind the spitting, for you know it is n't for the doctor to stand about being spit upon a little, when he's giving medicine. Just before the last ont, the poor Huntonites rolled their eyes dreadfully, and I believe some on 'em lost their senses a little; one of 'em took a notion that they were agoing to make him swallow a whole live goose, feathers and all; and he begged of 'em, if they would n't take out the gizzard and 'tother inside things, that they'd jest pull out the pin feathers, so that it would n't scratch his throat going down. But they did n't pay no attention to him, and just before the clock struck twelve they grabbed 'em by the throat, and pried their mouths open, and poured it in. The Huntonites guggled a little, but they had to swallow it. A day or two afterwards they made some of the Sinneters take it in the same way. They had a considerable tussle for it, but not quite so bad as they had in the House.

Some thought this healing dose would make the Huntonites worse, and some thought it would make 'em better. I've watched 'em ever since they took it whenever I dared to go near the Legislater, and I cant see much alteration in 'em. But that or something else has kicked up a monstrous dust amongst other folks all over the world amost. I've been looking over the newspapers a little, and I never see the world in such a terrible hubbub before in all my life. Every body seems to be running mad, and jest ready to eat each other up. There's Russia snapping her teeth like a great bear, and is just agoing to eat up the Poles, I dont mean Ephraim's bean poles, but all the folks that live in Poland; not that are Poland up there where Mr. Dunn lives, but that great Poland over along side of Russia. And there's the Dutch trying to eat up Holland, and the Belgians are trying to eat up the Dutch, and there's 'five great powers' trying to pour a healing dose down the throat of the king of the Netherlands, and there's Mr. O' Connell trying to make the king of England and Parliament take a healing dose, and there's Ireland jest ready to eat up Mr. O'Connell, and all the kings of Europe are trying to eat up the people, and the people are all trying to eat up the kings.

And our great folks in this country too, away off there to Washington, have got into such a snarl, I guess it would puzzle a Philadelphy lawyer to get 'em out of it. There's the President and Mr. Calhoun and Mr. Van Buren and the two great republican papers, and half a dozen more of 'em, all together by the ears; but which of 'em will eat up the rest I don't know. I've heard a good many guess that Mr. Van Buren would eat up the whole toat of 'em; for they say although he's a small man, there isn't another man in the country, that can eat his way through a political pudding so slick as he can. These are dreadful times, uncle; I don't know what 'll become of the world, if I dont get an office pretty soon.

It seems to me there must be something out of the way to make so much confusion in the world; and I hope the Legislater before they adjourn will pass a general healing act to cure all these difficulties. They've been talking about passing a healing act to cure our state house up to Augusta, for they say its too small, and they intend to bring it down here to Portland to cure it. But I guess it 'll give 'em a pull, for they say the Kennebeckers are master fellers to hold on.

They had a kind of a flusteration here to-day in the Legislater. The Speaker 's cleared out, and left 'em, because the Governor said he'd taken his turn sitting in the *Chair* long enough, and he must go and sit on the *Bench* awhile now. And then they went to work and chose that good-natured man from Monmouth for Speaker. I meant to a told you about them are two great meetings they 've had here to make Governors and Presidents and one thing another: but I hav'nt time to-day.

One of 'em made Mr. Smith Governor for next year and Gineral Jackson President; and 'tother made Mr. Sprague governor, and kind of put Mr. Clay a brewing for President.

If you think its best for me to run again for governor another year I wish you'd call our friends together up there and have me nominated, for there's nothing like starting in season in these matters.

Your loving neffu,

Jack Downing

Similarities of the Major Parties

35. George Combe

Lively Whig caucus in Massachusetts

Contemporaries who took party rhetoric literally got the impression that Democrats were markedly unlike Whigs in their beliefs and ideologies, their social status, and their economic standing. A modern variation on this theme has suggested that Whigs were stuffier and more decorous than Jacksonians. Neither the persons attending the 1839 Whig meeting in Boston described below nor their actions fit too well these analyses. The reporter was George Combe, a visiting phrenologist interested in more than the bumps on American heads.

Whig Caucus Meeting.—This is Sunday, and in the evening I attended a great Caucus meeting of the Whig party held in Faneuil Hall. It was called by public advertisements and placards, to-morrow being election-day for the great officers of State. No one could give me any reasonable explanation of the origin of the word *Caucus*, which is applied to political meetings. It is an unmeaning-looking vocable to a stranger, and, as used, it seems to imply a general in contra-distinction to a ward meeting of a

From George Combe, *Notes on the United States of North America, 1838–1840* (Edinburgh: Maclachlan, Stewart, 1841), 3 vols., III, pp. 146–149.

political party. I was tempted to invent an etymology for it, and to suppose it to be derived from the Latin *cœcus*, blind, because the people have at some period been viewed as giving themselves up at these meetings blindly to the guidance of their political leaders. The Sunday terminates at sunset, and the Caucus met at 7 P.M. The hall was densely crowded, and probably between two and three thousand persons were present. The youthfulness of the assembly was very striking. Without pretending to accuracy, I guessed the ages as follows. Five per cent. of the whole appeared to be boys under fourteen years of age; sixty per cent. young men between fourteen and twenty-eight; fifteen per cent. between twenty-eight and forty; fifteen per cent. between forty and fifty; and five per cent. above fifty. In size of brain and combination of organs, the speakers were inferior to the men whom I daily meet with in society. Their ideas were few; their words and figures many; and nearly all was assertion and declamation. Their speeches were addressed to Acquisitiveness, Self-Esteem, and Love of Approbation, much more than to Benevolence, Veneration, and Conscientiousness. The staple of their orations was praise of "*old* Massachusetts;" of "our *ancient* and beloved Commonwealth;" of prayers that she might be preserved from bowing the knee to Martin Van Buren; of denunciations against the Democrats, termed also the Locofocos; against specie, and the Treasury and Sub-Treasury bills; and of praises of paper currency, the "credit system," the Whigs, and Whiggery. The appeals which produced the loudest acclamations were those which embodied a warlike figure, or a witty and degrading representation of the Democrats. "To-morrow," said one speaker, "old Massachusetts will go to the poll like old Ironsides (the pet name of one of their frigates) to battle. She moved so calmly onward, and so silent were her crew, that the enemy expected her to strike without a contest; but when old Ironsides came up, yard-arm to yard-arm, every spirit flashed with energy and ardour; she sent from all her decks and tops such a storm of hail and thunder that no sound could be heard except that of her own mighty voice; when she held her arm, universal silence reigned; her prostrate enemy floated beside her sailless, mastless, and helmless, a pitiable wreck at the mercy of the waves. So shall old Massachusetts make the Locofocos float on the waters of the State to-morrow at sundown." This burst of eloquence called forth loud, long, and unanimous thunders of applause.

There was no discussion of principle in the speeches; no statement of facts; in short, very little intellectual substance of any kind. The object of them clearly was, not to operate on the understanding, for the whole audience was of one mind, but to produce *excitement*, with a view to rouse up the voters to go to the poll next day. Contemplated in this light, and seeing that the speeches were addressed to a young and essentially an unintellectual audience, they certainly had the merit of being well adapted to accomplish the end for which they were delivered.

I was much struck with the circumstance that the people must have remarkably few real grievances in any degree chargeable against the Government, when the opposition orators are able to muster only such slender materials for assailing them. The statement by one of them that the Sub-Treasury Bill would lead to a monarchy, was loudly applauded! One of the speakers compared the Democratic candidates to Milton's devils, and introduced Milton's verses descriptive of them, which he and his audience applied to particular "Locofocos;" but, from my not knowing the persons alluded to, the effect was lost on me. The personal appearance of the individuals who composed the assembly was highly respectable, and their conduct completely orderly.

The Rancor of Elections

36. Thurlow Weed

There was a violent outbreak

Students of international labor history know that paradoxically the history of no labor movement has been more violent and yet more conservative

From Harriet A. Weed, ed., *Autobiography of Thurlow Weed* (Boston: Houghton Mifflin, 1883), 2 vols., I, pp. 448, 449.

than the American. In the antebellum decades American party battles similarly were waged bitterly, even violently, while political issues were often bland and peripheral or subordinated to personalities. Thurlow Weed, a master strategist first of the Whig party of New York State and subsequently of the nation, describes the stormy scenes attendant on Albany elections, 1835 to 1837.

My residence in Albany as the editor of an Anti-Masonic journal promised small social enjoyment. There had been, up to this time, scarcely a dozen reputable citizens who openly avowed themselves political Anti-Masons. Of that very limited number, Weare C. Little and William White alone survive. While, therefore, the Anti-Masonic idea was decidedly distasteful, the "Evening Journal," even with that drawback, was made first endurable, and afterwards popular, especially in families. And while the paper was growing in favor I was personally wearing out the prejudices encountered at the beginning. Friendships, alike enduring and endearing, were formed. Business men, who had previously taken no active part in politics, became and ever after remained zealous and influential politicians. Lewis Benedict was for more than twenty years a member of the Whig State committee, and one of its most earnest and efficient workers. Merchants and business men, who had previously contented themselves with simply depositing their ballots on election days, now taking a broader view of the question, saw that something more was due and expected from them, and it was largely due to the zeal and liberality of that class that, after a long struggle, we were enabled to overthrow Regency rule, first in Albany, then in the State, and in 1840 to elect a Whig President. The scene of most exciting action in our early struggle with the Regency was the fourth ward of the city of Albany. That ward was the residence of Captain James Maher, a popular, adroit, and clear-headed Democratic leader, and myself, who were respectively charged with the organization and conduct of the elections, then occupying three days. I had known Captain Maher in command of a company of "Irish Greens" at Sackett's Harbor in 1813. Though politically opposed, a warm personal friendship existed between us, a circumstance which, in the most exciting fourth ward elections, on more than one occasion prevented violent outbreaks. There was a large number of canal and river men always drifting about the poll of the fourth ward, whose votes gave the ward to the party that succeeded in obtaining them. For many years the Regency, physically too strong for us, carried the ward by a decisive majority. That physical superiority not only gave them "the drift-wood," as it was called, but by violence and intimidation kept quiet and infirm Whig electors from the polls. To obviate this difficulty, it became necessary to meet force by force. I therefore, in 1835, organized a force, avowedly to preserve order, and enable all peaceable electors to reach the ballot-boxes. I apprised Captain Maher of our intention to protect our electors, "peaceably if we could, forcibly if we must." He approved of this determination, and endeavored to induce his hard-fisted men to act with ours in preserving order. But that was impossible; and soon after the polls were opened a collision occurred, in which our man, "Bob Chesebro," a stage-driver, was victor.

That quieted things for several hours, when another fight came off between a Democratic bully and George W. Daly, which resulted in favor of Daly. The first day of the election, therefore, closed auspiciously. This so much exasperated our opponents, that a large number of them appeared the next morning with concealed weapons, and bent upon mischief. Captain Maher, however, was enabled to control his followers, and the second day passed off quietly. But on the third and last day, an hour or two after the polls opened there was a violent outbreak, in which twenty or thirty men with clubs were engaged, and in which Bob Chesebro, Henry Y. Webb, George W. Daly, Samuel Strong, and other Whigs, not only stood their ground, but bore themselves, as Polonius advised Laertes, "so that the opposer 'might' beware of them." That election resulted in a handsome Whig gain. Our physical force was therefore maintained and augmented, and in 1837, after a desperate struggle, we carried the ward, as we did the State. Thenceforward the fourth ward became a sort of political barometer, both parties accepting the idea that "as goes the fourth ward so goes the State." To the men whom I have named, and other devoted workers in the fourth ward, including James Weldon, Chauncey Dexter, Thomas Hillson, David Nelligan, Stephen Thorn, Shepard, the Winnes, Stillman Witt, now a millionaire of Cleveland, Ohio, Provost Vesey, the Whelpleys, and others, I became much attached. Most of these men were dependent upon their labor for the support of their families, but such was their zeal for the Whig cause that all other considerations became secondary, and, with one exception, they have remained faithful through life.

37. Michael Chevalier

The spirit of anarchy in American elections

Chevalier records the amazement of a sensitive European to the widespread outbreak of electoral violence in 1834.

During the last six months, the spirit of anarchy had raised its head in the United States in such a manner as to inspire serious alarm, even among those not prone to be timid. You know what happened in New York during the April [1834] elections; several months later, in July, the city became the theatre of a series of outrages against the poor blacks, which were repeated several nights. In August the same excesses were committed in Philadelphia, under the same pretext, and with no less audacity and perseverance: then came the brutal assault on the convent in Charlestown [Mass.]*, when the retreat of peaceful nuns devoted to the education of young girls was attacked, plundered, and burnt down, without the Selectmen of the town having the power or the courage to make head against the rioters, and without the well-disposed citizens, taken by surprise by this act of savage intolerance, venturing to interfere. Hardly a month since, there

From Michael Chevalier, *Society, Manners and Politics*, pp. 161, 162.

* See document 25—Ed.

was also an incendiary conflagration at Philadelphia on the evening of the election; six houses were burnt, and the fire-men were driven off by the rioters, as at Charlestown, by main force. The same evening, an event of a more grave character occurred; several muskets were discharged by some of the Opposition whom the mob had assailed with stones, several persons were wounded, and one or two killed. A week before, during the preparatory elections, an obscure and peaceable individual was killed by a stab with a dagger.

A repetition of these scenes of disorder was feared in New York; but nothing of the sort occurred. Nearly 36,000 voters exercised their right of suffrage without any disturbance, although both parties were highly excited. The merit of this wise conduct is wholly due to the people; the Common Council had, indeed, taken extraordinary measures for the preservation of the peace, but what is here considered extraordinary, hardly comes up to the ordinary police in Europe. If the multitude in the United States abstain from acts of violence, it is because they choose to do so; if they preserve order, it is because they love order. Three hundred constables more or less, in a city of 260,000 souls, like New York, could do nothing. Some persons, however, attribute this moderation of the democracy wholly to its confidence in success, and insist, that, if there had been any symptoms of the elections going the other way, the streets would have been thronged, as in April, by bodies of men armed with clubs.

National Electioneering

38. ANONYMOUS

Such a sight was never seen before

The 1828 campaign for the presidency was one of the most scurrilous in American history. Issues were studiously avoided as partisans of Andrew Jackson and John Quincy Adams concentrated on personalities and

A Brief Account of the Execution of the Six Militia Men (1828 unpaged handbill).

mud-slinging. A coffin hand bill" was circulated by John Binns, an anti-Jackson newspaper editor, reminding voters that fourteen years earlier Jackson had executed six militia men for alleged desertion during the fighting against the Creek Indians. The flyer was enlivened by a picture of six coffins. The following selection is from a lengthier handbill that focused on a "factual" rather than a pictorial rendering.

> As we soon expect to have *official* documents in relation to the SIX MILITIA MEN, arrested, tried, and put to death, under the orders of General Andrew Jackson, this may not be an improper time to give to the public some of the particulars of the execution, as we have them from "AN EYE WITNESS," who appeals to Col. Russell, for the truth of every word he relates.
>
> *Democratic Press*

Harris was a Baptist preacher, with a large family. He had hired as a substitute for three months. This was the case with most of them. They were ignorant men, but obstinate in what they believed right; and what they had been told by their officers was right. They were all sure they could not be kept beyond three months, and they give up their muskets, and had provisions dealt out to them, from the public stores, before they left the camp. This confirmed their convictions that they were right and doing what was lawful.

Col. Russell commanded at the execution. The Militia men were brought to the place in a large wagon. The military dispositions being made, Col. Russell rode up to the wagon and ordered the men to descend. Harris was the only one who betrayed feminine weakness.—The awfulness of the occasion; his wife and nine children; the parting with his son; and the fear of a quickly approaching ignominious death! quite overcame him, and he sunk in unmanly grief. No feeling of military pride could brace him up.

Col. Russell, doubtless, felt as a man, but he felt also for the pride of the army, and desired to animate the men with fortitude. "You are about to die," said he, "by the sentence of a Court Martial—die like men; *like soldiers*. You have been brave in the field—you have fought well, do no discredit to your country, or dishonor to the army, or yourselves, by any unmanly fears. Meet your fate with courage."

Harris attempted to make some apology for his conduct, but while he spoke, he wept bitterly. The fear of death, the idea that he should never again behold his wife and little ones, and his son weeping near him, had taken such entire possession of his mind, that it was impossible he should rally.

Lewis, the gallant Lewis, said in a clear and manly tone, "Colonel, I have served my country well. I love it dearly, and would, if I could, serve it longer and better. I have fought bravely—*you know* I have, and HERE I have a right to say so MYSELF. I would not wish to die in this way"—here his voice faltered, and he passed the back of his right hand over his eyes—"I did not expect it: But, I am now as firm as I have been in battle, and you shall see that I will die as becomes a soldier.—You know I am a brave man." "Yes, Lewis," said the Colonel, "you have always behaved like a brave man."—Other sentences were uttered, other declarations were made, and other words of comfort spoken, but they were lost on me; my attention, says an Eye Witness, being chiefly directed to Lewis.

Six coffins were ranged as directed, and on each of them knelt one of our American Militia Men. Such a sight was never seen before! I trust in God it never will be seen again! Six soldiers were detailed and drawn up to fire at each man. What an awful duty! Their white caps were drawn over the faces of the unhappy men. Harris evidently trembled, and I could almost persuade myself that the heart of Lewis was enlarged, and that his bosom rose with manly courage to meet death.—The fatal word was given, and they all fell.

As we approached the scene of blood and carnage, Lewis gave signs of life—the rest were all dead—he crawled upon his coffin. After the lapse of a few minutes he said—I give his very words—"Colonel," the Col. was close to him, "Colonel, I am not killed, but I am sadly cut and mangled." His body was now examined, and it was found that but four balls had wounded him. "Colonel," said he, "did I behave well." "Yes, Lewis," said the Col. in the kindest tone of voice, "like a man." "Well sir," . . . , "have I not atoned for this offence? *Shall I not live?*" The Colonel was much agitated, and gave orders that the Surgeon should, if possible, preserve his life. They did all that skill and humanity could do—it was of no avail. Poor Lewis expressed a great desire to live—"not," said he at one time, "that I fear death, but I would repent me of some sins, and I desire to live yet a little longer in the world." He suffered inconceivable agony from his wounds, and died on the fourth day.

Many a soldier has wept over his grave. He was a brave man and much beloved. He suffered twenty deaths. I have seen the big drops chase each other down his forehead with pain and anguish. There was much sensibility and sympathy throughout the camp. I would not have, unjustly and unnecessarily, signed this death warrant for all the wealth of all the Indies. The soldiers detailed to shoot Lewis had, from strong feelings of sympathy, or mistaken humanity, failed to shoot him—but four balls had entered his body.

"An Eye witness" appeals to Col. Russell, who he thinks now lives in Alabama, for the perfect truth of this sketch. He does not fear but the Col. will keenly recollect and faithfully depict the horrors of the day on which six Americans were shot to death under his command—but not by his orders.

The order bears date the very day after *General Jackson* returned in triumph to New-Orleans, and the day before he joyfully went, under triumphal arches, to the Temple of the . . . God: where, says the historian, "They CROWNED their adored General with laurels." The order for the execution of these six unhappy men bears date January 22, 1815. His crown of laurels had not yet withered, when blood, the life's blood of his countrymen, of his fellow soldiers, flowed plentifully by his order. May that order and its consequences, sink deep into the hearts of the American people, and steel them against him who had no flesh in his obdurate heart; who did not feel for man; in the midst of joy and revelry, almost in the more immediate presence of his Creator, who issued the fatal order to put his creatures to death, and to make their wives and children, widows and orphans.

THE SIX MILITIA MEN

On Friday the 26th inst. the official documents in this case were put in possession of the Speaker, and on Wednesday the 30th inst. he announced the fact to the house. It is not suspected that in the intermediate five days the Speaker and a select body of Jackson men were examining the documents to ascertain what course it would be best to adopt when they were announced to the House. When Mr. Sloane, to whom the country is under great obligations, moved that the documents be printed, Mr. Wickliffe opposed it vehemently. He feared the consequence to the character of Gen. Jackson—he appealed to the candor of Mr. Sloane—he appealed to his magnanimity—to the magnanimity of the house—and did most piteously beseech them not to print these documents until he had made inquiry whether there were not in existence some other papers which might soften the darkness, and shade the cruelty of the picture, as it was exhibited in the papers before them. The subject was postponed—but the documents must be printed. There must be no opposing, no garbling, no obstructing—we must have the whole of the documents. The people demand them; and the people will have them; and a majority of their representatives will not venture to withhold them. Whatever may be the writhings and twistings, the moanings and complainings, which precede the publication of the documents, published they must be. We do not fear but we shall have them.

Dem. Press.

THE CASE OF SERGEANT MORROW

The Militia documents have been furnished to the House of Representatives. When they shall be published, *then the public will see a case that leaves every thing which has yet been said as to the six militia men, far behind.* If it be possible, let the public mind be prepared for the case of Sergeant Morrow.

We give an outline. He was one of the party of Militia that left Fort Strother on the 19th September. On the 1st of November, he surrendered himself, of his own accord, to Gen. Taylor, of the Tennessee militia, who commanded at Camp Stewart, stating, in substance, that he was convinced of the error of his conduct; that he was penitent for his offence, and anxious to return to his post and serve out his time, as a faithful soldier. Gen. Taylor gave him a certificate of his having surrendered himself, and in it granted him a pardon, on condition of his returning to his post; subject however, to the will of the commanding general. Morrow did return to his post—he was received, and he was used as a witness on the part of the prosecution of some of the Militia Men. He . . . upon his own trial; he stated in his defence that he was ignorant of any law requiring him to serve longer than *three* months—that he was confirmed in his opinion by Gen. ———, by Col. ———, and by Capt. ———, giving the names of the officers to the Court. He then threw himself upon the mercy of the Court. He was found guilty and sentenced to be shot. The sentence was approved *and he was executed!*

This case is horrible in all its aspects without any regard being had to the question of *time* of service. It is revolting to every feeling of humanity and at war with every acknowledged principle of justice.

Ibid.

39. Centreville Committee

Voters known to be favorable furnished with conveyance to the polls

The following circular indicates that Andrew Jackson's friends did not have a monopoly on political know-how. Distributed by Indiana supporters of John Quincy Adams in 1828, it specifies in detail the practical steps to be taken to assure victory.

Centreville, July 19th, 1828

Dear Sirs—You were appointed at a county meeting of the friends

William Chambers, Chairman Committee of Correspondence, *The Centreville Circular* (Centreville, Indiana, July 19, 1828).

of the Administration, held in this place, in May, 1827, a committee of vigilance for your district, and being uncertain whether you have been informed of that appointment, we beg leave now to notify you of it, and at the same time to solicit your co-operation and unremitting exertions to the duties which will be required of you. It is probably not unknown to you, that our opponents are daily making privately, as well as publicly, the most strenuous efforts, and unless we meet them in a correspondent manner, *showing an imposing front*, and a *bold, determined courage*, we may be defeated, although we believe that a great majority of the people of the county, and electoral district, are with us. The importance *of securing the delegation* to the Assembly in October is so obvious, and known to possess *so powerful a bearing* on that which is *to follow in November*, that we think it unnecessary to dwell on that subject; we would however, remark; that four gentlemen of undoubted abilities and unquestionable integrity have been selected by the general committee; for the promotion of whose election the friends of the administration have pledged themselves to give their individual and united support.

It is proposed and *will become a part of your duty to endeavor to discover the political sentiments of every voter in your district, to take down the names of all*, designating *for whom* they intend to *vote*, the *objections* of those opposed to the re-election of Mr. ADAMS, *and the cause of those objections;* on the other hand, *you are to acquaint yourselves with the reasons* of those *who prefer* General JACKSON, and endeavour to *put them right*. The list of persons so made out, to which you will add all voters deemed *doubtful*, and to whom *GREAT and POINTED attention must be paid*, is to be given in to the chairman of your district committee, or to the secretary with whom each committee man is frequently to communicate during the canvass, whose duty it will be to report their communications personally, together with all other information, to the corresponding committee at Centreville, every other Saturday in August. The chairman of the district committee, and the secretary must urge upon the several committee men *the necessity to see that all voters known to be favorable, and those who may be deemed* DOUBTFUL, BE FURNISHED WITH THE MEANS OF CONVEYANCE, *to the polls, and when there* KEPT IN VIEW *by the persons who convey them,* UNTIL THEY HAVE VOTED; *each committee man* to be as active and industrious as possible on the day of election, *a part of whom, the* MOST POWERFUL, *both in* PERSONAL STRENGTH *and* COURAGE, not less than six, must be appointed to stand constantly at the polls for the purpose as well of defending the rights of our friends, as to object to illegal voters, many of whom, particularly young men, nearly of age, will no doubt be pushed forward. The chairman and secretary ought immediately to add to your number of committee men, at least twenty, or more if necessary—*taking them out of every neighborhood* in the district, and also *taking care to select as many young and active men as possible.* We beg leave also to recommend to the chairman and secretary *to have frequent and* PRIVATE *meetings, taking always such precautions that we may act completely and fully organized before those in opposition to us are* AWARE OF WHAT WE ARE ABOUT. We cannot close this communication *without urging it as of the* UTMOST *importance*, that this and all other matters connected with our arrangements, should be kept ENTIRELY TO OURSELVES, at any rate until the ORGANIZATION of our PLANS *is fully matured.*—When you get well under way, sub-committees would essentially, we think, aid our cause, they might then be formed for each neighborhood, under the direction of the chairman and secretary of the district committee. The committee of correspondence will give all the aid in their power in furnishing political papers and documents as they may be wanting. We beg leave, also, to impress on you the policy of a calm and temperate deportment towards those on whom you wish *to make an impression*, believing likewise, that towards those who are our determined adversaries the same line of conduct is the preferable one to pursue. We feel assured that you fully appreciate the cause in which we are engaged, and consider it of such vital importance to the existence of our republican institutions, that your exertions will be used and your *ingenuity* exercised to insure success.

We are with great esteem, very respectfully,
Your most obedient servants,

WM. CHAMBERS, *Chairman*
Committee of Correspondence

40. CENTRAL CLAY COMMITTEE
Have Whigs stolen the people's money

Not all electioneering documents eschewed issues completely. The following flyer, issued during the 1844 presidential contest, posed the issues as seen by Clay partisans. The "Locofoco party" referred to is actually the Democratic party. Since the actual Locofocos were a dissident New York faction of Democrats with a reputation for radicalism, Whigs sought to gain political capital by stigmatizing the Jackson-Van Buren party as "Locos."

THE QUESTIONS TO BE DECIDED IN THE ELECTION OF TUESDAY, NOVEMBER 5, 1844, ARE

I.—Were the people of the United States sober and sane in November, 1840,—when by a popular majority of **140,000,** and by an Electoral vote of **nineteen** States out of twenty-six, they rejected the policy and administration of the Locofoco party, and accepted the proposed policy of the Whigs,—*or* were they *drunk* and *crazy?* This question was first raised by Martin Van Buren and Thomas H. Benton, and has been taken up as the first great point in dispute by the *Democratic Review*, by the Washington Globe, the Albany Argus, the Evening Post, and by all the recognized organs and agents of the Locofoco party. Were "the democracy of numbers" then out of their wits; and did they by that vote declare themselves "incapable of self-government?" Were they intoxicated with hard cider?—and blinded by coon-skins shaken in their

Flyer "printed by order of the Central Clay Committee, on the Printers' Car, in the Grand Procession of the Democratic Clay Clubs, New-York, October 30, 1844."

faces, when they voted that those who said that "*the people expect too much of the* government" should cease to govern?—when they decided that those who declared that "*the government would take care of itself, and the people might take care of themselves*"—should give place to those who *would exercise the people's power for the people's good?*

II.—Did those to whom the people in 1840 *(drunk or sober)* voted to entrust that power—FAIL TO REDEEM THEIR IMPLIED PLEDGES? Did *they* fail to perform what they promised? Their President died within thirty days after his inauguration. The man who succeeded to power, restored to office the party that went out convicted of thefts of public money to the amount of **$3,000,000,**—declared himself the Presidential candidate of that ejected, condemned, thieving party, and used all the veto power, the governmental patronage, and the condemned Executive violations of the Constitution,—for the subversion of the people's will, and the restoration to power of those whom the people in **1840,** branded as faithless and infamous? Was John Tyler right when he thus, like Benedict Arnold, trafficked with the people's foes on their promise of promotion? Or were those wrong who, representing the people in Congress, opposed the consummation of that bargain? Was it *their* fault that the voice of the people calling for "A CHANGE" was not obeyed? Was it their fault that the change which the people demanded was not completely effected—both as to the measures and *men?*

III.—Have those thus ejected, and *thus restored*, retracted their charges against "the democracy of **NUMBERS**"? Have they promised that they will not again effect the measures on which they were so thoroughly beaten and infamously routed in **1840**? Or do they again present those questions and ask "the sober second-thoughts of the people" on their favorite scheme of the Sub-treasury, the hard-money system—the "exclusive metallic currency?"

IV.—What did the Whigs do in Congress, when thus deprived of the co-operation and constitutional subordination of the Executive power? Did the Representatives of the Whigs *do all that they could* to fulfill their promises? Did they yield to proffered bribes—to tenders of office—to the seductions of power? Or did they go on fearlessly and honestly to execute the people's will—doing what they promised the people to do? What did they effect in their "exercise of *the people's power*, for the *people's good?*"

V.—Is THE TARIFF (passed by those Whigs of **1840** and opposed by the defeated Locofocos of **1840**) a measure that oppresses the true Democracy,—the working-men, the business-men, the professional-men, the mechanics, the farmers, the manufacturers, or the *American* merchants? Do the actual laborers of this city or of the country call for its repeal? Has it diminished the Revenue?—Has it reduced the *amount* of importations? Have American laborers been **PROTECTED** by it, against the unjust anti-republican competition of English paupers and European slaves? Has agricultural production decreased,—or have the farmers been impoverished? Are *wages* lower than in **1840** or **1841**? Has commerce been destroyed? Are there fewer ships built, or *smaller* ships?

VI.—Have those few Whigs who have enjoyed office since **1840**, *stolen* the people's money as did so many Locofocos who preceded them? Does any Whig at this time owe the Federal Treasury any thing? Is there *any* **MORAL** *difference* between these two parties, implied in this difference of practice? Which party have proved themselves the most honest keepers of the people's money?—Have the outcast Locofocos grown honest since their ejection? **WHO TAUGHT THEM HONESTY?** When it was asked as to any Whig in office—"Is he *honest?* Is he faithful?"—who ever answered in the negative?

VII.—Why did the Whigs lose the patronage of the Federal Government? Why did they fall under the displeasure of the man to whom they had entrusted the *possible* secondary possession of the Executive control? Was it by too much servility, too much cowardice, too much distrust of popular intelligence and justice, or too great corruption or willingness to barter principle for office?

VIII.—WHO lifted the Locofocos out of the dust into which the people crushed them in their wrath? Who raised them again to power, by thwarting the declared will of the people, and discouraging the Whigs from action?—Who raised the beaten party from death to life, from infamy to new insolence and pride, from despair to new hope? Who was seduced by them with proffers of re-nomination, promotion and support? Who, thus raised, was by them betrayed, even as *he* betrayed others?

IX.—What new issues have that beaten party made, when thus revived, and thus restored? Have they shown themselves the *friends of protection?* Or have they declared themselves the enemies of the Whig Tariff? Have they pledged themselves against a war of conquest, declared in favor of peace, of the preservation of the National faith and honor, and against measures for the extension and perpetuation of slavery? Have they added the abominations of the Sub-treasury, low prices and an exclusive metallic currency, added the heresies of free-trade, nullification, mob-law and war for the protection of slavery and the opening of new slave-markets?—for the assumption of **$25,000,000** of foreign debts, and the refusal to the States of their right to the income of the public lands out of an over flowing Treasury?

X.—Who is JAMES K. POLK? Why was he nominated? Why was Van Buren rejected? What measure does Polk favor, that Van Buren opposed? Did Van Buren give good reasons against the annexation of Texas?—Did his party reject him for giving such reasons! What good reason does Polk give, in opposition to Van Buren, in favor of annexing Texas? Was Van Buren wrong, and is Polk in the right?

XI.—Who is HENRY CLAY? What would be the answer to this question in Europe, in South America, or in Athens or Sparta? How is the country to be injured by his election? How is it to be benefited by his defeat?—Why should any American hate him for his public services through the last forty years?

Answer these questions in your heart! Answer at the ballot-box, —as you shall answer in the day of account!

Local Electioneering

41. New Orleans Daily Picayune

With our parish office-seekers national politics are thrown out

Students of national politics of the second quarter of the nineteenth century know that it was an age of demagogy. Some of the choicest specimens of opportunistic political rhetoric were furnished in local contests. The following selection, drawn from the editorial page of a leading New Orleans journal, describes the characteristic tactics employed by seekers after parish office.

The Candidate

The business of electioneering is one that engrosses the thoughts of many of our candidates at this time in our city, and the near approach of the election has warmed up the feelings of those of our citizens who take a deep interest in such matters. At the North the newspapers fight the battles of the different candidates, after the latter have been nominated in caucus or convention. In the West the candidate takes the stump and "explains his position." In this city, candidates for Governor or member of Congress usually address the public at large meetings, called particularly for that purpose. The election to take place on the 5th of November next, is for many Parish officers, such as sheriff, coroner, assessors, tax collectors, clerks of courts, justices of the peace and constables. These form a distinct class of candidates and manage the business of electioneering in a peculiar way. In most cases of elections the candidates rely on party politics to help them to the majority of votes, but with our parish office-seekers national politics are thrown out of the question. Any peculiar fitness for the office, it may be said, is overruled by the peculiar shrewdness of obtaining votes. These parish officers nominate themselves, pay their own expenses and do most of their own electioneering. The principal object is to convince the public that

Unsigned editorial in the New Orleans *Daily Picayune*, September 9, 1849.

the candidate is a "mighty clever fellow." The shrewdness necessary to accomplish this object, when there are active opposing candidates, is immense. A man should be cool, cautious, cunning and persevering; he should never be thrown off his guard, and be always ready to turn any slight circumstance to his own advantage. Our candidates do not mount the stump or speak at meetings, but they are as universally present as the plagues of Egypt. In the streets, about the bar-rooms, around the work shops, and in every crowd, they may be found. They are no presuming, domineering or unpleasant persons to meet, but on the contrary, patterns of good nature, politeness and civility.

Let us look for a moment at some of the good natured ways practised by a first rate electioneerer. If a man has any blind side or peculiar foible, the candidate will infallibly find it out, and make his approaches like a skilful general, from the most exposed and undefended quarter. Begin the conversation with him as you may, he gradually brings it round to the subject uppermost in his mind; makes new issues, and before you are aware of it, he is presenting new reasons why it would be a good plan for you to support him. This meeting of the candidates face to face with the sovereigns, in familiar intercourse, is productive of much good, and gives occasion to some funny scenes. On yonder corner stands a candidate. Observe him. His dress is plain and his manner unassuming. His tongue is oily and constantly in motion, dropping honey or manna at every breath. You see at once that he is one of the people, that he possesses a great regard to free institutions, and conspicuous above all, he generally has a thirsty crowd around him. Mark his interview with Jones, who is a voter. The candidate's good natured face is wreathed in smiles as Jones approaches. He grips Jones's hand and shakes it with a hearty earnestness. Is really very glad to see Jones. Hopes he is well. Never saw him look better. Inquires after madam and the children. If there is any measles about, he shows a first rate remedy. Is acquainted with almost all Jones's kinsfolks. Always liked the people from that part of the world that Jones came from. Those people have a way about them that suits him, as they are generous whole-souled fellows. Has no doubt the Council will soon pave the street that Jones lives in. They ought to have done so a long time ago. Thinks the Council rather a humbug, as they ought to take more interest in the affairs of the people. If Jones has had a difficulty with Muggins, candidate thinks that Muggins was decidedly to blame in the matter. If Jones prides himself on his horse, candidate says that he was noticing that horse last week, thinks that if he was pushed he would beat almost any horse on the road; the horse is worth more money than he cost, and would like to buy him himself at an advance, during the fall. Candidate thinks that Jones was right in knocking down Smith some weeks ago, as Smith should have known better than to have talked in the way he did. If Jones drives a slow horse, the candidate remarks that this way some people have of going hallooing and smashing along over the road, he doesn't like, it doesn't look well. If the candidate has ever served his country, in "tented field," he remembers every relation or friend of Jones's that was in the campaign, and extols their merits and their bravery.

The candidate visits Jones's shop, where there is a large number of workmen employed, who are good voters. He inspects the work. Takes great interest in every mechanical art. Never has seen such work turned out in this city. Thinks the Government ought to do something to help the mechanics. Has had that idea in his head for a long time. Thinks of putting his oldest boy to a trade. It's the surest way to make a good living after all.

The candidate does not abuse his opponent, not he; that might offend the "sovereign voter." He frankly admits that his opponent is a very good man, and wishes that he could be elected, but at this particular time there is a pressing reason why he should not be. The candidate is never so rude as to omit giving a man a title. He makes every body a General, Colonel, Doctor or 'Squire. If he sees a hole in your old coat or boots, he at once remarks that it is of no consequence—he always likes to see a man's clothes sit easy—never feels at home but when he has on his old clothes. He hints these lots of yours out of town will turn out to be a good speculation, and wonders why your wife never called to see his wife, and take tea. His wife would always be glad to see her, but is at this moment out of town. Speaking of guns, he has noticed that pointer dog of yours frequently, and thinks he has the best nose of any dog in town. Speaking of children, reminds him to tell you that he thinks that boy of yours a remarkable smart boy for his age; saw him flog a boy in the streets, the other day, twice as big as himself. He had not the least idea you had a girl so old, until he met the young miss at a fancy ball last winter; every body said that she danced the Polka better than any other girl in the room.

He generally tells a good story, and is sure to agree with you about the weather "any way you can fix it." He always thought that he was a good fisherman, but he tells you that he never was lucky enough to take so large a fish as the one you caught over the lake. He lays great stress on the fact that if elected he shall accommodate the public; and wonders that you never thought of running for Alderman, or a seat in the Legislature, believing you would be sure to be elected, as you have so many friends. He is very apt to think that Mr. Grab pushed you too hard on that note of yours that you failed to pay; and ventures the remark that some people were too greedy by half. He feels proud to be introduced to your dull friend, Mr. Simpkins, and as you touch glasses while drinking, hopes he shall have the pleasure of a better acquaintance with him. The model candidate is an insinuating, pleasant companion, and it does a person good to listen to him. He makes you feel so happy and comfortable. He induces you to have such a good opinion of yourself and all your friends. We really wish that all the different candidates could be elected, but grieve to think that the vast majority will be disappointed.

Demagogic Oratory

42. DAVY CROCKETT

Promise all that is asked and more

One of the virtuosi of political buncombe was the Tennessee Congressman, Davy Crockett. A formidable opponent of the Jacksonian party, Crockett was an effective orator who shrewdly cultivated a natural,

From David Crockett, *The Life of Colonel David Crockett* (Philadelphia: Porter and Coates, 1865), 275–278.

backcountry style that appealed to unsophisticated voters. In this selection Crockett advises his Little Rock audience in 1835 of the chief tricks of the political orator's trade.

Having gone through with the regular toasts, the president of the day drank, "Our distinguished guest, Col. Crockett," which called forth a prodigious clattering all around the table, and I soon saw that nothing would do, but I must get up and make them a speech. I had no sooner elongated my outward Adam, than they at it again, with renewed vigor, which made me sort of feel that I was still somebody, though no longer a member of Congress.

In my speech I went over the whole history of the present administration; took a long shot at the flying deposites, and gave an outline, a sort of charcoal sketch, of the political life of "the Government's" heir-presumptive. I also let them know how I had been rascaled out of my election, because I refused to bow down to the idol; and as I saw a number of young politicians around the table, I told them, that I would lay down a few rules for their guidance, which, if properly attended to, could not fail to lead them on the highway to distinction and public honor. I told them, that I was an old hand at the business, and as I was about to retire for a time I would give them a little instruction gratis, for I was up to all the tricks of the trade, though I had practised but few.

"Attend all public meetings," says I "and get some friends to move that you take the chair; if you fail in this attempt, make a push to be appointed secretary; the proceedings of course will be published, and your name is introduced to the public. But should you fail in both undertakings, get two or three acquaintances, over a bottle of whisky, to pass some resolutions, no matter on what subject; publish them even if you pay the printer—it will answer the purpose of breaking the ice, which is the main point in these matters. Intrigue until you are elected an officer of the militia; this is the second step towards promotion, and can be accomplished with ease, as I know an instance of an election being advertised, and no one attending, the innkeeper at whose house it was to be held, having a military turn, elected himself colonel of his regiment." Says I, "You may not accomplish your ends with as little difficulty, but do not be discouraged—Rome wasn't built in a day.

"If your ambition or circumstances compel you to serve your country, and earn three dollars a day, by becoming a member of the legislature, you must first publicly avow that the constitution of the state is a shackle upon free and liberal legislation; and is, therefore, of as little use in the present enlightened age, as an old almanac of the year in which the instrument was framed. There is policy in this measure, for by making the constitution a mere dead letter, your headlong proceedings will be attributed to a bold and unshackled mind; whereas, it might otherwise be thought they arose from sheer mulish ignorance. 'The Government' has set the example in his attack upon the constitution of the United States, and who should fear to follow where 'the Government' leads?

"When the day of election approaches, visit your constituents far and wide. Treat liberally, and drink freely, in order to rise in their estimation, though you fall in your own. True, you may be called a drunken dog by some of the clean shirt and silk stocking gentry, but the real rough necks will style you a jovial fellow, their votes are certain, and frequently count double. Do all you can to appear to advantage in the eyes of the women. That's easily done—you have but to kiss and slabber their children, wipe their noses, and pat them on the head; this cannot fail to please their mothers, and you may rely on your business being done in that quarter.

"Promise all that is asked," said I, "and more if you can think of anything. Offer to build a bridge or a church, to divide a county, create a batch of new offices, make a turnpike, or anything they like. Promises cost nothing, therefore deny nobody who has a vote or sufficient influence to obtain one.

"Get up on all occasions, and sometimes on no occasion at all, and make long-winded speeches, though composed of nothing else than wind—talk of your devotion to your country, your modesty and disinterestedness, or on any such fanciful subject. Rail against taxes of all kinds, office-holders, and bad harvest weather; and wind up with a flourish about the heroes who fought and bled for our liberties in the times that tried men's souls. To be sure you run the risk of being considered a bladder of wind, or an empty barrel, but never mind that, you will find enough of the same fraternity to keep you in countenance.

"If any charity be going forward, be at the top of it, provided it is to be advertised publicly; if not, it isn't worth your while. None but a fool would place his candle under a bushel on such an occasion.

"These few directions," said I, "if properly attended to, will do your business; and when once elected, why a fig for the dirty children, the promises, the bridges, the churches, the taxes, the offices, and the subscriptions, for it is absolutely necessary to forget all these before you can become a thoroughgoing politician, and a patriot of the first water."

My speech was received with three times three, and all that; and we continued speechifying and drinking until nightfall, when it was put to vote, that we would have the puppet show over again, which was carried *nem. con.* The showman set his wires to work, just as "the Government" does the machinery in his big puppet show; and we spent a delightful and rational evening. We raised a subscription for the poor showman; and I went to bed, pleased and gratified with the hospitality and kindness of the citizens of Little Rock. There are some first-rate men there, of the real half horse, half alligator breed, with a sprinkling of the steamboat, and such as grow nowhere on the face of the universal earth, but just about the back bone of North America.

43. Seba Smith

Major Downing ridicules the buncombe of politics

In this selection Smith satirizes the hyperbole indulged in by Democrats and National Republicans alike during Andrew Jackson's first administration.

From Seba Smith, *The Life and Writings of Major Jack Downing*, pp. 96–99.

GRAND DEMOCRATIC NATIONAL REPUBLICAN CONVENTION

Downingville, Monday, July 19, 1830

At a large and respectable meeting of the democratic national republicans of Downingville and the neighboring parts of the state, convened this day at the centre school house, the meeting was called to order by the venerable and silver-haired patriarch, old *Mr. Zebedee Downing,* who had not been out to a political meeting before for the last twenty-five years. The venerable old gentleman stated in a few feeling remarks the object of the meeting; that he had not meddled with politics since the days of Jefferson; but that now in view of the awful calamities which threatened to involve our country in total ruin, he felt it his duty the little remaining time he might be spared from the grave, to lift up his voice and his example before his children, grand children, and great grand children whom he saw gathered around him, and encourage them to save the country for which he had fought and bled in his younger years. After the enthusiastic applause elicited by these remarks, the old gentleman called for the nomination of a chairman, and JOSHUA DOWNING, ESQUIRE, was unanimously called to the chair, and *Mr. Ephraim Downing* appointed Secretary.

On motion of Mr. Jacob Downing, voted, that a committee of five be appointed to draft resolutions to lay before this meeting. Whereupon Jotham Downing, Ichabod Downing, Zenas Downing, Levi Downing, and Isaiah Downing, were appointed said committee, and after retiring about five minutes, they returned and reported the following preamble and resolutions.

Whereas an awful crisis has arrived in the political affairs of our country, our public men all having turned traitors, and resolved to ruin the country, and make us and our children all slaves forever; and whereas our ship of state and our ship of the United States, are both driven with tremendous violence before the fury of the political tempest, and are just upon the point of being dashed upon the breakers of political destruction; and whereas, nothing short of the most prompt and vigorous exertions of the patriotic democratic national republicans of this state and of the United States can avert the impending danger,

And whereas, the Jacksonites, and Adamsites, and Huntonites, and Smithites, have so multiplied in the land, and brought things to such a pass, that our liberties are unquestionably about to receive their doom forever:

Therefore Resolved, that it is the highest and most sacred duty of every patriotic Democratic National Republican in the State, to arouse himself and buckle on his political armour, and make one last, one mighty effort, to save the state and the country, and place the constitution once more upon a safe and firm foundation.

Resolved, that the awful crisis of affairs in this State requires a firm devoted patriot, a high-minded and gifted statesman, and a uniform unwavering Democratic National Republican, for chief magistrate.

Resolved, that in this awful crisis, we believe the eyes of all true patriots are turned upon

THE HON. JACK DOWNING,

late of Downingville, but since last winter a resident in Portland, the capital of the State.

Resolved, that we have the fullest confidence in the talents, integrity, moral worth, tried patriotism, and unwavering and unchangeable sterling Democratic National Republicanism of the *Hon. Jack Downing,* and that his election to the office of Governor in September next, and nothing else, can save the State from total, unutterable, and irretrievable ruin.

Resolved therefore, That we recommend him to the electors of this State as a candidate for said office, and that we will use all fair and honourable means, and, if necessary, will not stick at some a little *dis*honourable, to secure his election.

Resolved, That we disapprove of personal crimination and re-crimination in political contests, and therefore will only say of our opponents, that we think them no better than they should be, and that they unquestionably mean to destroy the land we live in.

Resolved, That it be recommended to all the patriotic democratic national republicans throughout the State, to be up and doing; to call county meetings, town meetings, school district meetings, and village and bar-room meetings, and proceed to organize the party as fast as possible, by appointing standing committees, and central committees, and corresponding committees, and bearers and distributers of handbills; and in short by doing every thing that the good of the cause and the salvation of the country requires.

Resolved, conditionally, That in case General Jackson should be likely to be re-elected, we highly and cordially approve of his administration, and believe him to be second to none but Washington; but in case he should stand no chance of re-election, we resolve him to be the ignorant tool of a corrupt faction, plotting to destroy the liberties of the country.

Resolved, That the thanks of this convention be presented to Miss Abigail Downing, for the use of her school room this afternoon, she having with a generous patriotism dismissed her school for that purpose.

Resolved, That the proceedings of this convention, signed by the Chairman and Secretary, be published in the *Portland Daily Courier*, and the *Family Reader*, the official organs of the Hon. Jack Downing's correspondence, and any other genuine Democratic National Republican papers in the State.

Joshua Downing, *Chairman*

Attest: Ephraim Downing, *Secretary*

We are assured by Lieutenant Timothy Downing, with whom we had a short interview, that the best spirit prevailed in the convention; not a dissenting voice was heard, and all the resolutions passed unanimously.

The Spoils System

44. Francis J. Grund

Nothing less than an appointment of two thousand dollars a year

Andrew Jackson's party did not initiate the so-called spoils system. Their popular reputation for having done so stems from Jackson's wholesale replacement of incumbents in federal office by the Democratic party faithful and by the comment made by the New York Democratic leader, William L. Marcy, that to the victor belong the spoils. Actually the turnover was not as great as had been supposed, nor were the Democratic appointees significantly more plebeian than previous office holders. What was new was the frankness with which party loyalty replaced talent as the chief criterion for appointive office. In the following selection Grund records the sarcastic commentary on the system by an anonymous informant in Washington, D.C.

When they [office seekers] first come here, they expect nothing less than an appointment of two thousand dollars a year; but by degrees their expectations become more moderate: they would then be satisfied with a clerkship; by and by with a still more subordinate station; and at last they would be glad if any one would pay their bill, and enable them to get home again. I remember a most remarkable story, which was current here shortly after the election of General Jackson, and which is singularly characteristic of the notions of our people as respects the power of the executive.

> One morning, scarcely a fortnight after the General's arrival at the White-house, a shabby-genteel looking man presented himself at his parlour, and, after the usual salutation and shaking of hands, expressed his joy at seeing the venerable old gentleman at last hold the situation of chief magistrate of the country, to which his bravery, his talents, and his unimpeachable rectitude fully entitled him. "We have had a hard time of it," said he, "in our little place; but our exertions were unremitting: I myself went round to

From Francis J. Grund, *Aristocracy in America*, pp. 250–251.

> stimulate my neighbours, and at last the victory was ours. We beat them by a majority of ten votes, and I now behold the result of that glorious triumph!" The General thanked him in terms of studied politeness, assuring him that he would resign his office in an instant if he did not think his election gave satisfaction to a vast majority of the people; and at last regretted his admirer's zeal for the public weal should have been so severely taxed on his account. "Oh, no matter for that, sir!" said he; "I did it with pleasure,—I did it for myself and for my country" (the General bowed); "and I now come to congratulate you on your success" (the General bowed again). "I thought, sir," continued he, "that, as you are now President of the United States, I might perhaps be useful to you in some official capacity." (The General looked somewhat embarrassed.) "Pray, sir, have you already made a choice of your cabinet ministers?"—"I have," was the reply of the General.—"Well, no matter for that; I shall be satisfied with an embassy to Europe."—"I am sorry to say there is no vacancy."—"Then you will perhaps require a head-clerk in the department of State?"—"These are generally appointed by the respective secretaries."—"I am very sorry for that: then I must be satisfied with some inferior appointment."—"I never interfere with these: you must address yourself to the heads of departments." —"But could I not be postmaster in Washington? Only think, General, how I worked for you!"—"I am much obliged to you for the good opinion you entertain of me, and for your kind offices at the last election; but the postmaster for the city of Washington is already appointed."—"Well, I don't particularly care for that; I should be satisfied with being his clerk."—"This is a subject you must mention to the postmaster."—"Why, then, General," exclaimed the disappointed candidate for office, "haven't you got an old black coat?" You may well imagine that the General gave him one.

As extravagant as this story appears, I can assure you that there are at any time in Washington hundreds of persons seeking employment of some sort or other; nine-tenths of whom return home disappointed, cursing the ingratitude of those whom they have elevated by their suffrages, and who are now so monstrously ungrateful as to suffer them to gain a livelihood by common labour. All these men finish by joining the opposition, expecting to be treated with more consideration by the next administration.

45. John B. Derby
A Federalist office holder in the Jackson administration

The following selection recounts the experience of a Boston Federalist, John B. Derby, first in winning an appointment from the Old General, and then in trying to hold the appointment. The latter portion of the account indicates the financial squeeze put on office holders by the party machine. Unpleasant as such pressure may have been to poorly paid incumbents, it was in a sense what the new political system was all about.

The following day [in July 1829] I was invited to eat a family dinner with the President. . . .

The dinner being ended, the President called for his pipe, and, seating himself in a recess at the window, drew a chair near his own, and beckoned me to occupy it. The members of his family retired, and I was left alone with the great man. He said, "he had known something of me before, through the newspapers, and of the trials I had sustained during the late political contest." I told him that I had no claims on his approbation for any thing I had suffered;—that I had only done my duty as a faithful citizen, and the consciousness of that was reward enough. That I was a federalist,—and all the members of the family to which I belonged, were federalists;—but, as I had maintained my attachment to a party, for many years, against all hope of its future restoration to power, I had, like the other young federalists of New England, acquired the principle of fidelity, and proved the sincerity of my opinions. That a large proportion of his adherents in New-England, and particularly in Massachusetts, were federalists, or the sons of federalists, and they would be the last to desert him, if he "ruled righteously," or to annoy him with mercenary importunities. He snatched his pipe from his mouth, and said, with great vehemence, "I believe it, every word of it;—I shall know nothing in my Administration, of the old party distinctions;

From John B. Derby, *Political Reminiscences* (Boston: Homer and Palmer, 1835), 59–61, 88–89, 92–97. Footnote is in the original.

all I require in the public servants is capacity, honesty, and fidelity to the Constitution. You have done much,—and tell me, what station would you desire to fill under my government?" I replied, it was reported in Boston that Mr. Gerry, the Surveyor of the District, would be removed, and I believed that if I was appointed in his place, it would be in my power to render essential services to the republican party in Massachusetts, by contributions to the party newspapers, and more especially, by presenting in myself the evidence that the young men who had the misfortune to be the descendants of old federalists, were not proscribed by his administration. He answered. "I have promised not to remove Mr. Gerry, but I have not promised to re-appoint him, and his commission does not expire until next January. Perhaps you cannot wait so long?" Oh yes, I replied, it will take me quite as long to bring my professional business to a close, and to prepare to enter on my new duties. The President reflected a moment and then said, "had you any other appointment in contemplation?" Yes Sir, I answered, I had thought that if I failed in the more desirable object, I would propose the Consulate at Naples, with an agency for the American claims on that Government. "But there is no appropriation for such an office," the President exclaimed, "we want young men to be educated as diplomatists, our country is deplorably deficient in such men, we have no corps of diplomatic agents, there are no schools for the instruction of such a corps. This project of yours will not answer; there are no funds to send you forth. I will consult my Secretaries, and you may, I think, consider the Surveyorship, at Boston, as your own." I clasped the hand of the President, with affection and reverence, and retired to Gadsby's; without feeling that my feet touched the earth, I seemed to tread on air.

The next morning I called at the "white house," and was informed, by the Secretaries, that it had been determined to appoint me Surveyor of Boston, and that if I had no other business at Washington, I might consider my business as completed, and my hopes attained. . . .

For a time, the business throughout the Custom House was carried on smoothly and harmoniously. The Collector felt and enjoyed his new power and dignity; and as Bonaparte declared that "*He* was the *State*," so he looked and acted as if *he* was the Custom House. I made occasional visits to the Statesman office, and whenever I could snatch a moment of leisure, wrote communications for the papers. [*The Statesman* was the newspaper published by the dominant, "pragmatic" wing of the Jacksonian party in Massachusetts. The faction came to be known as the Statesman faction—Ed.] It was not long, however, before I discovered that General McNeil's appointment was not agreeable to "the party," and that it had probably eclipsed the brilliant expectations of some member of their confederacy. And in a conversation at the Statesman office, I learnt with contempt and indignation, that my allegiance was due to *them*, and not to my patron. I instantly remarked, that the General's interests would always claim my first care, and that I should maintain them against every other interest. On now looking back to this period of my official life, I am convinced that I derived my appointment, either through instructions given to Gen. McNeil at Washington, (as some equivalent for broken promises,) or through the influence of the "Statesman leaders," exerted with the design that I should act as a spy on the General's movements, and keep him in subjection to their authority. They justly supposed, that the General was not the sort of man to *serve* under such officers, when he had been in the habit of *leading* in contests rather more perilous than party warfare. Accordingly, he was never admitted into their political consultations, but pointedly excluded; and on every inviting occasion was treated with neglect, and subjected to mortification. At the 4th July dinner of the Washington Society, (in 1830,) at Concert Hall, the General was left to find a seat at the bottom of the table, while Henshaw, Simpson, Dunlap, Brodhead, Greene, and even some *petty* Custom House officers, took possession of the "chief seats,"—at the head. But these *newspaper patriots* did not perceive, that the *place* occupied by a gentleman, who had proved his patriotism by real services to his country, and carried about with him the evidence of it, and of his valour, viz: his wounds, was the actual *head of the table.*

The Statesman leaders being confirmed in their official possessions, next turned their power and avarice against their own humble dependants. They had grasped all the lucrative offices in Boston in the gift of the Government, but were not satisfied. Alexander wept for new worlds to conquer; and while a single dollar was to be had the Statesman leaders thirsted to pocket it.

There was in the project I am about to unfold a meanness and extortion wholly unexampled, and almost beyond belief, could it not be substantiated by many respectable witnesses before any tribunal possessing the power to compel their attendance. I know that the Post and Statesman in the most emphatic language have repeatedly declared its falsity. Nevertheless, *it is true*. . . .

To return to the *Tax*. The first intimation I ever heard of it was from Nathaniel Greene, in his private room over the old Post Office, and but a short time after I became a public officer. Supposing that it was mere badinage, in which he habitually indulged, I treated it accordingly. But in July 1830, I received an invitation in writing, to "attend a meeting of the *Central Committee*," (to which I did not belong,) "at the Navy Agent's office in State-street." I remarked, as singular at the time, that General McNeil did *not* receive any invitation. I went there on the appointed evening, ignorant of the business which required so formidable a summons. In a short time some *ten* or *twelve* public officers made their appearance. I suppose *all* who were invited; for the usual plan was to assemble those who could be relied upon to *pass* a measure, and then, afterwards to *enforce* it on the rest, as the fiat of the party, from which there was no appeal. Mr. John Crowninshield, an appraiser, was chosen Chairman, and Mr. J. P. Robinson, (Public Store-keeper, formerly a Clerk in the House of Henshaw & Co.) Secretary. Then uprose Mr. Simpson with an aspect of solemn and melancholy concern. He said, substantially, "That it probably was known to every office-holder present that Mr. Nathaniel Greene, the Editor of the Boston Statesman had conducted the late political contest, in that paper, with singular zeal and ability. That he had contracted in these generous efforts *large debts*, amounting to over thirty thousand dollars—about $33,000;* that the officers of the government in Boston must be

* It was 15,000 only at Washington the year before.

conscious that they obtained their offices through the distinguished exertions of the Statesman and the party which sustained it; that Mr. Greene, although he had obtained a valuable office, could not, out of the profits which remained after deducting his necessary expenses, pay off much of the *principal* of the $33,000 debt, if at the same time he was obliged to keep down the *interest.* That political affairs were uncertain, and it was an object with Mr. Greene to exonerate himself from debt as soon as possible, and he would limit his expenses to only 1200 dollars a year! He (Mr. Simpson,) therefore thought, upon the whole view of the case, that it was not only proper, but incumbent on all the public officers in Boston to club together, and annually, by an assessment, pay the *interest* of Mr. Greene's debts, ($1,980) while he was diligently sweeping off the *principal!*" Mr. Simpson had no sooner taken his seat, than Mr. Brodhead, who sat on my left at a round table, "moved that a committee be appointed to retire and doom the several officers of the District in an annual sum each, for the purpose suggested."

I never was more completely thunderstruck. The word *"doom,"* (used to me, in a novel sense,) rang in my ears. Owing money myself, and receiving but a small salary in comparison with the expenses of my station, I was chilled to the bone by such a ruinous proposition. I thought to remonstrate, but was kindly informed that probably the assessment on the Surveyor's Department would be only 250 dollars per annum! Another officer, however, who felt his gains leaking from him like quicksilver, rose and proposed that before the fatal doom was pronounced, a Committee should be chosen to investigate the *actual amount* of the debt, *when contracted,* and for *what considerations.* A request so reasonable could not be refused, although evidently a disappointment, and the Committee was appointed. . . .

. . . on the morning of the 14th we were informed, by a faithful and honest man who was present, that the Committee appointed at the *first* meeting reported Nathaniel Greene's debts at 30,000 dollars, contracted for political purposes. All the public officers were doomed by the Committee. Our informant further stated, that *he* told the meeting "that in January, 1828, Nathaniel

Greene assembled "the party" in Boston, and represented to them his embarrassments, confessing that *two thousand* dollars would clear him of debt on the Statesman account; and that then he" (our informant,) "and other zealous Jacksonmen went forth and obtained new subscribers to that amount, and supposed they had entirely relieved the publishers." Upon this statement one of the "Leaders" remarked, with much vehemence, that "the *nine* gentlemen who were sureties for the debt of 30,000 knew five years ago all about it." Our informant suggested that the debt was a private debt, contracted some years before, for very different than political transactions. There was so much dissatisfaction expressed by the under officers at the report of the Committee, that the Leaders had to give way for a time and appoint a *new Committee* to investigate the amount and causes of the debt. . . .

An assessment on the public officers was therefore finally declared for the payment of 1200 dollars per year, the interest of twenty thousand, a debt due from the Postmaster to the Collector and his associates. It amounted to about 5 per cent. of their salaries; or rather I conclude so, because the annual sum demanded of General McNeil was in that ratio. The General was called upon by Mr. J. P. Robinson, the Secretary of the first meeting, and the agent for the collection, to pay 150 dollars per annum. He refused. In a week or two afterwards, Mr. Robinson called again, and stated that 125 dollars would be considered sufficient. The General declined paying any thing. I was invited, but peremptorily expressed my disgust at the whole project. Two or three of the under officers refused. They were told by Robinson that the Collector approved of the scheme and they would lose their offices by their pertinacity. . . .

Separate from the *corrupt* character of the transactions I have been stating, so remarkable under a *Reform* Administration, its enormity is more fully disclosed when it is known, that every under officer, monthly, before receiving his pay, takes and subscribes the following Oath.

> I, A. B———, do hereby certify on oath, that I have performed the services stated in the above account; that I have received the

> full sum therein charged, *to my own use and benefit, and that I have not paid, deposited or assigned, nor contracted to pay, deposit or assign any part of such compensation to the use of any other person, nor in any way, directly or indirectly, paid or given, nor contracted to pay or give, any reward or compensation for my office or employment, or the emoluments thereof—So help me God.*

Corrupt Practices

46. Thomas Brothers

It is called log-rolling

In 1840, Thomas Brothers, an Englishman, published a book describing the evils of American society. The author, who a few years earlier had published one of the leading trade union journals in the United States, had returned to England after the Panic of 1837. He had grown disappointed with almost all aspects of American civilization, particularly the gulf between democratic political theory and American practice. In the following passages Brothers discusses political wheeling-and-dealing in the States. His book took the form of letters to various acquaintances.

There, Sir; I have gently lifted the veil, so that the foreigners who have been tempted by *exorbitant interest* to lend their money to that gang of "speculators," who have, as Governor Wolf said, "*in defiance of the people's seal of reprobation,*" taken possession of the government, and call themselves Pennsylvania Legislatures—I have lifted the veil, Sir, so that these foreigners may have a peep at the manner in which their money has been divided among these legislatures, and that they may have some idea as to what must be the final result. Do the foreigners know what this Governor means by "*log-rolling legislation?*" They are queer words for a Governor to make use of, but, when understood, will be found to be very appropriate. Perhaps, to make the matter sure, I may as well give

From Thomas Brothers, *The United States of North America as They are: Not as They are Generally Described: Being a Cure for Radicalism* (London: Longman, Orne, Brown, Green and Longmans, 1840), 87–89.

their meaning; and, to save myself the trouble, I take the following from a newspaper of your city, called the *Pennsylvania*:—

At Harrisburg it is called log-rolling. Anywhere else it would be called bribery and corruption. On the frontiers of this country, when land is to be cleared, the trees are cut down, rolled together, and burnt. This, which cannot be done by one man, is effected by the joint efforts of the neighbourhood; and thus, by mutual aid, all the lands in the settlement are in their turn cleared and cultivated. The term by which this necessary act of fraternity is known has been applied, in practical legislation, to combinations of members who league together and carry a set of measures, each of which if judged of alone would stand no chance of success. Vote for my bill, and I will vote for yours; or when, as often happens, these political brokers are afraid to trust each other, they put the whole into one general bill, which with closed eyes they swallow. A great deal of skill is shown in admitting just such a sufficient number of sections as will carry the bill, and no more. If the friends of a good and particularly a popular measure can be induced to join the unholy alliance, so much the better. The title of the bill is sure to make this known, while all the doubtful or unpopular objects are included under the comprehensive words, "and for other purposes." Such is log-rolling, an art, it will be admitted, of great power when skilfully exercised.

Perhaps two or three members of the legislature have purchased a track of worthless land at their own price; they say it cost us but a few cents an acre, but, if we could get the State to make a canal, or a rail-road through it, we shall, in the excitement occasioned by such a measure, perhaps, make one or two hundred dollars an acre of it. These "legislatures" meet from all parts of the State, and they have their various schemes; some want a charter for a bank, others for the sole right of navigating a river, others for a rail-road; in short, their modes of robbing are by far more numerous, as well as more ingenious, than are those of the common thieves that infest London or Paris. They then, in their private capacity, make known their projects to each other, and the bargain is made. "I will help you *roll your log* through the forms of legislation if you will help me roll mine;" and in this manner is the whole session consumed. Then there are the lobby-members, a race very little if any inferior to the real members. Your friend M'Ilwain, at that time the recorder of the city and county of Philadelphia, you know, Sir, was a lobby member, in the case of obtaining a charter for the bank. It is the business of a lobby member to bribe the real members, in any way that seemeth to them best. The following account of one of these members I take from a New York paper of last year.

A case is reported in the Journal of Commerce, tried before Judge Ulchoeffer, New York, which was brought by the plaintiff to recover of the defendant compensation for work and labour done: amount claimed, 2000 dollars. The services rendered, and for which pay was claimed, were for "lobbying," as it is usually called, or endeavouring to procure the passage of the Bergen Port Company bill, by the legislature of New Jersey, in 1837. The bill in question was passed, and the defendant became president of the company.

A witness stated that one of the means which the plaintiff used to facilitate the passage of the bill was by treating the members to champagne and suppers, and that he gave a supper on the 22d of February while the bill was pending. Another, J. C. Zabriskte, of New Brunswick, said the defendant tried to engage him to assist in getting the bill through, and told him he might dictate his own terms, and if he wanted means to operate at Trenton, any reasonable amount would be furnished him.

"What would be a reasonable amount to operate with at Trenton, in such a case?—I should have required 500 dollars to operate with.

"Cross examined.—When you say you would require 500 dollars to operate with in such a case, what do you mean by that?—I mean I should have applied it in paying for wine and terrapin suppers, as that is about as efficient a mode of operating as I know of.

"Do you mean, by that answer, wine and terrapin suppers for the members of the legislature?—Yes, Sir.

"What was the general character of Mr. Hillyer's service?—He operated among the members generally and particularly. Mr.

Hillyer was esteemed one of the best Lobby members that ever appeared at Trenton for the last eight years. I do not know what Mr. Hillyer's particular mode of operation was in this case. I know the efficient mode of operation was the same in every case, by calling on the members and impressing on them favourably in regard to the measure before them; sometimes making the worst appear the better reason, and giving the members EXPLANATORY SUPPERS. Such was Mr. Hillyer's general mode of operations.

"The court charged the jury, and, among other things, remarked that,

" 'A legislator selected by the people to discharge a public trust ought to discharge it independently and honestly, but the legislator who votes from private influence acts dishonestly and corruptly. And every effort to obtain votes through private influence is adverse to public policy and legislative purity, and at variance with every sense of propriety.

" 'It is, therefore, scarcely necessary to observe, that to procure votes by means of suppers, or harassing legislators by making application to them, is dishonest in the extreme, and that no person can recover compensation for it.'

"The jury retired for nearly four hours, and brought in a verdict for the defendant."

So much for lobbying, log-rolling, and dividing the spoil of the people. "And what has all this to do with the foreigners," you will shrewdly remark, "who have the *State* for their security?" Sir, do you seriously think that any State in the world can, without becoming bankrupt, endure proceedings like these? You know that Pennsylvania has been on the very brink of bankruptcy half a dozen times within these few years, and has only been saved for a short time from that calamity by subterfuges such as no other nation in the world would ever think of resorting to. We are told by the biographer of the banker [Stephen] Girard, that Girard saved the State several times from bankruptcy by the timely loan of a few bank-notes, when nobody else on earth could be found to trust it with a cent. And [Nicholas] Biddle is continually boasting of having "saved the State." The shattered fragments of the old United States' Bank having been got together, and chartered as a

State bank, under the imposing name of "The Bank of the United States," did wonders, he says, for the State, and, to use his own words, "probably saved that city (Philadelphia) and the whole State, from general bankruptcy, which would have followed the winding up of its affairs."

American Politics Evaluated

47. John Quincy Adams

A sour view of national parties and politics

John Quincy Adams was hardly an objective source. He had a well-deserved reputation for suffering fools badly and was clearly not overjoyed with a state of political affairs that appeared too often to reward fools and knaves with high office. Nor had the incessant harassment Jacksonians had subjected him to during his presidency (1825–1829) done much to soften his attitude toward the American political system. Yet Adams was an informed, highly intelligent, and honest political man, whose trenchant observations are well worth recording.

Oct. 9. [1834]—The prosperity of the country, independent of all agency of the Government, is so great that the people have nothing to disturb them but their own waywardness and corruption. They quarrel upon dissensions of a doit, and split up into gangs of partisans of A, B, C, and D, without knowing why they prefer one to another. Caucuses, County, State, and National Conventions, public dinners, and dinner-table speeches two or three hours long, constitute the operative power of electioneering; and the parties are working-men, temperance reformers, Anti-Masons, Union and States-Rights men, Nullifiers, and, above all, Jackson men, Van Buren men, Clay men, Calhoun men, Webster

From Charles Francis Adams, ed., *The Memoirs of John Quincy Adams* (Philadelphia: J. B. Lippincott, 1874–1877), 12 vols., IX, p. 187; X, pp. 181, 182.

men, and McLean men, Whigs and Tories, Republicans and Democrats, without one ounce of honest principle to choose between them. New Hampshire is goverened by a knave of the name of Isaac Hill, editor of a newspaper, mail contractor, and now a Senator of the United States—just cunning enough to grow rich by railing against the rich, and to fatten upon the public spoils, bawling Democracy. This is the besetting sin of popular governments, and it is now as it always has been. Van Buren is a demagogue of the same school, with a tincture of aristocracy—an amalgamated metal of lead and copper. There are five or six candidates for the succession to the Presidency, all of them demagogues, and not one of them having any consistency of system for the government of the Union.

Jan. 1, 1840.—From eleven in the morning till four p.m. there was a succession of friendly visitors, as has been usual on the New Year's day since we left the President's house. Neither my wife nor Mary received visitors, and I was left to entertain the ladies as I could. This ceremony grows more and more irksome to me every year. The young and the prosperous may take pleasure in the recollections of the past and the anticipations of the future which associate themselves with the commencement of the year; but the idea which ought first and last to present itself to the mind of one who has already passed through so many New Year's days as I have, is the great probability that it will be the last.

Among the visitors of this day was General Scott, who has been recently talked of as a Whig candidate for the office of President of the United States. William H. Harrison was however, preferred both to him and to Henry Clay. A very curious philosophical history of parties might be made by giving a catalogue raisonné of the candidates for the Presidency voted for in the Electoral Colleges since the establishment of the Constitution of the United States. . . . Would not the retrospect furnish as practical principles in the operation of the Constitution—1, that the direct and infallible path to the Presidency is military service coupled with demagogue policy; 2, that in the absence of military service, demagogue policy is the first and most indispensable element of success, and the art of party drilling is the second; 3, that the drill consists in combining the Southern interest in domestic slavery with the Northern riotous Democracy; 4, that this policy and drill, first organized by Thomas Jefferson, first accomplished his election, and established the Virginia dynasty of twenty-four years, a perpetual political contradiction of his own principles; 5, that the same policy and drill, invigorated by success and fortified by experience, has now placed Martin Van Buren in the Presidential chair, and disclosed to the unprincipled ambition of the North the art of rising upon the principles of the South? . . . Meanwhile, the consummation of the peace and alliance between Van Buren and Calhoun was manifested by the appearance of Calhoun this day at the New Year's gathering at the President's house.

48. James Fenimore Cooper

The besetting vice of democracies

Although he admired Andrew Jackson, Cooper was highly critical of the politics practised by the general's party. In the following selection from *The American Democrat*, Cooper discusses the chief negative features of American democracy. Cooper believed these weaknesses to be inevitable consequences of a system that enfranchised and thus empowered the propertyless masses. The intelligence of the author adds weight to his observations, making of them something more durable than mere partisan, biased carping.

On the Disadvantages of Democracy

Democracies are liable to popular impulses, which, necessarily arising from imperfect information, often work injustice from good motives. Tumults of the people are less apt to occur in democracies than under any other form of government, for, possessing the legal means of redressing themselves, there is less necessity to resort to force, but, public opinion constituting, virtually, the power of the state, measures are more apt to be

From James Fenimore Cooper, *The American Democrat*, pp. 61–66.

influenced by sudden mutations of sentiment, than under systems where the rulers have better opportunities and more leisure for examination. There is more feeling and less design in the movements of masses than in those of small bodies, except as design emanates from demagogues and political managers.

The efforts of the masses that are struggling to obtain their rights, in monarchies and aristocracies, however, are not to be imputed to democracy; in such cases, the people use their natural weapon, force, merely because they are denied any participation in the legal authority.

When democracies are small, these impulses frequently do great injury to the public service, but in large states they are seldom of sufficient extent to produce results before there is time to feel the influence of reason. It is, therefore, one of the errors of politicians to imagine democracies more practicable in small than in large communities, an error that has probably arisen from the fact that, the ignorance of masses having hitherto put men at the mercy of the combinations of the affluent and intelligent, democracies have been permitted to exist only in countries insignificant by their wealth and numbers.

Large democracies, on the other hand, while less exposed to the principal evil of this form of government, than smaller, are unable to scrutinize and understand character with the severity and intelligence that are of so much importance in all representative governments, and consequently the people are peculiarly exposed to become the dupes of demagogues and political schemers, most of the crimes of democracies arising from the faults and designs of men of this character, rather than from the propensities of the people, who, having little temptation to do wrong, are seldom guilty of crimes except through ignorance.

Democracies are necessarily controlled by publick opinion, and failing of the means of obtaining power more honestly, the fraudulent and ambitious find a motive to mislead, and even to corrupt the common sentiment, to attain their ends. This is the greatest and most pervading danger of all large democracies, since it is sapping the foundations of society, by undermining its virtue. We see the effects of this baneful influence, in the openness and audacity with which men avow improper motives and improper acts, trusting to find support in a popular feeling, for while vicious influences are perhaps more admitted in other countries, than in America, in none are they so openly avowed.

It may also be urged against democracies, that, nothing being more corrupting than the management of human affairs, which are constantly demanding sacrifices of permanent principles to interests that are as constantly fluctuating, their people are exposed to assaults on their morals from this quarter, that the masses of other nations escape. It is probable, however, that this evil, while it ought properly to be enumerated as one of the disadvantages of the system, is more than counterbalanced by the main results, even on the score of morals.

The constant appeals to public opinion in a democracy, though excellent as a corrective of public vices, induce private hypocrisy, causing men to conceal their own convictions when opposed to those of the mass, the latter being seldom wholly right, or wholly wrong. A want of national manliness is a vice to be guarded against, for the man who would dare to resist a monarch, shrinks from opposing an entire community. That the latter is quite often wrong, however, is abundantly proved by the fact, that its own judgments fluctuate, as it reasons and thinks differently this year, or this month even, from what it reasoned and thought the last.

The tendency of democracies is, in all things, to mediocrity, since the tastes, knowledge and principles of the majority form the tribunal of appeal. This circumstance, while it certainly serves to elevate the average qualities of a nation, renders the introduction of a high standard difficult. Thus do we find in literature, the arts, architecture and in all acquired knowledge, a tendency in America to gravitate towards the common center in this, as in other things; lending a value and estimation to mediocrity that are not elsewhere given. It is fair to expect, however, that a foundation so broad, may in time sustain a superstructure of commensurate proportions, and that the influence of masses will in this, as in the other interests, have a generally beneficial effect. Still it should not be forgotten that, with the exception of those works, of which, as they appeal to human sympathies or the practices of men, an intelligent public is the best judge, the mass of no community is qualified to decide the most correctly on any thing, which, in its nature, is above its reach.

It is a besetting vice of democracies to substitute publick opinion for law. This is the usual form in which masses of men exhibit their tyranny. When the majority of the entire community commits this fault it is a sore grievance, but when local bodies, influenced by local interests, pretend to style themselves the publick, they are assuming powers that properly belong to the whole body of the people, and to them only under constitutional limitations. No tyranny of one, nor any tyranny of the few, is worse than this. All attempts in the publick, therefore, to do that which the publick has no right to do, should be frowned upon as the precise form in which tyranny is the most apt to be displayed in a democracy.

Democracies, depending so much on popular opinion are more liable to be influenced to their injury, through the management of foreign and hostile nations, than other governments. It is generally known that, in Europe, secret means are resorted to, to influence sentiment in this way, and we have witnessed in this country open appeals to the people, against the acts of their servants, in matters of foreign relations, made by foreign, not to say, hostile agents. Perhaps no stronger case can be cited of this weakness on the part of democracies, than is shown in this fact, for here we find men sufficiently audacious to build the hope of so far abusing opinion, as to persuade a people to act directly against their own dignity and interests.

The misleading of publick opinion in one way or another, is the parent of the principal disadvantages of a democracy, for in most instances it is first corrupting a community in order that it may be otherwise injured. Were it not for the counteracting influence of reason, which, in the end, seldom, perhaps never fails to assert its power, this defect would of itself, be sufficient to induce all discreet men to decide against this form of government. The greater the danger, the greater the necessity that all well-intentioned and right-minded citizens should be on their guard against its influence.

It would be hazardous, however, to impute all the peculiar faults of American character, to the institutions, the country existing under so many unusual influences. If the latter were overlooked, one might be induced to think frankness and sincerity of character were less encouraged by popular institutions than was formerly supposed, close observers affirming that these qualities are less frequent here, than in most other countries. When the general ease of society is remembered, there is unquestionably more deception of opinion practised than one would naturally expect, but this failing is properly to be imputed to causes that have no necessary connection with democratical institutions, though men defer to publick opinion, right or wrong, quite as submissively as they defer to princes. Although truths are not smothered altogether in democracies, they are often temporarily abandoned under this malign influence, unless there is a powerful motive to sustain them at the moment. While we see in our own democracy this manifest disposition to defer to the wrong, in matters that are not properly subject to the common sentiment, in deference to the popular will of the hour, there is a singular boldness in the use of personalities, as if men avenged themselves for the restraint of the one case by a licentiousness that is without hazard.

The base feelings of detraction and envy have more room for exhibition, and perhaps a stronger incentive in a democracy than in other forms of government, in which the people get accustomed to personal deference by the artificial distinction of the institutions. This is the reason that men become impatient of all superiority in a democracy, and manifest a wish to prefer those who affect a deference to the publick, rather than those who are worthy.

PART FOUR

An Inegalitarian Society

Prosperity

49. Samuel Goodrich
Consider the rapid increase of wealth

Impressionistic evidence—which is all that contemporaries had to go by in an era prior to the development of statistics or the appearance of detailed census reports—convinced many observers that the American economy turned out a vast quantity of things easily available to most persons. A depression such as the one following the panics of 1837 and 1839 slowed the march of prosperity but it was followed by an upward movement that was believed to have attained unprecedented heights of abundance. This message was conveyed by visiting travelers, by publishers such as Moses Yale Beach, by such political figures as Daniel Webster and Henry Clay, by the famous orator Edward Everett, and by the influential writer Samuel G. Goodrich. Goodrich's "Peter Parley" books won a great vogue, achieving spectacular publishing success in the children's market. As the following selection indicates, they painted a roseate picture of American life.

Having taken a backward glance at the history of our country, let us consider for a moment its present condition. Look at the towns and cities that are scattered over the country. Look at the hills and valleys, covered with fruit trees and gardens, and yielding their annual harvests.

Look at the rivers, ploughed with whizzing steamboats; look at the canals, bearing along their burden of produce and merchandise. Look at the steam-cars, hurrying along like birds upon the wing; look at our seaports, and see the forest of shipping that is crowded into their harbors.

Visit the city of New York, a busy, buzzing hive of men,

From Samuel G. Goodrich, *Peter Parley's Common School History* (Philadelphia: Butler and Williams, 1845), 287, 288.

containing nearly three hundred thousand people. Observe its beautiful streets, its fine houses, the banks, the churches, and other public edifices.

Enter the shops and notice the beautiful articles of merchandise brought from China, from Java, from Hindostan, from Arabia, from all the shores of the Mediterranean Sea, from England, France, Holland, and all the borders of the Baltic.

Go to the top of the City Hall, where you can have a view of the surrounding waters; notice the fringe of masts encircling the southern portion of the city. See there the flag of every commercial country under heaven. See there, too, ships, sloops, schooners, and steamboats, coming and going like bees in a summer morning, all bringing their burden to the hive.

What a beautiful sight is this, and in a country, too, which has been settled but little more than two hundred years! And, if you would know more of our country, get into a steamboat and sail up the Hudson, one of the finest streams on the face of the globe.

Visit Troy, Albany, Utica, Rochester, and Buffalo; all of them interesting and flourishing towns. Observe the numerous villages, the handsome houses, and the throngs of happy people that inhabit the state of New York.

If you are fond of travelling, cross Lake Erie in a steamboat, and proceed to Ohio. See there a country that has not been settled fifty years, now studded over with thriving towns and villages. Go to Cincinnati, Louisville, Nashville, St. Louis, and proceed on the bosom of the great Mississippi to New Orleans.

Consider the great valley through which the Mississippi flows; the millions of people that are already there; the rapid increase of wealth, the progress of refinement, and the multiplication of the inhabitants.

When you have seen these interesting things, go home and reflect upon them. Sit quietly down, review the past, consider the present, and look forward to the future. What a glorious prospect for our country, if our present government continues, if the people are true to their own interests, and maintain the liberty their fathers left them!

Equality of Condition

50. Alexis de Tocqueville

There are but few wealthy persons

Alexis de Tocqueville was the chief architect of the egalitarian version of antebellum American society. As has been noted by Tocqueville scholars, the brilliant French aristocrat relied more on logic than on empirical data in constructing his social theorems. The varied ingredients of his comprehensive thesis were interdependent, fitting together in an admirably balanced and logically consistent pattern. Of course there is much question as to the accuracy of Tocqueville's assumptions. There can, however, be no denying their great influence. The following selection illustrates the persuasiveness of the egalitarian model he posited for Jacksonian America, marked by social mobility and equality both of condition and opportunity.

In America there are but few wealthy persons; nearly all Americans have to take a profession. Now, every profession requires an apprenticeship. The Americans can devote to general education only the early years of life. At fifteen they enter upon their calling, and thus their education generally ends at the age when ours begins. If it is continued beyond that point, it aims only towards a particular specialized and profitable purpose; one studies science as one takes up a business; and one takes up only those applications whose immediate practicality is recognized.

In America most of the rich men were formerly poor; most of those who now enjoy leisure were absorbed in business during their youth, the consequence of this is that when they might have had a taste for study, they had no time for it, and when the time is at their disposal, they have no longer the inclination.

There is no class, then, in America, in which the taste for intellectual pleasures is transmitted with hereditary fortune and leisure and by which the labors of the intellect are held in honor. Accordingly, there is an equal want of the desire and the power of application to these objects.

From Alexis de Tocqueville, *Democracy in America*, I, chap. 3, pp. 53–55; II, chap. 10, pp. 137, 138.

A middling standard is fixed in America for human knowledge. All approach as near to it as they can; some as they rise, others as they descend. Of course, a multitude of persons are to be found who entertain the same number of ideas on religion, history, science, political economy, legislation, and government. The gifts of intellect proceed directly from God, and man cannot prevent their unequal distribution. But it is at least a consequence of what I have just said that although the capacities of men are different, as the Creator intended they should be, the means that Americans find for putting them to use are equal.

In America the aristocratic element has always been feeble from its birth; and if at the present day it is not actually destroyed, it is at any rate so completely disabled that we can scarcely assign to it any degree of influence on the course of affairs.

The democratic principle, on the contrary, has gained so much strength by time, by events, and by legislation, as to have become not only predominant, but all-powerful. No family or corporate authority can be perceived; very often one cannot even discover in it any very lasting individual influence.

America, then, exhibits in her social state an extraordinary phenomenon. Men are there seen on a greater equality in point of fortune and intellect, or, in other words, more equal in their strength, than in any other country of the world, or in any age of which history has preserved the remembrance. . . .

I never met in America any citizen so poor as not to cast a glance of hope and envy on the enjoyments of the rich or whose imagination did not possess itself by anticipation of those good things that fate still obstinately withheld from him.

On the other hand, I never perceived among the wealthier inhabitants of the United States that proud contempt of physical gratifications which is sometimes to be met with even in the most opulent and dissolute aristocracies. Most of these wealthy persons were once poor; they have felt the sting of want; they were long a prey to adverse fortunes; and now that the victory is won, the passions which accompanied the contest have survived it; their minds are, as it were, intoxicated by the small enjoyments which they have pursued for forty years.

Not but that in the United States, as elsewhere, there is a certain number of wealthy persons who, having come into their property by inheritance, possess without exertion an opulence they had not earned. But even these men are not less devotedly attached to the pleasures of material life. The love of well-being has now become the predominant taste of the nation; the great current of human passions runs in that channel and sweeps everything along in its course.

51. Michael Chevalier

The appearance of general ease

Chevalier added his own touches to the egalitarian social portrait of the United States in the early nineteenth century. According to him, no paupers were to be found in the free states, while even unskilled Irish immigrant laborers fared relatively well.

There is one thing in the United States that strikes a stranger on stepping ashore, and is of a character to silence his sentiments of national pride, particularly if he is an Englishman; it is the appearance of general ease in the condition of the people of this country. While European communities are more or less cankered with the sore of pauperism, for which their ablest statesmen have as yet been able to find no healing balm, there are here no paupers, at least not in the Northern and Western States, which have protected themselves from the leprosy of slavery. If a few individuals are seen, they are only an imperceptible minority of dissolute or improvident persons, commonly people of colour, or some newly landed emigrants, who have not been able to adopt industrious habits. Nothing is more easy than to live and to live well by labour. Objects of the first necessity, bread, meat, sugar, tea, coffee, fuel, are in general cheaper here than in France, and

From Michael Chevalier, *Society, Manners and Politics in the United States*, pp. 107–109.

wages are double or triple. I happened, a few days ago, to be on the line of a railroad in process of construction, where they were throwing up some embankments. This sort of labour, which merely requires force, without skill, is commonly done in the United States by Irish new-comers, who have no resource but their arm, no quality but muscular strength. These Irish labourers are fed and lodged, and hear their bill of fare; three meals a day, and at each meal plenty of meat and wheat bread; coffee and sugar at two meals, and butter once a day; in the course of the day, from six to eight glasses of whiskey are given them according to the state of the weather. Beside which they receive in money 40 cents a day under the most unfavourable circumstances, often from 60 to 75 cents. In France the same labour is worth about 24 cents a day the labourers finding themselves.

This positive and undeniable fact of the general ease, is connected with another, which gives it a singular importance in the eyes of a European, who is the friend of progressive reforms, and the enemy of violence; the prevalence of radicalism in politics. The term *democrat,* which elsewhere would fill even the republicans with terror, is here greeted with acclamations, and the name of *Democratic* is zealously claimed by every party as its exclusive property. But this is the only kind of property which is called in question; it is true that material property rapidly disappears in this country, unless it is preserved by the most constant vigilance, and renewed with untiring industry. But as long as it exists, it is the object of profound respect, which, I must confess, has rather surprised me. I should have expected that the social theory would have borrowed some notions from the predominant political theory; but there are those in Europe, who are not there considered the boldest speculators on this subject, who here would be looked upon as the most audacious innovators. From this simple statement, it seems natural to infer, that valuable lessons are to be learned here by those who seek to solve the great question that now agitates Europe, the amelioration of the greatest number. It would be interesting to inquire into the causes of this state of things, and to examine whether, with certain modifications, it could not be transferred to Europe, and particularly to France.

Equality Questioned

52. James Fenimore Cooper

The equality is no more absolute than that of any other country

There were of course dissenters. As shall be indicated, champions of the "laboring masses" challenged the prevailing consensus. Middle and upper class nay-sayers were more rare. James Fenimore Cooper, always sensitive to the deficiencies of what he feared was a dehumanizing new order, found varied traces of inequality in the United States. As the following passage indicates, Cooper believed that inequalities were not only inevitable but in some cases desirable.

On American Equality

The equality of the United States is no more absolute than that of any other country. There may be less inequality in this nation than in most others, but inequality exists, and, in some respects, with stronger features than it is usual to meet with in the rest of christendom.

The rights of property being an indispensable condition of civilization, and its quiet possession every where guarantied, equality of condition is rendered impossible. One man must labor, while another may live luxuriously on his means; one has leisure and opportunity to cultivate his tastes, to increase his information, and to refine his habits, while another is compelled to toil, that he may live. One is reduced to serve, while another commands, and, of course, there can be no equality in their social conditions.

The justice and relative advantage of these differencies, as well as their several duties, will be elsewhere considered.

By the inequality of civil and political rights that exists in

From James Fenimore Cooper, *The American Democrat*, pp. 39–43.

certain parts of the Union, and the great equality that exists in others, we see the necessity of referring the true character of the institutions to those of the states, without a just understanding of which, it is impossible to obtain any general and accurate ideas of the real polity of the country.

The same general exceptions to civil and political equality, that are found in other free countries, exist in this, though under laws peculiar to ourselves. Women and minors are excluded from the suffrage, and from maintaining suits at law, under the usual provisions, here as well as elsewhere. None but natives of the country can fill many of the higher offices, and paupers, felons and all those who have not fixed residences, are also excluded from the suffrage. In a few of the states property is made the test of political rights, and, in nearly half of them, a large portion of the inhabitants, who are of a different race from the original European occupants of the soil, are entirely excluded from all political, and from many of the civil rights, that are enjoyed by those who are deemed citizens. A slave can neither choose, nor be chosen to office, nor, in most of the states, can even a free man, unless a white man. A slave can neither sue nor be sued; he can not hold property, real or personal, nor can he, in many of the states be a witness in any suit, civil or criminal.

It follows from these facts, that absolute equality of condition, of political rights, or of civil rights, does not exist in the United States, though they all exist in a much greater degree in some states than in others, and in some of the states, perhaps, to as great a degree as is practicable. In what are usually called the free states of America, or those in which domestic slavery is abolished, there is to be found as much equality in every respect as comports with safety, civilization and the rights of property. This is also true, as respects the white population, in those states in which domestic slavery does exist; though the number of the bond is in a large proportion to that of the free.

As the tendency of the institutions of America is to the right, we learn in these truths, the power of facts, every question of politics being strictly a question of practice. They who fancy it possible to frame the institutions of a country, on the pure principles of abstract justice, as these principles exist in theories know little of human nature, or of the restraints that are necessary to society. Abuses assail us in a thousand forms, and it is hopeless to aspire to any condition of humanity, approaching perfection. The very necessity of a government at all, arises from the impossibility of controlling the passions by any other means than that of force.

The celebrated proposition contained in the declaration of independence is not to be understood literally. All men are not "created equal," in a physical, or even in a moral sense, unless we limit the signification to one of political rights. This much is true, since human institutions are a human invention, with which nature has had no connection. Men are not born equals, physically, since one has a good constitution, another a bad; one is handsome, another ugly; one white, another black. Neither are men born equals morally, one possessing genius, or a natural aptitude, while his brother is an idiot. As regards all human institutions men are born equal, no sophistry being able to prove that nature intended one should inherit power and wealth, another slavery and want. Still artificial inequalities are the inevitable consequences of artificial ordinances, and in founding a new governing principle for the social compact, the American legislators instituted new modes of difference.

The very existence of government at all, infers inequality. The citizen who is preferred to office becomes the superior of those who are not, so long as he is the repository of power, and the child inherits the wealth of the parent as a controlling law of society. All that the great American proposition, therefore, can mean, is to set up new and juster notions of natural rights than those which existed previously, by asserting, in substance, that God has not instituted political inequalities, as was pretended by the advocates of the Jus Divinum, and that men possessed a full and natural authority to form such social institutions as best suited their necessities.

There are numerous instances in which the social inequality of America may do violence to our notions of abstract justice, but the compromise of interests under which all civilized society must exist, renders this unavoidable. Great principles seldom escape working injustice in particular things, and this so much the more, in establishing the relations of a community, for in them many great, and frequently conflicting principles enter, to maintain the more essential features of which sacrifices of parts become necessary. If we would have civilization and the exertion indispensable to its success, we must have property; if we have property, we must have its rights; if we have the rights of property, we must take those consequences of the rights of property which are inseparable from the rights themselves.

The equality of rights in America, therefore, after allowing for the striking exception of domestic slavery, is only a greater extension of the principle than common, while there is no such thing as an equality of condition. All that can be said of the first, is that it has been carried as far as a prudent discretion will at all allow, and of the last, that the inequality is the simple result of civilization, unaided by any of those factitious plans that have been elsewhere devised in order to augment the power of the strong, and to enfeeble the weak.

Equality is no where laid down as a governing principle of the institutions of the United States, neither the word, nor any inference that can be fairly deduced from its meaning, occurring in the constitution. As respect the states, themselves, the professions of an equality of rights are more clear, and slavery excepted, the intention in all their governments is to maintain as far as practicable, though equality of condition is no where mentioned, all political economists knowing that it is unattainable, if, indeed, it be desirable. Desirable in practice, it can hardly be, since the result would be to force all down to the level of the lowest.

All that a good government aims at, therefore, is to add no unnecessary and artificial aid to the force of its own unavoidable consequences, and to abstain from fortifying and accumulating social inequality as a means of increasing political inequalities.

53. Thomas Hamilton

As much practical equality in Liverpool as New York

Armed with data compiled by modern researchers, the American sociologist Seymour Martin Lipset has recently argued that mobility and opportunity patterns in the contemporary United States and Britain are not nearly so unlike as had been supposed. One hundred and thirty-five years earlier the sensible and admired English visitor, Thomas Hamilton, noted similar conditions of equality—and inequality—in American and English society.

On the whole, the difference is not striking, I should imagine, between the social habits of the people of New York, and those prevalent in our first-rate mercantile cities. In both, the faculties are exerted in the same pursuits; in both, the dominant aristocracy is that of wealth; and, in both, there is the same grasping at unsubstantial and unacknowledged distinctions.

It is the fashion to call the United States the land of liberty and equality. If the term equality be understood simply as implying, that there exists no privileged order in America, the assertion, though not strictly true,* may pass. In any wider acceptation it is mere nonsense. There is quite as much practical equality in Liverpool as New York. The magnates of the Exchange do not strut less proudly in the latter city than in the former; nor are their wives and daughters more backward in supporting their pretensions. In such matters legislative enactments can do nothing. Man's vanity, and the desire of distinction inherent in his nature, cannot be repressed. If obstructed in one outlet, it will only gush forth with greater vehemence at another. The most contemptible of mankind has some talent of mind or body, some attraction—virtue—accomplishment—dexterity—or gift of for-

From Thomas Hamilton, *Men and Manners in America*, pp. 64–67.

* Not strictly true, because in many of the States the right of suffrage is made dependent on a certain qualification in property. In Virginia, in particular, this qualification is very high.

tune,—in short, something real or imaginary, on which he arrogates superiority to those around him. The rich man looks down upon the poor, the learned on the ignorant, the orator on him unblessed with the gift of tongues, and "he that is a true-born gentleman, and stands upon the honour of his birth," despises the *roturier*, whose talents have raised him to an estimation in society, perhaps, superior to his own.

Thus it is with the men, and with the fairer sex assuredly it is not different. No woman, conscious of attraction, was ever a republican in her heart. Beauty is essentially despotic—it uniformly asserts its power, and never yet consented to a surrender of privilege. I have certainly heard it maintained in the United States, that all men were equal, but never did I hear that assertion from the lips of a lady. On the contrary, the latter is always conscious of the full extent of her claims to preference and admiration, and is never satisfied till she feels them to be acknowledged. And what zephyr is too light to fill the gossamer sails of woman's vanity! The form of a feature, the whiteness of a hand, the shade of a ringlet, a cap, a feather, a trinket, a smile, a motion—all, or any of these, or distinctions yet finer and more shadowy, if such there be—are enough, here as elsewhere, to constitute the sign and shibboleth of her fantastic supremacy. It is in vain, therefore, to talk of female republicans; there exists, and can exist, no such being on either side of the Atlantic, for human nature is the same on both.

In truth, the spirit of aristocracy displays itself in this commercial community in every variety of form. One encounters it at every turn. T'other night, at a ball, I had the honour to converse a good deal with a lady, who is confessedly a star of the first magnitude in the hemisphere of fashion. She inquired what I thought of the company. I answered, "that I had rarely seen a party in any country in which the average of beauty appeared to me to be so high."

"Indeed!" answered my fair companion, with an expression of surprise; "it would seem that you English gentlemen are not difficult to please; but does it strike you, that the average is equally high as regards air, manner, fashion?"

"In regards to such matters," I replied, "I certainly could not claim for the party in question any remarkable distinction; but that, in a scene so animated, and brilliant with youth, beauty, and gaiety of spirit, I was little disposed to play the critic."

"Nay," replied my opponent, for the conversation had already begun to assume something of the form of argument, "it surely requires no spirit of rigid criticism, to discriminate between such a set of vulgarians, as you see collected here, and ladies who have been accustomed to move in a higher and better circle. Mrs. ——— is an odd person, and makes it a point to bring together at her balls all the riff-raff of the place—people whom, if you were to remain ten years in New York, you would probably never meet any where else. I assure you, there are not a dozen girls in this room that I should think of admitting to my own parties."

Thus driven from the field, I ventured to direct her notice to several elegant and pretty girls, about whom I asked some questions. Their attractions, however, were either not admitted, or when these were too decided to allow of direct negation, the subject was ingeniously evaded. If I talked of a pretty foot, I was told its owner was the daughter of a tobacconist. If I admired a graceful dancer, I was assured (what I certainly should not have discovered) that the young lady was of vulgar manners, and without education. Some were so utterly unknown to fame, that the very names, birth, habits, and connexions, were buried in the most profound and impenetrable obscurity. In short, a Count of the Empire, with his sixteen quarterings, probably would not have thought, and certainly would not have spoken, with contempt half so virulent of these fair plebeians. The reader will perhaps agree, that there are more *exclusives* in the world than the lady-patronesses of Almack's.

I shall now give an instance of the estimation in which wealth is held in this commercial community. At a party a few evenings ago, the worthy host was politely assiduous in introducing me to the more prominent individuals who composed it. Unfortunately, he considered it necessary to preface each repetition of the ceremony with some preliminary account of the pecuniary circumstances of the gentleman, the honour of whose acquaintance was about to be conferred on me. "Do you observe," he asked, "that tall thin person, with a cast in his eye, and his nose a little cocked? Well, that man, not three months ago, made a hundred thousand dollars by a single speculation in tallow. You must allow me to introduce you to him."

The introduction passed, and my zealous cicerone again approached, with increased importance of aspect—"A gentleman," he said, "worth at least half a million, had expressed a desire to make my acquaintance." This was gratifying, and, of course, not to be denied. A third time did our worthy entertainer return to the charge, and before taking my departure, I had the honour of being introduced to an individual, who was stated to be still more opulent than his predecessors. Had I been presented to so many bags of dollars, instead of to their possessors, the ceremony would have been quite as interesting, and perhaps less troublesome.

Aristocracy amid Democracy

54. J. S. Buckingham

There is a decided aristocracy of family connexion

Buckingham had come to this country to write a sympathetic account of the young republic, hoping to undo the mischief he felt had been done by hostile observers. Such motives add to the force of his judgment that for all the lip-service paid to egalitarianism here, an aristocratic elite presided over this nation's cities, whose "style of living . . . would be deemed elegant in any part of Europe."

The classes into which the population are divided in Philadelphia, are very similar to those of New York and Baltimore. Though there is no titled nobility, or hereditary aristocracy, there is a decided aristocracy of family connexion, as well as of wealth; and

From J. S. Buckingham, *America*, II, pp. 80–82.

of the two, the first are the most fastidious about the rank and station of their associates. The expressions of respect for those who are descended from the first families, or who belong to some of the oldest families of Pennsylvania, or Maryland, or New Jersey, or Virginia, are as frequently heard from the lips of Americans, as from those of the most aristocratic circles in our small country towns in England; and the phrases "they are people of yesterday," and "people of no family," convey as much odium to an American ear as to an English one.

The greater number of those select gentry inherit land, or houses, or stock, from their parents, and are not engaged in trade. They are occasionally joined by families who have acquired fortunes in business, and retire, when they form a small leisure class, whose chief occupation is visiting, and social intercourse when at home, and travelling to the sea-side, or to the springs of Virginia or Saratoga, in the warm season. The style of living observed by this class, is what would be deemed elegant in any part of Europe; their houses are large and well furnished; their domestics numerous, though nearly all coloured; their parties gay and brilliant; their manners polished and refined; and their conversation intelligent and agreeable.

The class next in order of consequence or consideration, is the aristocracy of wealth, which is more extended in numbers, not so exclusive or scrupulous about the rank or fortune of their associates, and more easily accessible to persons of inferior pretensions to themselves. Their style of living is more profuse and expensive, though not so refined and elegant; their parties are larger and more costly, and their visiting more frequent and more general.

Among these, however, are to be found many philanthropic and benevolent individuals, who devote a large portion of their wealth, as well as their labour and their time, to the promotion of charitable and religious objects. There is no country on earth, perhaps, where so large a portion of the wealthy are generous philanthropists as in America; and in no city of America are there more of this class than in Philadelphia. Mr. Matthew Carey, an Irishman and a Catholic—Mr. William Birch, an Englishman and a Unitarian—and Mr. Matthew Newkirk, an American and a Presbyterian—are splendid examples of this; and show that neither origin, country, or peculiarity of creed, prevents the exercise of the higher virtues of charity and benevolence, by the most wealthy individuals who have hearts to feel for the woes of others.

The middle class of society in Philadelphia,—removed from either extreme, of bare competency (for of abject poverty there is very little) and great wealth—is composed of merchants, traders, professional men, including the clergy, physicians, lawyers, and sojourners from different parts of the country. These form, of course, a very mixed and miscellaneous class, but they are, on the whole, the most intelligent, and most agreeable to strangers. No scrupulous apprehensions about low birth, or want of high family connexions—and no dread of associating with a man of small fortune or none at all—ever interrupts the full flow of hilarity and good humour, which is so characteristic of this mixed class, among whom there is a sufficient amount of intelligence on all general subjects, and a sufficient frankness in the expression of their opinions, to render their society both instructive and entertaining.

55. FRANCIS J. GRUND

Impossible to consider a man independently of his circumstances

Urban elites in the United States aspired to a status similar to that commanded by the upper crust on the Continent. Prestigious clubs were formed largely to enable wealthy men of eminent family to achieve exclusivity and standing comparable to that possessed by European nobility in a society lacking in the formal trappings of aristocracy. Several of Cooper's novels portray satirically the aristocratic pretensions of parvenu Americans. Grund had the gift of eliciting frank comment from

From Francis J. Grund, *Aristocracy in America*, I, pp. 190–199, 206–208, 269, 270; II, 104–108.

the 'aristocrats' he talked with and the ability to record it succinctly. No one has depicted better the social pretensions of leading men in the country's great cities.

It was half-past ten when I made my appearance at Mrs.———'s "rout." The rooms were richly decorated, and the company in excellent spirits. My friend had already arrived, and was talking to a young lady in one of the corners of the dancing-room; which was called "a desperate flirtation," inasmuch as the young lady appeared to be past sixteen, and not yet twenty, and the gentleman in circumstances which enabled him to support a wife. Similar flirtations were going on in other parts of the room; the married ladies being seated on benches or settees near the walls, and acting, if not as judges, at least as recorders of the events. The music, consisting chiefly of clarionets, flutes, and horns, was stationed to great advantage in the entry; leaving not only more room for the dancers in the parlour, but softening also the harmony of sounds by the greater distance. The ladies, especially those who danced, were, in point of dress, the exact copies of the patterns issued weekly in the French metropolis; and the gentlemen, though apparently timid in the presence of so many beauties, looked, nevertheless, sufficiently smart and enterprising for men of business.

I looked for a while on the group of dancers, in hopes of perceiving some slight variation, but was not a little annoyed by seeing continually the same figures and the same dancers. I afterwards communicated my surprise to my friend, but was told that I was in a fashionable house, in which none but fashionable young ladies and gentlemen could be expected "to have the floor;" and that if, from courtesy, some other people had been invited, it was expected they would have sufficient good sense not to obtrude themselves on the notice of the company, and least of all to make themselves conspicuous by joining in a quadrille or a waltz. "There are," added he, "some dozen of young girls here dying to show their 'steps,' but none of the fashionable young men would risk his standing in society by bringing them out; and, as for the young men of neither family nor wealth, who are only asked because they are relations of the house, (a custom which is by no means general in the United States,) they know their place too well to be guilty of such an impropriety.

"Whenever one of our wealthy stock-holders," continued he, "invites a poor devil to his house, the particular relation of entertainer and guest changes nothing in the relative position of the parties: the rich man still continues to assume the peculiar insolent condescension of a patron; while the man without credit will exhibit in his conduct the humiliating consciousness of his 'insufficiency.' If you took notice of the manner in which the lady of the house courtesyed to the gentlemen that were presented to her, you must have been able to distinguish the capitalist from the poor beginner, or unsuccessful speculator, as effectually as if their property had been announced with their names. Every additional thousand produces a new smile; for it is impossible for our people to consider a man independently of his circumstances."

"This," observed I, "is the fault of every practical nation, especially of the English, who are the most purse-proud and exclusive people in Europe."

"I know that," replied he: "but the English reward talent of every description higher than any other nation in the world; so that money is, in a certain sense, the just measure of capacity. In America, on the contrary, there are but few branches of *industry*, and almost none of *learning*, which are sure of meeting with an adequate remuneration in money; so that, if men are merely judged by their wealth, the meanest bank or counting-house clerk, or a common shopkeeper, has a better chance of arriving at respectability than the most successful scholar in the most difficult branches of human learning. Society, in this manner, must become lower and lower every day; there being no entailed estates or large hereditary possessions in the United States, securing to a privileged class the necessary means and leisure for the gratuitous pursuit of arts and sciences. And, as for the English being exclusive, you forget that, when English people assume that character, they possess generally the tact and *à-plomb* necessary for carrying it off; whereas, here you often meet the same spirit among people whose wealth is *credit* and *expectancy*, and whose manners and education are identified solely with the desk and ledger. Thus the terms 'patron' and 'client' are in New York, for instance, synonymous with 'creditor' and 'debtor;' and as the banks, according to the prevalent system of credit, must inevitably be the creditors of nine-tenths of the community, every person connected with them—and, above all, a stock-holder, cashier, or president—must necessarily be a patrician. The whole composition of our society is arithmetical; each gentleman ranking according to the numerical index of his property. You need only watch the conduct of the society in this room, and you will satisfy yourself of the truth of my assertion.

"Do you know that lady in pink satin," he continued, "who is talking to the lady dressed in white, across that modest-looking woman with the pale face, who is evidently embarrassed by this rudeness?"

I replied in the negative.

"The first," he said, "is the daughter of an honest shoemaker, who has become very rich by his industry, and is bitterly grieved by the aristocratic haughtiness of his daughter. I have heard it asserted that he often threatened her to hang up a last in his parlour, instead of a coat of arms, to punish the ridiculous pretensions of his family."

"Such a character," said I, "would have done credit to a Dutch burgomaster in the best times of the republic. But who is the lady thus planted between two of her sex, who are determined to take no more notice of her than if her chair were empty?"

"She is the wife of an American commodore," replied he; "one of the most gallant officers in the navy, who has shed his blood in his country's service. What further comment does this require?—what greater proof would you have of the insufferable arrogance of our moneyed aristocracy?"

"Let us follow that young lady, whose face I have never seen before in society," observed my friend after a short pause: "she looks as though she had never been used to company, and will probably become the butt of the aristocratic misses who keep possession of the floor."

The unfortunate girl, led by a young man, who, to judge from his manners, was a stranger in the city, had scarcely entered the dancing-room before every eye was turned upon her, and the most insolent, half-loud inquiry instituted as to "who she was," and "where she came from?"

"Do you know that girl?" demanded a young lady, who had just stopped dancing, loud enough for her to hear.

"I never saw her before in my life, *I* am sure," replied the *ballerina* who had been addressed, with a toss of her head; "do *you* know her?"

"Indeed I don't; I wonder how she got here!" resumed the first.

Here a third lady walked up, and examined the dress of the stranger; then, joining a small circle, "I am sure," said she, in an audible whisper, "it's not worth seventy-five cents a yard."

"And who is that unlicked cub that's with her?" demanded another lady.

"Heaven alone knows!" answered a voice; "I dare say, just come from the woods!"

"With his mouth full of tobacco!"

"I hope she isn't going to dance; if she does, I shall leave the room."

"I sha'n't stay either."

One half of this conversation the poor girl must have heard, as she was standing close to the speakers, and could not even escape from the sting of their remarks through the crowd that obstructed the passage; for it is the custom in America, as in England, for people who give parties to invite as many persons as possible, in order to have the satisfaction of a full room. She was on the point of bursting into tears; and yet the young, fashionable tigresses, of from sixteen to twenty years of age, had not feeling enough to take pity on her. I am aware that, in describing that of which I was an eye-witness, I shall scarcely be believed by my English or German readers, because it is almost impossible for an educated European to conceive the degree of rudeness, insolence, and effrontery, and the total want of consideration for the feelings of others, which I have often seen practised in what is called the "first society" of the United States. I have seen in Boston, or rather in Nahant, a small watering-place in the neighbourhood of that city, two girls,—one the daughter of a president of an insurance-office, and the other the child of a merchant,—supporting their heads with their elbows, and in this position staring at each other for several minutes across a public table; each believing that her standing in society entitled her to the longest stare, and that the other, being the daughter of a man of less consideration and property, should have modesty enough to cast down her eyes. . . .

The fashionable people of the Atlantic cities, who give dinner and evening parties either for the purpose of maintaining or acquiring a high rank in society, have themselves little or no disposition for company. With them society does not offer an agreeable and necessary respite from toil; but is merely a means of acquiring influence, &c. For this purpose it is not necessary to treat all persons with equal sincerity and politeness. "*La politesse nous tient lieu du cœur,*" say the French; but the fashionable people of the United States manage to get on without either. There is nothing in the composition of a fashionable American to compensate for the loss of natural affections,—nothing in his manner to soften the egotism which manifests itself in every motion, every gesture, every word which drops from his lips. And the worst of it is, that he imagines all this to be a successful imitation of English manners! He forgets entirely that, in imitating the manners of the higher classes in England, he is very much in the position of a sailor on horseback; showing by his whole carriage that he is out of his element, and, though straining every nerve to maintain his place, ready to tumble off at the first motion for which he is not previously prepared.

As regards the exclusiveness of the higher classes, and especially of the women, the instance before me was certainly one calculated to excite my indignation, had I not known fashionable young ladies that refused to walk in the streets of Philadelphia until the dinner-hour of "the common people," when they would be sure of having the sidewalk to themselves.

But what is all this, compared to the artificial distinctions introduced into their churches? It has always been the pride of the Catholic church in Europe to offer a place of worship to every man, without distinction of rank, title, or wealth. The utmost a man pays for a chair in any of the churches of France or Italy is one *sou;* the fashionable American Catholics, however, imitate the practice of those gentlemanly followers of Christ who choose to worship God in good company. Thus the respectable Catholics of New York, "who do not wish to be annoyed by the presence of an Irish mob," being for the most part composed of their own servants, have built a church for their own specific use,—a snug little concern, just large enough for a *genteel* audience to hear the Lord *en famille.*

In order to exclude effectually everything that might be disagreeable, no one is allowed to stand in the aisles; so that those poor devils who cannot afford to pay for a pew must be content to seek the Lord elsewhere *among their equals.*

"Another species of tyranny," continued my friend, "exercised by the higher classes of Americans consists in the proscription of all people belonging, or rather attempting to belong, to different sets. If you belong to the first society, you must not by any chance accept an invitation to the second, or shake hands in a friendly manner with people who are supposed to be of an inferior standing, except it be on election day for a political purpose. If you belong to the second, you may; of course, try with all your might 'to push for the first;' but, if you are once seen with the third, you have done even with the second: and so on. . . . Our second society, namely, has again its first, second, and third rank, each of which is again subdivided into still smaller circles, which are again numbered; so that it requires the nicety of a mathematician to ascertain what sort of company a man is likely to be with when invited to a party. Owing to this trifling circumstance, the members of the second society live with each other somewhat after the manner of cats and dogs; making but too frequently foreigners witnesses of their broils, and affording them, as will appear from my story, occasionally an opportunity of acting the peace-makers.

"An instance of this kind happened last year, when a Polish gentleman arriving in Boston, and finding the town too hot in the summer, was induced to take up his residence at the 'Washington

Hotel,' which he was told, and with great justice too, furnished excellent accommodations at moderate prices, and commanded a fine view of the harbour.

"Scarcely had he removed thither, before his being announced 'as a count,' 'a real count,' 'a count that was *known* to be a count,' and who had brought letters proving him to be 'every inch a count,' caused such a sensation in the house, that the ladies refused to eat, drink, and even *talk*, except in company of 'the count.' The count could not but be flattered by these attentions, and in turn omitted nothing by which to testify his gratitude. He listened with the utmost patience to the accounts of their chivalrous ancestors,—for in Boston even the second society have *ancestors*,—sat without opening his lips when they mutually abused one another, and with incredible skill managed to remain on good terms with the various sets, divisions, and subdivisions, whose every-day regret it was to be obliged, 'owing to the ridiculous American custom,' *to dine together at the same table*.

"At last the melancholy hour drew near when the count was about to depart. When this sad intelligence was received, the ladies, with that tenderness which belongs to their sex, and the peculiar generosity which marks 'the second society,' determined to pay to the count a tribute of their respect, and accordingly met in conclave to consult as to the best manner of manifesting their sentiments. At first, the first section of the second society met, and agreed to give the count *a ball*. Then came the second, then the third, then again the *élite* of each section; and, wonderful! on this subject they all agreed.

"It was therefore intimated to the count that he must defer his departure until after the ball, to which the cavalier readily consented; assuring the ladies that their kindness should be engraven on his heart, and that he should never forget the amicable reception he had met with in Boston. The rest of my story is easily told. The evening was fixed for the party, the 'ladies patronesses' chosen from each set, (because, the count having been polite to all, none could very well be omitted,) and invitations sent out to three or four hundred people to pay to the count the tribute due to his rank and quality.

"At last the appointed evening arrived. The ball was superb,—the hall magnificently decorated,—the music exquisite,—the refreshments in excellent taste and in the greatest profusion. There was also a supper;—not indeed equal to one of Crockford's, but, notwithstanding, nice, delicate, blending the French with the English art of cookery, and arranged in a style worthy of a *prince.* The selection of madeira and sherry corresponded with the supper; and there was a profusion of iced champaign for the ladies. The whole went off prosperously, with the exception of a single mistake; which, however, the count did not discover till the next morning, when the landlord, stepping into his room, presented him with a small piece of paper containing the disagreeable item of—

To Ball, 1000 dollars.

"The count was stupified,—changed colour,—declared that the ball had been given to him, and that he had nothing to do with settling the bill.

"The landlord withdrew; handed the bill to the 'ladies patronesses,' and respectfully demanded an explanation. Hereupon a grand meeting of all the sets was immediately convened, at which the best understanding prevailed throughout, the whole assembly coming to the unanimous resolution 'that the count was a shabby fellow.'

Lot of the Farmer

56. J. S. Buckingham

American farmers are much better off than the same class in England

Contemporary journals published for western farmers indicate their sense of grievance, not least at the great gulf that allegedly separated the happy ideal state of American agriculturists from the meager, marginal reality of

From J. S. Buckingham, *America,* II, pp. 412–415.

their life and work. Contrasting their situation with that of English farmers, however, Buckingham believed that by any comparative standard the situation of American farmers was superior.

The occupier of a farm, whether large or small, is almost invariably the owner of the land he cultivates; and therefore all the disagreeable differences between landlords and tenants, with the vexations of the game laws, the authority of country squires and clerical magistrates, so fertile a source of annoyance in England, are here unknown. There being no tithes, great or small, for the support of a State clergy, all that large class of evils growing out of tithe disputes and tithe compositions, are here also unheard of. The labourers being fewer than are required, and wages being high, there are neither paupers nor poor-rates, and neither workhouses nor jails are required for the country population, since abundance of work and good pay prevents poverty, and takes away all temptation to dishonesty. There being no ranks or orders, such as the esquire and the baronet, the baron and the earl, the marquis and the duke, each to compete with and outvie the other in outward splendour, which too often leads to inward embarrassment, as in England, the country residents are free from that foolish ambition which devours the substance of too many at home; and all those idle disputes and distinctions about old families and new ones, people of high birth and people of low, country families and strangers, which so perplex the good people of England when a county meeting or a county ball takes place, so as to set persons in their right places, to admit some, exclude others, and so on, are here happily unthought of. The consequence is, that with more sources of pleasure, and few sources of dissatisfaction, the American country gentry and farmers are much better off, and much happier than the same class of people in England. No corn laws exist to vex the landowner with a fear of their abolition, no non-payment of rents, and abatements to tenants, are ever heard of, for landlord and tenant are here merged in one. No distraint for tithes, or writs of ejectment, ever occur; and in short, scarcely anything ever happens to ruffle the serenity of a country life in the well-settled parts of America.

The greatest difference of all, however, between the agricultural population of England and those of the United States, is to be seen in their relative degrees of intelligence. In England, no one, I presume, will deny the fact, of the farmers and farm-labourers being among the least intelligent and most uneducated portion of the population. Here, on the contrary, they are among the most intelligent and best informed. A great number of the occupiers of farms are persons who, having been successful in business in cities, have retired at an early period of life, bought an estate, take delight in cultivating it on their own account for income, and as from seven to ten per cent. is realized on farming capital where carefully attended to, it is at once a safe and profitable investment.

These gentlemen having a good deal of leisure, little parish business to occupy them, and a taste for books and love of information, read a great deal more than the busy inhabitants of commercial cities, and have the power of exercising their judgment and reflection more free from the bias of party views and sectarian feelings, than those who live in large communities. Their previous education and ample means dispose others also to works of benevolence; and the consequence is, that while their conversation is more intelligent, and their manners greatly superior to that of English farmers generally, they devote a large portion of their time and means to the establishment and support of Sunday schools, district schools, societies for mutual improvement, country libraries, temperance societies, savings' banks, and in short every thing that can elevate those below them, and make them better and happier in their stations.

There are no taverns, as in the market-towns of England, to absorb half the profits made at market by the drinking and carousing of the buyers and sellers, as is the case with English farmers; and as their mode of visiting and entertaining is social and economical, families are continually interchanging evening visits with each other, to take a cup of tea, fruit, ice-cream, and sweetmeats or other delicacies, but without spirits, wine, beer, or cider—retiring early, and all coming or going in vehicles adapted to their means, from gigs and phaetons, to carriages and family waggons, for there is neither tax nor duty on carriages, horses, or servants, all being free to ride or walk as suits their pleasure.

If the contrast is striking between the English and American farmer, it is still more so between the farm-labourers of the two countries. In England it is well known what miserable wages agricultural labourers receive; 10 to 12 shillings, perhaps the average;—what scanty fare they are obliged to subsist upon—flesh meat once or twice a week, at the utmost; and how perpetually they stand in danger of the workhouse, with all their desire to avoid it, with no education themselves, and no desire to procure any for their children. Here, there is not a labourer on the farm who receives less than a dollar a day, or 24 shillings per week; while many receive more; and those who are permanently attached to the farm have wages equal to that throughout the year. Besides this, they have as good living at the farm-house as prosperous tradesmen in the middle ranks of life enjoy in England; three substantial meals a day, and in hay and harvest time four, with abundance and variety at each. At the same time they enjoy the advantages of excellent schools for the almost gratuitous education of their children, neat little cottages for themselves and wives to live in, a little plot of ground for gardening, and privileges in great number.

The consequence is, that the farm-labourers and their families are all well-fed, well-dressed, well-educated in all the ordinary elements of knowledge, intelligent in conversation, agreeable in manners, and as superior to the corresponding class of farm-labourers in England as all these advantages can indicate. There are no beer shops at which they spend their substance; no haunts of vice and debauchery at which they concoct the plans of the poacher, the smuggler, or the robber, to make up by illicit gains the deficiencies of honest industry; and, consequently, no need of prosecutions at the sessions, with all the array of constables, police, magistracy, and treadmills, to punish them and keep them in order.

57. Charles A. Murray

The American farmer is no better off than the British

Charles A. Murray, an English visitor, who spent much time traveling in the American West, disagreed with Buckingham about the relative situation of English and American farmers. According to Murray, the "superficial observer" was easily blinded by surface appearances in the United States.

I remember talking to an intelligent American farmer upon the subject of public burthens; and, upon comparing the sum paid by him in proportion to the yearly profit of his farm, I calculated that it was much in the same ratio with that paid by a farmer in the north of England or south of Scotland. Nor are the other circumstances connected with his position so much more favourable to the American farmer as they would appear to a superficial observer. He can buy his horses cheaper, his food cheaper, his land cheaper, and his taxes, direct and indirect, are lower; but his shoes, and linen, and cloth, are dearer and worse in quality; his labour is dearer; his farming utensils are also dearer: in fact, the chief advantage which he enjoys can scarcely be termed such in fair or philosophical language, namely, he *can* (and frequently *does*) exhaust his land, by demanding from it a perpetual succession of strong crops; knowing that when he has worked it out he can take in more in his neighbourhood, or move off to the West, where the proceeds of sale, even of his exhausted farm, will enable him to purchase as much of the finest soil in the world as he can attempt to cultivate.

Of course, these remarks only apply, in comparison, to the proprietary class of farmers in England, who are much fewer in number than those who pay rent. This is a separate branch of the subject, and cannot be touched upon here, as it depends altogether on the amount of rent in proportion to profit or

From Charles Augustus Murray, *Travels in North America, 1834–1836* (London: Richard Betley, 1841), 2 vols., I, pp. 147–149.

produce. That there are profits, is undoubtedly true; but they are not so high, nor so enviable, as they are usually represented. Nor does the American occupant of four hundred acres of the best land spend more upon the comforts and *luxuries* of life, than the occupant of two hundred acres of similar land in Yorkshire or in the Lothians,—although the produce of his farm returns him nominally twelve per cent. for his invested capital; that of the British farmer scarcely six, exclusive of expenses.

This question requires a closer examination of detail than can be expected in a narrative like this, before its discussion can lead to any useful result; especially as the soil, climate, public burthens, price of labour, and other circumstances, vary so widely in the different states, that an estimate formed accurately in Virginia or Massachusetts will be quite erroneous if applied to Ohio or Michigan.

The American agriculturists seem to have little local attachment. A New Englander or Virginian, though proud and vain of his state, will move off to Missouri or Illinois, and leave the home of his childhood without any visible effort or symptom of regret, if by so doing he can make ten dollars where he before made eight. I have seen such repeated instances of this that I cannot help considering it a national feature.

How different this is from the Scottish character may be gathered from the fact that a band of highlanders, of the Cameron and other Jacobite clans, left Scotland, after the rebellion of '45, and settled in Virginia. They were so numerous, that for many years afterwards the local courts were obliged to have a Gaelic interpreter, in order to carry on the requisite business in regard to witnesses and juries; and although the place where they fixed their abode was cheerless in appearance and the soil very poor, they have by perseverance and industry improved and rendered it comfortable; and are as unwilling to quit that spot, in search of the fertile plains of the Mississippi, as they were to leave their original country.

58. William Cooper Howells

The social condition was primitive

The "agrarian myth" was a creation largely of urbanites bemoaning lost innocence and extolling the life of the soil in which diverse virtues supposedly flourished. Working American farmers appear not to have subscribed widely to the concept. In the following passage the father of the novelist William Dean Howells recalls that farm life was hard and not very profitable.

The social condition of the people was rather primitive and very simple. None of them were wealthy. The possession of a quarter section or two of land, pretty well cleared up—that is, about a third or half of it under culture—with a log-house and barn, was thought to make a man well off. The money value of the wealth of the average of farms, would not be over $2,000, including the improvements. Nearly every man lived on a piece of land of his own, and this was usually in eighty or one hundred and sixty acre tracts. Their stock was small, and mostly their families were large. Almost every man was the son of a farmer in an older settlement who had come in to this to have a farm of his own, out of what his father could spare; or some man who had been a farm laborer or renter in an older place, had bought land and was opening out a home. Among such a people there were no rich, and none very poor. Most of them lived very plainly. They usually had enough to eat, though they were liable to run short a while before harvest. All that would bring money was sold to provide for taxes and such payments as only money would make; and those who had payments to make on their land were pretty sure to sell themselves bare, and were often hard put to it to maintain themselves in provisions.

As for dress, that was very plain, and fortunately, there was but little temptation to extravagance in this way. The women of the family, in almost every instance, produced something to wear.

From William Cooper Howells, *Recollections of Life in Ohio From 1813 to 1840* (Cincinnati: Robert Clarke, 1895), 122–125.

Besides the knitting and sewing, which was the work of the older women, the wool of the few sheep each farmer kept was spun in the family. So also was the flax that grew on the flax-patch, which was regularly cleared off in the winter, sowed with flax in March, harvested in June, and immediately planted with potatoes—yielding two important Irish crops in one year. The wool was sometimes carded at home, but usually it was sent off to one of the carding machines that would be put up in a mill, for the purpose of preparing the wool for spinning by carding and making it into rolls, that were about a yard long and three-fourths of an inch in diameter, light and soft, and from which an even thread was easily spun, either on a large spinning-wheel or the little treadle-wheel used also for flax. The quarter acre flax patch and the few sheep would, almost without noticing the expense or labor, produce the material for clothing a large family. The women pulled the flax, or at least helped to pull it, and helped in dressing it, and always spun it up. One or two grown up daughters would dispose of a large supply of flax and wool. The best flax was spun into a fine thread for linen, of which shirts and like wear were made; a coarser quality was made into sheeting and summer pantaloons. Summer coats were never worn, for when it was too warm for a cloth coat, men went in their shirt sleeves. The same short method was adopted as to summer shoes—omitting the shoes and stockings. The wool was spun into an average grade for cloth and flannel. A mixed cloth was made with a linen warp and woolen filling, which they called *linsey*, that was worn mostly by the women and children. It was made lighter than cloth, and cost less than flannel. Very often it was woven in plaid figures, and when new looked well, and was esteemed quite a desirable article for every-day dresses. The young women always thought themselves well dressed in a new linsey dress for winter, which, when new, would be worn to meeting, singing schools and "frolics," as they called all social gatherings where the young people made merry together. As the colors faded the dresses came into every-day wear, and they were so durable that they lasted till the next year's manufacture was brought in. Sometimes people made their flannels in plaids, which were nice and wore well. Fulled cloth was made at home till it was woven, when it would be taken to the fulling-mill to be finished. This was worn by the men and big boys, and made excellent clothing, though it was not fine, and the color was apt to fade. There was hardly a family of girls where one of them did not have a loom and weave all the plainer kinds of stuff for themselves and for others, so that the spinning and weaving was practically done at home. The prices of these manufactures are worthy of remark when compared to other produce. The stuff was woven one yard wide, which was the width when finished, except the fulled cloth, which shrunk to three-fourths. This cloth was estimated at one dollar and twenty-five cents to one dollar fifty cents per yard; linsey was about fifty cents; flannel, seventy-five; flax linen, fine, fifty; coarser kinds, twenty-five to thirty-seven and a half. At the same time wheat was very rarely over thirty-five cents a bushel; corn, twenty-five; and oats, twelve and a half. This was a great disproportion, in comparison with the present rates, when the quantity of wheat that would buy that coarse cloth would now buy broadcloth of the finest quality worn.

Another manufacture of these times, and which flourished through all changes, was whiskey. No difference if grain was scarce or dear, or times hard, or the people poor, they would make and drink whiskey. And the number of little distilleries was wonderful. Within two miles of where we lived there were three of them. They were small concerns, but they produced enough. They were commonly fitted up with a twenty-five or forty-gallon still and half a dozen tubs. They might, perhaps, have produced a barrel a day, if pushed to their capacity. The distillers would exchange a gallon of whiskey for a bushel of corn or rye, and when the whiskey-jug was empty, a boy would be sent on a bag of grain, perched on an old horse, to the still-house to make the exchange and renew the supply. People were not particular about the age of their liquor, and it was often drank on the day it was made. The custom was for every man to drink it, on all occasions that offered; and the women would take it sweetened and reduced to toddy. At raisings, huskings, log-rollings, and all manner of social gatherings, it was used as an invigorator.

Lot of the Worker

59. Harriet Martineau

Most favoured class I have ever known

Much modern evidence on the actual and real wages of American labor and the minuscule proportion of wealth owned by workers appears to refute Miss Martineau's glowing picture of the American worker's situation. Her version of contented factory girls working happily amidst clean and pleasant surroundings is sharply refuted by the modern scholarly studies done by Hannah Josephson and Vera Shlakman. The latter gloomy assessments, resting as they do on a great weight of evidence, suggest that Miss Martineau's tour of New England factory towns may have been a kind of "Potemkin village" trip in which she saw what factory owners wished her to see.

I visited the corporate factory-establishment at Waltham, within a few miles of Boston. The Waltham Mills were at work before those of Lowell were set up. The establishment is for the spinning and weaving of cotton alone, and the construction of the requisite machinery. Five hundred persons were employed at the time of my visit. The girls earn two, and some three, dollars a-week, besides their board. The little children earn one dollar a-week. Most of the girls live in the houses provided by the corporation, which accommodate from six to eight each. When sisters come to the mill, it is a common practice for them to bring their mother to keep house for them and some of their companions, in a dwelling built by their own earnings. In this case, they save enough out of their board to clothe themselves, and have their two or three dollars a-week to spare. Some have thus cleared off mortgages from their fathers' farms; others have educated the hope of the family at college; and many are rapidly accumulating an independence. I saw a whole street of houses built with the earnings of the girls; some with piazzas, and green venetian blinds; and all neat and sufficiently spacious.

From Harriet Martineau, *Society in America*, II, pp. 57–63. Footnote is in original.

The factory people built the church, which stands conspicuous on the green in the midst of the place. The minister's salary (eight hundred dollars last year) is raised by a tax on the pews. The corporation gave them a building for a lyceum, which they have furnished with a good library, and where they have lectures every winter,—the best that money can procure. The girls have, in many instances, private libraries of some merit and value.

The managers of the various factory establishments keep the wages as nearly equal as possible, and then let the girls freely shift about from one to another. When a girl comes to the overseer to inform him of her intention of working at the mill, he welcomes her, and asks how long she means to stay. It may be six months, or a year, or five years, or for life. She declares what she considers herself fit for, and sets to work accordingly. If she finds that she cannot work so as to keep up with the companion appointed to her, or to please her employer or herself, she comes to the overseer, and volunteers to pick cotton, or sweep the rooms, or undertake some other service that she can perform.

The people work about seventy hours per week, on the average. The time of work varies with the length of the days, the wages continuing the same. All look like well-dressed young ladies. The health is good; or rather, (as this is too much to be said about health any where in the United States,) it is no worse than it is elsewhere.

These facts speak for themselves. There is no need to enlarge on the pleasure of an acquaintance with the operative classes of the United States.

The shoe-making at Lynn is carried on almost entirely in private dwellings, from the circumstance that the people who do it are almost all farmers or fishermen likewise. A stranger who has not been enlightened upon the ways of the place would be astonished at the number of small square erections, like miniature school-houses, standing each as an appendage to a dwelling-house. These are the "shoe shops," where the father of the family and his boys work, while the women within are employed in binding and trimming. Thirty or more of these shoe-shops may be counted in a walk of half-a-mile. When a Lynn shoe manufacturer receives an order, he issues the tidings. The leather is cut out by men on his premises; and then the work is given to those who apply for it; if possible, in small quantities, for the sake of dispatch. The shoes are brought home on Friday night, packed off on Saturday, and in a fortnight or three weeks are on the feet of dwellers in all parts of the Union. The whole family works upon shoes during the winter; and in the summer, the father and sons turn out into the fields, or go fishing. I knew of an instance where a little boy and girl maintained the whole family, while the earnings of the rest went to build a house. I saw very few shabby houses. Quakers are numerous in Lynn. The place is unboundedly prosperous, through the temperance and industry of the people. The deposits in the Lynn Savings' Bank in 1834, were about 34,000 dollars, the population of the town being then 4,000. Since that time, both the population and the prosperity have much increased. It must be remembered, too, that the mechanics of America have more uses for their money than are open to the operatives of England. They build houses, buy land, and educate their sons and daughters.*

It is probably true that the pleasures and pains of life are pretty equally distributed among its various vocations and positions: but it is difficult to keep clear of the impression which outward circumstances occasion, that some are eminently desirable. The mechanics of these northern States appear to me the most favoured class I have ever known. In England, I believe the highest order of mechanics to be, as a class, the wisest and best men of the community. They have the fewest base and narrow interests: they are brought into sufficient contact with the realities of existence, without being hardened by excess of toil and care; and the knowledge they have the opportunity of gaining is of the best kind for the health of the mind. To them, if to any, we may look for public and private virtue. The mechanics of America have nearly all the same advantages, and some others. They have better means of living: their labours are perhaps more honoured; and

* The deposits in the Lowell Savings' Bank for 1834, were upwards of 114,000 dollars.

they are republicans, enjoying the powers and prospects of perfectly equal citizenship. The only respect in which their condition falls below that of English artisans of the highest order is that the knowledge which they have commonly the means of obtaining is not of equal value. The facilities are great: schools, lyceums, libraries, are open to them: but the instruction imparted there is not so good as they deserve. Whenever they have this, it will be difficult to imagine a mode of life more favourable to virtue and happiness than theirs.

There seems to be no doubt among those who know both England and America, that the mechanics of the New World work harder than those of the Old. They have much to do besides their daily handicraft business. They are up and at work early about this; and when it is done, they read till late, or attend lectures; or perhaps have their houses to build or repair, or other care to take of their property. They live in a state and period of society where every man is answerable for his own fortunes; and where there is therefore stimulus to the exercise of every power.

What a state of society it is when a dozen artisans of one town,—Salem,—are seen rearing each a comfortable one-story (or, as the Americans would say, two-story) house, in the place with which they have grown up! when a man who began with laying bricks criticises, and sometimes corrects, his lawyer's composition; when a poor errand-boy becomes the proprietor of a flourishing store, before he is thirty; pays off the capital advanced by his friends at the rate of 2,000 dollars per month; and bids fair to be one of the most substantial citizens of the place!

Such are the outward fortunes of the mechanics of America. Of their welfare in more important respects, to which these are but a part of the means, I shall have to speak in another connexion.

There are troubles between employers and their workmen in the United States, as elsewhere: but the case of the men is so much more in their own hands there than where labour superabounds, that strikes are of a very short duration. The only remedy the employers have, the only safeguard against encroachments from their men, is their power of obtaining the services of foreigners, for a short time. The difficulty of stopping business there is very great; the injury of delay very heavy: but the wages of labour are so good that there is less cause for discontent on the part of the workmen than elsewhere. All the strikes I heard of were on the question of hours, not of wages.

The employers are, of course, casting about to see how they can help themselves; and, as all are not wise and experienced, it is natural that some should talk of laws to prohibit Trades Unions. There is no harm in their talking of such; for the matter will never get beyond talk;—unless, indeed, the combinations of operatives should assume any forms, or comprehend any principles inconsistent with the republican spirit. The majority will not vote for any law which shall restrain any number of artisans from agreeing for what price they will sell their labour; though I heard several learned gentlemen agreeing, at dinner one day, that there ought to be such laws. On my objecting that the interest of the parties concerned would, especially in a free and rising country, settle all questions between labour and capital with more precision, fairness, and peace, than any law, it was pleaded that intimidation and outrage were practised by those who combined against those who would not join them. I found, on inquiry, that there is an ample provision of laws against intimidation and outrage; but that it is difficult to get them executed. If so, it would be also difficult to execute laws against combinations of workmen, supposing them obtained: and the grievance does not lie in the combination complained of, but somewhere else. The remedy is, (if there be indeed intimidation and outrage,) not in passing more laws, to be in like manner defied, while sufficient already exist; but in enlightening the parties on the subjects of law and social obligation.

One day, in going down Broadway, New York, the carriage in which I was, stopped for some time, in consequence of an immense procession on the side-walk having attracted the attention of all the drivers within sight. The marching gentlemen proceeded on their way, with an easy air of gentility. Banners were interposed at intervals; and, on examining these, I could scarcely believe my eyes. They told me that this was a procession of the journeymen mechanics of New York. Surely never were such dandy mechanics seen; with sleek coats, glossy hats, gay watch-guards, and doe-skin gloves!

I rejoice to have seen this sight. I had other opportunities of witnessing the prosperity of their employers; so that I could be fairly pleased at theirs. There need be no fear for the interests of either, while the natural laws of demand and supply must protect each from any serious encroachment by the other. If they will only respect the law, their temporary disagreement, and apparent opposition of interests will end in being mere readjustments of the terms on which they are to pursue their common welfare.

60. Seth Luther

As great a humbug as ever deceived any people

The following selection from a popular lecture, first given in 1832, by Seth Luther offers a far more critical portrait of the American factory system. Luther was one of the best known labor figures of the time, a leader of the Boston Trades' Union. Although he was a carpenter by trade, Luther was essentially a propagandist. His *Address to the Working Men of New England* won wide popularity among working-class audiences. Luther ridiculed the rose-colored version of factory conditions popularized by factory owners and their friends. Yet as his concluding remarks make clear he was not an inveterate foe of factories. He would not turn back the clock: the system was not to be scrapped but reformed.

We have shown how great a mass of human misery is hidden in England, under the glare of *National* wealth, and the splendor of National glory. You have visited the thick and crowded *manufacturing town,*

> Where avarice plucks the staff away,
> Whereon the weary lean,

From Seth Luther, *An Address to the Working Men of New England* (Boston: published by the author, 1832), 16–25, 30–31. Footnotes are in original.

And vice reels o'er the midnight bowl,
With song, and jest, obscene.

To hide existing, or anticipated and *inevitable* evils, of the like kind, resulting from like causes, our ears are constantly filled with the cry of *National* wealth, National glory, *American* System, and American industry. We are told that operatives are happy in our mills, and that they want no change in the regulations,[1] and that they are getting great wages, saving 25 per cent[2] over and above their living. This stuff is retailed by owners, and agents, and sold wholesale at the rate of eight dollars for a day's work of four hours in the capital at Washington. This cry is kept up by men who are endeavouring *by all the means in their power* to cut down the wages of *our own people,* and who send agents to *Europe,* to induce *foreigners* to come here, to underwork *American* citizens, to support *American* industry, and the *American* system.

The whole concern, (as now conducted) is as great a humbug as ever deceived any people. We see the system of manufacturing lauded to the skies; senators, representatives, owners, and agents of cotton mills using all means to keep out of sight the evils growing up under it. Cotton mills where cruelties are practised, excessive labour required, education neglected, and vice, as a matter of course, on the increase, are denominated 'the[3] principalities of the destitute, the palaces of the poor.' We do not pretend to say that this description applies in all its parts, to all mills alike—but we do say, that most of the causes described by Dr Kay of Manchester are in active operation in New England, and as sure as effect follows cause, the result must be the same. A member of the United States Senate seems to be *extremely* pleased with cotton mills; he says in the senate, 'Who has not been delighted with the clockwork movements of a large cotton manufactory, he had visited them often, and *always* with

1. So say the owners of slaves in all countries where human flesh and blood is bought and sold to pamper the luxury of *'we the people'* alias *we* who wield might for right.
2. See Cozzens' Report on the Manufactures of Rhode Island.
3. We imagine he never worked in one 13 or 14 hours per day.

increased delight.' He says the women work in large airy[4] apartments well warmed, they are neatly dressed, with ruddy complexions, and happy countenances; they mend the broken threads and replace the exhausted balls or broaches, and at stated periods they go to and return from their meals with light and cheerful step. (While on a visit to that pink of perfection, Waltham, I remarked that the females moved with a very light step, and well they might, for the bell rung for them to return to the mill from their homes in 19 minutes after it had rung for them to go to breakfast: some of these females boarded the largest part of a half a mile from the mill). And the grand climax is, that at the end of the week, after working like slaves for 13 or 14 hours every day, 'they enter the temples of God on the Sabbath, and thank him for all his benefits'—and the *American System* above all requires a peculiar outpouring of gratitude. We remark, that whatever girls or others may do west of the Alleghany mountains, we do not believe there can be a *single person found* east of those mountains, who ever *thanked God* for *permission* to work in a *cotton mill.*

Without being obliged to attribute wrong or mercenary motives to the Hon. Senator [Clay] (*whose talents certainly must command respect from all,* let their views in other respects be what they may), we remark, that we think he was most grossly deceived by the circumstances of his visit. We will give our *reasons,* in a few words spoken (in part) on a former occasion, on this subject. It is well known to all that when *Honourables* travel, that timely notice is given of their arrival and departure in places of note. Here we

4. So far from this, in some establishments the windows have been nailed down, and the females deprived of even fresh air, in order to support the '*American System.*'

An actual rebellion took place not long since, in consequence of this high-handed and tyrannical measure, among the 1000 females in a vast overgrown establishment. We learn that frequently the females have become entirely unmanageable in consequence of various cruelties practised on them at that place. We learn that not long since the agent newly appointed, made a rule that 'all who were not within the gates at the last stroke of the bell, was to pay a fine of 12½ cents,' whereupon the girls rose en masse. The confusion was great and the order revoked. How delightful to live in 'a principality of the destitute, a palace of the poor.'

have a case—the Honourable Senator from Kentucky is about to visit a *cotton mill*—due notice is given; the men, girls, and boys, are ordered to array themselves in their best apparel. Flowers of every hue are brought to decorate the mill, and unwreath the brows of the fair sex. If nature will not furnish the materials from the lap of summer, art supplies the deficiency. Evergreens mingle with the roses, the jasmine, and the hyacinth, to honour the *illustrious* visitor, the champion, the very Goliath of the American System. He enters! Smiles are on every brow. No *cow-hide*, or *rod*, or *'well seasoned strap'* is suffered to be seen by the Honourable senator, or permitted to disturb the enviable happiness of the inmates of this almost *celestial* habitation. The Hon. Gentleman views with keen eye the 'clock work.' He sees the rosy faces of the Houries[5] inhabiting this palace of beauty; he is in ecstasy—he is almost *dumfounded*—he enjoys the enchanting scene with the most intense delight. For an hour or more (not 14 hours) he seems to be in the regions described in Oriental song, his feelings are overpowered, and he retires, almost unconscious of the cheers which follow his steps; or if he hears the ringing shout, 'tis but to convince him, that he is in a land of reality, and not of fiction. His mind being filled with sensations, which, from their novelty, are without a name, he exclaims, 'tis a paradise; and we reply, if a Cotton Mill is a 'paradise,' it is *'Paradise Lost.'*

If we might be permitted to use a yankee privilege, and *guess* what would be the *drift* of the meditations of a person so happily wrought up, we might suppose he would *think poetically* as follows:

> I've seen them elegantly move
> Where shuttles swiftly slide,
> Methinks the *'Clock-work'* I do love,
> O'er which their fingers glide.
>
> 'Their auburn tresses carelessly
> O'erhang a neck of snow,
> And dazzlingly they glitter
> In sunset's crimson glow.'

5. Fabled beauties of the Mahometan paradise.

'They are more fair to look upon
Than sylph or fairy thing,'
More pleasant to enraptured eyes
Than budding flowers of spring.

We believe there are *many* beautiful and virtuous ladies employed in cotton mills, but we do know, notwithstanding this, that the *wives* and *daughters* of the *rich* manufacturers would no more associate with a *'factory girl,'* than they would with a *negro slave.* So much for equality in a *republican* country.

We would respectfully advise the honourable senator to travel *incognito,* when he visits Cotton Mills. If he wishes to come at the *truth,* he must not be known. Let him put on a *short jacket and trowsers,* and join the 'LOWER ORDERS' for a short time; then let him go into a factory counting room, and pull off his hat, which he will be told to do in some of our *'Republican Institutions'* [6] called Cotton Mills; then let him attempt to get work for 75 cents, or 100 for 14 hours per day instead of *eight* dollars for *four hours,* and he will then discover some of the *intrinsic beauties* of factory 'clockwork.' In that case we could show him in some of the prisons in New England, called cotton mills, instead of rosy cheeks, the *pale, sickly, haggard* countenance of the ragged child. Haggard from the *worse* than *slavish* confinement in the cotton mill. He might see that child driven up to the 'clockwork' by the cowskin, in some cases; he might see in some instances, the child taken from his bed at four in the morning, and plunged into cold water to drive away his slumbers, and prepare him for the labors in the mill. After all this he might see that child *robbed,* yes, *robbed* of a part of his time allowed for meals by moving the hands of the clock backwards, or forwards, as would best accomplish that purpose. We could show him 'clockwork' with a peculiar escapement, having power to move a whole factory village from three to six hundred miles east or west (from any other place, no *matter where*), by calculation of longitude. In one case we find Exeter N. H. 600 miles west of Boston, by the operation of this factory *'clockwork.'* The honorable gentleman might see *patent*

6. John Q. Adams' Report on Manufactures.

lever 'clockwork' of the *first quality* running on *diamonds*, which never was *guilty* of keeping the *true* time, while in the atmosphere of a manufacturing village, or in the pocket of an agent, overseer, or owner of a cotton mill. He might see in some, and not unfrequent instances, the child, and the female child too, driven up to the clockwork with the cowhide, or well seasoned strap of 'AMERICAN MANUFACTURE.' We could show him *many* females who have had corporeal punishment inflicted upon them; one girl eleven years of age who had her leg broken with a billet of wood; another, who had a board split over her head by a heartless monster in the shape of an overseer of a cotton mill 'paradise.'[7]

We, shall for want of time, (not stock) omit entering more largely into detail for the present, respecting the cruelties practised in some of the American mills. Our wish is to show that education is neglected, and that as a matter of course, because if 13 hours actual labour, is required each day, it is *impossible* to attend to education among children, or improvement among adults. With regard to hours of labour in cotton mills, there is a difference here as well as in England. In Manchester 12 hours *only* is the rule, while in some other towns in England many more are required.[8] The mills *generally* in New England, run 13 hours the year round, that is, actual labour for all hands; to which add one hour for two meals, making 14 hours actual labour—for a man, or woman, or child, must labour hard to go a quarter, and sometimes half a mile, and eat his dinner or breakfast in 30 minutes and get back to the mill. At the Eagle mills, Griswold, Connecticut, 15 hours and 10 minutes actual labour in the mill are required; at another mill in the vicinity, 14 hours of actual labour are required.

7. We do not pretend to say that all overseers are thus cruel, but we do say, that foreign overseers are frequently placed over American women and children, and, we are sorry to add, that sometimes foreigners in this country have employed American overseers to carry into effect their tyrannical rules in these mills.

8. In the cotton mills in France, 'during the longest days in summer, the help commence work at 6 o'clock A. M., work till nine, when *one hour* is allowed for breakfast, and another hour at dinner between 2 and 3 P. M., and the daily labour of 12 hours is finished about sunset.'—*Allen's Practical Tourist.* It appears, that the 'help' in Free America, are driven harder than they are in Europe. American Citizens! will you longer submit to worse tyranny than your enslaved brethren in the old world? or the slaves, in the southern parts of your own country.

It needs no argument, to prove that education *must* be, and is almost entirely neglected. Facts speak in a voice not to be misunderstood, or misinterpreted. In 8 mills all on one stream, within a distance of two miles, we have 168 persons who can neither read nor write. This is in Rhode Island. A committee of working men in Providence, report 'that in Pautucket there are at least *five hundred children,* who scarcely know what a school is. These facts, say they, are adduced to show the blighting influence of the manufacturing system as at present conducted, on the progress of education; and to add to the darkness of the picture, if blacker shades are necessary to rouse the spirit of indignation, which should glow within our breasts at such disclosures, in all the mills which the enquiries of the committee have been able to reach, books, pamphlets, and newspapers are *absolutely prohibited.* This may serve as a tolerable example for every manufacturing village in Rhode Island.' In 12 of the United States, there are 57,000 persons, male and female, employed in cotton and woollen mills, and other establishments connected with them; about two-fifths of this number, or 31,044 are under 16 years of age, and 6000 are under the age of 12 years. Of this 31,044, there are in Rhode Island *alone,* 3,472 under 16 years of age. The school fund is, in that State, raised in considerable part by lottery.

Now we all know, that the poor are generally the persons who support this legalized gambling; for the rich as a general rule, seldom buy tickets. This fund then, said to be raised by the rich, for the education of the poor, is actually drawn from the pockets of the *poor,* to be expended by the rich,[9] *on their own children,* while this large number of children, (3,472), are entirely, and totally deprived of all benefit of the school fund, by what is *called* the *American System.* Actually *robbed* of what is *emphatically* their own, by being *compelled* to labour in these *'principalities of the destitute'* and these *'palaces of the poor,'* for 13 hours per

9. By the *rich,* we here mean those, who are able to educate their own children, without resorting to the school fund. Among them will be found owners, agents, and overseers, who, many of them, take good care that their own children are educated, while the really poor children must remain ignorant, from the nature of the case.

diem, the year round. *What must be* the result of this state of things? 'We cannot regard even in anticipation, the contamination of moral and political degradation spreading its baleful influence throughout the community, through the medium of the uneducated part of the present generation, promulgated and enhanced in the future, by the increase of posterity, without starting with horror from the scene, as from the clankings of a TYRANT's chain.' [10] Perhaps, some may (as they have done) ask why do so many go to these mills, if they are such evil places. We answer, that the public are entirely deceived, as to the facts of the case. We have endeavoured to expose that deception; and further, we are authorized to say to *any man*, be he who he may, who represents the population employed in cotton mills, to be a happy and contented people, and who wish no amelioration in their condition, that the statements to that effect are FALSE. We appeal to the tens of thousands, under the *tyrannical government* of the mills, to support us in that assertion. Not only so, those who misrepresent the population thus employed, *know their own statements to be false*. It cannot be otherwise. We have said the public are deceived; we have shown in part how they are deceived; we will give more evidence to that point. If *one girl* in a mill, earns, by extra exertion, $4 per week, it is blazed abroad, from Mainc to Mexico, that the *girls* in that mill earn from one to four dollars per week; if an overseer gets 43 dollars per month, and the men under him from 10 to 20 clear of board, it is proclaimed that the men get from 10 to 43 dollars per month, 'according to their strength.' This is the same as saying, that all the officers of the United States, get from $300 to $25,000 per annum, according to their strength; and there is as much sense in one as the other, and one proves as much as the other.[11]

10. Memorial to Congress, from the Providence and Pautucket Association of Working Men.

11. A letter from Waltham to the author, says, that of all the hands there, only one gets 43 dollars per month, and that is the overseer of the machine shop; and many do not get 10 dollars per month. But a writer in the Concord paper says, they get from 10 to 43 dollars per month, *according to their strength*. We should think the Agent must be a powerful strong man, for we believe he gets 12 or 1500 dollars per year.

These factory owners are very fond of using the rule of AVERAGE, and they prove everything by that rule. One of them who said, 'the poor must work or starve,' used this rule to prove that the profit on manufacturing, was but 4 per cent. He said one factory commenced operation in 1806, and by 'judicious management,' cleared $300,000; another commencing at the same time, sunk $150,000 by 'careless and injudicious management.' Now, strike an average on this loss on one hand, and gain on the other, and the profit on Cotton mills is four per cent;[12] only give us this rule of average, and let us use it in this way, and we will prove that Washington and Arnold were both traitors, or patriots, which you please; because we will *average* the TREASON of one, with the PURE PATRIOTISM of the other, and the sum is done. By such means are the public deceived. Again, people are induced to go into mills to work, by a direct and false appeal to the passion of avarice; but why do they not leave, when they find they are deceived? We will give some of the reasons. In many mills, the overseers are ordered by the agents, to tell the help, that if they leave that establishment, the agents will write to all the other Factories, and tell their agents not to employ them. At Dover this has been done, and we know of other places where the same thing is practised. Other means are practised. If a girl is discharged from the service of the Company for any fault, and the agent is the judge in all cases, she cannot get her pay short of two weeks; so that if she has two or three dollars due, and belongs 100 or more miles from home, she must wait on that MAMMOTH COMPANY a fortnight for her pay; by this time, she is in debt for her board, and she must either go to the agent, and *humbly* ask him to give her employment, or starve. He, knowing that 'the poor must work or starve, and that the rich will take care of themselves,' *humanely* takes her into the cotton mill 'palace' on his own terms.

We do not say that this is the exact mode of procedure; but we do say, that it is a natural consequence of that one-sided and arbitrary rule. The hands are compelled to work for 'such wages as the Company sees fit to pay,' to pay all fines assessed, without

12. See answer to Interrogatories by Hon. John Whipple.

knowing what the prices or fines may be. Hands are liable to be discharged at any moment, but they cannot discharge themselves, short of a fortnight's notice. Cotton mills are called 'Republican Institutions.' At Dover, we understand, when any of the workmen go into the *'presence'* in the counting-room, they are told to pull off their hats: one man who entered the *'presence chamber'* did not do this, and gave as his reason, that no person was in when he entered; therefore, he did not conceive it necessary. He was told, 'I will let you know, you must take off your hat to respect the 'Office!' [13]

We must here give one more proof of the *Republican* nature of these institutions. Mr F.[14] a machinist of Dover, was a candidate for the Legislature of New Hampshire, set up by the Working Men. On the day of election, he was asked by S., foreman of the Company's Machine shop, if he meant to stand as a candidate. F. replied, you have had conversation enough with me to know my opinion on that subject. S. said I am authorized to say to you, that if you do stand or are elected, you will be *discharged*, and that *tomorrow morning*. F. said, if you say positively I shall be discharged, I shall not take myself out of the way on any consideration whatever. S. faltered a little, and said, I will not say positively, but probably. F. said to S., if you think I will be deprived of my rights by such threats, you don't know me. Am I to be deprived of my rights? my citizenship by a *Manufacturing Company?* On this they separated. F. was not discharged the next day, because the supposition is, the Company had no excuse which would satisfy the public. Mr F. was elected, and attended the session of the legislature. On his return he called on the Agent, who told him he had no more work for him, and said F. had broken his contract. He asked, what is the contract? You agreed to work for a year. You are mistaken, I am under no such contract. The agent said, I directed Mr S., an officer under me, to make such a contract with all who would do so. Now said F. I can tell

13. It is customary in London, to bow to a nobleman's carriage as it passes, whether empty or not.

14. The names of Parties are in possession of the Author of this address, and can be known at any time.

you to what time you allude. At that time there was a considerable complaint of low wages. Mr S. came into the shop, and said, to all those who were satisfied with the wages, that would or should be the standard for the year. I said for one I shall be satisfied. Now suppose I had gone to see my friends three or four weeks, would you have discharged me? No, said the Agent. If I had been unwell, or about street, or any where *else*, except at the Legislature, would you have discharged me? No, said the Agent. I am informed that this Mr F. bears a character without reproach, and was before on friendly terms with S. During the conversation on election day, F. said to S., It has always been said, that Manufacturing Corporations are aristocratical, and although they deny it in all cases, this proves the allegation to a demonstration.[15] But how does this affect the persons who are not employed in the mills? what have we to do with this tyranny in the mills? We answer, that the owners of mills oppose all reduction in the hours of labour, for the purposes of mental culture. Not that they care about hours of labour in *Cities*, but they fear the 'contagion' will reach their SLAVE MILLS. Hence they go into the shop of the Carpenter, and others who carry on business, and actually *forbid* them to employ what they sneeringly call '*ten hour* men.' Telling the employers, you shall not have our work unless you do as WE say. We have appealed to their sense of justice, their sense of humanity, their love of country, to consider the evils they are bringing on the poor, through ignorance. What has been the reply? one says 'if a man offers to work for me ten hours, I will kick him off my premises;' another says, I will shut down my gates, and you will starve in a week, and rather than do *that*, you will work on our terms. Another says, 'O, they can't stand it more than a day or two, and they will soon come back and BEG to go to work.' While the official[16] organ of Rhode Island Manufacturers

15. Mr W. G. of Lowell, we understand, was discharged from employ, for attending a Convention of Working men, in Providence, Rhode Island, December 5, 1831. In retaliation for this violation of all right principle, the Working men of Lowell turned Mr K. B. (Agent at Lowell) out of the Legislature of Massachusetts, and put Mr W. G. in his place.

16. Benjamin Cozzens.

gravely asserts, that these same people are saving 25 per cent of their wages, clear gain, and a Rhode Island Representative is telling us how much better we are situated than *southern* slaves. Now when these same men want the votes of the Working men, they will say, 'in strains as sweet as angels use,' Fellow Citizens, we want your assistance, give us 'your voices, your voices, your *sweet* voices.' But if you want time to improve your minds, take care of your families, and educate your children, you are called '*Disturbers of the peace*,' 'Agitators,' 'An unholy alliance,' Disorganizers, a 'Dangerous Combination' against the *higher* ORDERS. Such, Fellow Citizens of New England, is the language used to you and respecting you. While these men are boasting that they 'can take care of themselves;' while they are dependent on you every moment for the protection of that property, which they have obtained from your *bones*, and *sinews*, and *hearts-blood*, they are using it in an attempt to starve you into submission. This is no fiction; the speaker has heard merchants say, in a public room, in a public Hotel in Boston, that 'the Shipwrights, Caulkers and Gravers, had given up, and thrown themselves entirely on our mercy.' 'OUR MERCY!' are we ready for that word? Does not your hearts throb with one pulsation as you answer No! Is not that reply echoed from old Bunker's Height, where *Freemen* stood and *Freemen* fell *rejecting* the *mercy*, and *scorning* the *power* of TYRANTS.

Are not our feelings the same in this case? If they are not, we may well ask ourselves, as we falter from our duty to ourselves and country,

Where shall we bury our shame?
  Where, in what desolate place,
Hide the last wreck of a name,
  Thus broken and stained by disgrace?

. . . It has been said, that the speaker is opposed to *the* American System. It turns on one single point,—If these abuses are *the* American System, he is opposed. But let him see *an* American System, where education and intelligence is generally diffused, and the enjoyment of *life* and *liberty* secured to all; he then is ready to support *such* a system. But so long as our government secures exclusive privileges to a *very small part of the community*, and leaves the majority the '*lawful prey*' to avarice—so long does he contend against *any* 'System' so exceedingly unjust and unequal in its operation. He knows, that we must have manufactures. It is impossible to do without them; but he is yet to learn that it is necessary, or just, that manufactures must be sustained by injustice, cruelty, ignorance, vice, and misery; which is now the fact to a startling degree. If what we have stated be true, and we challenge denial, what must be done? Must we fold our arms and say, It always was so, and always will be. If we did so, would it not almost rouse from their graves the heroes of our revolution? Would not the cold marble, representing our beloved Washington, start into *life*, and reproach us for our *cowardice?* Let the word be—Onward! onward! We know the difficulties are great, and the obstacles many; but, as yet, we 'know our rights, and knowing, dare maintain.' We wish to injure no man, and we are determined not to be injured as we have been; we wish nothing, but those equal rights, which were designed for us all. And although wealth, and prejudice, and slander, and abuse, are all brought to bear on us, we have one consolation—'*We are the Majority.*'

Lot of the Free Negro

61. Edward Abdy

Colored people are not admitted to places of worship

Slaves were not the only black people in antebellum America. According to the modern scholar Leon Litwack the only significant advantage free

From Edward Abdy, *Journal of a Residence and Tour in the United States of North America, 1833–1834* (London: John Murray, 1835), 3 vols., I, pp. 133–135.

Negroes had over slaves was the ability of the former to criticize or protest against their treatment. Nothing offended most visitors more than America's treatment of its colored population. Some of the most trenchant observations of this unattractive phenomenon were made by the English Quaker visitor, Edward Abdy.

The people of Boston are, indeed, as civil and obliging as any I ever saw. One person took me through his house to direct me on my way to a street I wanted to find; and another sent her boy with me to point out a house I was looking for in the neighbourhood.

How far the aristocracy of the skin is carried in this pious city, may be seen by a curious document that was put into my hands by an abolitionist. A free black, some few years ago, came into possession of a pew in one of the churches here. It was the only thing he could obtain from a man who was unable, or unwilling, to pay a legal claim he had upon him. Having furnished it, he offered it for sale. Not finding a purchaser at the price he demanded,—and few would be likely to give the full value for what no one imagined the owner would dare to make use of,—he determined to occupy it himself;—whether he was unconscious of the offence he was about to give, or thought he might as well speculate upon the white man's pride, as, it would seem, the white man had speculated upon his submissiveness. The sensation produced by his unexpected appearance among the favored children of Nature in the very sanctum sanctorum of their distinctions, can be described by those only who witnessed it. The next Sunday, he took his wife and children with him.—It should be observed that the colored people are not admitted to places of worship, except to small pews or boxes set apart expressly for them, and so placed that they can hear without offending the fastidious delicacy of the congregation.—At Albany, there is one where a curtain is placed in front to conceal the occupants, when there are any; for those for whom they are destined, seldom enter them, and speak of them with the contempt they deserve, as "martin-holes" and "human menageries." It was now high time that notice should be taken of this contumacious spirit; and the intruder received the two following notes.

Mr. Brinsley
Sir,

IF you have any pew-furniture in pew No. 38, Park Street Meeting-house, you will remove it this afternoon.

GEORGE ODIORNE, *for the Committee.*

March 6, 1830

With the above was a copy of a note, written the day before to this Agent of the Committee, in these words.

Dear Sir,

PEW No. 38 in Park Street Church is let to Mr. Andrew Ellison.

Yours respectfully,
J. BUMSTEAD

The other letter was addressed "to Mr. Frederick Brinsley, colored man, Elm Street"; the contents are as follow.

Boston, March 6, 1830

Mr. Frederick Brinsley
Sir,

THE Prudential committee of Park Street Church, notify you not to occupy any pew on the lower floor of Park Street Meeting-house on any Sabbath, or on any other day, during the time of Divine worship, after this date—and, if you go there, with such intent, you will hazard the consequences. The pews in the upper galleries are at your service.

GEORGE ODIORNE, *for the Committee.*

Mr. Brinsley, on going again, found a constable at the pew-door. No further attempt was made to assert the rights of property against such a formidable combination; and we may seek in vain for the consequences, which Mr. Odiorne, with official brevity, says, would have been hazarded by another visit to the house of God. The offender is now removed from this scene of persecution and mortification, to a place "where the wicked cease from troubling and the weary are at rest."

62. Thomas Hamilton

A Negro is a creature marked out for degradation

The following selection is interesting as much for the light it throws on the observer as on what he has observed. In pondering the *de facto* in contrast to the *de jure* status of the free Negro of the North, a fairminded English visitor finds American civilization inferior to European at least in this not insignificant respect.

Having resolved to devote the day to the inspection of schools, I went from that under the superintendence of Professor Griscom, to another for the education of children of colour. I here found about a hundred boys, in whose countenances might be traced every possible gradation of complexion between those of the swarthy Ethiop and florid European. Indeed, several of the children were so fair, that I certainly never should have discovered the lurking taint of African descent. In person, they were clean and neat; and, though of course, the offspring of the very lowest class of the people, there was nothing in their dress or appearance indicative of abject poverty. The master struck me as an intelligent and benevolent man. He frankly answered all my questions, and evidently took pride in the proficiency of his pupils.

It has often happened to me, since my arrival in this country, to hear it gravely maintained by men of education and intelligence, that the Negroes were an inferior race, a link as it were between man and the brutes. Having enjoyed few opportunities of observation on people of colour in my own country, I was now glad to be enabled to enlarge by knowledge on a subject so interesting. I therefore requested the master to inform me whether the results of his experience had led to the inference, that the aptitude of the Negro children for acquiring knowledge was inferior to that of the whites. In reply, he assured me they had not done so; and, on the contrary, declared, that, in sagacity,

From Thomas Hamilton, *Men and Manners in America* (Philadelphia: Carey, Lea and Blanchard, 1833), 55–60. Footnote is in the original.

perseverance, and capacity for the acquisition and retention of knowledge, his poor despised scholars were equal to any boys he had ever known. "But, alas, sir!" said he, "to what end are these poor creatures taught acquirement, from the exercise of which they are destined to be debarred, by the prejudices of society? It is, surely, but a cruel mockery to cultivate talents, when, in the present state of public feeling, there is no field open for their useful employment. Be his acquirements what they may, a Negro is still a Negro, or, in other words, a creature marked out for degradation, and exclusion from those objects which stimulate the hopes and powers of other men."

I observed, in reply, that I was not aware that, in those States in which slavery had been abolished, any such barrier existed as that to which he alluded. "In the State of New York, for instance," I asked, "are not all offices and professions open to the man of colour as well as to the white?"

"I see, sir," replied he, "that you are not a native of this country, or you would not have asked such a question. "He then went on to inform me, that the exclusion in question did not arise from any legislative enactment, but from the tyranny of that prejudice, which, regarding the poor black as a being of inferior order, works its own fulfilment in making him so. There was no answering this, for it accorded too well with my own observations in society, not to carry my implicit belief.

The master then proceeded to explain the system of education adopted in the school, and subsequently afforded many gratifying proofs of the proficiency of his scholars. One class was employed in navigation, and worked several complicated problems with great accuracy and rapidity. A large proportion was perfectly conversant with arithmetic, and not a few with the lower mathematics. A long and rigid examination took place in geography, in the course of which questions were answered with facility, which, I confess, would have puzzled me exceedingly, had they been addressed to myself.

I had become so much interested in the little party-coloured crowd before me, that I recurred to our former discourse, and inquired of the master, what would probably become of his scholars on their being sent out into the world? Some trades, some description of labour of course were open to them, and I expressed my desire to know what these were. He told me they were few. The class studying navigation, were destined to be sailors; but let their talents be what they might, it was impossible they could rise to be officers of the paltriest merchantman that entered the waters of the United States. The office of cook or steward was indeed within the scope of their ambition; but it was just as feasible for the poor creatures to expect to become Chancellor of the State, as mate of a ship. In other pursuits, it was the same. Some would become stonemasons, or bricklayers, and to the extent of carrying a hod, or handling a trowel, the course was clear before them; but the office of master-bricklayer was open to them in precisely the same sense as the Professorship of Natural Philosophy. No white artificer would serve under a coloured master. The most degraded Irish emigrant would scout the idea with indignation. As carpenters, shoemakers, or tailors, they were still arrested by the same barrier. In either of the latter capacities, indeed, they might work for people of their own complexion, but no *gentleman* would ever think of ordering garments of any sort from a *schneider* of cuticle less white than his own. Grocers they might be, but then who could perceive the possibility of a respectable household matron purchasing tea or spiceries from a vile "Nigger?" As barbers, they were more fortunate, and in that capacity might even enjoy the privilege of taking the President of the United States by the nose. Throughout the Union, the department of domestic service particularly belongs to them, though recently they are beginning to find rivals in the Irish emigrants, who come annually in swarms like locusts.

On the whole, I cannot help considering it a mistake to suppose, that slavery has been abolished in the Northern States of the Union. It is true, indeed, that in these States the power of compulsory labour no longer exists; and that one human being within their limits, can no longer claim property in the thews and sinews of another. But is this all that is implied in the boon of freedom? If the word mean any thing, it must mean the enjoyment of equal rights, and the unfettered exercise in each individual of such powers and faculties as God has given him. In this true meaning of the word, it may be safely asserted, that this poor degraded caste are still slaves. They are subjected to the most grinding and humiliating of all slaveries, that of universal and unconquerable prejudice. The whip, indeed, has been removed from the back of the Negro, but the chains are still on his limbs, and he bears the brand of degradation on his forehead. What is it but the mere abuse of language to call him *free,* who is tyrannically deprived of all the motives to exertion which animate other men? The law, in truth, has left him in that most pitiable of all conditions, *a masterless slave.*

It cannot be denied, that the Negro population are still compelled, *as a class,* to be the hewers of wood, and drawers of water, to their fellow-citizens. *Citizens!* there is, indeed, something ludicrous in the application of the word to these miserable Pariahs. What privileges do they enjoy as such? Are they admissible upon a jury? Can they enrol themselves in the militia? Will a white man eat with them, or extend to them the hand of fellowship? Alas! if these men, so irresistibly manacled to degradation, are to be called *free,* tell us, at least, what stuff are slaves made of!

But on this subject, perhaps, another tone of expression—of thought, there can be no other—may be more judicious. I have already seen abundant proofs, that the prejudices against the coloured portion of the population, prevailed to an extent, of which an Englishman could have formed no idea. But many enlightened men, I am convinced are above them. To these I would appeal. They have already begun the work of raising this unfortunate race from the almost brutal state to which tyranny and injustice had condemned it. But let them not content themselves with such delusive benefits as the extension of the right of suffrage, recently conferred by the Legislature of New York.* The opposition to be overcome, is not that of *law,* but of

* The Legislature of New York, in 1829, extended the right of suffrage to men of colour, *possessed of a clear freehold estate, without encumbrance, of the value of 250 dollars.* A very safe concession, no doubt, since to balance the *black interest,* the same right of suffrage was granted to *every* white male of twenty-one years,

opinion. If, in unison with the ministers of religion, they will set their shoulders to the wheel, and combat prejudice with reason, ignorance with knowledge, and pharisaical assumption with the mild tenets of Christianity, they must succeed in infusing a better tone into the minds and hearts of their countrymen. It is true, indeed, the victory will not be achieved in a day, nor probably in an age, but assuredly it will come at last. In achieving it, they will become the benefactors, not only of the Negro population, but of their fellow-citizens. They will give freedom to both; for the man is really not more free, whose mind is shackled by degrading prejudice, than he who is its victim.

As illustrative of the matter in hand, I am tempted here to relate an anecdote, though somewhat out of place, as it did not occur till my return to New York the following spring. Chancing one day at the Ordinary at Bunker's to sit next an English merchant from St. Domingo, in the course of conversation, he mentioned the following circumstances. The son of a Haytian general, high in the favour of Boyer, recently accompanied him to New York, which he came to visit for pleasure and instruction. This young man, though a mulatto, was pleasing in manner, and with more intelligence than is usually to be met with in a country in which education is so defective. At home, he had been accustomed to receive all the deference due to his rank, and when he arrived in New York, it was with high anticipations of the pleasure that awaited him in a city so opulent and enlightened.

On landing, he inquired for the best hotel, and directed his baggage to be conveyed there. He was rudely refused admittance, and tried several others with similar result. At length he was forced to take up his abode in a miserable lodging-house kept by a Negro woman. The pride of the young Haytian (who, sooth to say, was something of a dandy, and made imposing display of gold chains and brooches,) was sadly galled by this, and the experience of every hour tended farther to confirm the conviction, that, in this country, he was regarded as a degraded being, with whom the

who has been one year in the State. It might be curious to know how many coloured voters became qualified by this enactment. They must, indeed, have been *rari nantes in gurgite vasto* of the election.

meanest white man would hold it disgraceful to associate. In the evening, he went to the theatre, and tendered his money to the box-keeper. It was tossed back to him, with a disdainful intimation, that the place for persons of his colour was the upper gallery.

On the following morning, my countryman, who had frequently been a guest at the table of his father, paid him a visit. He found the young Haytian in despair. All his dreams of pleasure were gone, and he returned to his native island by the first conveyance, to visit the United States no more.

This young man should have gone to Europe.—Should he visit England, he may feel quite secure, that, if he have money in his pocket, he will offer himself at no hotel, from Land's End to John O'Groat's house, where he will not meet with a very cordial reception. Churches, theatres, operas, concerts, coaches, chariots, cabs, vans, wagons, steam-boats, railway-carriages and air-balloons, will all be open to him as the daylight. He may repose on cushions of down or of air, he may charm his ear with music, and his palate with luxuries of all sorts. He may travel *en prince*, or *en roturier*, precisely as his fancy dictates, and may enjoy even the honours of a crowned head, if he will only pay like one. In short, so long as he carries certain golden ballast about with him, all will go well. But when that is done, his case is pitiable. He will then become familiar with the provisions of the vagrant act, and Mr. Roe or Mr. Ballantine will recommend exercise on the treadmill, for the benefit of his constitution. Let him but show his nose abroad, and a whole host of parish overseers will take alarm. The new police will bait him like a bull; and should he dare approach even the lowest eating-house, the master will shut the door in his face. If he ask charity, he will be told to work. If he beg work, he will be told to get about his business. If he steal, he will be found a free passage to Botany Bay, and be dressed gratis on his arrival, in an elegant suit of yellow. If he rob, he will be found a free passage to another world, in which, as there is no paying or receiving in payment, we may hope that his troubles will be at an end for ever.

Lot of the Woman

63. Harriet Martineau

Indulgence is given her as a substitute for justice

The belief was widespread that women in America were treated better and were more respected than elsewhere. Tocqueville went so far as to attribute America's greatness primarily to its allegedly remarkable and happy women. Feminists and their sympathizers did not agree. Few denied that American women were freer and shown more outward signs of respect than were their sisters abroad. What critics decried were the subordinate status and the lack of opportunity for self-realization of American women, that were no less objectionable for being in some respects subtle. Harriet Martineau believed that in terms of their material conditions American women *were* well off. But as the following passage indicates, she was dismayed at a treatment in which women were regarded not as equal to men but as adornments, even if sometimes pampered.

If a test of civilisation be sought, none can be so sure as the condition of that half of society over which the other half has power,—from the exercise of the right of the strongest. Tried by this test, the American civilisation appears to be of a lower order than might have been expected from some other symptoms of its social state. The Americans have, in the treatment of women, fallen below, not only their own democratic principles, but the practice of some parts of the Old World.

The unconsciousness of both parties as to the injuries suffered by women at the hands of those who hold the power is a sufficient proof of the low degree of civilisation in this important particular at which they rest. While woman's intellect is confined, her morals crushed, her health ruined, her weaknesses encouraged, and her strength punished, she is told that her lot is cast in the paradise of women; and there is no country in the world where

From Harriet Martineau, *Society in America*, II, pp. 226–230, 245, 255–257.

there is so much boasting of the "chivalrous" treatment she enjoys. That is to say,—she has the best place in stage-coaches: when there are not chairs enough for everybody, the gentlemen stand: she hears oratorical flourishes on public occasions about wives and home, and apostrophes to woman: her husband's hair stands on end at the idea of her working, and he toils to indulge her with money: she has liberty to get her brain turned by religious excitements, that her attention may be diverted from morals, politics, and philosophy; and, especially, her morals are guarded by the strictest observance of propriety in her presence. In short, indulgence is given her as a substitute for justice. Her case differs from that of the slave, as to the principle, just so far as this; that the indulgence is large and universal, instead of petty and capricious. In both cases, justice is denied on no better plea than the right of the strongest. In both cases, the acquiescence of the many, and the burning discontent of the few, of the oppressed, testify, the one to the actual degradation of the class, and the other to its fitness for the enjoyment of human rights.

The intellect of woman is confined. I met with immediate proof of this. Within ten days of my landing, I encountered three outrageous pedants, among the ladies; and in my progress through the country I met with a greater variety and extent of female pedantry than the experience of a lifetime in Europe would afford. I could fill the remainder of my volume with sketches: but I forbear, through respect even for this very pedantry. Where intellect has a fair chance, there is no pedantry, among men or women. It is the result of an intellect which cannot be wholly passive, but must demonstrate some force, and does so through the medium of narrow morals. Pedantry indicates the first struggle of intellect with its restraints; and it is therefore a hopeful symptom.

The intellect of woman is confined by an unjustifiable restriction of both methods of education,—by express teaching, and by the discipline of circumstance. The former, though prior in the chronology of each individual, is a direct consequence of the latter, as regards the whole of the sex. As women have none of the objects in life for which an enlarged education is considered requisite, the education is not given. Female education in America is much what it is in England. There is a profession of some things being taught which are supposed necessary because everybody learns them. They serve to fill up time, to occupy attention harmlessly, to improve conversation, and to make women something like companions to their husbands, and able to teach their children somewhat. But what is given is, for the most part, passively received; and what is obtained is, chiefly, by means of the memory. There is rarely or never a careful ordering of influences for the promotion of clear intellectual activity. Such activity, when it exceeds that which is necessary to make the work of the teacher easy, is feared and repressed. This is natural enough, as long as women are excluded from the objects for which men are trained. While there are natural rights which women may not use, just claims which are not to be listened to, large objects which may not be approached, even in imagination, intellectual activity is dangerous: or, as the phrase is, unfit. Accordingly, marriage is the only object left open to woman. Philosophy she may pursue only fancifully, and under pain of ridicule: science only as a pastime, and under a similar penalty. Art is declared to be left open: but the necessary learning, and, yet more, the indispensable experience of reality, are denied to her. Literature is also said to be permitted: but under what penalties and restrictions? . . . Nothing is thus left for women but marriage.—Yes; Religion, is the reply.—Religion is a temper, not a pursuit. It is the moral atmosphere in which human beings are to live and move. Men do not live to breathe: they breathe to live. A German lady of extraordinary powers and endowments, remarked to me with amazement on all the knowledge of the American women being based on theology. She observed that in her own country theology had its turn with other sciences, as a pursuit: but nowhere, but with the American women, had she known it make the foundation of all other knowledge. Even while thus complaining, this lady stated the case too favourably. American women have not the requisites for the study of theology. The difference between theology and religion, the science and the temper, is yet scarcely known among them. It is religion which they pursue as an occupation; and hence its small results upon the conduct, as well as upon the intellect. We are driven back upon marriage as the only appointed object in life: and upon the conviction that the sum and substance of female education in America, as in England, is training women to consider marriage as the sole object in life, and to pretend that they do not think so.

The morals of women are crushed. If there be any human power and business and privilege which is absolutely universal, it is the discovery and adoption of the principle and laws of duty. As every individual, whether man or woman, has a reason and a conscience, this is a work which each is thereby authorised to do for him or herself. But it is not only virtually prohibited to beings who, like the American women, have scarcely any objects in life proposed to them; but the whole apparatus of opinion is brought to bear offensively upon individuals among women who exercise freedom of mind in deciding upon what duty is, and the methods by which it is to be pursued. There is nothing extraordinary to the disinterested observer in women being so grieved at the case of slaves,—slave wives and mothers, as well as spirit-broken men,—as to wish to do what they could for their relief: there is nothing but what is natural in their being ashamed of the cowardice of such white slaves of the north as are deterred by intimidation from using their rights of speech and of the press, in behalf of the suffering race, and in their resolving not to do likewise: there is nothing but what is justifiable in their using their moral freedom, each for herself, in neglect of the threats of punishment: yet there were no bounds to the efforts made to crush the actions of women who thus used their human powers in the abolition question, and the convictions of those who looked on, and who might possibly be warmed into free action by the beauty of what they saw. . . .

The greater number of American women have home and its affairs, wherewith to occupy themselves. Wifely and motherly occupation may be called the sole business of woman there. If she has not that, she has nothing. The only alternative, as I have said, is making an occupation of either religion or dissipation; neither of which is fit to be so used: the one being a state of mind; the other altogether a negation when not taken in alternation with business.

It must happen that where all women have only one serious object, many of them will be unfit for that object. In the United States, as elsewhere, there are women no more fit to be wives and mothers than to be statesmen and generals; no more fit for any responsibility whatever, than for the maximum of responsibility. There is no need to describe such: they may be seen everywhere. I allude to them only for the purpose of mentioning that many of this class shirk some of their labours and cares, by taking refuge in boarding-houses. It is a circumstance very unfavourable to the character of some American women, that boarding-house life has been rendered compulsory by the scarcity of labour,—the difficulty of obtaining domestic service. The more I saw of boarding-house life, the worse I thought of it; though I saw none but the best. Indeed, the degrees of merit in such establishments weigh little in the consideration of the evil of their existence at all. . . .

As for the occupations with which American ladies fill up their leisure; what has been already said will show that there is no great weight or diversity of occupation. Many are largely engaged in charities, doing good or harm according to the enlightenment of mind which is carried to the work. In New England, a vast deal of time is spent in attending preachings, and other religious meetings: and in paying visits, for religious purposes, to the poor and sorrowful. The same results follow from this practice that may be witnessed wherever it is much pursued. In as far as sympathy is kept up, and acquaintanceship between different classes in society is occasioned, the practice is good. In as far as it unsettles the minds of the visitors, encourages a false craving for religious excitement, tempts to spiritual interference on the one hand, and cant on the other, and humours or oppresses those who need such offices least, while it alienates those who want them most, the practice is bad. I am disposed to think that much good is done, and much harm: and that, whenever women have a greater charge of indispensable business on their hands, so as to do good and reciprocate religious sympathy by laying hold of opportunities, instead of by making occupation, more than the present good will be done, without any of the harm.

All American ladies are more or less literary: and some are so to excellent purpose: to the saving of their minds from vacuity. Readers are plentiful: thinkers are rare. Minds are of a very passive character: and it follows that languages are much cultivated. If ever a woman was pointed out to me as distinguished for information, I might be sure beforehand that she was a linguist. I met with a great number of ladies who read Latin; some Greek; some Hebrew; some German. With the exception of the last, the learning did not seem to be of much use to them, except as a harmless exercise. I met with more intellectual activity, more general power, among many ladies who gave little time to books, than among those who are distinguished as being literary. I did not meet with a good artist among all the ladies in the States. I never had the pleasure of seeing a good drawing, except in one instance; or, except in two, of hearing good music. The entire failure of all attempts to draw is still a mystery to me. The attempts are incessant; but the results are below criticism. Natural philosophy is not pursued to any extent by women. There is some pretension to mental and moral philosophy; but the less that is said on that head the better.

This is a sad account of things. It may tempt some to ask 'what then are the American women?' They are better educated by Providence than by men. The lot of humanity is theirs: they have labour, probation, joy, and sorrow. They are good wives; and, under the teaching of nature, good mothers. They have, within the range of their activity, good sense, good temper, and good manners. Their beauty is very remarkable; and, I think, their wit no less. Their charity is overflowing, if it were but more enlightened: and it may be supposed that they could not exist without religion. It appears to superabound; but it is not usually of a healthy character. It may seem harsh to say this: but is it not the fact that religion emanates from the nature, from the moral state of the individual? Is it not therefore true that unless the nature be completely exercised, the moral state harmonised, the religion cannot be healthy?

One consequence, mournful and injurious, of the 'chivalrous' taste and temper of a country with regard to its women is that it is difficult, where it is not impossible, for women to earn their bread.

Where it is a boast that women do not labour, the encouragement and rewards of labour are not provided. It is so in America. In some parts, there are now so many women dependent on their own exertions for a maintenance, that the evil will give way before the force of circumstances. In the meantime, the lot of poor women is sad. Before the opening of the factories, there were but three resources; teaching, needle-work, and keeping boarding-houses or hotels. Now, there are the mills; and women are employed in printing-offices; as compositors, as well as folders and stitchers.

I dare not trust myself to do more than touch on this topic. There would be little use in dwelling upon it; for the mischief lies in the system by which women are depressed, so as to have the greater number of objects of pursuit placed beyond their reach, more than in any minor arrangements which might be rectified by an exposure of particular evils.

64. Frances Trollope

The lamentable insignificance of the American woman

Mrs. Trollope like Miss Martineau was a well-educated woman who believed that American civilization was seriously flawed by its treatment of females. No one has written better accounts of the insipid lives led by American women of the middle and upper classes. Their chief purpose in life was to marry. After marriage many of them appeared to spend a day typically with no loftier objective than somehow getting through it.

Let me be permitted to describe the day of a Philadelphian lady of the first class, and the inference I would draw from it will be better understood.

It may be said that the most important feature in a woman's history is her maternity. It is so; but the object of the present

From Frances Trollope, *Domestic Manners of the Americans*, pp. 280–285.

observation is the social, and not the domestic influence of woman.

This lady shall be the wife of a senator and a lawyer in the highest repute and practice. She has a very handsome house, with white marble steps and door-posts, and a delicate silver knocker and door-handle; she has very handsome drawing-rooms, very handsomely furnished, (there is a sideboard in one of them, but it is very handsome, and has very handsome decanters and cut glass water-jugs upon it); she has a very handsome carriage, and a very handsome free black coachman; she is always very handsomely dressed; and, moreover, she is very handsome herself.

She rises, and her first hour is spent in the scrupulously nice arrangement of her dress; she descends to her parlour neat, stiff, and silent; her breakfast is brought in by her free black footman; she eats her fried ham and her salt fish, and drinks her coffee in silence, while her husband reads one newspaper, and puts another under his elbow; and then, perhaps, she washes the cups and saucers. Her carriage is ordered at eleven; till that hour she is employed in the pastry-room, her snow-white apron protecting her mouse-coloured silk. Twenty minutes before her carriage should appear, she retires to her chamber, as she calls it, shakes, and folds up her still snow-white apron, smooths her rich dress, and with nice care, sets on her elegant bonnet, and all the handsome *et cætera;* then walks down stairs, just at the moment that her free black coachman announces to her free black footman that the carriage waits. She steps into it, and gives the word, "Drive to the Dorcas society." Her footman stays at home to clean the knives, but her coachman can trust his horses while he opens the carriage door, and his lady not being accustomed to a hand or an arm, gets out very safely without, though one of her own is occupied by a work-basket, and the other by a large roll of all those indescribable matters which ladies take as offerings to Dorcas societies. She enters the parlour appropriated for the meeting, and finds seven other ladies, very like herself, and takes her place among them; she presents her contribution, which is accepted with a gentle circular smile, and her parings of broad cloth, her ends of ribbon, her gilt paper, and her minikin pins, are added to the parings of broad cloth, the ends of ribbon, the gilt paper, and the minikin pins with which the table is already covered; she also produces from her basket three ready-made pincushions, four ink-wipers, seven paper-matches, and a paste-board watch-case; these are welcomed with acclamations, and the youngest lady present deposits them carefully on shelves, amid a prodigious quantity of similar articles. She then produces her thimble, and asks for work; it is presented to her, and the eight ladies all stitch together for some hours.

Their talk is of priests and of missions; of the profits of their last sale, of their hopes from the next; of the doubt whether young Mr. This, or young Mr. That should receive the fruits of it to fit him out for Liberia; of the very ugly bonnet seen at church on Sabbath morning, of the very handsome preacher who performed on Sabbath afternoon, and of the very large collection made on Sabbath evening. This lasts till three, when the carriage again appears, and the lady and her basket return home; she mounts to her chamber, carefully sets aside her bonnet and its appurte-nances, puts on her scolloped black silk apron, walks into the kitchen to see that all is right, then into the parlour, where, having cast a careful glance over the table prepared for dinner, she sits down, work in hand, to await her spouse. He comes, shakes hands with her, spits, and dines. The conversation is not much, and ten minutes suffices for the dinner; fruit and toddy, the newspaper and the work-bag succeed. In the evening the gentleman, being a savant, goes to the Wister society, and afterwards plays a snug rubber at a neighbor's. The lady receives at tea a young missionary and three members of the Dorcas society.

And so ends her day.

For some reason or other, which English people are not very likely to understand, a great number of young married persons board by the year, instead of "going to house-keeping," as they call having an establishment of their own. Of course this statement does not include persons of large fortune, but it does include very many whose rank in society would make such a mode of life quite impossible with us. I can hardly imagine a contrivance more effectual for ensuring the insignificance of a woman, than marrying her at seventeen, and placing her in a boarding-house. Nor can I easily imagine a life of more uniform dulness for the lady herself; but this certainly is a matter of taste. I have heard many ladies declare that it is "just quite the perfection of comfort to have nothing to fix for oneself." Yet despite these assurances I always experienced a feeling which hovered between pity and contempt, when I contemplated their mode of existence.

How would a newly-married Englishwoman endure it, her head and her heart full of the one dear scheme—

Well ordered home, *his* dear delight to make?

She must rise exactly in time to reach the boarding table at the hour appointed for breakfast, or she will get a stiff bow from the lady president, cold coffee, and no egg. I have been sometimes greatly amused upon these occasions by watching a little scene in which the bye-play had much more meaning than the words uttered. The fasting, but tardy lady, looks round the table, and having ascertained that there was no egg left, says distinctly, "I will take an egg if you please." But as this is addressed to no one in particular, no one in particular answers it, unless it happen that her husband is at table before her, and then he says, "There are no eggs, my dear." Whereupon the lady president evidently cannot hear, and the greedy culprit who has swallowed two eggs (for there are always as many eggs as noses) looks pretty considerably afraid of being found out. The breakfast proceeds in sombre silence, save that sometimes a parrot, and sometimes a canary bird, ventures to utter a timid note. When it is finished, the gentlemen hurry to their occupations, and the quiet ladies mount the stairs, some to the first, some to the second, and some to the third stories, in an inverse proportion to the number of dollars paid, and ensconce themselves in their respective chambers. As to what they do there it is not very easy to say; but I believe they clear-starch a little, and iron a little, and sit in a rocking-chair, and sew a great deal. I always observed that the ladies who boarded wore more elaborately worked collars and petticoats than any one else. The plough is hardly a more blessed instrument in America than the needle. How could they live without it? But time and the needle wear through the longest morning, and happily the American morning is not very long, even though they breakfast at eight.

It is generally about two o'clock that the boarding gentlemen meet the boarding ladies at dinner. Little is spoken, except a whisper between the married pairs. Sometimes a sulky bottle of wine flanks the plate of one or two individuals, but it adds nothing to the mirth of the meeting, and seldom more than one glass to the good cheer of the owners. It is not then, and it is not there, that the gentlemen of the Union drink. Soon, very soon, the silent meal is done, and then, if you mount the stairs after them, you will find from the doors of the more affectionate and indulgent wives, a smell of cigars steam forth, which plainly indicates the felicity of the couple within. If the gentleman be a very polite husband, he will, as soon as he has done smoking and drinking his toddy, offer his arm to his wife, as far as the corner of the street, where his store, or his office is situated, and there he will leave her to turn which way she likes. As this is the hour for being full dressed, of course she turns the way she can be most seen. Perhaps she pays a few visits; perhaps she goes to chapel; or, perhaps, she enters some store where her husband deals, and ventures to order a few notions; and then she goes home again—no, not home—I will not give that name to a boarding-house, but she re-enters the cold heartless atmosphere in which she dwells, where hospitality can never enter, and where interest takes the management instead of affection. At tea they all meet again, and a little trickery is perceptible to a nice observer in the manner of partaking the pound-cake, &c. After this, those who are happy enough to have engagements, hasten to keep them; those who have not, either mount again to the solitude of their chamber, or, what appeared to me much worse, remain in the common sitting-room, in a society cemented by no tie, endeared by no connection, which choice did not bring together, and which the slightest motive would break asunder. I remarked that the gentlemen were generally obliged to go out every evening on business, and, I confess, the arrangement did not surprise me.

It is not thus that the women can obtain that influence in society which is allowed to them in Europe, and to which, both sages and men of the world have agreed in ascribing such salutary effects. It is in vain that "collegiate institutes" are formed for young ladies, or that "academic degrees" are conferred upon them. It is after marriage, and when these young attempts upon all the sciences are forgotten, that the lamentable insignificance of the American women appears, and till this be remedied, I venture to prophesy that the tone of their drawing-rooms will not improve.

Lot of the Woman Worker

65. Mathew Carey

The misery and distress that prevail among this class

Women of the working class suffered during the "era of the common man" but for reasons that had little to do with the ennui found so enervating by the women described by Frances Trollope. The distressing working and living conditions of female workers are described in the appended report published by a committee of Philadelphians, under the chairmanship of Mathew Carey. Carey was a successful publisher, very much a "self-made" man, who believed that wealthy persons had the social obligation of alleviating the distress of the suffering poor.

Report on Female Wages

Philadelphia, March 25, 1829

The Subscribers, a committee appointed by the Town Meeting of the citizens of the city and county of Philadelphia, on the 21st ult. "to ascertain whether those who are able and willing to work, can in general procure employment—what is the effect upon the comfort, happiness and morals of the females who depend on their work for a support, of the low rate of wages paid to that class of

From Mathew Carey, *Miscellaneous Essays* (Philadelphia: Carey, Lea and Blanchard, 1830), 266–272. Footnotes are in the original.

society—to what extent the sufferings of the poor are attributable to those low wages—and what is the effect of benevolent or assistance societies on the industry of the labouring poor,"—beg leave to report,

That they have attended to the duties confided to them with a due sense of their importance, not merely to the comfort, happiness, and morals of that distressed, interesting and numerous portion of our population, whose case was particularly referred to them, but to the character of the community at large, which is deeply involved in the question of the justice done to that class, and the care and attention bestowed on their welfare:—

That they are convinced, from a careful examination of the subject, that the wages paid to seamstresses who work in their own apartments—to spoolers—to spinners—to folders of printed books—and in many cases to those who take in washing, are utterly inadequate to their support, even if fully employed, particularly if they have children unable to aid them in their industry, as is often the case; whereas, the work is so precarious that they are often unemployed—sometimes for a whole week together, and very frequently one or two days in each week. In many cases no small portion of their time is spent in seeking and waiting for work, and in taking it home when done:

That in the different branches above specified, industrious and expert women, unencumbered with families, and with steady employment, cannot average more than a dollar and a quarter per week; that their room rent is generally fifty cents, sometimes sixty-two and a half; and fuel probably costs about a quarter of a dollar per week, on an average through the year.[1] Thus, in the case of constant unceasing employment, (a case that rarely occurs,) there remains but about half a dollar per week, or twenty-six dollars per annum, for meat, drink, and clothing; and supposing only eight weeks in the year unemployed through sickness, want of work, or attention to children, (and this is but a moderate calculation) the amount for food and clothing would be reduced to the most miserable pittance of sixteen dollars per

1. This is probably too high, by a few cents.

annum! Can we wonder at the harrowing misery and distress that prevail among this class, under such a deplorable state of things?

That it is a most lamentable fact, that among the women thus "ground to the earth" by such inadequate wages, are to be found numbers of widows, with small children, who, by the untimely death of their husbands, and those reverses of fortune to which human affairs are liable, have been gradually reduced from a state of comfort and affluence to penury, and thrown upon the world, with no other dependence than their needles to support themselves and their offspring:

That although it is freely admitted that great distress and poverty arise from habits of dissipation and intemperance of husbands, and their shameful neglect to make that provision for their wives and children which they are bound to do by the laws of God and man, (and which, it is to be deeply regretted, the laws do not duly enforce,) yet we feel satisfied that those deplorable and pernicious habits do not produce half the wretchedness to which meritorious females are subjected in this city, of which the greater portion arises from the other source which we have stated, and which places before this class the alternatives of begging—applying to the overseers of the poor—stealing—or starving. We might add another—but we forbear.

That the scenes of distress and suffering which we have witnessed in our various visits to the dwellings of women who depend on their labour for support, resulting from inadequate wages, are of the most afflicting kind, and can scarcely be believed but by those by whom they have been beheld. We have found cases of women, whose husbands have been for weeks disabled by accidents, or by sickness produced by working on canals, surrounded by pestiferous miasmata—who have had to support their husbands and three or four children, by spooling at 20 cents per hundred skeins—by spinning at as low a rate of compensation—by washing and rough drying at 20 or 25 cents per dozen—or by making shirts and pantaloons at 12½ cents each:

That it is a great error to suppose, as is too frequently supposed, that every person in this community, able and willing to work, can procure employment; as there are many persons, of both sexes, more particularly females, who are at all times partially, and frequently wholly unemployed, although anxious to procure employment. There is almost always a great deficiency of employment for females, which is the chief reason why their wages are so disproportioned to those of males:

That there are few errors more pernicious, or more destitute of foundation, than the idea which has of late years been industriously propagated, that the benevolent societies of this city produce idleness and dissipation, by inducing the poor to depend on them, instead of depending on industry. The whole of the *annual subscriptions* for last year, to seven of the most prominent of these societies, embracing, it is believed, nearly all of any importance, was only 1069 dollars—and the whole of their disbursements, only 3740 dollars, a sum which obviously could not materially affect the industry of the many thousands, male and female, who have to work for their living. And it is of the last importance, in the consideration of this question, to take notice, that most part of these disbursements, was for *work done by aged women, and for food and clothing furnished to superannuated men and women, and destitute children:*

That those societies, far from increasing idleness and pauperism, have a directly contrary tendency; as, by the timely aid they afford, in seasons of distress and pressure, they very frequently produce the important effect of rescuing deserving persons from sinking into hopeless poverty, and thus becoming chargeable as paupers. Cases of this kind are of frequent occurrence. And it is not improbable that the consequent annual diminution of the poor tax exceeds the whole amount contributed to those societies by our citizens:

That the funds of those societies are managed with great prudence and circumspection—as the ladies humanely visit the poor in their habitations—ascertain the extent of their sufferings, as well as the nature of their claims for relief—and afford such aid as the cases respectively may require, and as their very limited means warrant. We think it but justice to declare, that we cannot conceive of any mode in which the same amount of money could do more effectual good—and we believe that the beneficence of the managers adds lustre to the character of the city. They are admirably calculated to be almoners to the wealthy, who are unable to seek out proper objects of charity, and are constantly liable to gross imposition:

That numerous proofs of the industry of the classes which depend for support upon their labour, and of the injustice of the denunciations levelled against them, might be produced; but we shall confine ourselves to two, one as regards males, the other as regards females. The first is, the thousands of men, who eagerly seek for labour on canals, often in pestilential situations, with death staring them in the face—the second, the fact that from 1000 to 1100 women have weekly travelled three, four, six, eight or ten squares, and anxiously waited for hours at the Provident Society's rooms for work, although it was known that they could not procure more than enough to employ themselves two, three or four days in the week. These two facts alone, ought to settle this question beyond the power of cavil or appeal.[2]

For evils of the magnitude and inveteracy of those under which the women suffer, who depend on their labour for support, it is difficult to devise a remedy. A complete remedy is perhaps impracticable. They may, however, and we hope will, be mitigated. The mitigation must wholly depend on the humanity and the sense of justice of those by whom they are employed, who, for the honour of human nature, it is to be supposed, have not been aware of the fact, that the wages they have been paying, were inadequate to the purchase of food, raiment and lodging; and who, now that the real state of the case is made manifest, will probably, as they certainly ought to, increase those wages. Although the great and increasing competition in trade, renders it necessary to use rigid economy in the expense of producing articles for market, it can never palliate, far less justify the oppression of the ill-fated people engaged in the production, by whose labours large fortunes are made, and their employers enabled to live in ease and opulence.

2. Subsequent inquiries have established the fact, that numbers of those women came from Kensington, a distance of two miles from the society's rooms, and of course had to travel four miles, for four shirts, which would require three days' labour, and for which they received but half a dollar!!!

It is peculiarly incumbent on those wealthy ladies, who employ seamstresses or washerwomen, and who ought to feel sympathy for the sufferings of their sex, to give them such wages as will not only yield them a present support, but enable them to make provision for times of sickness or scarcity of employment. It is painful to state, but regard for truth obliges us to state, that in this respect sufficient attention is not generally paid to the sacred rule of "doing unto others as we would have others do unto us." A moderate degree of attention to this rule, would annihilate a great portion of the distress of hundreds of suffering females.

One important means of mitigating the distress of this class, would be, to increase as far as possible the diversity of female employments, by which that competition which has produced the pernicious reduction of wages, would be diminished.

The Committee hope they will be pardoned for touching on a subject analogous to the object of their appointment, although not embraced in its terms. It is to recommend to the most serious consideration of the benevolent of their fellow citizens, the establishment of "a society for bettering the condition of the poor," [3] by encouraging habits of order, regularity and cleanliness in their persons and apartments; by instructing them in the most economical modes of cooking their food; by inducing them to send their children to school, and, when arrived at a proper age, to bind them apprentices to useful trades, and to lodge the little surplus of their earnings, when they have any surplus, in the saving fund; by enabling them to purchase fuel and other necessaries at reasonable rates; in a word, by inculcating on them those principles and that kind of conduct, which are calculated to elevate them in their own estimation, and in that of society at large. Societies of this description have produced the most salutary effects on the comfort and morals of the poor in various parts of Great Britain.

And while the Committee press on the humane and wealthy part of the community, the propriety of aiding in a greater degree

3. [July 8, 1830.] Two societies on this plan have been since formed in this city—one for bettering the condition of the poor, generally,—and the other for bettering the condition of indigent Roman Catholics.

than heretofore, (by their own exertions and through the various benevolent societies that exist among us, and whose funds are at present greatly reduced,) to alleviate the distresses of the numerous widows and orphans, and the really deserving poor and helpless of every description; they would likewise suggest to housekeepers and heads of families the propriety of seeking out and employing in the situation of domestics in their several families, destitute females, who, by the frowns of fortune, have been reduced to distress. Hundreds of this description are to be found within the precincts of the city and liberties, who, if properly encouraged, would be grateful for the means of employment thus afforded them, and who might profit by the precept and example set before them in the houses of respectable citizens. Perhaps there are few ties in common life, more binding than those that are found to exist between a benevolent master and mistress, and a faithful female servant who has grown up under their own eyes, and under their care and protection, and that of their descendants.

Lot of the Slave Woman

66. FANNY KEMBLE

Can you conceive a more wretched picture

If the plight of upper-class white women was a subtle matter, marked more by psychological than by material deprivation, the case was different for slave women. The difficulties they suffered were tangible. The observations by Fanny Kemble offer testimony that is fascinating for what it reveals of the mind of the observer. Miss Kemble was a well-known English actress, who had married a southern planter. The interest of her hearsay accounts of the sufferings and humiliations experienced by female slaves is increased by the fact that they involve

From Frances Anne Kemble, *Journal of a Residence on a Georgia Plantation in 1838–1839* (New York: Harper and Brothers, 1863), 174, 175, 189–192, 198–200.

her husband's own "property" and by the evidence that Miss Kemble herself was not altogether free of feelings of paternalism and condescension toward slaves.

Dear E——I can not give way to the bitter impatience I feel at my present position, and come back to the North without leaving my babies; and though I suppose their stay will not in any case be much prolonged in these regions of swamp and slavery, I must, for their sakes, remain where they are, and learn this dreary lesson of human suffering to the end. The record, it seems to me, must be utterly wearisome to you, as the instances themselves, I suppose, in a given time (thanks to that dreadful reconciler to all that is evil—habit), would become to me.

This morning I had a visit from two of the women, Charlotte and Judy, who came to me for help and advice for a complaint, which it really seems to me every other woman on the estate is cursed with, and which is a direct result of the conditions of their existence; the practice of sending women to labor in the fields in the third week after their confinement is a specific for causing this infirmity, and I know no specific for curing it under these circumstances. As soon as these poor things had departed with such comfort as I could give them, and the bandages they especially begged for, three other sable graces introduced themselves, Eddie, Louisa, and Diana; the former told me she had had a family of seven children, but had lost them all through "ill luck," as she denominated the ignorance and ill treatment which were answerable for the loss of these, as of so many other poor little creatures their fellows. Having dismissed her and Diana with the sugar and rice they came to beg, I detained Louisa, whom I had never seen but in the presence of her old grandmother, whose version of the poor child's escape to, and hiding in the woods, I had a desire to compare with the heroine's own story. She told it very simply, and it was most pathetic. She had not finished her task one day, when she said she felt ill, and unable to do so, and had been severely flogged by Driver Bran, in whose "gang" she then was.

The next day, in spite of this encouragement to labor, she had again been unable to complete her appointed work; and Bran having told her that he'd tie her up and flog her if she did not get it done, she had left the field and run into the swamp. "Tie you up, Louisa!" said I; "what is that?" She then described to me that they were fastened up by their wrists to a beam or a branch of a tree, their feet barely touching the ground, so as to allow them no purchase for resistance or evasion of the lash, their clothes turned over their heads, and their backs scored with a leather thong, either by the driver himself, or, if he pleases to inflict their punishment by deputy, any of the men he may choose to summon to the office; it might be father, brother, husband, or lover, if the overseer so ordered it. I turned sick, and my blood curdled listening to these details from the slender young slip of a lassie, with her poor piteous face and murmuring, pleading voice. "Oh," said I, "Louisa; but the rattlesnakes—the dreadful rattlesnakes in the swamps; were you not afraid of those horrible creatures?" "Oh, missis," said the poor child, "me no tink of dem; me forget all 'bout dem for de fretting." "Why did you come home at last?" "Oh, missis, me starve with hunger, me most dead with hunger before me come back." "And were you flogged, Louisa?" said I, with a shudder at what the answer might be. "No, missis, me go to hospital; me almost dead and sick so long, 'spec Driver Bran him forgot 'bout de flogging." I am getting perfectly savage over all these doings, E——, and really think I should consider my own throat and those of my children well cut if some night the people were to take it into their heads to clear off scores in that fashion. . . .

Old Molly, of whom I have often before spoken to you, who lived here in the days of the prosperity and grandeur of "Hampton," still clings to the relics of her old master's former magnificence, and with a pride worthy of old Caleb of Ravenswood showed me through the dismantled decaying rooms and over the remains of the dairy, displaying a capacious fish-box or well, where, in the good old days, the master's supply was kept in fresh salt water till required for table. Her prideful lamentations over the departure of all this quondam glory were ludicrous and pathetic; but, while listening with some amusement to the jumble of grotesque descriptions, through which her impression of the immeasurable grandeur and nobility of the house she served was the predominant feature, I could not help contrasting the present state of the estate with that which she described, and wondering why it should have become, as it undoubtedly must have done, so infinitely less productive a property than in the old major's time.

Before closing this letter, I have a mind to transcribe to you the entries for to-day recorded in a sort of daybook, where I put down very succinctly the number of people who visit me, their petitions and ailments, and also such special particulars concerning them as seem to me worth recording. You will see how miserable the physical condition of many of these poor creatures is; and their physical condition, it is insisted by those who uphold this evil system, is the only part of it which is prosperous, happy, and compares well with that of Northern laborers. Judge from the details I now send you; and never forget, while reading them, that the people on this plantation are well off, and consider themselves well off, in comparison with the slaves on some of the neighboring estates.

Fanny has had six children; all dead but one. She came to beg to have her work in the field lightened.

Nanny has had three children; two of them are dead. She came to implore that the rule of sending them into the field three weeks after their confinement might be altered.

Leah, Cæsar's wife, has had six children; three are dead.

Sophy, Lewis's wife, came to beg for some old linen. She is suffering fearfully; has had ten children; five of them are dead. The principal favor she asked was a piece of meat, which I gave her.

Sally, Scipio's wife, has had two miscarriages and three children born, one of whom is dead. She came complaining of incessant pain and weakness in her back. This woman was a mulatto daughter of a slave called Sophy, by a white man of the name of Walker, who visited the plantation.

Charlotte, Renty's wife, had had two miscarriages, and was with child again. She was almost crippled with rheumatism, and showed me a pair of poor swollen knees that made my heart ache.

I have promised her a pair of flannel trowsers, which I must forthwith set about making.

Sarah, Stephen's wife—this woman's case and history were alike deplorable. She had had four miscarriages, had brought seven children into the world, five of whom were dead, and was again with child. She complained of dreadful pains in the back, and an internal tumor which swells with the exertion of working in the fields; probably, I think, she is ruptured. She told me she had once been mad and had ran into the woods, where she contrived to elude discovery for some time, but was at last tracked and brought back, when she was tied up by the arms, and heavy logs fastened to her feet, and was severely flogged. After this she contrived to escape again, and lived for some time skulking in the woods, and she supposes mad, for when she was taken again she was entirely naked. She subsequently recovered from this derangement, and seems now just like all the other poor creatures who come to me for help and pity. I suppose her constant childbearing and hard labor in the fields at the same time may have produced the temporary insanity.

Sukey, Bush's wife, only came to pay her respects. She had had four miscarriages; had brought eleven children into the world, five of whom are dead.

Molly, Quambo's wife, also came to see me. Hers was the best account I have yet received; she had had nine children, and six of them were still alive.

This is only the entry for to-day, in my diary, of the people's complaints and visits. Can you conceive a more wretched picture than that which it exhibits of the conditions under which these women live? Their cases are in no respect singular, and though they come with pitiful entreaties that I will help them with some alleviation of their pressing physical distresses, it seems to me marvelous with what desperate patience (I write it advisedly, patience of utter despair) they endure their sorrow-laden existence. Even the poor wretch who told that miserable story of insanity, and lonely hiding in the swamps, and scourging when she was found, and of her renewed madness and flight, did so in a sort of low, plaintive, monotonous murmur of misery, as if such sufferings were all "in the day's work."

I ask these questions about their children because I think the number they bear as compared with the number they rear a fair gauge of the effect of the system on their own health and that of their offspring. There was hardly one of these women, as you will see by the details I have noted of their ailments, who might not have been a candidate for a bed in a hospital, and they had come to me after working all day in the fields. . . .

I have been interrupted by several visits, my dear E——, among other, one from a poor creature called Judy, whose sad story and condition affected me most painfully. She had been married, she said, some years ago to one of the men called Temba, who, however, now has another wife, having left her because she went mad. While out of her mind she escaped into the jungle, and contrived to secrete herself there for some time, but was finally tracked and caught, and brought back and punished by being made to sit, day after day, for hours in the stocks—a severe punishment for a man, but for a woman perfectly barbarous. She complained of chronic rheumatism, and other terrible ailments, and said she suffered such intolerable pain while laboring in the fields, that she had come to entreat me to have her work lightened. She could hardly crawl, and cried bitterly all the time she spoke to me.

She told me a miserable story of her former experience on the plantation under Mr. K——'s overseership. It seems that Jem Valiant (an extremely difficult subject, a mulatto lad, whose valor is sufficiently accounted for now by the influence of the mutinous white blood) was her first-born, the son of Mr. K——, who forced her, flogged her severely for having resisted him, and then sent her off, as a farther punishment, to Five Pound—a horrible swamp in a remote corner of the estate, to which the slaves are sometimes banished for such offenses as are not sufficiently atoned for by the lash. The dismal loneliness of the place to these poor people, who are as dependent as children upon companionship and sympathy, makes this solitary exile a much-dreaded infliction; and this poor creature said that, bad as the flogging was, she would sooner have taken that again than the dreadful lonely days and nights she spent on the penal swamp of Five Pound.

I make no comment on these terrible stories, my dear friend, and tell them to you as nearly as possible in the perfectly plain, unvarnished manner in which they are told to me. I do not wish to add to, or perhaps I ought to say take away from, the effect of such narrations by amplifying the simple horror and misery of their bare details.

My dearest E—— I have had an uninterrupted stream of women and children flowing in the whole morning to say "Ha de, missis?" Among others, a poor woman called Mile, who could hardly stand for pain and swelling in her limbs; she had had fifteen children and two miscarriages; nine of her children had died; for the last three years she had become almost a cripple with chronic rheumatism, yet she is driven every day to work in the field. She held my hands, and stroked them in the most appealing way while she exclaimed, "Oh my missis! my missis! me neber sleep till day for de pain," and with the day her labor must again be resumed. I gave her flannel and sal volatile to rub her poor swelled limbs with; rest I could not give her—rest from her labor and her pain—this mother of fifteen children.

Another of my visitors had a still more dismal story to tell; her name was Die; she had had sixteen children, fourteen of whom were dead; she had had four miscarriages: one had been caused with falling down with a very heavy burden on her head, and one from having her arms strained up to be lashed. I asked her what she meant by having her arms tied up. She said their hands were first tied together, sometimes by the wrists, and sometimes, which was worse, by the thumbs, and they were then drawn up to a tree or post, so as almost to swing them off the ground, and then their clothes rolled round their waist, and a man with a cowhide stands and stripes them. I give you the woman's words. She did not speak of this as of any thing strange, unusual, or especially horrid and abominable; and when I said, "Did they do that to you when you were with child?" she simply replied, "Yes, missis." And to all this I listen—I, an English woman, the wife of the man who owns these wretches, and I can not say, "That thing shall not be done again; that cruel shame and villainy shall never be known here again." I gave the woman meat and flannel, which were what she came to ask for, and remained choking with indignation and grief long after they had all left me to my most bitter thoughts.

Poverty amid Prosperity

67. John H. Griscom

The helpless and noisome manner in which they live

Evidence compiled by modern researchers discloses that the overwhelming majority of urban residents owned no real or personal property during the "age of egalitarianism." In the following selection John Griscom describes the appalling housing conditions of New York City's more marginal population. The contemporary labor press offered many reports testifying to similar conditions in cities in all sections of the country.

If not on a par, in importance, with the improvement in education, which has of late made such rapid strides, it certainly is second only to it, and indeed it may well be questioned, whether improvement in the physical condition of the lower stratum of society, is not a necessary precedent, in order that education of the mind may exercise its full and proper influence over the general well-being. Teach them how to live, so as to avoid diseases and be more comfortable, and then their school education will have a redoubled effect, in mending their morals, and rendering them intelligent and happy. But without sound bodies, when surrounded with dirt, foul air, and all manner of filthy associations, it is vain to expect even the child of education, to be better than his ignorant companions, if indeed you do not, by educating him, give him an additional weapon, by which he may prey more successfully upon his fellows.

From John H. Griscom, *The Sanitary Condition of the Laboring Population of New York*, pp. 6–9.

This country, and especially this city, it is hoped, will not much longer be behind others in this cause of the suffering poor and depressed humanity. Some movements, promoting this investigation, have recently been commenced, but much is yet to be done. The path has been pointed out to us by pioneers across the Atlantic; there is abundant disposition to pursue the object, which only requires to be sought out, and put to work by the authorities, to procure all the desirable results of such labours.

The system of tenantage to which large numbers of the poor are subject, I think, must be regarded as one of the principal causes, of the helpless and noisome manner in which they live. The basis of these evils is the subjection of the tenantry, to the merciless inflictions and extortions of the *sub-landlord.* A house, or a row, or court of houses, is hired by some person of the owner, on a lease of several years, for a sum which will yield a fair interest on the cost. The *owner* is thus relieved of the great trouble incident to the changes of tenants, and the collection of rents. His income is sure from one individual, and obtained without annoyance or oppression on his part. It then becomes the object of the lessee, to make and save as much as possible, with his adventure, sufficient sometimes to enable him to purchase the property in a short time.

The tenements, in order to admit a greater number of families, are divided into small apartments, as numerous as decency will admit. Regard to comfort, convenience, and health, is the last motive; indeed, the great ignorance of this class of speculators (who are very frequently foreigners and keep a grog shop on the premises) would prevent a proper observance of these, had they the desire. These closets, for they deserve no other name, are then rented to the poor, from week to week, or month to month, the rent being almost invariably required in advance, at least for the first few terms. The families moving in first, after the house is built, find it clean, but the lessee has no supervision over their habits, and however filthy the tenement may become, he cares not, so that he receives his rent. He and his family are often found steeped as low in depravity and discomforts, as any of his tenants, being above them only in the possession of money, and doubtless often beneath them in moral worth and sensibility.

It is very frequently the case that families, after occupying rooms a few weeks, will change their location, leaving behind them all the dirt which their residence has occasioned. Upon this the next comers will sit down, being so much occupied with the hurry of moving, and with the necessity of placing their furniture immediately in order, that attention to cleansing the apartment is out of the question, until they are "settled," and then, if done at all, it is in the most careless and inefficient manner. Very often, perhaps in a majority of the cases in the class of which I now speak, no cleaning other than washing the floor, is ever attempted, and that but seldom. Whitewashing, cleaning of furniture, of bedding, or persons, in many cases is *never* attempted. Some have old pieces of carpet, which are never shaken, (they would not bear it,) and are used to hide the filth on the floor. Every corner of the room, of the cupboards, of the entries and stairways, is piled up with dirt. The walls and ceilings, with the plaster broken off in many places, exposing the lath and beams, and leaving openings for the escape from within of the effluvia of vermin, dead and alive, are smeared with the blood of unmentionable insects, and dirt of all indescribable colours. The low rooms are diminished in their areas by the necessary encroachments of the roof, or the stairs leading to the rooms above; and behind and under them is a hole, into which the light of day never enters, and where a small bed is often pushed in, upon which the luckless and degraded tenants pass their nights, weary and comfortless.

In these places, the filth is allowed to accumulate to an extent almost incredible. Hiring their rooms for short periods only, it is very common to find the poor tenants moving from place to place, every few weeks. By this practice they avoid the trouble of cleansing their rooms, as they can leave behind them the dirt which they have made. The same room, being occupied in rapid succession, by tenant after tenant, it will easily be seen how the walls and windows will become broken, the doors and floors become injured, the chimneys filled with soot, the whole premises populated thickly with vermin, the stairways, the common passage of several families, the receptacle for all things noxious, and whatever of self-respect the family might have had, be crushed under the pressure of the degrading circumstances by which they are surrounded.

Another very important particular in the arrangements of these tenements must here be noticed. By the mode in which the rooms are planned, *ventilation is entirely prevented.* It would seem as if most of these places were built expressly for this purpose. They have one or two windows, and a door at one side of the room, but no opening anywhere else. A draught of air *through,* is therefore an utter impossibility. The confined position of the dwelling itself, generally, prevents the access of the external currents of air, even to the outside, to any considerable extent. The window sashes, in addition, perhaps are so arranged, that the upper one (if there are two) cannot be let down, being permanently fastened up; hence the external air, poor as it is, cannot visit the upper section of the room, unless by opening the door, by which the interior of the room is exposed to view. If there is a sleeping apartment, it is placed at the extremity of the room farthest from the windows, is generally but little larger than sufficient to hold a bedstead, and its area is reduced, for air, by the bed furniture, trunks, boxes, &c. and having no windows, fresh air and sun light are entire strangers to its walls. In this dark hole there is, of course, a concentrated accumulation of the effluviæ of the bodies and breaths of the persons sleeping in it, (frequently the whole family, several in number,) and this accumulation goes on from night to night, without relief, until it can easily be believed the smell becomes intolerable, and its atmosphere productive of the most offensive and malignant diseases. There is no exaggeration in this description. I cannot too highly colour the picture, if I would. What, then, will be thought of the condition of thousands of our fellow-citizens in the *winter season,* when every crevice is closed to keep out the cold air, and when I state, that what I have described, I have repeatedly seen and felt in the *summer,* when the windows and doors are opened to the fullest extent, day and night, admitting all the ventilation possible, small as it is.

I have had recent occasion to visit several of these pestiferous places, and I pen these paragraphs in the month of August, with their sight and smell fresh upon my senses.

The almost entire absence of household conveniences, contributes much to the prostration of comfort and self-respect of these wretched people. The deficiency of water, and the want of a convenient place for washing, with no other place for drying clothes than the common sitting and bed room, are very serious impediments in the way of their improvement. Without any convenient or safe place to deposit wood, or coal, or food in large quantities, all their purchases are by "the small," from the neighbouring grocer, (who is perhaps the landlord,) at prices from 10 to 50 per cent. above the rates at which they might be obtained, under better circumstances.

But the most offensive of all places for residence are the *cellars.* It is almost impossible, when contemplating the circumstances and condition of the poor beings who inhabit these holes, to maintain the proper degree of calmness requisite for a thorough inspection, and the exercise of a sound judgment, respecting them. You must descend to them; you must feel the blast of foul air as it meets your face on opening the door; you must grope in the dark, or hesitate until your eye becomes accustomed to the gloomy place, to enable you to find your way through the entry, over a broken floor, the boards of which are protected from your tread by a half inch of hard dirt; you must inhale the suffocating vapor of the sitting and sleeping rooms; and in the dark, damp recess, endeavor to find the inmates by the sound of their voices, or chance to see their figures moving between you and the flickering blaze of a shaving burning on the hearth, or the misty light of a window coated with dirt and festooned with cobwebs—or if in search of an invalid, take care that you do not fall full length upon the bed with her, by stumbling against the bundle of rags and straw, dignified by that name, lying on the floor, under the window, if window there is;—all this, and much more, beyond the reach of my pen, must be felt and seen, ere you can appreciate in its full force the mournful and disgusting condition, in which many thousands of the subjects of our government pass their lives.

> There vapors, with malignant breath
> Rise thick, and scatter midnight death.

There are two features of a cellar residence which more especially render them objectionable; 1st, the dampness, and 2d, the more incomplete ventilation. In *any* cellar the impossibility of access for the heat of the sun to the parts of the soil adjacent to the floor and walls, and the absence of currents of air through the room, keep it much more damp than rooms above ground, where the heat and air have freer access. This is emphatically the case with *inhabited* cellars, inasmuch as the inmates are careful to exclude the external air, by closing all the avenues of its approach, in order to preserve the temperature high in winter and low in summer. The moisture, whose escape is thus prevented, is in itself a very prolific source of disease, and combined with the darkness and impure air of these places, is actually productive of a great amount of sickness. Could the sun and air be made to reach them, and were it possible to establish a sufficient ventilation through them, much of their noxiousness would be relieved; but under no circumstances can they be made fit for the residence of *living* beings; they are properly adapted only as receptacles for the dead.

In addition to these impediments to the drying of these places, they are very often so situated, that the surface water finds its way into them at every rain storm. It may be remembered that in the summer of 1843 all the underground apartments in many sections of the city were completely flooded by a deluge of rain. In the eastern part of the city, in Delancy, Rivington, Stanton, and many other of the neighbouring streets, almost every cellar (and great numbers of them are inhabited) were half filled with water. This evil will not recur to so great an extent, in the neighbourhood alluded to, sewers having been built in some of the streets. But in other sections, indeed in every section, where the position of the basement is unaltered, and sewers are not constructed, the nuisance must be suffered at every rain storm. In some courts to which I can point, *the surface is below the level of the street*, and at every rain, the water being unable to run off into the street, is all discharged down into the adjacent areas and cellars, keeping them almost constantly wet. It was but a short time ago I met with the case of a woman, the wife of a tailor living in a noted court in Walkerstreet, and occupying partly a basement, in which she was compelled to pass much of her time. She has lived there six months, four of which she has been sick with rheumatism, and on that account, unable to work. Otherwise she would be able to earn considerable by assisting her husband. They have four children depending upon them, and are obliged to seek assistance from the public, in consequence of this sickness. She attributes her disease to the water in the cellar, which runs in, and obliges her to bale out, and wipe up, at every storm.

PART FIVE

Political Issues

The "Corrupt Bargain"

68. Corresponding Committee

For what end were the wishes of the people defeated and their will outraged

One of the chief issues of the presidential election of 1828 was the way in which John Quincy Adams had won the election of 1824. Following Adams's choice by the House of Representatives early in 1825 on the failure of any candidate to win an electoral majority, Andrew Jackson and his supporters charged that a "corrupt bargain" between Adams and Henry Clay had flouted the popular will. That the charge had little factual basis did not detract from its wide dissemination and great influence, as the following pro-Jacksonian circular indicates.

(Circular)

Sir,

A meeting of the electors of this Town, friendly to the interests of Gen. Jackson as a candidate for the next Presidency, having been held on the 22d inst., at which a Corresponding Committee was appointed for the purpose of promoting those interests, they take the liberty, in the discharge of a duty so congenial to their feelings, to address you—under the gratifying anticipation, that your activity and influence will be most cheerfully exerted, in the advancement of the object, sought to be effected.

The events connected with the last Presidential Election, fraught as they were, with painful interest to the American People; must be yet fresh and unobliterated in your recollection,

Circular printed by Joshua Bloore, Chairman of the Corresponding Committee of the town of Waterford, New York State, 1829.

and it will not they trust, be considered necessary, that they should go into a minute detail of matters so ungrateful to their feelings, so humiliating to our national character, and so utterly repugnant to the nature and purity of a free representative government. Let it suffice to state, that the election of Mr. Adams to the Executive chair of the Union, was in direct opposition to the wishes of a large majority of the nation, as emphatically expressed by the Electoral Colleges—that it was the result of intrigue and traffic, the most profligate and unholy, and was the mean of excluding from the Presidency, an individual, pre-eminently illustrious and distinguished, and who, more than "any other man now living," is best entitled to the warmest regards, and the deepest and most ardent gratitude, of the Republic. And for what end, were the declared wishes of the People to be defeated, and their will outraged? for what were the honor and integrity of the House of Representatives, to be surrendered into the hands of an unprincipled, political speculator? and for what was the Saviour of New-Orleans! the renowned Victor of the South!! to be debarred from an inheritance, to which, by a life devoted to the interests of his country, and by the benefaction of public services the most brilliant and unrivalled, he was so justly entitled? Was it, to promote the good and advance the prosperity of the Union? For the honor of our country, which has been so grossly sullied, most sincerely do this Committee wish, that a reply could be rendered in the affirmative—but the fact is otherwise; and it would require no ordinary degree of hardihood and effrontery to assert, and more than christian charity to believe, that any considerations of national good, could have had an influence, in generating intrigues and coalitions, to oppose and defeat the public will, and violate one of the most sacred and vital principles of all free governments. No! Such intrigues and such coalitions, have their origin in motives other than those of patriotism, and love of country, and can only be imputed to the instigation of designs, which an upright mind and an uncorrupted heart, never knew.

The fact will not be denied, that divested of the strength which Mr. Adams derived through the instrumentality of Mr. Clay, the friends of Gen. Jackson, in the House of Representatives, were, at the period of the last Presidential election, a decided majority over the friends of Mr. Adams; neither will it be denied, that of the three candidates returned to the House, viz. Gen. Jackson, Mr. Crawford, and Mr. Adams, that Mr. Clay had repeatedly declared it as his opinion, that Mr. Crawford was best entitled to the Presidency. What then, was the cause which induced Mr. Clay, in opposition to an opinion thus repeatedly expressed, and in violation of his duty to the People of the United States, entertaining as he did such opinion; to espouse the interests of Mr. Adams, without the use of a solitary effort to promote the choice of the candidate, whom he believed to be entitled to the Presidential chair? Was it, because he had been previously ignorant of the character or claims of Mr. Adams? No! they were co-commissioners at Ghent—had passed winter after winter together at the city of Washington, and had on a variety of occasions, acted in concert and in opposition to each other—Mr. Clay must therefore of necessity, have been intimately acquainted with the merits or demerits of Mr. Adams, and could have received no new revealings, either of his character or his claims. What then, it is again asked, was the cause which prompted Mr. Clay, to desert Mr. Crawford, and attach himself to the fortunes of Mr. Adams! and what was the cause, which could induce Mr. Clay, upon determining to abandon the candidate of his choice, to ally himself with Mr. Adams, in opposition to Gen. Jackson, the known Favorite of a majority of the Union? Who, but blushes for the violated honor, and bleeding reputation of his country, when he finds that *cause,* in the fulfilment of an understanding or the redemption of a pledge—in the nomination and appointment of Mr. Clay to the office of Secretary of State, and in the consummation of a bargain, paralleled only by the history of an ISCARIOT.

What then, under such circumstances, is the duty of the American People? They are under a sacred & imperative obligation, to rally round the illustrious individual, upon whom, at the last Presidential election, they would, as a mark of their gratitude, have conferred the highest honor in their gift—to defeat the re-election of a man, who now holds by usurpation, what otherwise, he could not have acquired, and to seat in the chair, which he now occupies, in the place of a *Cabinet Jesuit*—a politician of unsuspected virtue, and a statesman of incorruptible integrity—who was in his youth a soldier, and in his age a Hero.

To advance this most desirable object, the meeting under whose appointment this Committee now act, having previously "RESOLVED" to support no other candidate for Congress at the ensuing election, than "an open, avowed, and devoted friend of Andrew Jackson," unanimously "recommended to the numerous friends of Gen. Jackson in this county, without regard to State politics, county divisions, or local strifes, to assemble in their several towns as soon as practicable, and make choice of four delegates from each town to assemble in County Convention on the *twenty-first* day of October next, at two o'clock in the afternoon, at the Court House, in the village of Ballston Spa, for the purpose of nominating a suitable person to be supported as a candidate for Congress at the ensuing election," and this committee would most respectfully urge upon your consideration, the importance and necessity of such measure, by reminding you that upon the members of Congress to be elected at the next election, will devolve the duty, doubly responsible because of the occurrences of the last Presidential election, of making choice of the next President, should the Electoral Colleges fail to elect.

Relying upon your regard for the honor of a county, whose soil has been consecrated by the blood of patriots and whose sons should be on the alert to sustain in their purity, the principles of that government, which their fathers died to establish, this Committee flatter themselves, that no exertions of yours will be withheld in the promotion of the measure thus recommended, and in the election of the Candidate to be nominated by the contemplated convention.

It may be proper to add, to prevent misconception, that it is not the desire of this Committee, representing the feelings of the meeting, in whose behalf they have addressed you, to elect a candidate for the purpose of counteracting or embarrassing the measures of the present administration, any further than they may aim at the re-election of Mr. Adams, but that the object is, to elect a member of congress to represent this county, who, if necessary, would render his vote, and exert his influence in behalf of Andrew Jackson.

JOSHUA BLOORE,
Chairman of the Jackson
Corresponding Committee,
of the town of Waterford.

The Eaton Affair

69. ANDREW JACKSON DONELSON

The repugnance of society to recognize Mrs. Eaton

One of the leading issues of Andrew Jackson's first administration concerned the refusal by the wives of several cabinet members to entertain socially Peggy Eaton, wife of Jackson's secretary of war. Construing the snubs as a political as well as personal attack on himself, Jackson dissolved his first cabinet when he failed to receive assurances that Mrs. Eaton—a young woman of a certain reputation—would be treated differently. Jackson and some of his later admirers have sought to portray the affair as Jackson's rebuff to a masked attempt by Calhounites to dominate the administration. In the selection that follows, Jackson's nephew and private secretary offers a less admirable interpretation. Young Donelson and his wife Emily were banished from the White House for the latter's refusal to visit Mrs. Eaton.

STATEMENT OF ANDREW J. DONELSON*

Washington, November 10, 1830

On this day about 12 oclock the President remarked to me that he

From John Spencer Bassett, ed., *Correspondence of Andrew Jackson* (Washington: Carnegie Institution, 1928–1931), IV, pp. 200–202. Reprinted by courtesy of the publisher. Footnote is in the original.

* Copy. Jackson MSS., Presidential Messages and Misc., Box D. In the handwriting of A. J. Donelson.

had received my note of yesterday in relation to the difficulties which opposed the return of Mrs. Donelson to the city of Washington. The views which he took of that subject were so extraordinary and indicate so firm a determination to hold the members of his cabinet as well as myself who had not coerced their families into an intercourse with Mrs. Eaton, officially responsible to him, that I have felt it due to myself hereafter to reduce to writing what passes as leading to this object.

Tho well aware from the moment of the organization of the cabinet that the repugnance of society to recognize Mrs. Eaton as a proper associate would deeply affect the feelings of the President and expose his excitements to the arts of office seekers and to the many biasses which must naturally attend the incorporation of private feelings with the action of the Government, yet I relied upon the checks, which, an overruling sense of justice, the tendency of time and good counsels, and the inherent weakness of such combinations contained, to dispel the delusion, and ultimately redeem the administration from the odium of such a feature. This anticipation has been banished by the conversation which the President held with me to day. An infatuation kept alive by the timidity of weak friends and the interests of the political party which have used Majr. Eaton as an instrument first to obtain the confidence of the President and afterwards to controul him, has long since classed those who associated with Mrs. Eaton or who countenanced her pretensions to virtue and innocence, as the confidential friends of the President, and those who did not as secretly favoring the views of an opposition to his fame and character. The circumstances which ought to have removed this infatuation have confirmed it. It has now become a principle of the administration, and as such consigns to destruction those who do not subscribe to the means which are necessary to secure it power.

Independently of the importance of the subject in this point of view, it is more so to me individually, in another. My relation to the President as his private secretary, the object of his early favor and care, and but for this impediment the sharer with his adopted son of his estate—this and all the influences which it sets in motion calculated on the one hand to enjoin obedience, forbearance, conciliation, love and gratitude, as my duty; and on the other, opposite and corresponding vices or faults as the just measure of my character, if my agency in this event seperates me from his person; are considerations of the deepest import to my future happiness. That the world may know that they have been justly appreciated—that if I am borne down as others are by this evil tide, neither my honor, my character, nor my duties are sunk beneath it, by whatever standard they may be estimated, I have yielded to the necessity of preserving up to this period some evidences of my conduct in relation to the attempts of Mrs. Eaton to subdue the moral sentiment of society, which will be found in another part of this book. The same necessity has also induced me to reduce to writing the conversations which I hold with the President; and I commence with that of this day.

The following letter was before him dated 9th Nov. 1830

> *My Dear Uncle,* Understanding you in that part of our conversation last evening relating to the return of Mrs. Donelson to this city, to say, that I must not anticipate this happiness until I could consent to her visiting Mrs. Eaton, or in other words would coerce an intercourse between Mrs. Eaton and Mrs. Donelson, out of your house as well as in it, as far as the latter was concerned, it becomes my painful duty to apprise you again that such terms cannot receive my approbation.
>
> If I have misconceived your meaning, pray, let me know what are the difficulties which I have to remove before my family can be allowed to occupy the same house that I do.
>
> *yr. grateful and affectionate nephew*
>
> P. S. I do not wish another correspondence on the subject—all that I desire is the knowledge of your wishes in relation to the extent of the intercourse in question, that I may be able to be governed by them, or occupy no longer than may be necessary a position which you think unfriendly to them.
>
> *yr. etc* A. *J. D.*

The President said he had read with much pain this letter, that I knew very well he would not part with his friend Majr. Eaton, and that this was the object of those who did not allow their families to associate with Mrs. Eaton. I replied to him that whatever might be the views of others in regard to Majr. Eaton that mine only looked to his fame and the protection of my own honor and character. That I had never seen any authority for his inference that a non intercourse with Mrs. Eaton was evidence of Political hostility to Majr. Eaton or himself.

The President continued. It is evidence of hostility to me. The refusal of my cabinet to associate with Mrs. E has already produced a coldness between several of them, which was daily exhibited. That he would not look to the cause of that coldness, but would at a proper time remove it by appointing officers that would harmonise in all their relations. I am, Sir, advised of the combinations which were formed in this city to keep Mrs. Eaton out of society, and the existence of similar ones at Nashville and elsewhere. They will fail. I shall never seperate from Majr. Eaton, no influence can ever force me to do it. The time is not far off when I will give the Gentlemen of my cabinet who cannot harmonise with Majr. Eaton some honorable proofs of my confidence in new stations: vacancies will shortly take place in the corps of foreign ministers: they must take these or retire. I can do without them.

I replied to him: This will be a fatal step. It is that which your enemies are looking for. You have not a right to interfere with the private family relations of the cabinet, and the attempt to do it must be seriously injurious. It was to avoid such an imputation that I chiefly desired the return of Mrs. Donelson, whose absence had been already ascribed to his determination to coerce her into an intercourse with Mrs. Eaton.

He said. It was not true that he wished to coerce the intercourse, but that Mrs. D should not return until such intercourse could be maintained, or until she could be on the same terms with the families of all the Heads of Departments. That forty members of Congress during the past winter, understanding that the female part of his family and the ladies of the cabinet officers did not associate with Mrs. Eaton, had asked him if Genl. Jackson was at the head of the Government, that this was the language of his friends every where. It was the language of truth, and he would shew the world that Genl. Jackson was at the head of Government, that he would not put up with what Mr. Monroe did. He knew his duty and would produce harmony. He also spoke in bitter terms of Govr. Branch as having treated Majr. Eaton cruelly (I was struck with this remark as corresponding with one of Mr. Triste's in which he mentioned that Westcott said every body knew that Eaton appointed the cabinet, and that Govr. Branch among other things was reproached with ingratitude to Majr. Eaton—Mr. Triste so informed me to day. It may be proper also to state that Westcott has recently been foiled in an attempt to get his Brother a midshipman reinstated, is one of Mr. Van Buren's officers, and has been quite indecorous in his official intercourse with the Secretary of the Navy. I was stating my opinions of the error into which the President had fallen by not discriminating between the rights of society as it regarded the character of Mrs. Eaton, and his own, when we were interrupted by the appearance of Sent Smith.

The Tariff

70. Andrew Jackson

I am in favor of a judicious examination of the tariff

Modern economic historians tend to discount the significance of tariffs in the economic development of the United States in the nineteenth century. Jackson's contemporaries had a very different perception, regarding the issue as a crucial one. In the following letter, Andrew Jackson as presidential candidate reveals his evasiveness toward an issue he knew was of great interest to voters. Even historians sympathetic to Jackson concede that he was all things to all men in this matter, Jacksonian campaign managers trimming their sails to the varied political

From John Spencer Bassett, ed., *Correspondence of Andrew Jackson*, III, pp. 249–251. Reprinted by courtesy of the Carnegie Institution of Washington.

winds in the different states. L. H. Coleman, a Jackson man of Warrentown, North Carolina, to whom Jackson wrote, later published this letter in the *Niles Register.*

To L. H. Coleman

Washington, April 26, 1824

Sir: I had the honor this day to receive your letter of the 21st instant and with candor shall reply to it. My name has been brought before the nation by the people themselves without any agency of mine: for I wish it not to be forgotten that I have never solicited office, nor when called upon by the constituted authorities have ever declined where I conceived my services would be beneficial to my country. But as my name has been brought before the nation for the first office in the gift of the people, it is incumbent on me, when asked, frankly to declare my opinion upon any political or national question pending before and about which the country feels an interest.

You ask my opinion on the Tariff. I answer, that I am in favor of a judicious examination and revision of it; and so far as the Tariff before us embraces the design of fostering, protecting, and preserving within ourselves the means of national defense and independence, particularly in a state of war, I would advocate and support it. The experience of the late war ought to teach us a lesson; and one never to be forgotten. If our liberty and republican form of government, procured for us by our revolutionary fathers, are worth the blood and treasure at which they were obtained, it surely is our duty to protect and defend them. Can there be an American patriot who saw the privations, dangers, and difficulties experienced for the want of a proper means of defense during the last war, who would be willing again to hazard the safety of our country if embroiled; or rest it for defense on the precarious means of national resources to be derived from commerce, in a state of war with a maratime power which might destroy that commerce to prevent our obtaining the means of defense, and thereby subdue us? I hope there is not; and if there is, I am sure he does not deserve to enjoy the blessing of freedom.

Heaven smiled upon, and gave us liberty and independence. That same providence has blessed us with the means of national independence and national defense. If we omit or refuse to use the gifts which He has extended to us, we deserve not the continuation of His blessings. He has filled our mountains and our plains with minerals—with lead, iron, and copper, and given us a climate and soil for the growing of hemp and wool. These being the grand materials of our national defense, they ought to have extended to them adequate and fair protection, that our own manufactories and laborers may be placed on a fair competition with those of Europe; and that we may have within our own country a supply of those leading and important articles so essential to war. Beyond this, I look at the Tariff with an eye to the proper distribution of labor and revenue; and with a view to discharge our national debt. I am one of those who do not believe that a national debt is a national blessing, but rather a curse to a republic; inasmuch as it is calculated to raise around the administration a moneyed aristocracy dangerous to the liberties of the country.

This Tariff—I mean a judicious one—possesses more fanciful than real dangers. I will ask what is the real situation of the agriculturalist? Where has the American farmer a market for his surplus products? Except for cotton he has neither a foreign nor a home market. Does not this clearly prove, when there is no market either at home or abroad, that there is too much labor employed in agriculture? and that the channels of labor should be multiplied? Common sense points out at once the remedy. Draw from agriculture the superabundant labor, employ it in mechanism and manufactures, thereby creating a home market for your breadstuffs, and distributing labor to a most profitable account, and benefits to the country will result. Take from agriculture in the United States six hundred thousand men, women, and children, and you at once give a home market for more bread stuffs than all Europe now furnishes us. In short, sir, we have been too long subject to the policy of the British merchants. It is time we should become a little more *Americanized*, and instead of feeding the paupers and laborers of Europe, feed our own, or else in a short time, by continuing our present policy, we shall all be paupers ourselves.

It is, therefore, my opinion that a careful Tariff is much wanted to pay our national debt, and afford us the means of that defense within ourselves on which the safety and liberty of the country depend; and last, though not least, give a proper distribution to our labor, which must prove beneficial to the happiness, independence, and wealth of the community.

This is a short outline of my opinions, generally, on the subject of your inquiry, and believing them correct and calculated to further the prosperity and happiness of my country, I declare to you I would not barter them for any office or situation of a temporal character that could be given me.

I have presented you my opinions freely, because I am without concealment, and should indeed despise myself if I could believe myself capable of acquiring the confidence of any by means so ignoble.

I am, sir, very respectfully, your obedient servant.

To Andrew J. Donelson

Washington, April 27, 1824

. . . . I will be home as soon as I can; but I cannot leave here before I vote upon the Tariff Bill: I have recd many letters on this subject, many as I suppose held forth in *terorum.* I mean to convince those who are not yet acquainted with me; that I cannot be intimidated from doing that, which my Judgment and conscience tells me is right; by any earthly power. I therefore will support the Tariff so far as I believe it will tend to *foster,* the means of national defence, and *procure it from [our] own means;* which will insure allways an ample suply within our country in a state of war; beyond this I will view it with an eye to Revenue to meet our national debt; give a proper distribution to labour, by which the agricultural interest will be promoted.

From these hints you will conclude I will vote for the Bill; as I believe it right and proper to feed our own labourers instead of those of Europe, and keep within us that capital that is drawn from us, and creates in part the wealth of England. The British merchants and British influence has had heretofore too much influence; we must in our policy look more to our national interest.

71. South Carolina Legislature

We look not to the President but to the Constitution alone

In the 1820s the Congress appeared to be institutionalizing the protective tariff. The South Carolina State Legislature, very much influenced by the ideas of John C. Calhoun, argued that the tariffs of 1824 and 1828 were unconstitutional and oppressive. The resolutions that follow anticipate the nullification argument of several years later.

WHEREAS the people of South Carolina in the exercise of their Sovereign Rights, have assembled in their respective Districts, and declared the Tariff Acts of 1824 and 1828, palpable infractions of the Constitution of the United States, and have urged their Representatives in the Legislature assembled, to adopt such measures as may protect, maintain and defend their Liberties. It becomes the duty of this Legislature after the appeals so emphatically made, to interpose the State government between the people and the Federal government, vigilantly to guard their reserved rights, and promptly to vindicate them when attacked—Fully aware how ardently the people of this State are attached to the Federal Union—how strenuous their endeavours to procure the adoption of that Instrument, which leagued Independent Sovereignties into one great Republic—how highly they prize Freedom of Trade and Liberty of Action, and how devoutly they cherished the expectation that all these would be preserved to them, and their Posterity in all time to come. This Legislature can not but view with profound astonishment the exercise by the

Resolutions approved by the South Carolina State Legislature, Charleston, S.C., 1828.

Federal Government of powers—abridging the freedom of Trade, circumscribing industry—violating the constitution, and weakening the Union.

Therefore Resolved, That the people of South Carolina have borne with patience, and endured with long suffering the oppressions of the general government, and the gross, palpable and alarming infractions of the Federal Constitution—That for eight years they have petitioned, argued, and remonstrated—that their Remonstrances have been disregarded—their arguments unheeded, and their most humble petitions treated with contempt—that whilst we have been arguing against power, and trusting to the persuasive arts to combat avarice, and subdue insatiable desire—the friends of manufactures have been up, and doing—until the time has at length arrived, when combinations have been formed sufficient to out-number us by large majorities, and bold enough to advance to the consummation of their schemes in defiance of Protests and solemn Remonstrance.

Resolved, that we will vindicate the Federal Constitution, and will no longer suffer what was established for our security to be perverted to our destruction—that our Liberties are endangered by a mournful progression of events; that for eight years, powers have been exercised by Congress to advance the Interests of the few, without regard to the grievances of the many—that if we now omit to resist, or negligently permit unconstitutional Laws to be enforced in our Territory, in a short period we may be despoiled of our Property, and our Liberties be wrested from us—that this State cannot, after the repeated unequivocal proofs it has experienced, of the utter inutility of Petitions and Remonstrances, reasonably expect that they would be hereafter effectual or productive—that the same local interests which have produced these calamities—militate against a compliance with our wishes and requests, and that it becomes this Legislature and this People, to recur to fundamental principles—that to delay at this time to act, would only render acting more difficult at a future time, and that however much we confide in the Integrity—Patriotism, and firmness of Gen. Jackson, it would be a dangerous delusion to suspend the assertion of our rights, from a confidence in the man of our choice—that we look not to the President, but to the Constitution alone, for the support of our rights, and the preservation of our Liberties.

Resolved, that the Tariff Laws are unjust, oppressive, and palpable Infractions of the Constitution, and as such are void, inoperative, and in no manner obligatory upon the People of this State—That this Legislature will devise such means as are requisite, and necessary to prevent our citizens from being further oppressed by them, and that a Committee be appointed to Draft and Report a Bill—the more effectually to protect our citizens in the exercise of their just rights, and to relieve them from the oppression of unconstitutional enactments.

Resolved, That a Committee be appointed for the purpose of drawing up (in bold, manly, and energetic language,) a memorial to the Congress of the United States, *in the nature of a bill of rights:* setting forth fully and distinctly the various encroachments, that have been of late years made on the Constitution of the United States, and on the rights of the several sovereign states, whose union forms our national confederacy. In particular, setting forth, in a strong light, the *manifest, unconstitutional, sectional,* and oppressive character, of the laws constituting the Tariff of protection, and earnestly requesting their repeal.

Resolved, That two citizens of this State, be specially appointed, to carry without delay, the aforesaid memorial to the Representatives of South Carolina, in the present Congress, with instructions to the said Representatives, to move as early as may be, for the repeal of the Tariff of 1828.

Resolved, That the Governor of this state, be directed to transmit a copy of said memorial, as soon as may be, to the Governor of every state in the union, accompanied by a letter requesting that it may be laid forthwith before the state legislature, and that a reply may be returned to him, as early as convenience will admit.

Resolved, That if the said laws, constituting the Tariff of protection, be not repealed, during the ensuing session of Congress, that the same, or a similar memorial, be transmitted to the succeeding Congress of 1829–30, *as the best appeal which this state ought to make to the good feelings, and wisdom of the Congress of the Union.*

Resolved, That a Committee of —— be raised to devise and report such measures as may be best calculated to carry into effect the foregoing resolutions.

Resolved, That our Senators in Congress be instructed to apply to Congress in the name of the State of South Carolina, to call a convention for proposing amendments to the Constitution of the United States, declaratory of the powers of Congress, enumerated in the Constitution, and restrictive of the exercise by them of any powers or rights not plainly expressed on the face of the instrument.

The Bank War

72. ANDREW JACKSON

The rich and powerful bend government to selfish purposes

The Bank War was the leading issue of Jackson's two administrations. Certainly the controversy over "Biddle's Bank" appeared to be the closest thing to a true ideological issue of the party battles of the era. As the following excerpt from Jackson's 1832 veto message indicates, Jackson—and Amos Kendall, the chief author of the message—sought to give the impression that their opposition to rechartering the second Bank of the United States after its charter lapsed in 1836, was animated largely by anticapitalistic sentiments. The effectiveness of this rhetoric is indicated by how seriously it was taken by Nicholas Biddle, the bank's president, who denounced its alleged "Jacobin" spirit.

From "The Veto of the Bill to Recharter the Second Bank of the United States," James D. Richardson, ed., *A Compilation of the Messages and Papers of the Presidents, 1789–1897* (Washington, D.C.: Government Printing Office, 1896), II, pp. 576, 577, 590, 591.

The bill "to modify and continue" the act entitled "An act to incorporate the subscribers to the Bank of the United States" was presented to me on the 4th July instant. Having considered it with that solemn regard to the principles of the Constitution which the day was calculated to inspire, and come to the conclusion that it ought not to become a law, I herewith return it to the Senate, in which it originated, with my objections.

A bank of the United States is in many respects convenient for the Government and useful to the people. Entertaining this opinion, and deeply impressed with the belief that some of the powers and privileges possessed by the existing bank are unauthorized by the Constitution, subversive of the rights of the States, and dangerous to the liberties of the people, I felt it my duty at an early period of my Administration to call the attention of Congress to the practicability of organizing an institution combining all its advantages and obviating these objections. I sincerely regret that in the act before me I can perceive none of those modifications of the bank charter which are necessary, in my opinion, to make it compatible with justice, with sound policy, or with the Constitution of our country.

The present corporate body, denominated the president, directors, and company of the Bank of the United States, will have existed at the time this act is intended to take effect, twenty years. It enjoys an exclusive privilege of banking under the authority of the General Government, a monopoly of its favor and support, and, as a necessary consequence, almost a monopoly of the foreign and domestic exchange. The powers, privileges, and favors bestowed upon it in the original charter, by increasing the value of the stock far above its par value, operated as a gratuity of many millions to the stockholders.

An apology may be found for the failure to guard against this result in the consideration that the effect of the original act of incorporation could not be certainly foreseen at the time of its passage. The act before me proposes another gratuity to the holders of the same stock, and in many cases to the same men, of at least seven millions more. This donation finds no apology in any uncertainty as to the effect of the act. On all hands it is conceded that its passage will increase at least 20 or 30 per cent more the market price of the stock, subject to the payment of the annuity of $200,000 per year secured by the act, thus adding in a moment one-fourth to its par value. It is not our own citizens only who are to receive the bounty of our Government. More than eight millions of the stock of this bank are held by foreigners. By this act the American Republic proposes virtually to make them a present of some millions of dollars. For these gratuities to foreigners and to some of our own opulent citizens the act secures no equivalent whatever. They are the certain gains of the present stockholders under the operation of this act, after making full allowance for the payment of the bonus.

Every monopoly and all exclusive privileges are granted at the expense of the public, which ought to receive a fair equivalent. The many millions which this act proposes to bestow on the stockholders of the existing bank must come directly or indirectly out of the earnings of the American people. It is due to them, therefore, if their Government sell monopolies and exclusive privileges, that they should at least exact for them as much as they are worth in open market. The value of the monopoly in this case may be correctly ascertained. The twenty-eight millions of stock would probably be at an advance of 50 per cent, and command in market at least $42,000,000, subject to the payment of the present bonus. The present value of the monopoly, therefore, is $17,000,000, and this act proposes to sell for three millions, payable in fifteen annual installments of $200,000 each.

It is not conceivable how the present stockholders can have any claim to the special favor of the Government. The present corporation has enjoyed its monopoly during the period stipulated in the original contract. If we must have such a corporation, why should not the Government sell out the whole stock and thus secure to the people the full market value of the privileges granted? Why should not Congress create and sell twenty-eight millions of stock, incorporating the purchasers with all the powers and privileges secured in this act and putting the premium upon the sales into the Treasury?

But this act does not permit competition in the purchase of this monopoly. It seems to be predicated on the erroneous idea that the present stockholders have a prescriptive right not only to the favor but to the bounty of Government. It appears that more than a fourth part of the stock is held by foreigners and the residue is held by a few hundred of our own citizens, chiefly of the richest class. For their benefit does this act exclude the whole American people from competition in the purchase of this monopoly and dispose of it for many millions less than it is worth. This seems the less excusable because some of our citizens not now stockholders petitioned that the door of competition might be opened, and offered to take a charter on terms much more favorable to the Government and country.

But this proposition, although made by men whose aggregate wealth is believed to be equal to all the private stock in the existing bank, has been set aside, and the bounty of our Government is proposed to be again bestowed on the few who have been fortunate enough to secure the stock and at this moment wield the power of the existing institution. I can not perceive the justice or policy of this course. . . .

It is to be regretted that the rich and powerful too often bend the acts of government to their selfish purposes. Distinctions in society will always exist under every just government. Equality of talents, of education, or of wealth can not be produced by human institutions. In the full enjoyment of the gifts of Heaven and the fruits of superior industry, economy, and virtue, every man is equally entitled to protection by law; but when the laws undertake to add to these natural and just advantages artificial distinctions, to grant titles, gratuities, and exclusive privileges, to make the rich richer and the potent more powerful, the humble members of society—the farmers, mechanics, and laborers—who have neither the time nor the means of securing like favors to themselves, have a right to complain of the injustice of their Government. There are no necessary evils in government. Its evils exist only in its abuses. If it would confine itself to equal protection, and, as Heaven does its rains, shower its favors alike on the high and the low, the rich and the poor, it would be an unqualified blessing. In the act before me there seems to be a wide and unnecessary departure from these just principles.

Nor is our Government to be maintained or our Union preserved by invasions of the rights and powers of the several States. In thus attempting to make our General Government strong we make it weak. Its true strength consists in leaving individuals and States as much as possible to themselves—in making itself felt, not in its power, but in its beneficence; not in its control, but in its protection; not in binding the States more closely to the center, but leaving each to move unobstructed in its proper orbit.

Experience should teach us wisdom. Most of the difficulties our Government now encounters and most of the dangers which impend over our Union have sprung from an abandonment of the legitimate objects of Government by our national legislation, and the adoption of such principles as are embodied in this act. Many of our rich men have not been content with equal protection and equal benefits, but have besought us to make them richer by act of Congress. By attempting to gratify their desires we have in the results of our legislation arrayed section against section, interest against interest, and man against man, in a fearful commotion which threatens to shake the foundations of our Union. It is time to pause in our career to review our principles, and if possible revive that devoted patriotism and spirit of compromise which distinguished the sages of the Revolution and the fathers of our Union. If we can not at once, in justice to interests vested under improvident legislation, make our Government what it ought to be, we can at least take a stand against all new grants of monopolies and exclusive privileges, against any prostitution of our Government to the advancement of the few at the expense of the many, and in favor of compromise and gradual reform in our code of laws and system of political economy.

I have now done my duty to my country. If sustained by my fellow-citizens, I shall be grateful and happy; if not, I shall find in the motives which impel me ample grounds for contentment and peace. In the difficulties which surround us and the dangers which threaten our institutions there is cause for neither dismay nor alarm. For relief and deliverance let us firmly rely on that kind Providence which I am sure watches with peculiar care over the destinies of our Republic, and on the intelligence and wisdom of our countrymen. Through *His* abundant goodness and *their* patriotic devotion our liberty and Union will be preserved.

Andrew Jackson

73. John Pendleton Kennedy

The "pet banks" satirized

Early in his second term Jackson again overrode Congressional opposition, deciding now that the bank was not a safe repository for government deposits, which instead would go into the vaults of selected state banks. The latter were rightly called "pet banks," since the chief criterion used in choosing them was not the ability or sound experience of their directors but rather their Democratic political preferences. These banks were as "capitalistic" in nature as the second Bank of the United States, perhaps more so. For where Biddle's bank had a quasi-public character and its objectives were other than maximum profit for its shareholders, the new repositories were interested in profit, pure and simple. The following selection is from a widely acclaimed spoof written by a Whig wit, John Pendleton Kennedy. It is set in "Quodlibet," a mythical borough controlled by Jacksonian opportunists delighted at the chance to get a piece of the action now that the deposits were removed from the second bank.

Quodlibet, or that which now is Quodlibet, was then as nothing. Michael's dwelling house and tanyard, Abel Brawn's blacksmith shop, Christy M'Curdy's mill and my schoolhouse made up the sum total of the settlement. It is now ten years, or hard on to it, since the commissioners came this way and put the cap-sheaf on Michael's worldly fortune by ruining his tanyard and breaking up

From John Pendleton Kennedy, *Quodlibet* (Philadelphia: Lea and Blanchard, 1840), 26–39.

his business, whereof the damage was so taken to heart by the jury, that, in their rage against internal improvements, they brought in a verdict which doubled Mr. Grant's estate in ready money, besides leaving him two acres of town lots bordering on the Basin, and which, they say, are worth more to-day than the whole tanyard with its appurtenances ever was worth in its best time. This verdict wrought a strange appetite in our county, amongst the landholders, to be ruined in the same way; and I truly believe it was a chief cause of the unpopularity of internal improvements in this neighbourhood, that the commissioners were only able to destroy the farms on the lowlands—which fact, it was said, brought down the price of the uplands on the whole line of the canal, besides creating a great deal of ill humor amongst all who were out of the way of being damaged.

With the money which this verdict brought him, Mr. Grant improved a part of his two acres—which he was persuaded to cut up into town lots—by building the brick tavern and the store that stands next door to it. These were the first buildings of any note in Quodlibet, and are generally supposed to have given rise to the incorporation of the Borough by the Legislature. Jesse Ferret took a lease of the tavern as soon as it was finished, and set up the sign of "The Hero"—meaning thereby General Jackson—which, by the by, was the first piece of historical painting that the celebrated Quipes ever attempted. The store was rented by Frederick Barndollar for his son Jacob, who was just then going to marry Ferret's daughter Susan, and open in the Iron and Flour Forwarding and Commission line, in company with Anthony Hardbottle, his own brother-in-law.

This was the state of things in Quodlibet five years before "The Removal," * from which period, up to the date of the Removal, although Barndollar & Hardbottle did a tolerable business, and Ferret had a fair run of custom, there were not above a dozen new tenements built in the Borough. But a bright destiny was yet in reserve for Quodlibet; and as I propose to unfold some incidents

* Jackson's decision to "remove the deposits" from the Second Bank of the United States and to store them instead in selected state banks—Ed.

of its history belonging to these later times, I cannot pretermit the opportunity now afforded me to glance, though in a perfunctory and hasty fashion, at some striking events which seemed to presignify and illustrate its marvellously sudden growth.

I think it was in the very month of the Removal of the Deposites, that Theodore Fog broke up at Tumbledown, on the other side of the Hog Back, and came over to Quodlibet to practise law. And it was looked upon as a very notable thing, that, in the course of the following winter, Nicodemus Handy should have also quitted Tumbledown and brought his sign, as a lottery agent, to Quodlibet, and set up that business in our Borough. There was a wonderful intimacy struck up between him and Fog, and a good many visits were made by Nicodemus during the fall, before he came over to settle. Our people marvelled at this matter, and were not a little puzzled to make out the meaning of it, knowing that Nicodemus Handy was a shrewd man, and not likely, without some good reason for it, to strike up a friendship with a person so little given to business as Theodore Fog—against whom I desire to say nothing, holding his abilities in great respect, but meaning only to infer that as Theodore is considered high-flown in his speech, and rather too fond of living about Ferret's bar-room, it was thought strange that Nicodemus, who is plain spoken, and of the Temperance principle, should have taken up with him. It was not long after Mr. Handy had seated himself in Quodlibet, and placed his sign at the door of a small weather-boarded office, ten feet by twelve, and within a stone throw of Fog's, before the public were favored with an insight into the cause of this intimacy between these two friends. This was disclosed in a plan for establishing The Patriotic Copper-Plate Bank of Quodlibet, the particulars whereof were made known at a meeting held in the dining room of "The Hero" one evening in March, when Theodore Fog made a flowery speech on the subject to ten persons, counting Ferret and Nim Porter the bar-keeper. The capital of the bank was proposed to be half a million, and the stock one hundred dollars a share, of which one dollar was to be paid in, and the remainder to be secured by promissory notes payable on demand, if convenient.

This excellent scheme found many supporters; and, accordingly, when the time came for action, the whole amount was subscribed by Handy and Fog and ten of their particular friends, who had an eye to being directors and officers of the bank—to whom might also be added about thirty boatmen, who, together with the boys of my academy, lent their names to Mr. Handy.

Through the liberality of Fog, the necessary cash was supplied out of three hundred dollars, the remains of a trust fund in his hands belonging to a family of orphans in the neighborhood of Tumbledown, who had not yet had occasion to know from their attorney, the said Theodore Fog himself, of their success in a cause relating to this fund which had been gained some months before. As Nicodemus managed the subscriptions, which indeed he did with wonderful skill, these three hundred dollars went a great way in making up the payments on considerably more than the majority of the stock: and this being adjusted, he undertook a visit to the Legislature, where, through the disinterested exertions of some staunch democratic friends, he procured a most unexceptionable charter for the bank, full of all sorts of provisions, conditions and clauses necessary to enable it to accommodate the public with as much paper money as the said public could possibly desire.

In consideration of these great services, Nicodemus Handy elected himself Cashier; and, at the same time, had well nigh fallen into a quarrel with Fog who had set his heart upon being President—which, in view of the fact that that gentleman's habits were somewhat irregular after twelve o'clock in the day, Nicodemus would by no means consent to. This dissention, however, was seemingly healed, by bringing in as President, my worshipful pupil, the honorable Middleton Flam, now our member of Congress, and by making Theodore one of the directors, besides giving him the law business of the bank. It was always thought, notwithstanding Fog pretended to be satisfied at the time with this arrangement, that it rankled in his bosom, and bred a jealousy between him and his associates in the bank, and helped to drive him to drinking faster than he would naturally have done, if his feelings had not been aggravated by this act of supposed ingratitude.

I should not omit to mention that Nicodemus Handy was a man of exact and scrupulous circumspection, and noted for the deliberation with which he weighed the consequences of his actions, or, as the common saying is, "looked before he leapt"—a remarkable proof of which kind of wisdom he afforded at this time. Having been compelled by circumstances to live beyond the avails of his lottery business, and thereby to bring himself under some impracticable liabilities, he made it a point of conscience before he could permit himself to be clothed with the dignity of a cashier, or even to place a share of stock in his own name on the books, to swear out in open court, and to surrender, for the benefit of his numerous and patient creditors, his whole stock of worldly goods—consisting, according to the inventory thereof on record, which I have seen, of a cylindrical sheet-iron stove, two chairs, a desk and a sign-board, this latter being, as I remember, of the shape of a screen, on each leaf of which, "NICODEMUS HANDY" was printed, together with the scheme of a lottery, set forth in large red and blue letters. He barely retained what the law allowed him, being his mere wearing apparel; to wit, a brand new suit of black superfine Saxony, one dozen of the best cambric linen shirts, as many lawn pocket handkerchiefs, white kid gloves, and such other trivial, but gentlemanlike appurtenances as denoted that extreme neatness of dress in which Mr. Handy has ever taken a just pride, and which has been so often remarked by his friends as one of the strong points in his character. These articles, it was said, he had procured not more with a provident eye to that state of destitution, into which the generous surrender of his property was about to plunge him, than with a decent regard to the respectability of appearance which the public, he conceived, had a right to exact from the Cashier of the Patriotic Copperplate Bank of Quodlibet. All right-minded persons will naturally commend this prudence, and applaud Mr. Handy's sense of the dignity proper to so important and elevated a station—a station which Theodore Fog, in his speech at "The Hero," so appropriately eulogised as one "of financial, fiscal and monetary responsibility."

There was one circumstance connected with the history of the establishment of the Bank that excited great observation amongst our folks:—that was the dislike Michael Grant took up against it from its very beginning. It was an indiscriminate, unmitigable, dogged dislike to the whole concern, which, by degrees, brought him into a bad opinion of our Borough, and I verily believe was the cause why, from that time forward, he kept himself so much at his farm near the Hog Back and grew to be, as if it were out of mere opposition, so unhappily, and indeed I may say, so perversely stubborn in those iniquitous Whig sentiments which he was in the habit of uttering. I have heard him say that he thought as badly as a man could think, of the *grounds* for starting the Bank, and still worse of the *men* who started it;—which, certainly, was a very rash expression, considering that our congressman, the Hon. Middleton Flam, was President and one of the first patrons of the institution, and that such a man as Nicodemus Handy was Cashier; to say nothing of Theodore Fog, whose habits we are willing to confess, might, in the estimation of some men, give some little color to my worthy friend's vituperation.

Now, there was no man in Quodlibet whom Handy and Fog so much desired, or strove so hard, to bring into the Bank scheme as Mr. Grant. They made every sort of effort and used all kinds of arguments to entice him. Nicodemus Handy on one occasion, I think it was in April, put the matter to him in such strong points of view, that I have often marvelled since how the good gentleman stood it. He argued, with amazing cogency, that General Jackson had removed the deposites for the *express purpose* of destroying the Bank of the United States, and giving the State Banks a fair field: that the Old Hero was an enthusiastic friend to State Rights, and especially to State Banks which it was the desire of his heart to see increased and multiplied all over the country; that he was actually, as it were, making pets out of these Banks, and was determined to feed them up with the public monies and give them such a credit in the land as would forever shut out all hope to the friends of a National Bank to succeed with their purpose: and finally that although Clay and the Whigs were endeavoring to resist the General in his determination to establish New Banks in the States, that resistance was already considered hopeless. It was with a visible air of triumph that Mr. Handy in confirmation of this opinion read from the Globe of the 21st of December previous, these words:

> The Intelligent people of the West know how to maintain their rights and independence and to repel oppression. Although foiled in the beginning, every Western State is about to establish a State Bank institution. They are resolved to avail themselves of their own state credit, as well as of the National credit, to maintain a currency independent of foreign control. Mr. Clay's presses in Kentucky begin now to feel how vain are all their efforts to resist the determination of the people of the West. Ohio, Indiana, Illinois, Missouri and Kentucky are resolved to take care of themselves, and no longer depend on the kind guardianship of Biddle, Clay & Co.

Having laid this fact before Mr. Grant, by way of clinching the argument Mr. Handy pulled out of his pocket a letter which he had just received from the Secretary of the Treasury. It contained a communication of the deepest import to the future fortunes of our Borough; which communication, as I have been favoured by Mr. Handy with a copy, I feel happy to transcribe here for the edification of my reader. It is a circular, and came to our cashier printed on gilt edged letter paper, having the title of the Bank, the date and some other items filled up in writing.

> *Treasury Department, April 1, 1834*
>
> Sir:—The Patriotic Copper-plate Bank of Quodlibet has been selected by this department as the depository of the public money collected in Quodlibet and its vicinity; and the Marshal will hand you the form of a contract proposed to be executed, with a copy of his instructions from this department. In selecting your institution as one of the fiscal agents of the government, I not only rely on its solidity and established character, as affording a sufficient guarantee for the safety of the public money entrusted to its keeping, but I confide also in its disposition to adopt the most liberal course which circumstances will admit, toward other moneyd institutions gener-

ally, and particularly those in your vicinity. The deposites of the public money will enable you to afford increased facilities to commerce, and to extend your accommodations to individuals; and as the duties which are payable to the government arise from the business and enterprise of the merchants engaged in foreign trade, it is but reasonable that they should be preferred in the additional accommodations which the public deposites will enable your institution to give, whenever it can be done without injustice to the claims of other classes of the community.

I am, &c.

R. B. TANEY,
Secretary of the Treasury

To the President of the Patriotic Copper-plate Bank of Quodlibet.

"There, sir,"—said Mr. Handy, after he had read this paper to Mr. Grant—"read that over again and tell me if there is any Quodlibetarian that ought not to rejoice in this great event, and lend his endeavors, with both heart and soul to promote and sustain an institution so favored by the government. The secretary, you perceive, has confidence in the 'solidity and established character' of our bank—how can you refuse *your* confidence after that? Sir, the Secretary is an honor to the democracy of Quodlibet:—what does he say? Does he tell us to keep the public moneys locked up only for the selfish purposes of the government? Oh no: far from it; 'the deposites,' says he, 'will enable you to afford increased facilities to commerce, and to extend your accommodations to individuals.' Mark that! there's a President and Secretary for you! True friends, Mr. Grant—true friends to the people. How careful are they of our great mercantile and trading classes! Sir, the government cannot do too much for such people as we are—that's the true democratic motto—we *expect* a great deal—but they outrun our expectations. No more low prices for grain, Mr. Grant—no more scarcity of money:—accommodation is the word—better currency is the word—high prices, good wages and plenty of work is the word now-a-days. We shall have a city here before you can cleverly turn yourself round. Depend upon it, sir, we are destined to become a great, glorious and immortal people."

"Sir," said Theodore Fog, interposing at this moment, with a look that wore a compound expression of thoughtful sternness and poetical phrensy—"when the historic muse shall hereafter contemplate the humble origin of Quodlibet——"

"Fog," interrupted Nicodemus somewhat petulantly—and I feel sorry to be obliged to record this inconsiderate language, "D—n the historic muse—we are now on business."

"As a director, sir," replied Fog with a subdued air, but with a dignified gravity, "I have a *right* to speak. I meant to say, sir, in plain phrase, that Quodlibet must inevitably, from this day forth, under the proud auspices of democratic principles—obedient to that native impulse which the profound statesmanship of this people-sustaining and people-sustained administration, has imparted to it, soar aloft to place herself upon the proud pinnacle of commercial prosperity, wealth and power. I have no doubt, Mr. Grant, your tavern lot will increase to three times its present value. You *ought* to take stock;—let me tell you, sir, as a citizen of Quodlibet, you ought. As to the cash, that's a bagatelle. Handy and I can let you have any number of shares on your own terms. Flam will do any thing we say to let you in. By the by, he got us the deposites. Flam's a man of influence—but whether on the whole he will make us the best President we could have procured, is perhaps somewhat apocryphal."

"You cannot fail to see," said Mr. Handy, "that we must all make our fortunes, if the government is only true to its word; and who can doubt it will be true? We start comparatively with nothing, I may say, speaking of myself—absolutely with nothing. We shall make a large issue of paper, predicated upon the deposites; we shall accommodate every body, as the secretary desires—of course, not forgetting our friends, and more particularly ourselves:—we shall pay, in this way, our stock purchases.—You may run up a square of warehouses on the Basin; I will join you as a partner in the transaction, give you the plan of operations, furnish architectural models, supply the funds, et cetera, et cetera. We will sell out the buildings at a hundred per cent. advance before they are finished; Fog here will be the purchaser. We have then only to advertise in the papers this extraordinary rise of property in Quodlibet—procure a map to be made of our new city; get it lithographed, and immediately sell the lots on the Exchange of New York at a most unprecedented valuation. My dear sir, I have just bought a hundred acres of land adjoining the Borough, with an eye to this very speculation. You shall have an interest of one half in this operation at a reasonable valuation—I shall want but a small profit, say two hundred per cent.—a mere trifle—in consideration of my labors in laying it off into streets, lanes and alleys;—and if there is any convenience in it to you—although I know you are a moneyed man—you have only to make a proposal for a slice of accommodation—just drop a note now and then into the discount box—you understand? The Secretary will be delighted, my dear sir, to hear of our giving an accommodation to you. But there's one thing, Mr. Grant, I must not forget to remark—the Secretary, in fact, makes it a sort of *sine qua non*—you must come out a genuine—declare yourself a Whole Hog—and go for Flam in the fall elections. The Secretary expects, you know,"—and as he said this he laid his finger significantly upon his nose, "that the accommodation principle—you know—is to be measurably—extended—you know—in proportion to the—democracy—of the applicants—you understand? —a word to the wise—that's all. It could n't be expected, you perceive, that *we*, holding the deposites, should be quite as favorable to the Whigs, who rather charge us with experimenting on the currency—you know—and who, in fact, don't scruple to say that our banking system will be a failure—it could n't be expected we should be as bountiful to them as to those who go with us in building up this concatenation—tweedle dum and tweedle dee, you know, betwixt you and me;—but it's made a point of—and has its effect on ulterior expectations, you understand. The long and the short is, without being mealy-mouthed, we must prefer the old Hero's friends;—but, after all, that's a small matter:—be a Democrat, and go for Flam!"

"Flam and the immutable principles of civil liberty!" said Fog, with great animation. "Middleton Flam, the embodyment and personification of those deep and profound truths, based upon the eternal distinctions of the greatest good to the greatest number! Diffusive wealth, combined capital, increased facilities to commerce, and accommodation to individuals—there is the *multum in parvo* of General Jackson's democratic creed!—there is the glorious consummation of the war with the great money power, which, like Juggernaut, was crushing down the liberties of our republic!"

Michael Grant was a patient listener, and, ordinarily, a man of few words. He stood all the time that Fog and Handy were plying him with this discourse, with his thumbs in his waistcoat pockets, looking down, with a grum cogitation, at his own image in the water of the basin, on the margin of which the parties had met, and every now and then rocking on his heels and flapping the soles of his feet sharply on the ground, denoting, by this movement, to those who knew his habit, that he was growing more and more positive in his opinion. Once or twice he was observed to raise his head, and, with one eye half shut, seemed as if studying the heavens. At length he broke out with an answer which, both from the vehemence of his tone and the unusual volubility of his words, caused Handy and Fog to prick up their ears, and gaze upon each other with a look of incredulous surprise.

"Look you, gentlemen," said he, "Nicodemus Handy and Theodore Fog: You have never heard me say that General Jackson was not a good general. I scorn to take any thing away from the reputation of an old soldier—I have never done it—I never mean to do it; I respect him for his services: but, curse me, if I believe he knows any more about banks than I do about bombshells! No, nor his secretary neither; or, if *he* does, he is not man enough to say no to the General. As for this Patriotic Copperplate Bank of Quodlibet, and others now springing up of the same kidney, they are just so many new Egyptian plagues, which our rascally magicians and false prophets have been conjuring up to harass the people with. It won't be long before we shall begin to find out that the frogs and the locusts and the lice of Pharaoh's kingdom have been all outdone by these new banks, which the General and his secretaries are so busy to hatch. Do you know what is coming, Nicodemus Handy? I'll tell you. Now your new banks are like these thundergust mills, over here in the mountain: just as long as you have showers from the treasury, so long will your wheels keep in motion; but the first dry spell at Washington shuts you up, and disappoints the whole country side in their grist. They are all eggs of the same basket, and this administration will be known, by and by, as the Thundergust Bank Administration. In four years from this day, there will be twice as many of these paper machines, big and little, as there are now; and bank notes will be thrashed out as fast as chaff at the tail of a fan. The country will be filled with toad stools—not mushrooms, for they are worth something. We shall see your toad-stool great men fetching up in a night, and ciphering out fortunes in a week. The world will turn crazy after speculations—just such speculations as your hundred acre purchase—bought without a cent of money, and paid for by accommodation, granted on what Fog here calls the great democratic principle. The public lands will be grabbed at by every rascal who has cunning and knavery enough to go to the President and his secretary, and flatter them on their Democracy. He who can dip deepest into that play will build towns for himself, lay out farms for his children by the mile square, and make nabobs of his sons; and, whilst he does so, he will vilify and bring into contempt all honestly gathered wealth, and prate about his friendship for the poor man, just to keep the reins in his own hands. We have had one of these paper money storms once before in this country. I remember it well. It came after the old bank went down, just as it is coming now, since President Jackson has set his heart upon strangling the monster, as he calls it. The old story will be told over again. By doubling the number of banks, you will double trade and speculation, and that will double our debts, without adding one bushel to our crops. Then look out for the day of reckoning! Coin will be wanting to pay for the silks and wines and fine linen, that we shall have got upon trust upon the other side of the ocean. Such banks as have the coin will be obliged to let it go, and they will call upon the people to pay up,—which the people will not be able to do. What follows? A suspension of specie payments, and along with that all manner of grumbling and discontent and ill will. Every man will be laying the blame upon his neighbor, and your thundergust banks will be the loudest in the whole crowd, crying out that a panic has been got up by the dying monster:—and you who call yourselves Democrats, to stave off all inquiry into the matter, will shout that the liberties of the country are in danger;—like a thief who has stolen a horse, you will get up into the saddle and strike off at full speed, foremost in the chase, bellowing 'stop thief!' After the crash, what becomes of your new banks, your new towns, your new stocks, and your new men? Soap bubbles bursted! Torn bladder skins, not fit to make a tobacco pouch! Fools will build houses, and wise men will live in them. Is not this plainly enough set down in past history? What more do you want? Take the trouble to read the speeches in congress, and you will find the whole course of the thing demonstrated by the wisest men at Washington. Listen to their counsels, and take heed in time. Forewarned is forearmed. Tell General Jackson that it is not beneath the wisdom of a great man to take a lesson from his adversary. The best friends of the people are those who tell them the truth, in time to put them on their guard,—no matter how harsh it may seem to the President or any body else. Now, sir, that is my opinion."

Monopoly

74. Roger Brooke Taney

The object of all government, to promote happiness and prosperity

The Jacksonians capitalized heavily on the issue of monopoly. This was a brillant achievement, inasmuch as in many states the Jacksonian legislatures were the truest exemplars of the system of monopoly they so delighted in excoriating in party propaganda. The democracy's antimo-

From Richard Peters, *Reports of Cases Argued and Adjudged by the Supreme Court*, January Term, 1837 (Philadelphia: Thomas, Cowperthwait, 1845), XI, pp. 557–563.

nopoly reputation owed much to the 1837 decision by the Supreme Court in the case of the *Charles River Bridge Company* v. *Warren Bridge Company.* While not the radical decision some opponents claimed it was, the ruling did refute the notion that a monopolistic right adhered to a company by implication from its possession of a charter. No such right existed, argued Roger Brooke Taney, Jackson's appointee to the High Court, particularly in areas where new enterprise was needed to keep up with demand. The other decisions of the Court, most of whose members were appointed by Jackson, make clear that the judicial branch of "Jacksonian Democracy" was dedicated to defense of private property, contracts, and the rights of corporations, while having little sympathy for debtors. The following selection contains the bulk of Taney's Charles River decision.

The case now before the court is, in principle, precisely the same. It is a charter from a state. The act of incorporation is silent in relation to the contested power. The argument in favour of the proprietors of the Charles river bridge, is the same, almost in words, with that used by the Providence Bank; that is, that the power claimed by the state, if it exists, may be so used as to destroy the value of the franchise they have granted to the corporation. The argument must receive the same answer; and the fact that the power has been already exercised so as to destroy the value of the franchise, cannot in any degree affect the principle. The existence of the power does not, and cannot depend upon the circumstance of its having been excised or not.

It may, perhaps, be said, that in the case of the Providence Bank, this court were speaking of the taxing power; which is of vital importance to the very existence of every government. But the object and end of all government is to promote the happiness and prosperity of the community by which it is established; and it can never be assumed, that the government intended to diminish its power of accomplishing the end for which it was created. And in a country like ours, free, active, and enterprising, continually advancing in numbers and wealth; new channels of communication are daily found necessary, both for travel and trade; and are essential to the comfort, convenience, and prosperity of the people. A state ought never to be presumed to surrender this power, because, like the taxing power, the whole community have an interest in preserving it undiminished. And when a corporation alleges, that a state has surrendered for seventy years, its power of improvement and public accommodation, in a great and important line of travel, along which a vast number of its citizens must daily pass; the community have a right to insist, in the language of this court above quoted, "that its abandonment ought not to be presumed, in a case, in which the deliberate purpose of the state to abandon it does not appear." The continued existence of a government would be of no great value, if by implications and presumptions, it was disarmed of the powers necessary to accomplish the ends of its creation; and the functions it was designed to perform, transferred to the hands of privileged corporations. The rule of construction announced by the court, was not confined to the taxing power; nor is it so limited in the opinion delivered. On the contrary, it was distinctly placed on the ground that the interests of the community were concerned in preserving, undiminished, the power then in question; and whenever any power of the state is said to be surrendered or diminished, whether it be the taxing power or any other affecting the public interest, the same principle applies, and the rule of construction must be the same. No one will question that the interests of the great body of the people of the state, would, in this instance, be affected by the surrender of this great line of travel to a single corporation, with the right to exact toll, and exclude competition for seventy years. While the rights of private property are sacredly guarded, we must not forget that the community also have rights, and that the happiness and well being of every citizen depends on their faithful preservation.

Adopting the rule of construction above stated as the settled one, we proceed to apply it to the charter of 1785, to the proprietors of the Charles river bridge. This act of incorporation is in the usual form, and the privileges such as are commonly given to corporations of that kind. It confers on them the ordinary faculties of a corporation, for the purpose of building the bridge; and establishes certain rates of toll, which the company are authorized to take. This is the whole grant. There is no exclusive privilege given to them over the waters of Charles river, above or below their bridge. No right to erect another bridge themselves, nor to prevent other persons from erecting one. No engagement from the state, that another shall not be erected; and no undertaking not to sanction competition, nor to make improvements that may diminish the amount of its income. Upon all these subjects the charter is silent; and nothing is said in it about a line of travel, so much insisted on in the argument, in which they are to have exclusive privileges. No words are used, from which an intention to grant any of these rights can be inferred. If the plaintiff is entitled to them, it must be implied, simply, from the nature of the grant; and cannot be inferred, from the words by which the grant is made.

The relative position of the Warren bridge has already been described. It does not interrupt the passage over the Charles river bridge, nor make the way to it or from it less convenient. None of the faculties or franchises granted to that corporation, have been revoked by the legislature; and its right to take the tolls granted by the charter remains unaltered. In short, all the franchises and rights of property enumerated in the charter, and there mentioned to have been granted to it, remain unimpaired. But its income is destroyed by the Warren bridge; which, being free, draws off the passengers and property which would have gone over it, and renders their franchise of no value. This is the gist of the complaint. For it is not pretended, that the erection of the Warren bridge would have done them any injury, or in any degree affected their right of property; if it had not diminished the amount of their tolls. In order then to entitle themselves to relief, it is necessary to show, that the legislature contracted not to do the act of which they complain; and that they impaired, or in other words, violated that contract by the erection of the Warren bridge.

The inquiry then is, does the charter contain such a contract on the part of the state? Is there any such stipulation to be found in that instrument? It must be admitted on all hands, that there is none—no words that even relate to another bridge, or to the diminution of their tolls, or to the line of travel. If a contract on that subject can be gathered from the charter, it must be by implication; and cannot be found in the words used. Can such an agreement be implied? The rule of construction before stated is an answer to the question. In charters of this description, no rights are taken from the public, or given to the corporation, beyond those which the words of the charter, by their natural and proper construction, purport to convey. There are no words which import such a contract as the plaintiffs in error contend for, and none can be implied; and the same answer must be given to them that was given by this court to the Providence Bank. The whole community are interested in this inquiry, and they have a right to require that the power of promoting their comfort and convenience, and of advancing the public prosperity, by providing safe, convenient, and cheap ways for the transportation of produce, and the purposes of travel, shall not be construed to have been surrendered or diminished by the state; unless it shall appear by plain words, that it was intended to be done.

But the case before the court is even still stronger against any such implied contract, as the plaintiffs in error contend for. The Charles river bridge was completed in 1786. The time limited for the duration of the corporation by their original charter, expired in 1826. When, therefore, the law passed authorizing the erection of the Warren bridge, the proprietors of Charles river bridge held their corporate existence under the law of 1792, which extended their charter for thirty years; and the rights, privileges, and franchises of the company, must depend upon the construction of the last mentioned law, taken in connection with the act of 1785.

The act of 1792, which extends the charter of this bridge, incorporates another company to build a bridge over Charles river; furnishing another communication with Boston, and distant only between one and two miles from the old bridge.

The first six sections of this act incorporate the proprietors of the West Boston bridge, and define the privileges, and describe the duties of that corporation. In the seventh section there is the following recital: "And whereas the erection of Charles river bridge was a work of hazard and public utility, and another bridge in the place of West Boston bridge may diminish the emoluments of Charles river bridge; therefore, for the encouragement of enterprise," they proceed to extend the charter of the Charles river bridge, and to continue it for the term of seventy years from the day the bridge was completed; subject to the conditions prescribed in the original act, and to be entitled to the same tolls. It appears, then, that by the same act that extended this charter, the legislature established another bridge, which they knew would lessen its profits; and this, too, before the expiration of the first charter, and only seven years after it was granted; thereby showing, that the state did not suppose that, by the terms it had used in the first law, it had deprived itself of the power of making such public improvements as might impair the profits of the Charles river bridge; and from the language used in the clauses of the law by which the charter is extended, it would seem, that the legislature were especially careful to exclude any inference that the extension was made upon the ground of compromise with the bridge company, or as a compensation for rights impaired.

On the contrary, words are cautiously employed to exclude that conclusion; and the extension is declared to be granted as a reward for the hazard they had run, and "for the encouragement of enterprise." The extension was given because the company had undertaken and executed a work of doubtful success; and the improvements which the legislature then contemplated, might diminish the emoluments they had expected to receive from it. It results from this statement, that the legislature in the very law extending the charter, asserts its rights to authorize improvements over Charles river which would take off a portion of the travel from this bridge and diminish its profits; and the bridge company accept the renewal thus given, and thus carefully connected with this assertion of the right on the part of the state. Can they, when holding their corporate existence under this law, and deriving their franchises altogether from it; add to the privileges expressed in their charter an implied agreement, which is in direct conflict with a portion of the law from which they derive their corporate existence? Can the legislature be presumed to have taken upon themselves an implied obligation, contrary to its own acts and declarations contained in the same law? It would be difficult to find a case justifying such an implication, even between individuals; still less will it be found where sovereign rights are concerned, and where the interests of a whole community would be deeply affected by such an implication. It would, indeed, be a strong exertion of judicial power, acting upon its own views of what justice required, and the parties ought to have done; to raise, by a sort of judicial coercion, an implied contract, and infer it from the nature of the very instrument in which the legislature appear to have taken pains to use words which disavow and repudiate any intention, on the part of the state, to make such a contract.

Indeed, the practice and usage of almost every state in the Union, old enough to have commenced the work of internal improvement, is opposed to the doctrine contended for on the part of the plaintiffs in error. Turnpike roads have been made in succession, on the same line of travel; the later ones interfering materially with the profits of the first. These corporations have, in some instances, been utterly ruined by the introduction of newer and better modes of transportation, and travelling. In some cases, rail roads have rendered the turnpike roads on the same line of travel so entirely useless, that the franchise of the turnpike corporation is not worth preserving.

Yet in none of these cases have the corporation supposed that their privileges were invaded, or any contract violated on the part of the state. Amid the multitude of cases which have occurred, and have been daily occurring for the last forty or fifty years, this is the first instance in which such an implied contract has been contended for, and this court called upon to infer it from an ordinary act of incorporation, containing nothing more than the usual stipulations and provisions to be found in every such law. The absence of any such controversy, when there must have been so many occasions to give rise to it, proves that neither states, nor individuals, nor corporations, ever imagined that such a contract could be implied from such charters. It shows that the men who voted for these laws, never imagined that they were forming such a contract; and if we maintain that they have made it, we must create it by a legal fiction, in opposition to the truth of the fact, and the obvious intention of the party. We cannot deal thus with the rights reserved to the states; and by legal intendments and mere technical reasoning, take away from them any portion of that power over their own internal police and improvement, which is so necessary to their well being and prosperity.

And what would be the fruits of this doctrine of implied contracts on the part of the states, and of property in a line of travel by a corporation, if it should now be sanctioned by this court? To what results would it lead us? If it is to be found in the charter to this bridge, the same process of reasoning must discover it, in the various acts which have been passed, within the last forty years, for turnpike companies. And what is to be the extent of the privileges of exclusion on the different sides of the road? The counsel who have so ably argued this case, have not attempted to define it by any certain boundaries. How far must the new improvement be distant from the old one? How near may you approach without invading its rights in the privileged line? If this court should establish the principles now contended for, what is to become of the numerous rail roads established on the same line of travel with turnpike companies; and which have rendered the franchises of the turnpike corporations of no value? Let it once be understood that such charters carry with them these implied contracts, and give this unknown and undefined property in a line of travelling; and you will soon find the old turnpike corporations awakening from their sleep, and calling upon this court to put down the improvements which have taken their place. The millions of property which have been invested in rail roads and canals, upon lines of travel which had been before occupied by turnpike corporations, will be put in jeopardy. We shall be thrown back to the improvements of the last century, and obliged to stand still, until the claims of the old turnpike corporations shall be satisfied; and they shall consent to permit these states to avail themselves of the lights of modern science, and to partake of the benefit of those improvements which are now adding to the wealth and prosperity, and the convenience and comfort, of every other part of the civilized world. Nor is this all. This court will find itself compelled to fix, by some arbitrary rule, the width of this new kind of property in a line of travel; for if such a right of property exists, we have no lights to guide us in marking out its extent, unless, indeed, we resort to the old feudal grants, and to the exclusive rights of ferries, by prescription, between towns; and are prepared to decide that when a turnpike road from one town to another, had been made, no rail road or canal, between these two points, could afterwards be established. This court are not prepared to sanction principles which must lead to such results.

Many other questions, of the deepest importance, have been raised and elaborately discussed in the argument. It is not necessary, for the decision of this case, to express our opinion upon them; and the court deem it proper to avoid volunteering an opinion on any question, involving the construction of the constitution, where the case itself does not bring the question directly before them, and make it their duty to decide upon it.

Some questions, also, of a purely technical character, have been made and argued, as to the form of proceeding and the right to relief. But enough appears on the record to bring out the great question in contest; and it is the interest of all parties concerned, that the real controversy should be settled without further delay: and as the opinion of the court is pronounced on the main question in dispute here, and disposes of the whole case, it is altogether unnecessary to enter upon the examination of the forms of proceeding, in which the parties have brought it before the court.

The judgment of the supreme judicial court of the commonwealth of Massachusetts, dismissing the plaintiffs' bill, must, therefore, be affirmed, with costs.

Nullification

75. Andrew Jackson

The sacred Union, hitherto inviolate

One of the most difficult problems faced by the Jackson administration was the nullification controversy. In 1832 South Carolina proclaimed its

From "A Proclamation to the People of South Carolina," Richardson, ed., *Messages and Papers of the Presidents*, II, pp. 640–642.

right to nullify the tariff act of that year, threatening secession if the federal government attempted to use coercion to enforce compliance with the law. Contributing to the crisis was the impression given by Old Hickory that his refusal to interfere with Georgia's snubbing of federal authority in the Cherokee case earlier in the year signified his unwillingness to act against any assertive state. Jackson dealt effectively with this thorny constitutional and political question. While the proclamation drawn up for him by his attorney general, Edward Livingston, was a forceful statement, Jackson's comprehensive policy in this instance was judicious and flexible. He permitted Calhoun to save face and Clay to gain credit for a compromise the ground for which had been prepared by Jackson himself.

Whereas a convention assembled in the State of South Carolina have passed an ordinance by which they declare "that the several acts and parts of acts of the Congress of the United States purporting to be laws for the imposing of duties and imposts on the importation of foreign commodities, and now having actual operation and effect within the United States, and more especially" two acts for the same purposes passed on the 29th of May, 1828, and on the 14th of July, 1832, "are unauthorized by the Constitution of the United States, and violate the true meaning and intent thereof, and are null and void and no law," nor binding on the citizens of that State or its officers; and by the said ordinance it is further declared to be unlawful for any of the constituted authorities of the State or of the United States to enforce the payment of the duties imposed by the said acts within the same State, and that it is the duty of the legislature to pass such laws as may be necessary to give full effect to the said ordinance; and

Whereas by the said ordinance it is further ordained that in no case of law or equity decided in the courts of said State wherein shall be drawn in question the validity of the said ordinance, or of the acts of the legislature that may be passed to give it effect, or of the said laws of the United States, no appeal shall be allowed to the Supreme Court of the United States, nor shall any copy of the record be permitted or allowed for that purpose, and that any person attempting to take such appeal shall be punished as for contempt of court; and, finally, the said ordinance declares that the people of South Carolina will maintain the said ordinance at every hazard, and that they will consider the passage of any act by Congress abolishing or closing the ports of the said State or otherwise obstructing the free ingress or egress of vessels to and from the said ports, or any other act of the Federal Government to coerce the State, shut up her ports, destroy or harass her commerce, or to enforce the said acts otherwise than through the civil tribunals of the country, as inconsistent with the longer continuance of South Carolina in the Union, and that the people of the said State will thenceforth hold themselves absolved from all further obligation to maintain or preserve their political connection with the people of the other States, and will forthwith proceed to organize a separate government and do all other acts and things which sovereign and independent states may of right do; and

Whereas the said ordinance prescribes to the people of South Carolina a course of conduct in direct violation of their duty as citizens of the United States, contrary to the laws of their country, subversive of its Constitution, and having for its object the destruction of the Union—that Union which, coeval with our political existence, led our fathers, without any other ties to unite them than those of patriotism and a common cause, through a sanguinary struggle to a glorious independence; the sacred Union, hitherto inviolate, which, perfected by our happy Constitution, has brought us, by the favor of Heaven, to a state of prosperity at home and high consideration abroad rarely, if ever, equaled in the history of nations:

To preserve this bond of our political existence from destruction, to maintain inviolate this state of national honor and prosperity, and to justify the confidence my fellow-citizens have reposed in me, I, Andrew Jackson, President of the United States, have thought proper to issue this my proclamation, stating my views of the Constitution and laws applicable to the measures adopted by the convention of South Carolina and to the reasons they have put forth to sustain them, declaring the course which duty will require me to pursue, and, appealing to the understanding and patriotism of the people, warn them of the consequences that must inevitably result from an observance of the dictates of the convention.

Strict duty would require of me nothing more than the exercise of those powers with which I am now or may hereafter be invested for preserving the peace of the Union and for the execution of the laws; but the imposing aspect which opposition has assumed in this case, by clothing itself with State authority, and the deep interest which the people of the United States must all feel in preventing a resort to stronger measures while there is a hope that anything will be yielded to reasoning and remonstrance, perhaps demand, and will certainly justify, a full exposition to South Carolina and the nation of the views I entertain of this important question, as well as a distinct enunciation of the course which my sense of duty will require me to purpose.

The ordinance is founded, not on the indefeasible right of resisting acts which are plainly unconstitutional and too oppressive to be endured, but on the strange position that any one State may not only declare an act of Congress void, but prohibit its execution; that they may do this consistently with the Constitution; that the true construction of that instrument permits a State to retain its place in the Union and yet be bound by no other of its laws than those it may choose to consider as constitutional. It is true, they add, that to justify this abrogation of a law it must be palpably contrary to the Constitution; but it is evident that to give the right of resisting laws of that description, coupled with the uncontrolled right to decide what laws deserve that character, is to give the power of resisting all laws; for as by the theory there is no appeal, the reasons alleged by the State, good or bad, must prevail. If it should be said that public opinion is a sufficient check against the abuse of this power, it may be asked why it is not deemed a sufficient guard against the passage of an unconstitutional act by Congress? There is, however, a restraint in this last case which makes the assumed power of a State more indefensible, and which does not exist in the other. There are two appeals from an unconstitutional act passed by Congress—one to the judiciary, the other to the people and the States. There is no appeal from the State decision in theory, and the practical illustration shows that the courts are closed against an application to review it, both judges and jurors being sworn to decide in its favor. But reasoning on this subject is superfluous when our social compact, in express terms, declares that the laws of the United States, its Constitution, and treaties made under it are the supreme law of the land, and, for greater caution, adds "that the judges in every State shall be bound thereby, anything in the constitution or laws of any State to the contrary notwithstanding." And it may be asserted without fear of refutation that no federative government could exist without a similar provision. Look for a moment to the consequence. If South Carolina considers the revenue laws unconstitutional and has a right to prevent their execution in the port of Charleston, there would be a clear constitutional objection to their collection in every other port; and no revenue could be collected anywhere, for all imposts must be equal. It is no answer to repeat that an unconstitutional law is no law so long as the question of its legality is to be decided by the State itself, for every law operating injuriously upon any local interest will be perhaps thought, and certainly represented, as unconstitutional, and, as has been shown, there is no appeal.

If this doctrine had been established at an earlier day, the Union would have been dissolved in its infancy. The excise law in Pennsylvania, the embargo and nonintercourse law in the Eastern States, the carriage tax in Virginia, were all deemed unconstitutional, and were more unequal in their operation than any of the laws now complained of; but, fortunately, none of those States discovered that they had the right now claimed by South Carolina. The war into which we were forced to support the dignity of the nation and the rights of our citizens might have ended in defeat and disgrace, instead of victory and honor, if the States who supposed it a ruinous and unconstitutional measure had thought they possessed the right of nullifying the act by which it was declared and denying supplies for its prosecution. Hardly and unequally as those measures bore upon several members of the Union, to the legislatures of none did this efficient and peaceable remedy, as it is called, suggest itself. The discovery of this important feature in our Constitution was reserved to the present day. To the statesmen of South Carolina belongs the invention, and upon the citizens of that State will unfortunately fall the evils of reducing it to practice.

If the doctrine of a State veto upon the laws of the Union carries with it internal evidence of its impracticable absurdity, our constitutional history will also afford abundant proof that it would have been repudiated with indignation had it been proposed to form a feature in our Government.

Jingoism

76. ANDREW JACKSON

The president prepares to insult France

Old Hickory's penchant for bluster brought the nation to the brink of war with France in 1835. The issue involved the footdragging of the French government in paying a debt it had agreed it owed the United States for earlier maritime violations. Jackson's public stance was belligerent enough. The following selection indicates that an earlier draft he had prepared was harsher still. While Jacksonian "diplomacy" did score a number of successes, it is almost a contradiction in terms to apply the word *diplomacy* to Jackson's highhanded and belligerent approach in the case of the French spoliation claims.

NOTES FOR THE ANNUAL MESSAGE

December 7, 1835

I regret to inform you that we have received no official information from France, since my last message to congress. From the publications in ministerial Journals of France we are informed that a bill has been passed by the chambers and peers and approved by the King making appropriations for the payment stipulated in the treaty of July 1831, with a proviso, as insulting to

From John Spencer Bassett, ed., *Correspondence of Andrew Jackson*, V, pp. 377–379. Reprinted by courtesy of the Carnegie Institution of Washington. Footnote is in the original.

us, and degrading to her, thus heaping insult upon injury. After a delay of upwards of four years based upon mere subterfuges, whilst France has been receiving all the benefits stipulated by us for her benefit and which have amounted nearly to as much, if not more, than the sum stipulated to be paid to our citizens for indemnities for spoliations on our commerce, and after acknowledging the justness of the debt stipulated to be paid as appears by her public journals, she passes the appropriation to pay the indemnity stipulated with the proviso, that the money is not to be paid until an apology or what is the same explanation, is made for a pretended insult to her in the President Message of 1834. What, France take offence at a message which detailed the truth, why it may be asked had not France paid the debt she acknowledged to be just and had pledged her national faith and the honor of her King long before that she would pay. if she had, she would have spared the Executive of the painful duty in exposing in his communication to congress in 1834 the facts detailing the bad faith of the Government of France, as he was bound to do by the requisitions of the constitution. What disgraceful and dishonorable attitude has France by this proviso placed herself? What after having acknowledged the justness of the debt, because she is asked to pay, being long due, and having failed to pay, she takes the requirement to pay as an insult and is contented to pockett the money which she acknowledges justly due to our citizens as an indemnity for this pretended insult—how degrading such conduct as this to that proud and chivalric nation? ?would this have been the conduct of her Frances the first, her Henry 4th, or her Boneparte, or even any high minded honorouble Frenchman. the answer of every honest highminded honorable man must be in the *negative*—the debt would have been first paid, and then the demand for satisfaction of her insulted honor.

But the very proposition is as insulting as it is degrading to our Government. By the constitution it is made the duty of the President, "from time to time to give to congress the state of the union and to recommend to their consideration such measures as he shall judge necessary and expedient." In pursuance of this injunction the President makes known to congress the state of our affairs with France, he states the treaty, and the stipulations under it with a religious exactness in which he was obliged to bring into review the unfaithfulness of France in not complying with her national engagements under the treaty made by her king, ratified and regurally exchanged by him and for which as her sovereign he had plighted his faith for its full execution, the various subterfuges and pretensions for the delays in non fulfilment, and from the reluctance and bad faith shewn on her part in noncomplience, when she was and had been from the exchange of ratification of the treaty in the receipt of all the benefits under it stipulated on our part, the President did then, as he seriously does now, recommend to congress the adoption of such energetic measures as would enforce a peaceful complience, letters of mark and reprisals and that was the only peaceful remedy, known to international law as pointed out by all who had written upon the laws of nations. and what has France presumed and arrogated to herself, to interfere with our domestic concerns and to dictate to the President of free and independent america, the Language he must use in fulfiling his constitutional duties, and that he must refrain from speaking the truth to the coordinate branches of the Govt as it relates to the infidelity of France or any other nation when they fail with their voluntary engagements by solemn treaty for wrongs inflicted upon our unofending commerce and declares herself insulted, is willing to put up with and puts into her pockett the five millions acknowledged to be justly due to our citizens.

And is this degradation to be submitted to, that the President must submit his communications to the agents here of foreign Governments and know from each whether it is worded, pointed and made suitable to eachs palate before he sends it to congress. there cannot be an individual american that would yield to such arrogant presumption in a foreign government, and if there are, he is unworthy of the name, and unworthy to live under blessings of freedom our Government affords. The history of the whole transaction of France shew not only a disregard for their national faith, but that the passage of the law with this proviso was to raise a pretext for violating the treaty on her part and by that means avoiding the payment of her just and acknowledged debt. she was informed by our minister the moment the insulting amendment was proposed and presented to the chambers, that if adopted we would view it as a rejection of the treaty—notwithstanding this information the Duck de Brolio prime minister accepts the amendment, the peers afterward pass it and the king approves and as private advices informs, the minister was encouraged to do this as he was informed that the senate would not support the President in his adhering to the treaty, by granting him the means to enforce it, and as evidence of this fact the rejection by the senate of the three millions of dollars appropriated by the House of representatives to enable the President to place our fortifications and our Navy in a proper state of preparation for defence is urged at Paris as proof of this fact and therefore they may trifle and sport with our national character and honor, violate her treaty, insult us by demanding apology for pretended insult when none was offerred or can be found, and that she will not comply with her treaty until a change of the Executive is made.

These are the pretensions of France. She must be misinformed, and misguided by bad men. There cannot be an american, that is not a traitor to his country and its best interest who would not resent such pretensions in a foreign government. She has heard already the voice from Main to Louisiana, no apology, no explanation. my heart cordially responds to that voice, no explanation, no apology, but what is to be found in the message and in our ministers letter explaining it before the insulting amendment was proposed. The treaty must be fulfilled, no war thro the custom houses, but the peaceful remedy, Letters of mark and reprisals, and when the debt is paid and France taught to know, that we ask nothing but what is shurly right, and permit nothing that is wrong, and how scrupilously we maintain our national faith and treaties we can return to our former intercourse and friendship. The treaty must be fulfilled responds every true american, and if congress responds to the voice of the people, with the smiles of heaven in every good cause the Treaty will be fulfilled.

Note. The rejection of the appropriation by the Senate relied on by France, that the Executive will not be sustained in enforcing a fulfilment of the Treaty—McKain.*

Note.

The charge of the French Government in 1797, of being insulted by the Presidents message (speech as then called) is simular to the present subterfuge resorted to by the French Government. What cause has not this Government to complain of insult and violated faith from the French Government were we to scan its public acts, the proviso on which she places the payment of indemnity passed by the chambers, accepted of by the minister, passed by the Peers, and approved by the King as a salvo for his violated faith in retaining the 25,000,000 Franks which all had acknowledged to be due, and *all* appear willing to pockett as a full indemnity for the complained of insult. In this early stage our Govt. repelled the arrogance of France for this attempt at interferrence with our domestic concerns, and every independent and true american will resent to death the hauteur demand for apology for any thing said by the President to congress in performing duties imposed upon him by the constitution.

Message to conclude—There has been nothing discoverable in the conduct of France which ought to relax our measures to enforce the treaty, but on the contrary to extend and invigorate it.

Abolitionist Literature

77. Amos Kendall and Andrew Jackson

These steps will pacify the South

The Jackson administration favored the suppression of antislavery writings in the South. On this issue too Jackson and Calhoun were at odds

From John Spencer Bassett, ed., *Correspondence of Andrew Jackson*, V, pp. 359–361. Reprinted by courtesy of The Carnegie Institution of Washington. Footnotes are in the original.

* Samuel McKean, U. S. senator from Pennsylvania 1833–1839.

but their differences were purely tactical. Old Hickory was ready to use federal power to close off the mails to abolitionist literature, while Calhoun would turn the job over to the states. Both men were as one with regard to the underlying issue: the need to use police power to prohibit the mails to critics of slavery.

POSTMASTER GENERAL KENDALL TO JACKSON

Washington, August 7, 1835

Dear Sir, I have been sick for two days and write you from my bed. Within a few hours I have much improved and hope to be up in a few more.

Herewith you have copies of a correspondence between me and the Postmaster at Charleston S. C. upon a subject of the utmost interest. Believing that nothing but the exclusion of the inflamatory matter spoken of from the mails,[1] can secure their transmission through the South and regarding the papers themselves as most flagitious, I have only thought of the means of intercepting them with as little noise and difficulty as possible. It has seemed to me best that I should give no instructions upon the subject, but let the several Postmasters act upon such intimations as are given in my first letter to the Postmaster at Charleston. I have received a request from Richmond to give orders to stop them there, and have sent a copy of that letter. I have also communicated it to the P.M. here and advised him verbally to hand out none of the papers except to such persons as claim them as actual subscribers. I think these steps carried out will pacify the South; but I should like to have your views. . . .

TO POSTMASTER GENERAL KENDALL.[2]

Rip Raps, August 9, 1835

. . . . I have read with sorrow and regret that such men live in our happy country—I might have said monsters—as to be guilty of the attempt to stir up amongst the South the horrors of a servile war—Could they be reached, they ought to be made to atone for

1. Incendiary publication respecting slavery, sent through the mails into the South by extreme abolitionists.

2. Cincinnati *Commercial*, Feb. 4, 1879.

this wicked attempt, with their lives. But we are the instruments of, and executors of the law; we have no power to prohibit anything from being transported in the mail that is authorized by the law. The only thing that can be done is what you have suggested, verbally, to the postmaster in the city, "*to deliver to no person these inflamatory papers,* but those who are really subscribers for them; and few men in society will be willing to acknowledge that they are encouraging by subscribing for such papers this horrid and most wicked proceedure; and when they are known, every moral and good citizen will unite to put them in coventry, and avoid their society. This, if adopted, would put their circulation down everywhere, for there are few so hardened in villainy, as to withstand the frowns of all good men.

Sincerely regret the breaking open the Post-office at Charleston, and seizing those inflamatory papers. This spirit of mob-law is becoming too common and must be checked, or ere long it will become as great an evil as a servile war, and as the innocent will be as much exposed to the cruelty and murderous [can not decipher] [3] as in the midst of a servile war—the instigators of both must be checked and punished, or we will soon have no safety under our happy Government of laws. But until Congress meets, and makes some arrangements by law, on this subject, we can do nothing more than direct that those inflamatory papers be delivered to none but who will demand them as subscribers; and in every instance the Postmaster ought to take the names down, and have them exposed thro the publik journals as subscribers to this wicked plan of exciting the negroes to insurrection and to massacre. This would bring those in the South, who were patronizing these incendiary works into such disrepute with all the South, that they would be compelled to desist, or move from the country. . . .

3. This bracketted statement is in the *Commercial's* text.

Abolitionism as a Political Issue

78. "LEONIDAS"

Did not the first framers of the American Constitution grant to the South certain rights

Abolitionism emerged as a mass movement in the 1830s. One of its consequences was a series of riots directed against abolitionists and Negroes in northern and western cities. Another was the fear it evidently inspired among some champions of slavery. In this document an alleged former northern abolitionist urges southern whites to take vigorous action against abolitionist radicals, who secretly long to march into the South and "demand the unconditional release of your slaves."

CIRCULAR LETTER,
TO THE CITIZENS OF THE SOUTHERN STATES

The individual who now addresses you is a citizen of the North, having spent the last twenty years of his life, (exceptting one) in the Northern States. He would not appear before the public as an advocate, or champion of slavery, but as a firm, unflinching, friend of Southern *institutions*, and Southern *rights*. Having not only been a witness of the first dissemination of those principles, which the great champions of immediate Emancipation strenuously and vigorously support, but having also been, but lately, *one* of their *number;* having mingled in their *councils*, and received the emoluments of office at their hands. I deem *it but* my duty solemnly to dissent from those principles, and to swear *eternal separation*. In so doing, I feel that I am discharging my duty, not only to my friends, but to my country and my *God*. In thus abandoning principles which I but lately advocated, justice indeed would call loudly *for my reasons*. By thus giving *them*, I would not wish to cast any reflections, upon the more enlightened

"Leonidas," *Circular Letter to the Citizens of the Southern States* (Raleigh, N.C.: T. Loring, December 25, 1837), 1–3.

and intelligent citizens of the North, who have been so unfortunate as to fall into these same errors. The great mass of Northern Abolitionists are by no means the most intelligent and virtuous! They have all embraced their principles from almost as various motives as there are classes and grades of society; some by a *love* of *popularity and fame;* others by a thirst of novelty and innovation; some by their ignorance have become the dupes of designing men, others have bowed like cringing slaves to the opinions of those more enlightened; but by far the greater proportion are the lower classes of society, the ignorant, the unenlightened.

These have been led on by partizans, both in politics and religion. The one seeking his own *interests* and fame, the other following a blind and bigoted zeal, and the wild and flashing fires of religious fanaticism. They have appealed to the passions of the people not only in all the mastery of their eloquence, but they have brought before them, slavery in all its loathsome and disgusting forms; they have pictured before them all the horrors of the rack, the torture, and the *Spanish inquisition.* They have brought before them the bleeding African, bound in chains, kneeling upon his mother earth, and with his eye upturned to Heaven exclaiming in agony, "am I not a friend and brother." Then they have appealed to their sympathies as *christians!* they have urged them for the sake of humanity, bleeding humanity, to arouse, and do their *duty.* Think you they have failed to *excite* their sympathies? No! would to heaven it had been *so!* They *have* painted the African in all the sufferings and agonies of which human nature is capable, bleeding, dying, goaded on by the merciless lash of the task-master. They have placed him in all the horrors of starvation, in the dungeon, and on the scaffold, and *even in the last* agonies of death, *unheeded, unpitied* and *unavenged.* With such a picture, embellished by the masteries of eloquence, think you they have failed to excite the sympathies of the ignorant? I fear lest they have produced feelings more to be dreaded, than those of *sympathy.* As a last appeal they *have* denounced slave-holders as tyrants, cruel relentless tyrants—who hold their slaves only as dependent on their will, and whose life or death was subject to their bidding. They have denounced them as destitute of the least feeling of sympathy or mercy. Aye, *and more than* once, I *have,* as these sentiments were uttered, seen *their* eyes gleam with vengeance, which told, too *well,* the consequences, had they the *slave-holders in their power.* I say not this to widen the breach already made, but rather to awaken the *southern people* to their interests. In thus saying that the great proportion of Northern Abolitionists, are of the ignorant and unenlightened, I will not deny that there are some of high and splendid acquirements, men of *distinguished* talents; distinguished alike for their powers of mind and rectitude of conduct. Among these, I might mention the names of Green, Smith, Garrison, and many others, whose transcendant talents *might* well *have* been engaged in some more glorious *cause,* than that of sewing the seeds of discord, which shall one day, unless blasted, *light the funeral pile of this republic.* I will not deny that there are some among them, *whose motives* are *just* and *honorable;* these have embraced their principles without a due examination; from false premises they could but arrive at *false conclusions.* Giving way to the sympathies of their nature, they have followed the impulses of *animal* feeling, rather their better *judgements.* Led on by bigots, and the servile minions of fanaticism, they have at length persuaded themselves into the *belief* that they were but *in* the way of their *duty;* for such indeed, would be *excited, feelings rather* of pity than *revenge.*

Having spoken of the different characters which have embraced these sentiments, and of the various motives which have actuated each, I will mention as briefly as possible their *opinions.* They believe, or pretend to believe, slavery not only morally, but religiously an evil! *This evil,* they think themselves bound, by all the laws of humanity and religion to destroy! Their motto is, "Let us do our duty fearless of consequences, though the Heavens should fall!" They affirm that in thus doing their duty, they are but doing *justice* to *the laws, their country, and their God.* They assert that they have nothing to do with the issue of this conflict, they leave that event solely and entirely to the *Supreme Ruler* of the destinies of nations. If indeed it might result in the *dissolution* of our holy UNION, they are not *responsible* for the consequences. If indeed the torch of internal dissensions, should light the funeral Pyre of America, and the iron hand of despotism sway his trident above the ruins of our liberties, they are *not* to be *accountable.* Though the life-blood of our citizens should flow in rivers from Maine to Louisiana, and from the Atlantic to the Rocky Mountains, their duty is paramount to *all.* Though the cries of *widows and orphans* should *fall upon their ears,* in all the notes of wo, beseeching them to pause in their career, they must *pursue* their duty and trust the *event* to *Heaven.* Though internal commotions should stop the rolling of the spheres, and hurl the Andes from their base, and this vast *Universe* roll back again to chaos, "let us do our duty fearless of consequences," is still their cry.

They do not indeed say that it is their duty to shoulder their musket and march into your Territory and demand an unconditional release of your Slaves, but I *stake* my *reputation* upon it, there are many who *would* do so, had they the *physical courage.* They contend that paying a master for his slave is *wrong,* because forsooth, it is a virtual acknowledgement, that the master has a right to hold his *fellow-man* in bondage, hence they are opposed to any compromise which might afford a *fair compensation* to the *master* for the loss of his *slave.* Thus they hold it not only the duty of southern citizens to *give their slaves* immediate and unconditional freedom, but do so without any *remuneration* either from individuals or Government. These are a few of the leading principles by which they *profess to be actuated!*

Of those among Abolitionists called Amalgamationists I will say but few words, for I detest alike, them and their principles. Suffice it to say that there are those who not only contend that the Africans should be admitted to a political equality, but that they should also be permitted to enter our households, to mingle in our *social circles,* and even *embrace* our sons and daughters in their arms as one of their own blood and kindred. But this subject is too loathing for human nature, and *I leave it!*

As one who *has* lately abandoned principles, most *destructive,* both to our country and liberty—I would say to the Abolitionists of the *North,* what can you expect to accomplish by *further pursuing your mad schemes?* Is not humanity, is not justice, is not the sacred Constitution of our common country firmly against you? Did not the first framers of the American Constitution grant to the South certain *rights,* which *rights* can *never* be surrendered but at the price of liberty? Is not each State of *itself, free, sovereign* and *independent?* What right has the parliament of Upper Canada to legislate for New York, or what right has New York to legislate for North Carolina? None surely! Did not the Southern People make the granting of these rights, the only conditions upon which they would consent to unite with the Northern States? Surely so! And but for these rights, they would have remained at this day a separate confederacy, guided by their own Rulers, and governed by their own Laws. What then can you effect in face of the sacred Constitution? Will you still persist? Go on then! Pursue your schemes! Light the torch of civil discord! Raise the hand of brother against brother, father against son, and friend against friend! Unfurl your banner of eternal hatred to mankind! Deluge the land in blood! Stop not! Urge on!! Heed not the cries of widows and orphans! But let the war of death roll on! Revere not the sacred name of WASHINGTON, and the long list of patriots slain! Now swear the dissolution of our holy Union, and let war, blood and carnage sweep on its purple tide of death from icy Labrador to the Arctic Zone! Let *slaughtered millions be the sacrifice!!* Hark! hear ye that thundering crash! It was the Temple of our Liberties! Raise high! Raise high the sacreligious arm, and fire its falling piles, and let its smoke ascend as incense to your God—and as its ashes shall scatter with the winds, sit down amidst its ruins, and with a demoniac smile, exclaim to Heaven *"we have but done our duty!"* Oh! my country! is this thy destiny! Is it for an end thus ignominous that thou art doomed! Shall the foes of liberty thus soon sport upon thy ruins? Was it for this our mothers taught us to lisp the sacred name of Washington, and the long list of patriot's names, enrolled in Fame? Was it for this the plains of Monmouth, of Camden, and of Bunker Hill, were dyed in purple and in gore? An end thus ignominous? Is this the funeral Pyre of *American Liberty?*

Fellow citizens of the South, let me beseech you, awake to your interests: Rouse for the conflict, and gird on your armor! You have a foe, ever vigilant, ever watchful! Will you suffer him to fall upon you sleeping on your post, and thus become an easy prey? The assassin of your Liberties is already on your threshold! Will you permit the dagger, already uplifted, to drink your hearts-blood, and fall *unavenged?* I do not ask you to gird on *your swords* or *march* to the battle field. No, yours is a conflict *of words,* of eloquence, more potent than *the sword!* Yours, must be a firm *resolve* to support your rights, *even* at the hazard of your lives, for *Liberty* is dearer *than life—speak* in *a* voice of thunder, *and* you *must* be *heard.* Tell these invaders of your rights, to pause, for the ground on *which* they *tread* is *holy! Tell them, that neither* the fear of threats, or the *hope* of *rewards* can ever induce you to relinquish the *price* of your *liberty!* Tell them, you have rights, guarantied by the sacred Constitution, which you never will yield, only at the forfeit of *your life.* In thus entreating you to awake from your slumbers, and *prepare for the conflict,* I would not indeed wish you to be hasty or rash in your actions—be *governed* by moderation, but with *firmness* and *decision.* Let your motto be—"the Union, it must and shall be preserved!!" Of one thing the Abolitionists *may* be assured, slavery *never* will, or *never* can be abolished, only by the consent of each State—by its own free and sovereign *Legislation.* Let me assure you, citizens of the South, that the pole star of hope *around which Northern Abolitionists cling with fervor* is that of the *Abolition* of slavery in the *District of Columbia*—this is to be the key which unlocks their designs, and leads them to *triumph!*—'tis here they have cast their anchor, which if it safely moors them, will carry them to certain victory!—'tis here they have planted *their* battery, and with a resolve, to carry the Fortress by storm, or die in the last ditch!—'tis here they are to pour all the fires of their *artillery,* and roll on their engines of destruction, in one vast phalanx joined, for Death or *Victory!* This is the Yorktown of their *hopes.* If they fail here, their defeat must drive them to shame and contempt, and as the sheet anchor of their safety is sundered and they cut from their *moorings,* they must retire in defeat from the contest, covered *with* the *shame,* the *contempt,* and the *ignominy* of *mankind!* If they succeed, their next step will, and must be, to *demand* of you, an *immediate* and *unconditional* surrender of your slaves. If *they succeed, they will not stop here*—they will not be satisfied with so *small a victory!* No! but the next sound that will fall upon your ears, will be the imperative demand, the *immediate* emancipation from slavery—or the dissolution of our Union!

But they cannot succeed, if you will but do your duty, if you will but sound the note of alarm until its peals of thunder shall echo from the *Atlantic waves* to the Rocky Mountains, and from Hudson's Bay to Panama, *they cannot succeed.* Then rouse for the conflict, and meet the foe! the victory *must be yours.* Let the eloquence of your citizens in the Senate Halls, pour fourth against these invaders of your rights, these *enemies of your Liberty!* Tell them not to dare to place their impious hands upon the Constitution, sealed by the blood of Patriots. Tell them at least to *revere* the name of WASHINGTON! Entreat them by all the ties of consanguinity, by all the bonds that unite them to friends they love, by all that is sacred, for the sake of the Instrument of our Independence, for the sake of our Country, and our Liberty, to pause in their mad career! Beseech them to remember the crimsoned plains of Monmouth, of Camden, of Orleans, and of Bunker Hill! If they will yet persevere, let them suffer the consequences, and let the vengeance, be upon *their own devoted Heads.* Let the double infamy of him who fired the Ephesian Temple rest upon their memories, and the imprecations and curses of *future* generations fall upon *them, and their posterity, and let their names enrolled, on* the annals of undying infamy, stand out to *future ages!* Upon their ashes rear the *eternal* granite, and let the inscription be—"Here rests the destroyer of the American Constitution and Liberty, whose sacrilegious hands applied the torch upon their smouldering piles." Rest assured, you have no reason to doubt the issue of this conflict; if you will but arouse from your slumbers, if you will but shake off that lethargy which seems to have bound you, if you will arouse then our glorious Country is yet saved! and we are free! You have with you the great *mass of the enlightened, the intelligent, and the virtuous,* of the North. You have her men of Science, her Philosophers, her Philanthropists and Statesmen! her good, her great, her learned!

With such an array of assistance, can you *refuse to act.* Once more I appeal to you, for the sake of humanity, for the sake of our beloved country, for the sake of the Constitution, for the sake of yourselves, your children, and your posterity, for the sake of Millions yet unborn; arise! arise! grid on your armor for the conflict, and go forth to meet the foe! You will then have the glorious reflection of having saved your country from the ruthless hand of *its* foes, and of rescuing the Constitution of our Liberties from *the vile grasp of these inveterate enemies* of mankind! How pleasing this reflection—countless millions, yet to be, shall rise to bless your names, and on the monumental marble which enshrines your ashes, burn incense of their gratitude. Yes, kneeling they will invoke Heaven's blessings forever upon your posterity! Your memories immortal as those of a *Wolf,* a *Montgomery,* a *Warren,* a *La Fayette,* and a *Washington,* shall stand engraved upon the archives of eternal Fame. Everduring through countless ages, *forever cherished, honored, and revered!* If indeed, I have failed in this my last appeal, in behalf of our beloved country, if you will not come to the rescue, then *farewell* Liberty! *farewell* the dearest hopes of Freemen! Farewell, all that we love, or fondly cherish! The genius of America, guided by the majestic Eagle, *shall* hover o'er the tomb of an *immortal* Washington, and snatching the Urn of his ashes from its deathless slumbers shall bear it Heavenward, and cast her last glance upon the smouldering piles of this Republic.

But methinks, through the deepening gloom, I see the dawning of a brighter day! Methinks I see you rising and exclaiming, *to the rescue!* joined as one band of brothers, rallying round the Constitution, and *swearing by all that is sacred,* to sustain it, and hand it down to future ages, as you have received it from your forefathers, or be buried, your-selves amidst its ruins! Methinks I hear you exclaiming, in a voice, loud as the death blast of Gabriel—"Wo to the hand, and Palsied be the arm that dares to light the sacrilegious torch upon the Temple of American Liberty."

Methinks I hear your voice as it echoes loud as the seven thunders "The Union," it must and shall be "preserved." Then indeed shall we behold the foes of your rights defeated, crowned with shame and contempt, and covered with the everlasting reproach and infamy of mankind! Then indeed shall nations learn that we are capable of self-government, and that as freemen, we can and will sustain our liberties, whether attacked by tyrants and despots without, or endangered by foes or commotions within. Then the great experiment, whether mankind can be free, will not have failed. Then we shall behold our beloved country, rising in greatness and glory, the *pride* of nations, and the *admiration* of the world! Our flag shall float in triumph on every ocean, the protection of our rights, the pride of our citizens, and the last hope of the free! Every gale shall greet our spreading canvass from icy Labrador to the Torrid Zone, and from Arctic's dashing tides to *Gambia's silver wave!* At the mention of our names, despots shall tremble on their thrones, and tyrants Quake! Ages shall circle away, and the memory of Washington and the long list of American worthies engraved on the battlements of freedom, shall shine in all the undying splendors of their fame. The magestic Eagle guided by the genius of patriotism, shall bear their names upon a car of clouds, above a flaming UNIVERSE, and wave our flag triumphant amid the *"wreck of matter, and the crush of worlds."*

Leonidas

79. LIBERTY PARTY

We believe that American slavery is contrary to all divine law

In 1840 a Liberty party was created, nominating James G. Birney, a former slaveholder, for president. Although the new party was opposed to slavery, it issued no formal program and was less than explicit in stating precisely what measures it favored. Bitterly opposed even by many

Resolutions adopted by the Liberty Party of Williamsburgh, Kings County, New York, December 29, 1841.

abolitionists, to whom the idea of a separate party was anathema, the Liberty party got only 6,225 votes in the presidential election. The following document illustrates the issues that caught the eye of local Liberty party men, their undoubted hostility toward slavery, and their lack of precision as to the policies the party should follow.

At a meeting of the LIBERTY PARTY, held December 29th, 1841, at the town of *Williamsburgh, Kings County, N. Y.*, on motion, JAMES WARNER, was appointed *Chairman*, and WILLIAM H. PILLOW, *Secretary* of the meeting.

The following Resolutions, after a calm and deliberate discussion of the principles contained in them, were *unanimously* adopted:

Resolved, That, in our opinion, the 21st rule of the House of Representatives, excluding all petitions on the question of Slavery, is unconstitutional, arbitrary, and tyrannical in the extreme, and that we hereby earnestly request that the aforesaid rule be rescinded.

Resolved, That if the 21st rule be not rescinded, it is the opinion of this meeting, that the seat of Government ought to be removed *North* of "Mason and Dixon's line," where "the peculiar institution" does not exist.

Resolved, That the slaves of the brig Creole, who rose and took possession of said vessel, thereby regaining their natural rights and Liberty, acted in accordance with the principles of our Declaration of Independence and the late decision of the Supreme Court; and have proved themselves in their whole conduct worthy of their freedom; and we trust that their noble example will be *imitated by all in similar circumstances.*

Whereas, according to the facts published in the papers of the day, it appears that the American consul at Nassau, N.P., did attempt to rescue the brig Creole by violence, and force back the freemen into slavery, Therefore,

Resolved, That President Tyler be, and is hereby requested to order said Consul home, provided said facts should be as is here stated.

Whereas, We believe that American slavery is contrary to all Divine law, and that to use the words of John Wesley, "it is the sum of all villany," Therefore,

Resolved, That should the slaves at the South endeavor to gain their natural rights and liberty, "peaceably if they can, *forcibly if they must,*" we should not feel bound to aid in extinguishing the sacred flame, but in the words of that noble-hearted Democrat, William Legget, "we would pray that the BATTLE might go with the oppressed."

Resolved, That the Inspection Law passed by the Legislature of Virginia, to take effect in May, 1842, and approved by South Carolina, Georgia, and Alabama, is unconstitutional, and calculated farther to disturb the *present* political relations subsisting between the several States, and to produce a *dissolution of the Union.*

Whereas, The Slave Power, by striking down the Right of Petition, lynching citizens of the free North, breaking open the mails, and passing inspection and other arbitrary laws, is making continual encroachments upon the Liberty of the States, therefore—

Resolved, That it is high time that these things should *cease,* for the time is fast approaching when slavery *must* be abolished, by peaceable means, OR ———

Resolved, That this meeting view the correspondence between our ex-minister, Andrew Stevenson, and Lord Palmerston, with feelings of grief and deep indignation, that our government should uphold the use of the American flag for the protection of the Slave Trade and other piracy.

Resolved, That these proceedings be signed by the Chairman and Secretary, and sent to every member of our national Congress, the President of the United States, and the Governors of the slaveholding States.

JAMES WARNER, *Chairman*

WILLIAM H. PILLOW, *Secretary*

Executive Tyranny

80. The National Intelligencer

The presidential office became the fountain of all power

The Whig party that emerged in 1834 by its choice of name sought to stigmatize President Andrew Jackson as a European-style monarch. In the following editorial the *National Intelligencer* summarizes the Whig case against the alleged tyranny practiced by the democracy. This journal, published in Washington City by Joseph Gales and William W. Seaton, was the most influential Whig newspaper in the country.

Constitutional law

The tendency of the politics of the party predominant during the last Administration, and by whose suffrage the present Administration came into power, was to convert the Government, in practical operation, into a monarchy, differing in hardly any respect from the monarchies of the old world, except in the monarch's being elective. There are few powers exercised by the King of Great Britain which have not, within the last nine years, been claimed, substantially, as powers inherent in the Executive of the United States, by those who damned and denounced, in the name of *Democracy*, all who dared to doubt either the omnipotence or the infallibility of the President. Under the operation of the new-light doctrine to which we refer, the Presidential office became, in fact, the fountain of all power, as well as of all political honor; and if the President did not exercise exclusive Legislative as well as Executive power, he was enabled, by his exercise of the veto power, to *prevent* any legislation whatever which he had not himself dictated. In so undisguised a manner were these pretensions made for the Executive, that the President of the United States in various instances himself avowed them, in his official communications to Congress, as his motives and rules of action.

So much has the public mind, and the attention of all parties,

From the editorial page of the *National Intelligencer*, March 15, 1838.

been occupied for the last twelve months with the evils which immediately beset us of a deranged currency and an obstructed commerce, that these monstrous pretensions of the Jackson school of politicians (of which pretension, however, all the late and present embarrassments are but the first fruits) have, in a great degree, as it were, faded from observation. But they have not faded from the record; and it is still useful and instructive occasionally to revive the recollection of them.

Among the favorite points in the political creed to which we refer was the construction put upon that provision of the Constitution which imposes upon the President the duty of "taking care that the laws be faithfully executed"; which provision was interpreted to subject the action of every officer of the Government, in the discharge of duties imposed upon him by law, to the absolute will and control of the President.

It was upon this principle that the removal of Secretary DUANE from office was made and justified by President JACKSON. He declared it, in his Message to the Senate of the 15th April, 1834, to be settled constitutional law,

> that the entire executive power is vested in the President of the United States; that, as incident to that power, the right of appointing and removing those officers who are to aid him in the execution of the laws, with such restrictions only as the Constitution prescribes, is vested in the President; that the Secretary of the Treasury is one of those officers; that the custody of the public property and money is *an executive function,* which, in relation to the money, has always been exercised through the Secretary of the Treasury and his subordinates; that, in the performance of these duties, he is subject to *the supervision and control of the President,* and in all important measures having relation to them consults the Chief Magistrate, and obtains his approval and sanction; that *the law* establishing the bank *did not, as it could not, change the relation between the President and Secretary*—did not release the former from his obligation to see the law faithfully executed, *nor the latter from the President's supervision and control.*

In a preceding part of the same Message, the President had laid it down that

> the custody of the public money, under such regulations as may be prescribed by legislative authority, has always been considered *an*

> *appropriate function* of the Executive Department in this and all other Governments;

and, further, that

> Congress cannot take out of the hands of the Executive Department the custody of the public property or money, without an assumption of Executive power, and subversion of the first principles of the Constitution.

Considering these passages in connection, the late President took the broad ground, as the reader will perceive, that this "Executive function," being one exercised by the President through the Secretary of the Treasury, *no law* COULD *change the relation* of absolute control of the President over the Secretary of the Treasury in relation to the discharge of his official duty in regard to it.

Analogous doctrines are to be found in other documents emanating from the late Administration, which we have not time to particularize, our object being, besides, only to direct the reader's attention, for the present, to this particular doctrine, as *exploded* by the Opinion of the Supreme Court, in the case of the Postmaster-General and Stockton and Stokes, delivered a few days ago.

The presumptuous and hectoring Letter by which the Postmaster-General replied, in June last, to the writ issued by the Circuit Court for this District, citing him before it, is of too recent date not to be freshly remembered by our readers. In that paper, the doctrine embodied in the Message of President JACKSON, which we have just quoted, was expanded and enlarged upon; (by the same pen, in all probability, as first traced it; for it is certainly no violent inference that the same pen to which the country was indebted for the "Reasons" for the removal of the Deposites was also employed to defend that illegal measure after its consummation.) At all events, the same *spirit* inhabits and pervades the two documents. In this Letter of the Postmaster-General we find the identical doctrine of the Protest Message, elaborated and illustrated through the space of several columns of the Globe, of which the cream may be found in the following extract:

> So far as regards their execution, no distinction is made by the Constitution, between special acts and general acts; between private acts and public acts. It is the duty of the President to take care that all alike "be faithfully executed." The Executive is *an unity*. The framers of the Constitution had studied history too well to impose on their country a divided Executive. The Executive power was vested *in a President*. The Executive officers *are his agents*, for whom he is held responsible by the People, whose agent he is. The acts of the Executive officers *are the acts of the President*. Constitutionally, he is as responsible for them as if they were done by himself, though not morally. So far as regards the execution of the laws, therefore, no distinction can be maintained between acts of the President and those of his subordinate officers. In law they are all acts of the President. When the Judiciary attempt to control those acts, they attempt to control the Executive power, to assume the functions of the President, to make themselves the Executive in the last resort, superior to the Executive created by the Constitution, and elected by the People.
>
> Suppose the laws require a specific act of the President himself, involving private rights, which he refuses to perform. The courts have as much law for issuing a mandamus against him as against any of his subordinates in a like case. It is a case, as much as that of which the Court has already assumed jurisdiction. The President disobeys their mandamus, and they send an attachment. By whom do they send it? By a Marshal, holding his office at the will of the President, WHO CAN STRIKE THEIR PROCESS DEAD IN HIS HANDS, *by dismissing him on the spot*. This fact proves the absurdity of the power assumed. And that which the President can legally do to protect himself, *he can do to protect any of his agents*, being always responsible to his country for the proper exercise of his power.

Struck with abhorrence, which we believe was generally participated by our readers, at this bold avowal of irresponsibility to the laws, and this contemptuous defiance of the authority of those who attempt judicially to cause them to be respected, we expressed the sensation thus produced in our minds; for which we were taken to task in the usual courteous terms of that urbane and dignified journal which reflects the opinions, but does not reflect the manners, of the present (as it did of the former) Administration. We then said, as we religiously believed,

> that, in the pretensions put forth in the argument of the Postmaster-General, we have the elements of a conflict between the Executive and Judicial authorities of the Government, in which if the Executive triumph, there is no longer any law in the land for the protection of the rights of individuals against the wrongs of any Executive officers whatever.

After perusing this brief review of occurrences which now belong to history, the reader will be able better to comprehend the feelings of gratification—ay, and of gratitude, too—with which we listened to the Opinion of the Supreme Court, in the case referred to, as it was read by one of those Judges whose integrity and purity no man will dare to call in question.

Desiring that our readers shall understand the full scope and bearing of those passages of the Court's Opinion which gave us so much pleasure, we have availed ourselves of the politeness of the officers of the Court to copy from it the two paragraphs which struck us with the greatest force, and now present them to our readers as follows:

EXTRACTS

From the Opinion of the Supreme Court of the United States, in the case of the Postmaster-General and Stockton & Stokes.

> Under the first head of inquiry, it has been considered by the counsel on the part of the Postmaster-General that this is a proceeding against him to enforce the performance of an *official duty*, and the proceeding has been treated as an infringement on the Executive Department of the Government, which has led to a very extended range of argument on the independence and duties of that Department, but which, according to the view taken by the Court of the case, is entirely misapplied. We do not think the proceeding in this case interferes in any respect whatever with the rights or duties of the Executive, or that it involves any conflict of powers between the Executive and Judicial Departments of the Government. The Mandamus does not seek to direct or control the Postmaster-General in the discharge of any official duty partaking in any respect of an Executive character, but to enforce the performance of a merely ministerial act, which neither he nor the President had any authority to deny or control.

We shall not therefore enter into any particular examination of the line to be drawn between the powers of the Executive and Judicial Departments of the Government. The theory of the Constitution undoubtedly is, that the great powers of the Government are divided into separate departments; and, so far as these powers are derived from the Constitution, the departments may be regarded as independent of each other. But, beyond that, all are subject to regulation by law, touching the discharge of the duties required to be performed.

The Executive power is vested in a President, and, so far as his powers are derived from the Constitution, he is beyond the reach of any other department, except in the mode prescribed by the Constitution, through the impeaching power. But it by no means follows that every officer in every branch of that department is under the exclusive direction of the President. Such a principle, we apprehend, is not, and certainly cannot be, claimed by the President. There are certain political duties imposed upon many officers in the Executive Department, the discharge of which is under the direction of the President. But it would be an alarming doctrine, that Congress cannot impose upon an Executive officer any duty they may think proper, which is not repugnant to any rights secured and protected by the Constitution. And, in such cases, the duty and responsibility grow out of, and are subject to, the control of the law, and not to the direction of the President. And this is emphatically the case when the duty enjoined is of a mere ministerial character.

It was urged at the bar that the Postmaster-General was alone subject to the direction and control of the President with respect to the execution of the duty imposed upon him by this law: and this right of the President is claimed as growing out of the obligation imposed upon him by the Constitution to take care that the laws be faithfully executed. This is a doctrine that cannot receive the sanction of this court. It would be vesting in the President a dispensing power, which has no countenance for its support in any part of the Constitution, and is asserting a principle which, if carried out in its results to all cases falling within it, would be clothing the President with a power entirely to control the legislation of Congress and paralyze the administration of justice.

81. An Anonymous Democrat

Obedient to their master's nod, they bowed to paper as their God

Democratic partisans did not agree with the Whig charge that Jackson's entire banking policy was unconstitutional. The following flyer satirizes the Whig attack, charging that it was a mere cover for a selfish policy designed to reward Nicholas Biddle and his friends. The flyer was probably published between 1837, the year of Van Buren's inauguration, and 1839. The references to Clay and "Godlike Dan" (Daniel Webster) indicate that William Henry Harrison, the actual Whig candidate in 1840, had not yet been nominated.

The Bleeding Constitution

Air–Teddy the Tiler

O will you hear my wond'rous tale
Of black and white, of blue and pale
Whiglings rare who sigh and wail
  O'er the "bleeding Constitution"!
In '34 James Watson Webb
Was by Nick Biddle put to bed,
Brought forth a "Whig," and now 'tis said
"Whigs" through the land like locusts spread.
They've Harry Clay and Godlike Dan,
Each vowing he's the proper man
To take the place of little Van
  And save the Constitution.

Chorus.—O Federal Whig, bank bought Webbite
  Nick Biddle can't with all his might
  Make us believe that all is right
  'Bout *his* "bleeding Constitution."

These Whiglings most live in great state,
They never work, but speculate
On lots and stocks, at highest rate,
  And "the bleeding Constitution";

The Bleeding Constitution [n.d.].

And when the people are distressed
'Tis just the time the Whigs are blest
With hopes to see the workeys pressed
To sell their birthright with the zest,
The same with which their bully Webb
Like cattle at the old Bull's Head—
Was sold, to eat "the monster's" bread
  For the "bleeding Constitution."

Chorus.—O Federal Whigs, &c.

Not long ago these Whiglings bold
Were by their master plainly told
To go for bank rags, not for gold
  And save the Constitution!
Obedient to their master's nod,
They bowed to paper as their God
While on their backs he laid the rod
By keeping gold beneath the sod;
Beneath the sod! Lord, did I say,
O no, he had'nt enough to pay
His customers from day to day
  To save the Constitution!

Chorus.—O Federal Whig, &c.

One day King Nick invited most
All of his subjects to a roast
For all the Banks gave up the ghost
  To save the Constitution!
Of all the gold we are bereft
And we have nought but paper left
Said he, with that we will make a shift
So for the spoils let's set off swift:
They went to work these bastard Whigs
And danced away, shinplaster jigs
And made themselves as fat as pigs
  For the "bleeding Constitution"!

Chorus.—O Federal Whig, &c.

By his request they met again
When he informed them " 'twas in vain
To antidote the paper bane

'Twould kill the Constitution!
You've too much eaten, drank, and worn
And better if we had ne'er been born
Than blow too soon the Specie horn
Twould help the *rabble* all forlorn
And make them cry aloud 'hurrah
For Jackson gold in peace or war
We'll not be Whig-bugged any more,'
Thus kill the Constitution!"

Chorus.—O Federal Whig, &c.

With awe profound they heard him out
Then wheeled, and turned, and jumped about
And then expressed a serious doubt
About *their* Constitutions!
Know ye most potent, honored Nick
That if we to your mandate stick,
The de'il himself cant keep the trick
Within our walls of stone and brick:
The People with their many eyes
Would to our tricks be overwise
And find out we'd been telling lies,
Thus lose *our* Constitutions!

Chorus.—O Federal Whig, &c.

Calm as a gentle summer's day
Nick rose in state and thus did say,
"Friends if you do your just debts pay
You'll kill the Constitution!
Let but the hand of plenty wave
O'er field and flood, 'twill many save
From want, destruction, and the grave,
And then the people wont behave.
Will ye not learn from lessons past
That Whiggery can never last
When poor men have a good repast!
You'll *kill* the Constitution!"

Chorus.—O Federal Whig, &c.

Some men are bad to a degree
Some are so comparatively,

Whigs are so superlatively,
  And all for the Constitution!
Like grave yard rats they thrive and grow
Best in times of famine and woe
When pestilence lays many low;
And panic stricken men don't know
But Mat Van Buren and the de'il
Have tyranized o'er Nich'las Biddle,
And brought upon the land great evil
  And *bled* the Constitution!

Chorus.—O Federal Whig, &c.

(Slow.)

Then rise en masse ye noble souls
With eagerness rush to the Polls,
A patriot band be thou enrolled
  In defence of the Constitution!
Be ready at your country's call
Strike ye for freedom one and all
For Whiggery, the tyrant's pall,
Before the light of truth must fall;
And in its stead DEMOCRACY
O'er this blest land triumphantly
Will wave the banner of the free,
  And save the Constitution!

Chorus.—Then rise en masse, &c.

Indian Expulsion

82. William Wirt

These people are now civilized in a very great degree

That neither the Jacksonians nor their National Republican and Whig opponents were radical parties in the ideological sense does not mean

From John P. Kennedy, ed., *William Wirt's Memoirs* (Philadelphia: Blanchard and Lea, 1849), 2 vols., II, pp. 253–259.

that they did not differ significantly on important issues. Whig leaders generally had a more humane and tolerant position toward racial minorities. The Jacksonians were dedicated to driving the Indians west of the Mississippi and were not fastidious about the means to be used. That previous federal guarantees to the southern tribes or Supreme Court decisions might have to be violated seemed of little concern to Andrew Jackson. One of Jackson's most notorious actions occurred during the controversy between the Cherokees and the state of Georgia, when Jackson aligned himself with the state's policy to expel the Indians. William Wirt, who was the attorney for the Cherokees, gives his version of the issues in the following selection.

To Judge Carr

Baltimore, June 21, 1830

My dear Friend:

. . . I wish to consult you on a matter of business so deeply interesting to my character both as a man and a lawyer, that I must claim from you the rights of friendship.

You are apprised of the proceedings of Georgia in reference to the Cherokee lands within her chartered limits, and her desire to expel the Cherokees from the State *per fas aut nefas*. She passed a law last winter to take effect at the beginning of this month, abolishing the Cherokee laws and usages within their own territory, —extending the whole of the Georgia laws over these people, and disqualifying them from giving evidence against a white man in a court of justice. The present administration, playing into her hand, caused a bill to be passed through Congress, authorizing the President to exchange with them for their present lands, other lands of equal value beyond the Arkansas Territory. This bill leaves it to the option of the Indians to accept the exchange or not: but the President has told them that although they are placed, by their treaties, expressly under the protection of the United States and of no other sovereign, yet he cannot protect them against the laws of Georgia, that State having a right to legislate over all persons within the limits of her territory. Thus they are oppressed by these obnoxious laws of Georgia, on the one hand, and allured by the exchange proposition on the other. But they have visited the lands offered to them, and find them unfit for agriculture, to which, under the influence of Mr. Jefferson and his advice given to them when he was president, they have devoted themselves for several years past. . . . I do not know whether you attended to the debate in Congress, last winter, on the Indian bill. If you did, you must have seen that the pretension of right in Georgia to legislate over the Cherokees was demonstrated to be utterly fallacious. These people, although partly within the chartered limits of the State, not being within her *territorial jurisdiction,* have been uniformly treated, both by the British Government and our own, as a sovereign people, with an acknowledged right to be governed only by their own laws and usages, within their territory, the exclusive possession of which has been so solemnly guaranteed to them by their treaties with the United States. In the estimation of many of the most enlightened men in Congress, the injury about to be inflicted on these people is shocking to justice and humanity. The Indian bill, nevertheless, passed by a slight majority. . . .

Some of the most distinguished men in Congress who had opposed its passage, Webster, Judge Spencer, Frelinghuysen and others, advised the Cherokee delegates then in Washington, to employ counsel to bring the various questions of their rights, under their treaties, before the Supreme Court of the United States: and for this purpose they were introduced to me, when in Washington on Judge Peck's case, some two or three weeks ago. I was aware of the delicacy of the situation in which this application placed me. I saw that I was about to be made instrumental in thwarting or impeding (or trying to do it, perhaps in vain,) a project on which the President and State of Georgia were bent, and which, but for my interference, might take immediate effect by the removal of the Indians—for they would sooner remove and die in the wilderness, than remain in subjection to the laws of Georgia. But, on the other hand, having been assured by so many distinguished men that the Supreme Court would protect them, and that they had only to secure eminent counsel to effect their object, they have resolved to bear the present oppression of Georgia until the question can be decided by the Supreme Court. Although the delicacy of the situation in which such an engagement would place me, glanced through my mind at the time of the application, yet as I was strongly impressed with the injustice about to be done to these people, I did not think it right to flinch from any considerations of personal ease and safety; and I promised to examine their case and give them my opinion, and, if necessary, my professional services in the Supreme

Court. On my return to Baltimore, I took up the question of the right of Georgia to extend her laws over these people, read all the speeches in Congress *pro* and *con,* on the subject, the opinion of the President communicated to the Cherokees through the Secretary of War, in favour of the right of the State, and gave the whole case a thorough examination. My conclusion was against the right of the State. But in making this examination, I was struck with the manifest determination, both of the President and the State, that the State laws should be extended over them, *at every hazard.* This led me to reflect more seriously on the predicament in which I was about to place myself, and perhaps involve the Supreme Court of the United States. . . .

There are many well-meaning men who think it the interest of the Cherokees to remove to a country where the whites will no longer annoy them, and where they may pass their lives in peace and quiet. The country offered to them in exchange has also been represented as a paradise in itself and a haven of perpetual repose to them. The country offered, I have already described. There are wild Indians in the neighbourhood who will probably contest the right of possession with them, and make that paradise a slaughter-house and a scene of mutual extermination. These people are now civilized in a very great degree, and do not wish to relapse into barbarism, nor to reside again near savage neighbours. It is, therefore, their most anxious desire to remain where they are, as they have a right to do. Yet if they had no hope from the Supreme Court, they would, I have no doubt, go—thinking it the least of evils. With regard to the Supreme Court, the Attorney-General is reported to have said, that the State of Georgia would not respect their decision, if against them, but would go on to enforce their rights according to their own opinion of them; and after what has already passed, I should not be surprised if the President should co-operate with them and render the decision abortive, by forbidding the Marshal and people of the country from obeying it. On the other hand it is *possible,* (though not very probable,) that the President may bow to the decision of the Supreme Court, and cause it to be enforced; and that Georgia may sullenly acquiesce. If the President saw the subject with the eyes of his predecessors, he could easily quiet the State of Georgia; but, unfortunately, he stands committed by the public expression of his opinion. And Georgia is determined to make hay while the sun shines, and enforce her great object of expulsion during the present administration. I have already addressed a letter to the Governor of Georgia, of which I send you a copy, and have also placed copies of it in the hands of the President, and of the Cherokees. I have given an opinion to the Cherokees, on their rights (or rather several opinions on several different questions) and have advised the measures by which I think these questions may be carried to the Supreme Court. Now, I wish to ask you whether there is any thing exceptionable against me either as a lawyer or a citizen of the United States, in the part I am taking in this case. I am, indeed, aiding these oppressed people against the President of the United States and the State of Georgia—but in conformity, as I think with the constitutional laws and treaties of the United States. I need not tell you that I have no fear of personal consequences, but I have a great fear of doing what any honourable man can think wrong. . . .

The opinion which I have given is this—that if these people shall be sued civilly, or criminally prosecuted before a State court of Georgia, under the Georgia law, they may defend themselves on the ground of their treaties, which regard them as a sovereign nation within their own territory, under the *exclusive government* of their own laws, usages and customs; that the law of Georgia is void, as being repugnant to these treaties; and that if the present court of Georgia shall decide in favour of the law against the right claimed under the treaty, the case may be carried for revision to the Supreme Court of the United States, under the 25th section of the Judiciary act: see the case of Cohens *v.* the State of Virginia, 6 Wheaton, 375—Chief Justice Marshall's opinion.

I think it clear that the jurisdiction must be founded upon that section, as it has been construed by the Supreme Court, whatever may be the ultimate decision on the right. This, however, is appellate jurisdiction and requires that the case should first have passed through the State courts, which will delay the decision and throw every impediment in our way. The Attorney-General says the State of Georgia will take care that no case shall ever come to the Supreme Court. They will probably refuse to receive and put upon their records any plea which will show that the construction of treaties was involved, so that the record will contain nothing to found the jurisdiction of the Supreme Court, under the 25th section. Hence, it became important for me to enquire whether these people had any right to apply at once to the original jurisdiction of the federal courts; and this I cannot perceive that they can do, unless the Cherokee Nation be *a foreign state* in the sense of the Constitution, in which case they would have a right under the Constitution to file an original bill against the State of Georgia, in the Supreme Court, and ask an injunction against the execution of her law within their territory; or, unless the individuals of the Cherokee Nation be *aliens,* and consequently have a right to sue a citizen of Georgia in the federal courts. The High Court of Errors and Impeachments of New York, have held unanimously that these tribes are *alien and sovereign nations,* and their citizens *aliens:* Godall *vs.* Jackson, 20 Johnson, 693. Webster advises that every suit shall be brought in the name of the Cherokee Nation: he must therefore regard them as a foreign state. Will you read the case in 20th Johnson? and tell me, since I have shown you how deeply the Supreme Court may be interested in this subject, whether there would be any impropriety in your conversing with the Chief Justice on this subject, as a brother judge, and giving me his impressions of the political character of this people, in the respect I have mentioned. I would not have you to conceal from him that the question may probably come before the Supreme Court. The subject will not be new to him. He has had occasion to consider several times the character and rights of these people. His opinion in the case of Johnson and McIntosh, (3 Wheaton, pages 571, 593,) seems to me to maintain the right of the Indians to govern themselves exclusively by their own laws, within their own territory, although their right to that territory be a mere right of possession.

If the individuals of the Cherokee Nation be *aliens,* so as to found the original jurisdiction of the Supreme Court, the principal Chief of that Nation might file a bill against those officers of the State of Georgia, who will probably be engaged in executing her law, and ask an injunction against them, although he could not sue the State herself. See the cases of Osborn *vs.* the Bank of the United States, (9 Wheaton, 733,) and Bank of the United States *vs.* Planter's Bank of Georgia, ib. 904. Have you time to read these cases and inform yourself on this subject? There is another point on which I wish it was possible to come at the opinion of the Chief Justice, with propriety. It is this:—treaties compose a part of the supreme law of the land by the sixth article of the Constitution,—and it is added that "the judges in any State shall be bound thereby, any thing in the constitution or laws of any State or territory, to the contrary notwithstanding." Now, by these treaties I hold the Cherokees to be "a sovereign nation." See the speeches of Frelinghuysen and Sprague in the Senate. But the President said they are not a sovereign state, but subject to the laws of the State of Georgia.

The Supreme Court has decided with regard to the new South American Republics while in a state of revolt, that the courts of the nation could not recognize them as States, until they had been recognized as such by the Executive of the United States. But I understand this to be limited to new States in that condition, and not to apply to old States whom the United States have continually acknowledged as such by treating with them as sovereign States. I wish to know whether the Chief Justice considers, according to the opinion already pronounced by him, the courts of the nation constitutionally bound by the declaration of the Executive branch of the government, (that is to say, the President of the United States,) that any people are or are not a sovereign state, so that the prior implications, by treaty, of their sovereignty, will be judicially considered as superseded by such presidential declarations. I can scarcely suppose that such is his notion: since otherwise the President might by his declaration, put Great Britain or any ancient sovereign, out of the family of nations. . . . If I were near the Chief Justice I would ask him at once, these questions myself,—and tell him as I wish you to do, that there is no case yet depending, which involves a decision on them; but that, unless the opinions of the Supreme Court, as already pronounced, prevent it, there may be questions of a delicate and embarrassing nature to the Supreme Court, which may be prevented by a correct understanding of the full scope of the decisions heretofore pronounced.

I would speak to him with the confidence of a friend, . . . and leave it to him to say, whether he would or would not be willing to come out with the expression of his opinion, so as to prevent embarrassment and mischief. I cannot discover that there would be any impropriety either in his saying whether the principles I have mentioned are involved in the former decision; or, what he may at present, think of these questions. . . . Unless I am restrained by your advice, I shall go on with this case in behalf of these people. But if you think it wrong, tell me so, and I shall as frankly draw off from these people and tell them why. I do not ask whether it be politic, but inherently right or wrong; for if right, I shall go on at any hazard. Pray give me your views fully of this matter; and if Cabell has not left Richmond for this place, (where I am expecting him

> every boat,) take him into the council,—and our trusty and well-beloved friend Coalter too. I shall be longing to hear from you on this subject.
>
> *Your friend,*
> WM. WIRT

This letter was submitted by Judge Carr to the Chief Justice, who, upon consideration of the subject, thought it his duty to refrain from indicating any opinion on the delicate and interesting questions suggested by Mr. Wirt. "I have followed"—he adds, in a letter to Judge Carr expressing this determination—"the debate in both houses of Congress, with profound attention and with deep interest, and have wished, most sincerely, that both the executive and legislative departments had thought differently on the subject. Humanity must bewail the course which is pursued, whatever may be the decision of policy."

As might have been expected, in a case which had enlisted so much feeling, the motives of the counsel for engaging in it were questioned with no little asperity by many who stood in the relation of partisans on the side of Georgia. The publication of Mr. Wirt's opinion in favour of the Cherokees, furnished occasion for much censure and detraction. He was accused of taking part against his own country. He was charged also with acting from considerations of personal pique against an administration which had supplanted him and his friends. Those who assailed him through the public press seemed to find it a difficult problem to solve—how any upright citizen could question an executive proceeding which was intended to enlarge the national domain: how any such citizen could be so bold as to assert the rights of the weak and defenceless, or plead the sanctity of the national faith embodied in treaties, against the usurpations either of national or state authorities.

Such attacks upon his motives Mr. Wirt did not think it becoming his own self-respect to repel by any public notice. In a letter to a friend, he writes:

> I am insisting only on what General Washington and all his successors have held to be right; namely, that the Indians are

entitled to the protection guaranteed to them by the treaties. If this administration, for the first time, has taken different ground, and shall deny that protection to them, I can perceive no principle of morality or patriotism that requires me to adopt this new-fangled notion in opposition to those of Washington, Jefferson, Madison, Monroe, and John Quincy Adams. With all these great men, I think the Indians entitled to this protection; and I think, too, that the Supreme Court can give it. In this last position I may be wrong. But thinking as I do, and holding the proceedings of Georgia towards these poor creatures to be most tyrannical, as well as unconstitutional, and, if suffered, that it would be a foul breach of faith on the part of the United States, the disgrace of which the waters of the ocean of Time can never wash out, what sort of *patriotism* is that which could require me to refuse my professional services, when properly asked, to uphold the honour of my own country, and the rights of these oppressed people? The *prudence* of the engagement is another thing. It will be pronounced prudent or imprudent, as any man shall apply *long* or *short* measure to the subject. Those who consult only the personal convenience of the moment, will pronounce it imprudent. This I call the *short* measure. But I hold it most prudent always to do our duty, whether convenient or inconvenient. This I call *long* measure. If I had declined this engagement from a cowardly fear of the consequences, I should never have been able to hold up my head again.

83. An Anonymous Feminist

Their land will be divided up among those who are seeking it

Helen Hunt Jackson gained fame after the Civil War by cataloging the list of atrocities perpetrated against the Indian tribes and exposing their plight. The following selection, written a half century earlier, indicates the sympathy felt by an anonymous feminist toward the southern tribes and her indignation at federal and state policies toward them. Of interest is her argument that women had a special role to play "in relation to this helpless race."

Circular Addressed to Benevolent Ladies of the United States (1829), 1–3.

Circular

Addressed to Benevolent Ladies of the United States

The present crisis in the affairs of the Indian Nations in the United States, demands the immediate and interested attention of all who make any claims to benevolence or humanity. The calamities now hanging over them, threaten not only these relics of an interesting race, but if there is a Being who avenges the wrongs of the oppressed, are causes of alarm to our whole country.

The following are the facts of the case. This continent was once possessed only by the Indians, and earliest accounts represent them as a race, numerous, warlike and powerful. When our forefathers sought refuge from oppression on these shores, this people supplied their necessities, and ministered to their comfort; and though some of them, when they saw the white man continually encroaching upon their land, fought bravely for their existence and their country, yet often too, the Indian has shed his blood to protect and sustain our infant nation.

As we have risen in greatness and glory, the Indian nations have faded away. Their proud and powerful tribes are gone, their noble Sachems and mighty warriors are heard of no more; and it is said the Indian often comes to the borders of his limited retreat, to gaze on the beautiful country no longer his own, and to cry with bitterness at the remembrance of past greatness and power.

Ever since the existence of this nation, our general government, pursuing the course, alike of policy and benevolence, have acknowledged these people as free and independent nations, and has protected them in the quiet possession of their lands. In repeated treaties with the Indians, the United States, by the hands of the most distinguished statesmen, after purchasing the greater part of their best lands, have *promised* them "*to continue the guaranty of the remainder of their country* FOREVER." And so strictly has government guarded the Indian's right to his lands, that even to go on to their boundaries to survey the land, subjects to heavy fines and imprisonment.

Our government also, with parental care, has persuaded the

Indians to forsake their savage life, and to adopt the habits and pursuits of civilized nations, while the charities of Christians, and the labors of missionaries have sent to them the blessings of the gospel to purify and enlighten. The laws and regular forms of a civilized government are instituted; their simple and beautiful language, by the remarkable ingenuity of one of their race, has become a written language with its own peculiar alphabet, and by the printing press, is sending forth among these people, the principles of knowledge, and liberty, and religion. Their fields are beginning to smile with the labors of the husbandman; their villages are busy with the toils of the mechanic and the artisan; schools are rising in their hamlets, and the temple of the living God is seen among their forests.

Nor are we to think of these people only as naked and wandering savages. The various grades of intellect and refinement exist among them as among us; and those who visit their chieftains, and families of the higher class, speak with wonder and admiration of their dignified propriety, nobleness of appearance, and refined characteristics as often exhibited in both sexes. Among them are men fitted by native talents, to shine among the statesmen of any land, and who have received no inferior degree of cultivation. Among them also, are those who by honest industry, have assembled around them most of the comforts, and many of the elegancies of life.

But the lands of this people are *claimed* to be embraced within the limits of some of our Southern States, and as they are fertile and valuable, they are demanded by the whites as their own possessions, and efforts are making to dispossess the Indians of their native soil. And such is the singular state of concurring circumstances, that it has become almost a certainty, that these people are to have their lands torn from them, and to be driven into western wilds and to final annihilation, unless the feelings of a humane and christian nation shall be aroused to prevent the unhallowed sacrifice.

Unless our general government interfere to protect these nations, as by solemn and oft-repeated treaties they are bound to do, nothing can save them. The states which surround them are taking such measures as will speedily drive them from their country, and cause their final extinction.

By enactments recently passed in some of these states, it is decided that the laws of these states shall be extended over the Indian territory in the course of the next year (1830). And the following specimen of their laws will show what will be the fate of the Indian when they take effect.

> ART. 8. All laws, usages and customs, made, established, and in force in the said territory, by the said Cherokee Indians, be, and are hereby, on and after the first day of June 1830, declared *null* and *void.*
>
> ART. 9. No Indian, or descendant of Indian, residing within the Creek or Cherokee nations of Indians, shall be deemed a *competent witness,* or a *party to any suit,* in *any court* created by the constitution, or laws of this state, to which a white man may be a party.

If these laws are permitted to take effect, the Indians are no longer independent nations, but are slaves, at the sovereign disposal of the whites, who will legislate for them. Their land will be divided up among those who are seeking it; their cattle may be driven off; their persons and their property abused; even their wives and children could be murdered before their eyes, and no Indian might approach a court of justice to testify of wrongs received. Should those who seek the Indian lands, be deterred from such open violence, other as ready and as effectual means could be adopted. Should their lands be divided among the whites, the Indians *cannot live* surrounded by their settlements. He has the spirit of freedom and nobility, and cannot consent to be trod down, reviled and scorned. He would fly to the ends of the earth to avoid the humiliation and ruin. Or should some portion of this race remain, still bound to their native soil, *intoxication* is a scourge the white man has well learned to wield. *Now,* by the Indian laws, whiskey is seized and destroyed on their lands; but *then,* when all their laws "become null and void," it would be brought to every man's door, and be presented to his lips. *Then,* feeble, dispirited, scorned and oppressed, what shadow of hope that this fiery temptation would not waste and destroy them, till desolation take its fill.

But it is said that our government has provided a refuge for them beyond the Mississippi, where they may retreat and be protected. But let the simple matter of fact be stated, and this seems but solemn mockery. The Indians have never been subject to any man. They consist of different free born, independent tribes. They are attached to their native soil, and have again and again refused to relinquish it. They know that they have a perfect *natural* right to it, and that the government of the United States by many treaties have solemnly *promised* to protect them in their lawful possessions of it. They know they have rights as independent nations and distinct communities, and in this character can make the most forcible appeals both to the justice and the magnanimity of the United States.

But they are required to give up their national character and rights, and become wandering emigrants. A small tract of wild and uncultivated land has been apportioned to them principally beyond the Arkansas; a territory found by examination to be deficient both in wood and water, which are articles of indispensable necessity to emigrants and from whence the Indians who have been persuaded to depart, are returning with dissatisfied complaints. To this wild and unpromising resort, it is proposed to remove 60,000 people of all ages, sexes and condition; to break up all their existing social, political and religious associations; to expose them to the hunger, nakedness, sickness and distress of a long and fatiguing journey, through unfrequented wilds; to crowd into this narrow space different tribes, speaking diverse languages, and accustomed to different habits of life; and to place them under the government of white agents, to be appointed by government. Here, they are expected to take up their residence, with no other hope than that when they have made their lands valuable by cultivation, they again must be driven into still more distant wilds; for if our government cannot fulfil its treaties and protect them *now,* well they know it could not do it then. Is the thing possible, that these 60,000 Indians can thus be stripped of all they hold dear on earth, and in direct violation of oft repeated treaties, and yet quietly and unresistingly submit to such oppression and robbery? Does not the very statement show, that in effecting this wicked project, the "voice of our brothers' blood" would cry unto God from this guilty land?

It appears then, that measures are fast ripening, which, if put in execution, are to exterminate the Indians. If they remain where they are, and the laws of the different states are permitted to be extended over them, and their lands divided among the whites, intoxication, quarrels and unrestrained oppressions will soon change them to vagabonds and ensure their final extinction. Should they be driven to the west, a fate no less cruel awaits them there, where they lose even the last sad hope of reposing from their oppressions in the sepulchres of their fathers, and beneath their native soil.

But why should this deed of infamy and shame be perpetrated before the nations of the earth, and in the face of high Heaven? Are the people who claim the Indian's country in need of land? They have more than they can possibly occupy, for a hundred years to come. Has not our government power to prevent this deed? If our government has not power to fulfil its treaties, it would be a most humiliating fact thus to be exposed before the nations of the earth. But our president is empowered by the constitution to issue his proclamation forbidding any such encroachments as are threatened, and if this is disregarded, he has power by his sole authority, to command *the whole military force of our nation,* to protect and sustain the Indian in his rights.

Can any difficulty or danger arise from allowing this small remnant of a singular and peculiar race to exist in the midst of us? Why should they not stand, the cherished relic of antiquity, protected and sustained in their rights, and becoming a free and christian people, under their own laws and government? Can the millions of our nation, fear any evil from their numbers or their power? Can *any thing* be feared but that their helplessness should be made the prey of the avaricious and the unprincipled?

But they are beginning to be oppressed and threatened, and when they have looked for protection and help it has been refused. Already we begin to hear them lamenting, that they must leave their home, their country, the land of their fathers, and all that is dearest to them on earth. At a late Indian council, after having been told by the agent of our government, that they no longer could be protected, the head chieftain thus replies in the simple language of sorrow and reproach.

> We do not wish to sell our lands and remove. This land our Great Father above gave us. We stand on it. We stood on it before the white man came to the edge of the American land. We stand on it still. It belongs to us. It belongs to no one in any place but ourselves. Our land is no borrowed land. White men came and sat down here and there and every where around us. When they wished to buy land of us, we have had good councils together. The white man always said "the land is yours—it is yours." We have always been true friends of the American people. We have not spoiled the least thing belonging to an American. Although it has been thus, a very different talk is now sent to us. We are told, that the King of Mississippi is about to extend his laws over us. We are distressed. Our hands are not strong. We are a small people; we do not know much. The King of Mississippi has strong arms, many warriors, and much knowledge. He is about to lay his laws upon us; we are distressed.
>
> Colonel Ward (the agent), knows we have just begun to build new houses, and make new fields, and to purchase iron, and set up blacksmith's shops with our annuity. We have some schools, we have begun to learn, and we have begun to embrace the gospel. We are like an infant *so high*, (here the chief bowed and extended his hand as low as his knee,) who has just begun to walk. So it is with us. We have just begun to rise and go. And our great Father who sits in the white house says to us—Unless you go yonder (pointing to the west) the white man will extend his laws over you. We do not say his words are lies—we believe they are true. We respect them as sacred. But we are distressed. Oh that our great Father would love us! Oh that the King of Mississippi would love us!

It cannot but seem a matter of grief and astonishment, that such facts exist in this country; in a nation blessed with wealth, and power, and laws, and religion; and whose possessions reach from ocean to ocean. But humiliating as is the reflection, *the*

Indians must perish, unless their destruction can be averted by a most decided and energetic expression of the wishes and feelings of a christian nation, addressed to the Congress now assembling, and which is soon to decide their doom.

Have not then the females of this country some duties devolving upon them in relation to this helpless race? They are protected from the blinding influence of party spirit, and the asperities of political violence. They have nothing to do with any struggle for power nor any right to dictate the decisions of those that rule over them. But they may *feel* for the distressed, they may stretch out the supplicating hand for them, and by their prayers, strive to avert the calamities that are impending over them. It may be, that female petitioners can lawfully be heard, even by the highest rulers of our land. Why may we not approach and supplicate that we and our dearest friends may be saved from the awful curses denounced on all who oppress the poor and needy, by Him, whose anger is to be dreaded more than the wrath of man; who can "blast us with the breath of his nostrils," and scatter our hopes like chaff before the storm. It may be this will be *forbidden;* yet still we remember the Jewish princess, who being sent to supplicate for a nation's life, was thus reproved for hesitating even when *death* stared her in the way. "If thou altogether hold thy peace at this time, then shall deliverance arise from another place; but thou and thy father's house shall be destroyed;" and who knoweth whether thou art come to the kingdom for such a cause as this?

To woman, it is given to administer the sweet charities of life, and to *sway the empire of affection;* and to her it may also be said, "who knoweth whether thou art come to the kingdom for such a cause as this?"

In the days of chivalry, at the female voice, thousands of lances would have been laid in rest to protect the helpless and oppressed. But these are days of literature, refinement, charity and religion; and may we not appeal to nobler champions, than chivalry could boast? Will the liberal and refined, those who are delighted with the charms of eloquence and poetry; those who love the legends of romance, and the records of antiquity; those who celebrate and admire the stern virtues of Roman warriors and patriots; will these permit such a race to be swept from the earth?—a nation who have emerged from the deepest shades of antiquity; whose story, and whose wild and interesting traits are becoming the theme of the poet and novelist; who command a native eloquence unequalled for pathos and sublimity; whose stern fortitude and unbending courage, exceed the Roman renown? Will the naturalist, who laments the extinction of the mammoth race of the forest, allow this singular and interesting species of the *human* race to cease from the earth? Will those who boast of liberty, and feel their breasts throb at the name of freedom and their country, will they permit the free and noble Indian to be driven from his native land, or to crouch and perish under the scourge of oppression? And those whose hearts thrill at the magic sound of *home*, and turn with delightful remembrance to the woods and the valleys of their childhood and youth, will they allow this helpless race to be forced for ever from such blessed scenes, and to look back upon them with hopeless regret and despair?

You who gather the youthful group around your fireside and rejoice in their future hopes and joys, will you forget that the poor Indian loves his children too, and would as bitterly mourn over all their blasted hopes? And, while surrounded by such treasured blessings, ponder with dread and awe these fearful words of Him, who thus forbids the violence, and records the malediction of those, who either as individuals, or as nations, shall oppress the needy and helpless.

> *Thou shalt not vex the stranger nor oppress him, for ye were strangers in the land. If thou afflict them, and they cry at all unto me, I will surely hear their cry; and my wrath shall wax hot, and I will kill you with the sword, and your wives shall be widows, and your children fatherless.*

P.S. Should the facts alluded to in the preceding be doubted, they can be fully substantiated by consulting the communications signed "William Penn," and the statements made and signed by many of the most distinguished philanthropists of our country, which are to be found in the recent numbers of our public prints.

This communication was written and sent abroad solely by the female hand. Let every woman who peruses it, exert that influence in society, which falls within her lawful province, and endeavor by every suitable expedient to interest the feelings of her friends, relatives and acquaintances, in behalf of this people, that are ready to perish. *A few weeks* must decide this interesting and important question, and after that time, sympathy and regret will all be in vain.

84. The Cherokee Nation

We wish to remain on the land of our fathers

The heads of the Cherokee Nation prepared an address to the people of the United States, patiently describing the bases of their claim to continued residence on territory within the state of Georgia. The Cherokee appeal "to the good sense of the American people" of course went unheeded, and shortly afterward they together with other southern tribes were forced to follow the "trail of tears" from their homes to west of the Mississippi.

Address

Of the Committee and Council of the Cherokee Nation in General Council convened, to the People of the United States.

Some months ago, a delegation was appointed by the constituted authorities of the Cherokee nation, to repair to the City of Washington, and, in behalf of this nation, to lay before the Government of the United States such representations as should seem most likely to secure to us as a people that protection, aid, and good neighborhood, which had been so often promised to us, and of which we stand in great need. Soon after their arrival in the

From *Address of the Committee and Council of the Cherokee Nation to the People of the United States* (New Echota, Cherokee Nation, July 17, 1830), 4–8.

City, they presented to Congress a petition from our National Council, asking for the interposition of that body in our behalf, especially with reference to the laws of Georgia, which were suspended in a most terrifying manner over a large part of our population, and protesting in the most decided terms against the operation of these laws. In the course of the winter they presented petitions to Congress, signed by more than four thousand of our citizens, including probably more than nineteen twentieths, and for ought we can tell ninety-nine hundredths, of the adult males of the nation (our whole population being about sixteen thousand,) pleading with the assembled representatives of the American people, that the solemn engagements between their fathers and our fathers may be preserved, as they have been till recently, in full force and continued operation; asking, in a word for protection against threatened usurpation, and for a faithful execution of a guaranty, which is perfectly plain in its meaning, has been repeatedly and rigidly enforced in our favor; and has received the sanction of the government of the United States for nearly forty years.

More than a year ago we were officially given to understand by the Secretary of War, that the President could not protect us against the laws of Georgia. This information was entirely unexpected; as it went upon the principle, that treaties made between the United States and the Cherokee Nation have a power to withstand the legislation of separate States; and of course, they have no efficacy whatever, but leave our people to the mercy of the neighboring whites, whose supposed interests would be promoted by our expulsion, or extermination. It would be impossible to describe the sorrow which affected our minds, on learning that the Chief magistrate of the United States had come to this conclusion, that all his illustrious predecessors had held intercourse with us on principles which could not be sustained; that they had made promises of vital importance to us, which could not be fulfilled—promises made hundreds of times, in almost every conceivable manner,—often in the form of solemn treaties, sometimes in letters written by the Chief Magistrate with his own hand, very often in letters written by the Secretary of

War under his direction, sometimes orally by the President and the Secretary to our chiefs, and frequently and always, both orally and in writing, by the Agent of the United States residing among us, whose most important business it was, to see the guaranty of the United States faithfully executed.

Soon after the war of the Revolution, as we have learned from our fathers, the Cherokees looked upon the promises of the whites with great distrust and suspicion; but the frank and magnanimous conduct of General Washington did much to allay these feelings. The perseverance of successive Presidents, and especially of Mr. Jefferson, in the same course of policy, and in the constant assurance that our country should remain inviolate, except so far as we voluntarily ceded it, nearly banished anxiety in regard to encroachments from the whites. To this result the aid which we received from the United States in the attempts of our people to become civilized, and the kind efforts of benevolent societies, have greatly contributed. Of late years, however, much solicitude was occasioned among our people by the claims of Georgia. This solicitude arose from an apprehension that by extreme importunity, threats, and other undue influence, a treaty would be made, which should cede the territory and thus compel the inhabitants to remove. But it never occurred to us for a moment, that without any new treaty, without any assent of our rulers and people, without even a pretended compact, and against our vehement and unanimous protestations, we should be delivered over to the discretion of those who had declared by a legislative act, that they wanted the Cherokee lands and would have them.

Finding that relief could not be obtained from the Chief Magistrate, and not doubting that our claim to protection was just, we made our application to Congress. During four long months our delegation waited, at the doors of the National Legislature of the United States, and the people at home, in the most painful suspense, to learn in what manner our application would be answered, and, now that Congress has adjourned, on the very day before the date fixed by Georgia for the extension of her oppressive laws over the greater part of our country, the distressing intelligence has been received that we have received no answer at all; and no department of the Government has assured us, that we are to receive the desired protection. But just at the close of the session, an act was passed, by which half a million of dollars was appropriated towards effecting a removal of the Indians; and we have great reason to fear that the influence of this act will be brought to bear most injuriously upon us. The passage of this act is certainly understood by the representatives of Georgia as abandoning us to the oppressive and cruel measures of the State, and as sanctioning the opinion that treaties with Indians do not restrain State Legislation. We are informed by those who are competent to judge, that the recent act does not admit of such construction; but that the passage of it, under the actual circumstances of the controversy, will be considered as sanctifying the pretensions of Georgia, there is too much reason to fear.

Thus have we realized with heavy hearts, that our supplication has not been heard; that the protection heretofore experienced is now to be withheld; that the guaranty, in consequence of which our fathers laid aside their arms and ceded the best portion of their country, means nothing; and that we must either emigrate to an unknown region, and leave the pleasant land to which we have the strongest attachments, or submit to the legislation of a State, which has already made our people outlaws, and enacted that any Cherokee, who shall endeavor to prevent the selling of his country, shall be imprisoned in the Penitentiary of Georgia not less than four years. To our countrymen, this has been melancholy intelligence, and with the most bitter disappointment has it been received.

But in the midst of our sorrows, we do not forget our obligations to our friends and benefactors. It was with sensations of inexpressible joy, that we have learned, that the voice of thousands, in many parts of the United States, has been raised in our behalf, and numerous memorials offered in our favor, in both houses of Congress. To those numerous friends, who have thus sympathized with us in our low estate, we tender our grateful acknowledgements. In pleading our cause, they have pleaded the cause of the poor and defenceless throughout the world. Our special thanks are due, however, to those honorable men, who so ably and eloquently asserted our rights, in both branches of the national legislature. Their efforts will be appreciated wherever the merits of this question shall be known; and we cannot but think, that they have secured for themselves a permanent reputation among the disinterested advocates of humanity, equal rights, justice, and good faith. We even cherish the hope, that these efforts, seconded and followed by others of a similar character, will yet be available, so far as to mitigate our sufferings, if not to effect our entire deliverance.

Before we close this address, permit us to state what we conceive to be our relation with the United States. After the peace of 1783, the Cherokees were an independent people; absolutely so, as much as any people on earth. They had been allies to Great Britain, and as a faithful ally took a part in the colonial war on her side. They had placed themselves under her protection, and had they, without cause, declared hostility against their protector, and had the colonies been subdued, what might not have been their fate? But her power on this continent was broken. She acknowledged the independence of the United States, and made peace. The Cherokees, therefore, stood alone; and in these circumstances, continued the war. They were then under no obligations to the United States any more than to Great Britain, France or Spain. The United States never subjugated the Cherokees; on the contrary, our fathers remained in possession of their country, and with arms in their hands.

The people of the United States sought a peace; and in 1785, the treaty of Hopewell was formed, by which the Cherokees came under the protection of the United States, and submitted to such limitations of sovereignty as are mentioned in that instrument. None of these limitations, however, affected, in the slightest degree, their rights of self-government and inviolate territory. The citizens of the United States had no right of passage through the Cherokee country till the year 1791, and then only in one direction, and by an express treaty stipulation. When the Federal Constitution was adopted, the treaty of Hopewell was confirmed, with all other treaties, as the Supreme law of the land. In 1791, the treaty of Holston was made, by which the sovereignty of the Cherokees was qualified as follows: The Cherokees acknowledged themselves to be under the protection of the United States, and of no other sovereign. They engaged that they would not hold any treaty with a foreign power, with any separate state of the Union, or with individuals. They agreed that the United States should have the exclusive right of regulating their trade; that the citizens of the United States should have a right of way in one direction through the Cherokee country; and that if an Indian should do injury to a citizen of the United States he should be delivered up to be tried and punished. A cession of lands was also made to the United States. On the other hand, the United States paid a sum of money; offered protection; engaged to punish citizens of the United States, who should do any injury to the Cherokees; abandoned white settlers on Cherokee lands to the discretion of the Cherokees; stipulated that white men should not hunt on these lands, nor even enter the country without a passport; and gave a solemn guaranty of all Cherokee lands not ceded. This treaty is the basis of all subsequent compacts; and in none of them are the relations of the parties at all changed.

The Cherokees have always fulfilled their engagements. They have never reclaimed those portions of sovereignty, which they surrendered by the treaties of Hopewell and Holston. These portions were surrendered for the purpose of obtaining the guaranty which was recommended to them as the great equivalent. Had they refused to comply with their engagements, there is no doubt the United States would have enforced a compliance. Is the duty of fulfilling engagements on the other side less binding than it would be if the Cherokees had the power of enforcing their just claims?

The people of the United States will have the fairness to reflect, that all the treaties between them and the Cherokees were made, at the solicitation, and for the benefit, of the whites; that valuable considerations were given for every stipulation, on the part of the United States; that it is impossible to reinstate the parties in their former situation; that there are now hundreds of thousands of citizens of the United States residing upon lands ceded by the

Cherokees in these very treaties; and that our people have trusted their country to the guaranty of the United States. If this guaranty fails them, in what can they trust, and where can they look for protection?

We are aware, that some persons suppose it will be for our advantage to remove beyond the Mississippi. We think otherwise. Our people universally think otherwise. Thinking that it would be fatal to their interests, they have almost to a man sent their memorial to Congress, deprecating the necessity of a removal. This question was distinctly before their minds when they signed their memorial. Not an adult person can be found, who has not an opinion on the subject, and if the people were to understand distinctly, that they could be protected against the laws of the neighboring states, there is probably not an adult person in the nation, who would think it best to remove; though possibly a few might emigrate individually. There are doubtless many who would flee to an unknown country, however beset with dangers, privations and sufferings, rather than be sentenced to spend six years in a Georgia prison for advising one of their neighbors not to betray his country. And there are others who could not think of living as outlaws in their native land, exposed to numberless vexations, and excluded from being parties or witnesses in a court of justice. It is incredible that Georgia should ever have enacted the oppressive law, to which reference is here made, unless she had supposed that something extremely terrific in its character was necessary in order to make the Cherokees willing to remove. We are not willing to remove; and if we could be brought to this extremity, it would be not by argument, not because our judgment was satisfied, not because our condition will be improved, but only because we cannot endure to be deprived of our national and individual rights and subjected to a process of intolerable oppression.

We wish to remain on the land of our fathers. We have a perfect and original right to remain without interruption or molestation. The treaties with us, and laws of the United States made in pursuance of treaties, guaranty our residence, and our privileges, and secure us against intruders. Our only request is, that these treaties may be fulfilled, and these laws executed.

But if we are compelled to leave our country, we see nothing but ruin before us. The country west of the Arkansas territory is unknown to us. From what we can learn of it, we have no prepossessions in its favor. All the inviting parts of it, as we believe, are pre-occupied by various Indian nations, to which it has been assigned. They would regard us as intruders, and look upon us with an evil eye. The far greater part of that region is, beyond all controversy, badly supplied with wood and water; and no Indian tribe can live as agriculturalists without these articles. All our neighbors, in case of our removal, though crowded into our near vicinity, would speak a language totally different from ours, and practice different customs. The original possessors of that region are now wandering savages, lurking for prey in the neighborhood. They have always been at war, and would be easily tempted to turn their arms against peaceful emigrants. Were the country to which we are urged much better than it is represented to be, and were it free from the objections which we have made to it, still it is not the land of our birth, nor of our affections. It contains neither the scenes of our childhood, nor the graves of our fathers.

The removal of families to a new country, even under the most favorable auspices, and when the spirits are sustained by pleasing visions of the future, is attended with much depression of mind and sinking of heart. This is the case, when the removal is a matter of decided preference, and when the persons concerned are in early youth or vigorous manhood. Judge, then, what must be the circumstances of a removal, when a whole community, embracing persons of all classes and every description, from the infant to the man of extreme old age, the sick, the blind, the lame,—the improvident, the reckless, the desperate, as well as the prudent, the considerate, the industrious, are compelled to remove by odious and intolerable vexations and persecutions brought upon them in the forms of law, when all will agree only in this, that they have been cruelly robbed of their country, in violation of the most solemn compacts, which it is possible for communities to form with each other; and that, if they should make themselves comfortable in their new residence, they have nothing to expect hereafter but to be the victims of a future legalized robbery!

Such we deem, and are absolutely certain, will be the feelings of the whole Cherokee people, if they are forcibly compelled by the laws of Georgia to remove; and with these feelings, how is it possible that we should pursue our present course of improvement, or avoid sinking into utter despondency? We have been called a poor, ignorant, and degraded people. We certainly are not rich; nor have we ever boasted of our knowledge, or our moral or intellectual elevation. But there is not a man within our limits, so ignorant as not to know that he has a right to live on the land of his fathers, in the possession of his immemorial privileges, and that this right has been acknowledged and guaranteed by the United States; nor is there a man so degraded as not to feel a keen sense of injury, on being deprived of this right and driven into exile.

It is under a sense of the most pungent feelings that we make this, perhaps our last appeal to the good people of the United States. It cannot be that the community we are addressing, remarkable for its intelligence and religious sensibilities, and pre-eminent for its devotion to the rights of man, will lay aside this appeal, without considering that we stand in need of its sympathy and commiseration. We know that to the Christian and the Philanthropist the voice of our multiplied sorrows and fiery trials will not appear as an idle tale. In our own land, on our own soil, and in our own dwellings, which we reared for our wives and for our little ones, when there was peace on our mountains and in our valleys, we are encountering troubles which cannot but try our very souls. But shall we, on account of these troubles, forsake our beloved country? Shall we be compelled by a civilized and christian people, with whom we have lived in perfect peace for the last forty years, and for whom we have willingly bled in war, to bid a final adieu to our homes, our farms, our streams and our beautiful forests?

No. We are still firm. We intend still to cling, with our wonted affection, to the land which gave us birth, and which, every day of our lives brings to us new and stronger ties of attachment. We appeal to the judge of all the earth, who will finally award us justice, and to the good sense of the American people, whether we are intruders upon the lands of others. Our consciences bear us witness that we are the invaders of no man's rights—we have robbed no man of his territory, nor have we deprived any man of his unalienable privileges. How then shall we indirectly confess the right of another people to our land by leaving it forever? On the soil which contains the ashes of our beloved men we wish to live—on this soil we wish to die.

We intreat those to whom the foregoing paragraphs are addressed, to remember the great law of love, "Do to others as ye would that others should do to you"—Let them remember that of all nations on the earth, they are under the greatest obligations to obey this law. We pray them to remember that, for the sake of principle, their forefathers were *compelled* to leave, therefore *driven* from the old world, and that the winds of persecution wafted them over the great waters and landed them on the shores of the new world, when the Indian was the sole lord and proprietor of these extensive domains. Let them remember in what way they were received by the savage of America, when power was in his hand, and his ferocity could not be restrained by any human arm. We urge them to bear in mind, that those who would now ask of them a cup of cold water, and a spot of earth, a portion of their own patrimonial possessions, on which to live and die in peace, are the descendants of those whose origin, as inhabitants of North America, history and tradition are alike insufficient to reveal. Let them bring to remembrance all these facts, and they *cannot*, and we are sure they *will not* fail to remember, and sympathize with us in these our trials and sufferings.

New Echota, C. N. July 17, 1830

Lewis Ross,
Pres't of Committee
Richard Taylor,
James Daniel,
Jos. Vann,
David Vann,
J. R. Daniel,
Slim Fellow,
Situake,
De-Gah-Le-Lu-Ge,
Robbin,
Tah-Lah-Doo,
John Timson,
W.S.Codey, Clerk
Going Snake, Speaker
of the Council
James Bigbey,
Deer-in-the-water,

Edward Gunter,	Nah-Hoo-Lah,	Charles Reese,
John Baldridge,	White Path,	Sleeping Rabbit,
Samuel Ward,	Ne-Gah-We,	Chu-nu-gee,
George Sanders,	Dah-Ye-Ske,	Bark,
Daniel Griffin, Jun.	John Ridge, Clerk of Council	Laugh-at-Mush,
James Hamilton,	Alex. M'Daniel,	Chuleowah,
Walking Stick,	Thos. Foreman,	Turtle.
Moses Parris,		

Local and Urban Issues

85. William H. Seward

The mayor shall be elected by the people

Although the attention of historians has long been focused on the national political issues of the "Jacksonian era," important developments were also occurring on the state and local levels. One of the most significant trends of the 1830s was toward the popular election of mayors. In this speech in the New York State Senate, April 22, 1831, William H. Seward, later Whig leader and governor of New York State, argues in favor of direct popular election of mayors. As a matter of fact, neither the kind of men elected nor their policies changed as a result of this democratic reform. The problem was not with the new electoral procedure but in the fact that "underlying realities" were impervious to the new procedure.

What is the state of the question before the Senate? The provision required by the city of New York is, that the mayor of that city shall be elected by the people. The amendment under consideration proposes that the legislature shall hereafter have the right to prescribe the manner in which that officer shall be elected or appointed.

It is admitted that the office of mayor is one of local interests, duties and responsibilities, and that it is, in the abstract, right and proper that the mayor should be elected by the people in that

From George E. Baker, ed., *The Works of William H. Seward* (New York: Redfield, 1853), I, pp. 10–13.

city. Why, then, should not this provision, conceded to be abstractly right and proper, be adopted? Is it to be rejected on the ground of distrust of the people? No such distrust is avowed, and I am therefore bound to believe none is indulged. Only one argument has been urged in support of the amendment, which was, that it was expedient that the mode of election or appointment of this officer should be made a subject of legislative discretion, in order that it might from time to time be varied according to the wishes of the people of that city. This argument supposes that the present application is based upon slight grounds, and that the city of New York would not long be content with any one mode of election or appointment. This presumption is altogether unwarranted. So far as concerns this application, we are distinctly informed that it is made because by the late alteration in the charter of that city—the Common Council was divided into two houses—and the mayor was vested with the power of negativing by his veto the ordinances of those houses—and it is submitted to us that the officer with whom this power is vested ought not to derive his office from that body, or be responsible to it in derogation of whose power he is to exercise his veto. Who will deny that there is merit in this proposition? Who will contend that the governor of this state, who is invested with concurrent legislative powers, should by derivation of his office or otherwise be made amenable to the legislature. This application, then, so far from being groundless, is correct in principle, and in harmony with the structure of our government. And what grounds are there for the presumption that the people of the city of New York will again require an alteration in the mode of electing their mayor if the present application shall prevail? Under the old Constitution of this state, the mayor was appointed by the council of appointment. Was the city of New York then restive and clamorous for change? No; that city acquiesced until the loud and deep-toned and universal popular complaint against the corruptions of the council of appointment demanded its abolition, and a new depository of the appointing power of the state. Then, in accordance with the more democratic principles which prevailed at that day, the appointment of mayor was confided to the immediate representatives of the people of the city in their Common Council. Have the people of that city since been unquiet on this subject? No, sir; they have never asked for a change, until by another radical alteration in the powers and duties of this office, and in the organization of the Common Council, a necessity has arisen for the application now made.

Again, sir, the tendency of all our principles of government is to democracy; the new Constitution took the appointment from the council of appointment, and conferred it upon the immediate representatives of the people. There is but one more change before you reach absolute democracy; that is the one now proposed, and conceded to be proper. Are gentlemen afraid that the people, once invested with this power, will come back again and sue us to relieve them from its responsibilities? Such an instance would be anomalous in the history of government.

But we are told that the appointment or election of this officer ought not to "be bound up in constitutional bonds"—that it ought to be left to the legislature. Sir, I think if there be any right of the people which ought to be bound up in constitutional bonds, it is the right of electing their magistrates. If there be any right belonging to the people of the city of New York which ought to be bound up "in constitutional bonds," it is the right guarantied to them of electing, either by their immediate representatives, or by their own ballots, the highest local magistrate in their city, without being subjected to the caprice of party in your legislature. Gentlemen who support the amendment say they are in favor of allowing the mayor to be chosen by the people; will *their* amendment carry out their views? Amend the Constitution as *they* propose, and will the people then have that right? No; but it will then be left to the legislature of the state to determine whether the mayor shall be elected by the people or by the Common Council, or appointed by the legislature, or by the governor and Senate—and to revoke that decision at pleasure.

Gentlemen do indeed assure us that the legislature will never deprive the people of that city of the privilege of electing this officer, unless at their own solicitation. We are asked if we believe any legislature would so deprive them, and we are even told that to entertain such an apprehension, is to arrogate to ourselves all the virtue and the purity of the present and future legislatures. I, sir, arrogate to myself no such extraordinary portion of virtue and purity, and yet I have less confidence in legislative bodies than is necessary to induce my consent to restore to this legislature a power, of which, within my own recollection, it has been solemnly, and for cause, deprived by the Constitution. I will not say that the legislature ever would deprive the people of New York of the right to elect the first magistrate of their city; but I can safely say that legislatures have reluctantly parted with power, and have sometimes upon poor pretexts assumed it. But, sir, the answer to the gentleman's inquiry is furnished by the Constitution. The incorporation of the provision in the Constitution which reserves the appointment of the mayor by the Common Council, shows that the people distrust the purity and virtue of the legislature. It is, I believe, a broad and living principle of democracy, that the tendency of delegated power is always to its own aggrandizement, and that the safety of the rights of the people is secured by their jealousy of encroachment. So much distrust of the legislature as the Constitution expresses, and so much as is founded in the maxims of our government, and no more, I entertain.

What was the evil which called into existence the convention which framed your Constitution? Other grounds of objection there were indeed to your old Constitution, but the crying evil was the corruption and abuses of the council of appointment, subjected to the exercise of a mighty and controlling central power of Albany. What was the great reform made by that convention? Other reforms there were, but that which was the most valuable was the abolition of the council of appointment, and the distribution among different depositories more immediately derived from and subjected to the popular will, and of the appointing power of the state. Will not the people regard this as an attempt to bring back to the central power this portion of the appointing power? Will they not regard it as a precursor of other attempts to restore that state of things which it demanded the convention of 1821 to overthrow? Yes, sir, they will so regard it, and I think I may say for that portion of them which are my constituents, that any proposition tending to increase at the expense of popular rights and privileges, the power of the legislature or executive, will be met and resisted as an encroachment.

For these reasons, I am opposed to that portion of the amendment which provides for subjecting to legislative action the mode of the appointment of the mayor of the city of New York. I am in favor of giving the election to the people, and of extending the same right of election to all the cities in the state, and I shall avail myself of a distinct motion to amend for that purpose.

86. Mechanics, Merchants, and Others

The auction system creates a monopoly in the hands of a few

Auctions played an important role in early nineteenth-century cities in the disposition of European, largely English, imports. The fortune of Philip Hone, mayor of New York City in the mid-1820s and prominent member of that city's elite, was grounded in the auction business. The system came to be opposed by diverse groups, importing merchants, small shopkeepers, manufacturers, and workingmen, all of whom felt aggrieved by what they dubbed the "monopolistic" system. Anti-auction sentiment cut across party lines, attracting, among others, supporters of Clay's "American System" and the conservative faction of the New York State Working Men's party.

Memorial to the New York Legislature, by the Executive Committee appointed by the "respectable meeting of Mechanics, Merchants and others," February 22, 1830.

CIRCULAR

New-York, February 22nd., 1830.

SIR:—The accompanying Resolutions were adopted at a large and respectable meeting of Mechanics, Merchants and others, convened according to public notice, at Tammany Hall, on the evening of the 20th inst.

The undersigned, the Executive Committee, appointed by that meeting, have thought it proper to address the Members of the Legislature on this subject. A bill has been introduced into the House of Assembly, which meets their approbation; because it goes in a great measure to remedy the evils of which the complaints have at length become so general. We would endeavor to press upon your judgment the facts here stated, and invite the attention of every unprejudiced mind, to a calm investigation of their consequences.

The tricks resorted to at Auction Sales, for the purpose of decoying bidders, have become so notorious as to leave little cause to doubt their demoralizing effects. The petty practices resorted to by *Auctioneers* and *Sellers*, have long deluded the honest purchaser, and it is not until he at length becomes convinced by his past experience of the frauds often practised upon him, that he is aware of the vortex into which he has plunged.

For fifteen years has the evil of the system of Auction Sales been accumulating. When it first appeared in the City of New-York, confined in its operations to its legitimate purposes, the public considered that it was circumscribed in its course. But when it came to be extended throughout the different sections of our country—and particularly throughout our State; destroying the business of the honest Mechanic, and through him the Manufacturing and Agricultural interests; introducing into our City spurious goods, made expressly for what is termed Auction Sales, but actually intended for purposes of deception: its evils have become insufferable, and it is for the purpose of destroying a system which has given rise to such a state of things that we have the honor to address you.

It is an established fact, susceptible of the clearest demonstration, that articles made for sale at Auction, are of an inferior quality both as it regards materials and workmanship, and this has an inevitable tendency to undermine the integrity of the Mechanic—retrograde his ability—and to destroy that just pride which every individual feels, when he has produced a piece of workmanship, that, while it affords him a just compensation for his skill, elevates his name and his country's honor. Next to intellectual attainments, the boast of every nation has been the skill and excellence of her Mechanics, and Scientific men. But this cannot be our situation if encouragement is not afforded to those who deserve a just and reasonable compensation for their labor, and this we believe to be the opinion of every intelligent and candid person, who has given the subject a full and proper attention; thus, while justice is rendered the Mechanic, the community at large receives a corresponding benefit in the superiority of the article they use. In this respect the consumer is as much interested in the suppression of Retail Auctions, as the Mechanic; for, while it may be the case that articles are bought at a less price than at the shop of the Working Man, the difference in the quality results in a manifest loss to the buyer and consumer. In fact no party is benefited but the Auctioneer, at the expense of both the Mechanic and Consumer.

In addition to this, by the continuance of Retail Auctions, the legitimate employment and business of the Mechanics of our City and State, is given to the Mechanics of the neighboring states, from whose workshops the Auctions of our City are inundated with inferior articles, and this by injuring the honest Mechanic and Working Man, depresses trade, and the value of every species of property in our city, both real and personal.

Nor is this all. The inseparable consequence of Retail Auctions tend to undermine and degrade the morals of a people among whom they exist; for truth and honesty are not very conspicuous traits in their operations. But deception and fraud have been known in numberless instances to be connected in their transactions, yet in such a manner that no redress could be had by the sufferer, there being no responsible person to reach. Where does such a case ever occur with a fair and honest dealer?

It is on such principles as are here stated, that the Retail Auctions in this City have been conducted—inferior articles sold for good—Mahogany tables have been presented to the eye of the purchaser, apparently well made and in good condition, when glue has been the only substance connecting the parts. This deception is likewise used in other articles of furniture, also as in wearing apparel. These facts the Committee are ready to substantiate by the most conclusive testimony; and in this manner is the Mechanic, the Working Man, and the industrious female portion of the community defrauded, as well as the consumer, by the prevalence of Retail Auctions.

In conclusion: The Committee think, that in no single point of view have the Retail Auctions any just claim on the community to sustain them. They contribute nothing of any amount to the Canal Fund, as the thirty-five Auctioneers, who are the retailers, paid the last year, only $3,992; whereas, were they required to take a license, as contemplated by the bill now before the House of Assembly, the amount accruing to the State would be $8,650, being $4,648 additional, admitting they sold nothing that paid duties to the Canal Fund. But it is believed that revenue will not be diminished at all.

Again: The Auction system creates a monopoly of business in the hands of a few, to the exclusion of many; and this appears to us as inconsistent with the rights of other citizens, who are equally entitled to participate in the legitimate prosperity of any business or calling—no one having a preference over others, except such as superior industry and merit shall deserve and command.

The undersigned feel that they are engaged in a just and righteous cause. That with this subject is connected not only the prosperity of our City, but the whole State. That they have no resource but by the Constitutional Right of petitioning the Legislature for that redress, which only IT can give; and, in respectfully recommending to your attention this business, we have confidence in your wisdom and justice, trusting that an appeal to either will not be made in vain.

We have the honor to remain,
Your obedient Servants,

THOMAS HUNT,
THOMAS DUNCAN,
GEORGE E. SMITH,
JAMES W. DOMINICK,
JOSEPH P. SIMPSON,
SILAS B. HAMILTON,
JOHN F. SIBELL,
ABIJAH MATHEWS,
RICHARD CROMWELL,
DANIEL SMITH,
ISAAC CROSS,
CORNELIUS SMITH,
RICHARD E. MOUNT,
WILLIAM SCOTT,
SHIVERS PARKER,
JOHN K. COWPERTHWATE,
JOHN LLOYD.

PART SIX

Reform, or The Issues Neglected

The American Penchant for Reform

87. Alexis de Tocqueville

Americans of all ages, all conditions, constantly form associations

No one has described more vividly than Tocqueville the disposition of Americans to form associations in order to do good. Actually, there is some question as to whether "all conditions" were represented in such organizations. In the nineteenth as in the twentieth century, middle- and upper-class Americans appear to have been most likely to participate in voluntary associations.

The political activity that pervades the United States must be seen in order to be understood. No sooner do you set foot upon American ground than you are stunned by a kind of tumult; a confused clamor is heard on every side, and a thousand simultaneous voices demand the satisfaction of their social wants. Everything is in motion around you; here the people of one quarter of a town are met to decide upon the building of a church; there the election of a representative is going on; a little farther, the delegates of a district are hastening to the town in order to consult upon some local improvements; in another place, the laborers of a village quit their plows to deliberate upon the project of a road or a public school. Meetings are called for the sole purpose of declaring their disapprobation of the conduct of the government; while in other assemblies citizens salute the authorities of the day as the fathers of their country. Societies are formed which regard drunkenness as the principal cause of the evils of the

From Alexis de Tocqueville, *Democracy in America*, I, chap. XIV, pp. 271, 272, chap. XII, pp. 204, 205; II, chap. V, pp. 114, 115, 117–118. Footnote is in the original.

state, and solemnly bind themselves to give an example of temperance.*

The great political agitation of American legislative bodies, which is the only one that attracts the attention of foreigners, is a mere episode, or a sort of continuation, of that universal movement which originates in the lowest classes of the people and extends successively to all the ranks of society. It is impossible to spend more effort in the pursuit of happiness.

It is difficult to say what place is taken up in the life of an inhabitant of the United States by his concern for politics. To take a hand in the regulation of society and to discuss it is his biggest concern and, so to speak, the only pleasure an American knows. This feeling pervades the most trifling habits of life; even the women frequently attend public meetings and listen to political harangues as a recreation from their household labors. Debating clubs are, to a certain extent, a substitute for theatrical entertainments: an American cannot converse, but he can discuss, and his talk falls into a dissertation. He speaks to you as if he was addressing a meeting; and if he should chance to become warm in the discussion, he will say "Gentlemen" to the person with whom he is conversing. . . .

In no country in the world has the principle of association been more successfully used or applied to a greater multitude of objects than in America. Besides the permanent associations which are established by law under the names of townships, cities, and counties, a vast number of others are formed and maintained by the agency of private individuals.

The citizen of the United States is taught from infancy to rely upon his own exertions in order to resist the evils and the difficulties of life; he looks upon the social authority with an eye of mistrust and anxiety, and he claims its assistance only when he is unable to do without it. This habit may be traced even in the

* At the time of my stay in the United States the temperance societies already consisted of more than 270,000 members; and their effect had been to diminish the consumption of strong liquors by 500,000 gallons per annum in Pennsylvania alone. Temperance societies are organizations the members of which undertake to abstain from strong liquors.

schools, where the children in their games are wont to submit to rules which they have themselves established, and to punish misdemeanors which they have themselves defined. The same spirit pervades every act of social life. If a stoppage occurs in a thoroughfare and the circulation of vehicles is hindered, the neighbors immediately form themselves into a deliberative body; and this extemporaneous assembly gives rise to an executive power which remedies the inconvenience before anybody has thought of recurring to a pre-existing authority superior to that of the persons immediately concerned. If some public pleasure is concerned, an association is formed to give more splendor and regularity to the entertainment. Societies are formed to resist evils that are exclusively of a moral nature, as to diminish the vice if intemperance. In the United States associations are established to promote the public safety, commerce, industry, morality, and religion. There is no end which the human will despairs of attaining through the combined power of individuals united into a society. . . .

. . . The political associations that exist in the United States are only a single feature in the midst of the immense assemblage of associations in that country. Americans of all ages, all conditions, and all dispositions constantly form associations. They have not only commercial and manufacturing companies, in which all take part, but associations of a thousand other kinds, religious, moral, serious, futile, general or restricted, enormous or diminutive. The Americans make associations to give entertainments, to found seminaries, to build inns, to construct churches, to diffuse books, to send missionaries to the antipodes; in this manner they found hospitals, prisons, and schools. If it is proposed to inculcate some truth or to foster some feeling by the encouragement of a great example, they form a society. Wherever at the head of some new undertaking you see the government in France, or a man of rank in England, in the United States you will be sure to find an association.

I met with several kinds of associations in America of which I confess I had no previous notion; and I have often admired the extreme skill with which the inhabitants of the United States succeed in proposing a common object for the exertions of a great many men and inducing them voluntarily to pursue it.

I have since traveled over England, from which the Americans have taken some of their laws and many of their customs; and it seemed to me that the principle of association was by no means so constantly or adroitly used in that country. The English often perform great things singly, whereas the Americans form associations for the smallest undertakings. It is evident that the former people consider association as a powerful means of action, but the latter seem to regard it as the only means they have of acting.

Thus the most democratic country on the face of the earth is that in which men have, in our time, carried to the highest perfection the art of pursuing in common the object of their common desires and have applied this new science to the greatest number of purposes. Is this the result of accident, or is there in reality any necessary connection between the principle of association and that of equality?

As soon as several of the inhabitants of the United States have taken up an opinion or a feeling which they wish to promote in the world, they look out for mutual assistance; and as soon as they have found one another out, they combine. From that moment they are no longer isolated men, but a power seen from afar, whose actions serve for an example and whose language is listened to. The first time I heard in the United States that a hundred thousand men had bound themselves publicly to abstain from spirituous liquors, it appeared to me more like a joke than a serious engagement, and I did not at once perceive why these temperate citizens could not content themselves with drinking water by their own firesides. I at last understood that these hundred thousand Americans, alarmed by the progress of drunkenness around them, had made up their minds to patronize temperance. They acted in just the same way as a man of high rank who should dress very plainly in order to inspire the humbler orders with a contempt of luxury. It is probable that if these hundred thousand men had lived in France, each of them would singly have memorialized the government to watch the public houses all over the kingdom.

Nothing, in my opinion, is more deserving of our attention than the intellectual and moral associations of America. The political and industrial associations of that country strike us forcibly; but the others elude our observation, or if we discover them, we understand them imperfectly because we have hardly ever seen anything of the kind. It must be acknowledged, however, that they are as necessary to the American people as the former, and perhaps more so. In democratic countries the science of association is the mother of science; the progress of all the rest depends upon the progress it has made.

African Colonization

88. American Colonization Society

An asylum for our free coloured population

The central problem of American society concerned the relationship of the races. The idea of removing free Negroes or colonizing them in Africa had appealed to Thomas Jefferson and to other whites who believed that the races would never be able to live in harmony in this country. The American Colonization Society had been formed in 1817 to support the emigration of willing Negroes to a colony in Liberia. The following message, written by R. R. Gurley, secretary of the society, argues that a flourishing Liberia would encourage manumission, and that the society's noble work is opposed only by unrealistic persons who would abolish slavery immediately and those other fanatics who would abolish it never.

To the people of the United States

The practicability of colonizing in Africa, any number of the Free People of Colour of the United States, that may choose to emigrate, being demonstrated; the Managers of the American Colonization Society, address their fellow-citizens, under a deep

From *Address of the Managers of the American Colonization Society to the People of the United States* (Washington: James C. Dunn, 1832), 3–8.

conviction, that this whole nation is now summoned to aid the work, by the most weighty considerations of interest, duty, and charity. Believing, as the Managers do, that it is a work of immediate and vast importance, on the accomplishment of which, depends the temporal and eternal happiness of millions in this country, and in Africa, and which can be adequately done only by the combined powers of the nation, they are urged irresistably, to make an appeal in its behalf to all the patriotic, humane, and religious of the land. Nor can they doubt that ten thousand hearts will respond to this appeal, and ten thousand hands be stretched out with offerings to a cause, invested, with all that can attract affection and kindle enthusiasm in the noblest minds. Of the success of the plan, they can now speak not merely with hope, but with confidence.—A Colony of more than two thousand persons, firmly established, well-ordered and well-governed; prosperous in trade; moral and religious in character; with schools and churches; courts of justice, and a periodical press; enlarging its territory, and growing in strength; respected by all who have visited it from Europe, and exerting a salutary and extensive influence over the native tribes, now offers an asylum for our free coloured population, and to our citizens, every means and motive for conferring freedom on those who enjoy it not, and imparting civilization and christianity to Africa.

Though the Managers regard the scheme of the Society, as essentially connected with the purity and stability of our political institutions, and the glory of our national character, yet it is rather in its benevolent aspect towards a long afflicted and degraded people, in the midst of us, and their more wretched brethren in Africa, that they would commend it to the patronage of the public.—That there are causes operating to retard the improvement and depress the minds of the free people of colour in the United States, which no benevolence nor even Religion, can for ages, if ever remove; and that the elevation, to any great degree, of our coloured population generally, depends upon their settlement as a distinct community, in some country beyond the reach of those embarrassing circumstances, from which, neither humanity nor legislation can relieve them here, the Managers consider decided both by reason and experience. It is not merely with law and prejudice that the free man of colour has here to contend; but with superior knowledge, wealth and influence, with a competition to which he is unequal, with a deep sense of the thraldom of his past, and the disadvantages of his present condition, with an inwrought conviction, that whatever may be the worthy temporal object, of his pursuit, he has little prospect of attaining it, and that neither he nor his brethren can stem the tide, which beats against him in almost every course of life.

In Liberia, he exhibits not the semblance, but the reality of freedom, stands forth conscious that no barrier opposes his progress in improvement, feels his spirit stirred by new motives and better hopes, is awakened to the conviction that a great practicable good is to be achieved by him, not for himself alone, but for his posterity, and his race throughout all time and throughout the world; experiences, in fine, almost the power of a new creation forming him for actions worthy of his nature and his destiny. That a change, so striking and beneficial, is realized by the intelligent and well-disposed man of colour on his arrival at the Colony, is proved by abundant and unquestionable testimony. The officers of our own Navy, as well as enlightened foreigners, have witnessed with wonder and delight this transformation, from imbecility and hopelessness, to activity, and confidence, and manliness and high anticipations.

But while the Society would confer upon free men of colour unspeakable blessings, it offers the best asylum for slaves manumitted from regard to interest, humanity or conscience. Who does not know that in many States, the right of emancipation has been denied to the master, on the ground, that the exercise of such right would be inconsistent with the public good? Yet the restrictions of law have to a great extent proved ineffectual to prevent manumission, and numerous slaves have been transferred to other States, wherein they might enjoy, at least, nominal freedom, though still untouched by the spirit, and denied the blessings of Genuine Liberty. The Society adhering closely to its original design and principles, and exerting no influence upon slavery, except a moral influence, through the will of the master;

gives freedom to that will, relieves it from every embarrassment, and demonstrates to the view of all concerned, how emancipation to any and every extent desired, may be effected, not with danger or detriment, but rather with advantage to the public, and vast and perpetual benefit to the slave. Certain it is, that thousands of our fellow-citizens, whose dearest interests are identified with the prosperity and honour of the South, give their countenance and aid to the Society, not merely because it is most beneficial to the people of colour already free, but as offering powerful inducements to voluntary manumission by individuals, and States. And true it is, that the enemies of the Society are reduced to two classes, those who would abolish slavery instantaneously, and those who desire it may never be abolished. Hundreds are now freemen in Liberia, who were recently slaves in the United States, and many others of the same class are held in trust for the Society whenever its means shall be adequate to their colonization.

But Africa makes her appeal to our sympathy and charity, in a tone of earnestness and distress to which we are bound to listen, and which the Board trust cannot be resisted. It is along her dark shores and over her immense but uncultivated fields, that the Society will dispense its richest blessings. What a night of gloom and terror has settled, for ages, on her land! Her immense population covered with barbarism, given up as prey to outrage and violence, cursed by a traffic which has set brother against brother, desolated families and villages, excited the worst passions of savage nature, ruthlessly sundered all the ties of kindred and affection, and seizing with merciless and unyielding grasp its bleeding and broken-hearted victims, borne them crowded and crushed and dying into foreign and hopeless bondage! And even now, when her cries have pierced the heart of Christendom, when states and kingdoms have legislated and united to put an end to her sufferings, still torn, plundered, and robbed of her children by the pirates of all nations; she stretches out her hands and casts an imploring eye towards the friends of God and man, in this free and blessed country, for that deliverance, which she has looked for in vain to all the world beside.

And who can doubt that to this Nation *the interests of the*

African race are, by Providence, especially entrusted. The means by which our high and solemn duty to her is to be discharged, is evident. Her exiled children in the midst of us, are waiting to return to her, not as they came, ignorant and enslaved barbarians, but free and instructed christians, capable with the aid that we can give them, of founding upon her shores civilized institutions, of becoming teachers and guides to her people, of inculcating among them, those lessons of wisdom, which men with few advantages are not always the last to learn, that the duty of man is never at war with his interest, and that happiness is the handmaid of virtue. Already in the vicinity of Liberia are they abandoning the traffic in slaves, for a more peaceful commerce and the humane arts of life, and numerous tribes have sought the protection and adopted, as their own, the laws of the Colony.

That similar colonies established at proper intervals along the whole coast of western Africa, by men of the same complexion and ancestry with the natives, and who, having suffered, themselves, can commisserate their afflicted brethren, who, consenting and assisted to emigrate, not from mere selfish views, but by the holier motives of philanthropy and religion, that such colonies will erect impassable barriers between the parties in the slave trade, and by opening to the African tribes the sources of a better commerce and communicating to them a knowledge of the Christian faith, win them over to the love and practice of truth, and social virtue, may be as confidently expected, as that any moral means, well directed, will reform a debased and uncivilized people.

True it is asked, will the ignorant and degraded men of colour of this country become the best missionaries to enlighten and regenerate Africa? To this we reply that there are men of colour in the U. S. who are well informed and exemplary christians, that such as these have founded our present African Colony, that the very work to which they are called will develope their powers, and give elevation to their character, and finally, that plans for education and improvement commensurate with the necessities of every settlement which may be made, enter essentially into the views of the society.

If in a little more than two centuries, our own country has by colonization been changed from a wilderness into a fruitful field, if a free and enlightened Nation of twelve millions has sprung up here, where but lately, the wolf and savage roamed unmolested amid boundless forests, where nature looked wild and rude as they; if beautiful villages, and populous cities, Halls of Legislation, magnificent Edifices, Temples of justice and a thousand Churches stand before us the monuments of our greatness; what may we not anticipate for Africa from the settlement of civilized and christian men upon her shores? And by whom can such settlements be so well founded, as by the free people of colour of the United States? Does not Providence clearly invite them to a work of unexampled promise, to their posterity and mankind? And is not this nation urged to assist them by the same Providence not less manifestly, and by motives as numerous and great as ever wrought upon the human mind.

The Managers feel that the time has come, when it were criminal on this subject, to be silent. *They feel that something should be done, compared with which all that has been done is nothing.*—They know that a spirit should go abroad throughout all the borders of the land, like that which kindled in the hearts of our fathers, when they staked their all for independence; that every lover of man and of God, is called, as by a mandate from Heaven, to lift up his voice and bring forward his contribution to effect an object, the doing of which, will in all after ages, be deemed our Nation's chief glory, while Africa will record and celebrate it, as the great moral revolution in her history. True, the work is a great one; and therefore, worthy of a nation like this. That it is practicable to any extent desired, is as evident as that it is great. The sum saved in a single year to the state of New York, by the partial reformation from intemperance, would transport to Africa the annual increase of the whole coloured population of the U.S. And shall we, the most prosperous people in the world, who are legislating not to increase, but reduce our revenue, want for such an object, a mere pittance of that which is, yearly, by luxury and intemperance worse than wasted? The magnitude of the work and the expense to be incurred in its accomplishment, constitute no valid objections to it, because the importance and glory of it exceed the former, and our means the latter. And that history gives no precedent for such a work, will prove but a miserable apology for neglecting it, unless it be reasonable to make the *standard of our duty and the measure of our renown* correspond to those of *long buried* nations, rather than to the *greatness* of our obligations to God, of our *opportunities* and *means* of usefulness and the *height* of christian *charity*. Surely the people of the United States cannot forget how God hath delivered and exalted them by his own right hand, that the light of their example might bless the world; nor will they sacrifice both duty and renown, for fear of showing to mankind that it is possible for nations as well as individuals to be magnanimous and illustrious for virtue.

The Managers appeal then to the clergy of every denomination, and invite them, annually, on or near the day consecrated to the memory of our Independence, to bring the claims of the Society before their people, and to receive, in furtherance of its object, such free-will offerings as gratitude to God and love to men may incline them to bestow.

They appeal to the Auxiliary Societies and urge them to come forward with increased power to the work, to assist in forming other kindred associations, and by widely diffusing information to excite the whole American community, duly to consider and promote the cause.

To their fair country-women, who are ever first to feel for the wretched, and foremost to administer relief, whose moral influence in society, though their own modesty may undervalue it, humanity and religion acknowledge to be of vast power and unspeakable worth, Africa, darker in her mourning than her complexion, offers in silent grief, her plea, which it were impossible to render more convincing by argument, or touching by eloquence. She looks to American benevolence as to that in which all her precious hopes are treasured up, and for their fulfilment, nature itself will plead more strongly than we can, in every female heart.

Nor would the Managers omit to say to those who control the public press, that almost omnipotent engine for moving human minds to action, that to them, belongs the power of securing to the design of this Society, the amplest means for its speedy consummation. Let every Editor in the country, feel himself responsible to make known throughout the limits of his influence, the views, operations and success of the Society; and that which it has been attempting in weakness, will be done with power, that which private charity has so well commenced, be completed by the bounty of the States and the Nation.

In concluding this, perhaps too protracted address, the Managers beg leave to say, that not less than one thousand emigrants are now seeking a passage to Liberia; that the Colony is prepared to receive them, that funds only are wanting to enable the society to prosecute its enterprise on a large scale, and that all which can appeal to our interests, encourage our hopes, or move our hearts to charity, now commends the cause of African Colonization to the affection and liberty of our countrymen. Nor will they, the Managers are persuaded, remain insensible to the merits of this cause. Every where meet us the indications of its growing popularity. Justice and Compassion, Mercy and Charity, have gone forth in fellowship, to plead for it, and the Managers trust in the great Author of all good to send forth his spirit to their aid—that Spirit—under whose divine illuminations and all-gracious but all-subduing energies, men of every country and condition shall finally rejoice in peace and love, sharers, in unity, of the same faith, and of the same hope of the great and common salvation. And if from the thick gloom overshadowing Africa, light begins to break forth, let us look for brighter glory, and believe that he who made Joseph's captivity the precursor of his honour, and his usefulness, and the death of his own Son, at which nature trembled, the means of human redemption, will finally change the evils which have cursed Africa, into blessings; that the slave trade and slavery, which have been to her a torrent of wrath, laying waste all her happiness and hopes, will end in a tide, deep, tranquil and refreshing, flowing forth to wake life and gladness in all her wildernesses and solitary places, and to make even her deserts to bud and blossom as the rose.

By order of the Board.

R. R. GURLEY, *Secretary*

89. "Cushing"

They hate and despise us; they wish us out of their sight

The following letter to the editor of a black weekly is interesting in several ways. It illustrates the hostility of some blacks toward the program of the colonization society, which, combined with the indifference of many others, helped account for the small success of the movement. It also indicates that for all the humiliations they suffered here, some blacks felt a strong "attachment to [their] native country"—the United States.

A few thoughts on colonization

Mr. Editor,—Knowing you to be a staunch opponent of Colonization, whether at home or abroad, I improve the present opportunity by making a few general observations in relation to that system, through the column of your paper, the "Colored American." I may be excused in doing so, when I state, for the especial consideration of Colonizationists, that I am one of that people whom they would expatriate—consequently, I have a *motive,* as well as a *right,* to protest against it; and, I doubt not, the sentiments that I hold will meet with a hearty response from every man of color, who has right views upon the subject.

I was asked the other day, by an intelligent colored brother, (a minister of the Gospel,) "Why do Colonizationists still persist in endeavoring to carry out their plans, since they encounter so decided an opposition from every quarter?" I replied, "It is because they have advanced so far that they cannot detract, without incurring the ridicule, as they now have the contempt and pity of all; and, sooner than incur that ridicule, they still persevere, although *themselves* conscious that they can never succeed." And so it is. The colored people of these United States

From letter by "Cushing" to the editor of *The Colored American,* published in Philadelphia and New York City, II, No. 39, November 17, 1838, p. 2.

have (thanks be to God) set their everlasting VETO upon their operations and designs, which has at once paralyzed their efforts, shut up their mouths, and settled all controversies in regard to their *willingness* to emigrate. Yet, notwithstanding all this—regardless of the odium and condemnation of the public generally, and the execration and contempt of the colored people particularly, which they are heaping upon themselves, they still continue to trumpet forth their praise into the ears of all—to employ and send out their agents and lecturers, and have the effrontery, the unparalleled audacity to class their society among the first and most deserving of the benevolent institutions which this country boasts! "Tell it not in Gath."

But to the subject. Fully sensible, as they are, that neither persuasion, entreaty or falsehood, or all combined can effect what they so ardently long for, (the banishment of American citizens into a foreign and a barbarous land) they have resorted to other, and as they think, more efficient methods of accomplishing the above *meritorious object,* namely: a regular system of proscription and insult, leaving nothing undone which can promote their efforts and advance their cause, and undoing everything calculated to operate in the way of the colored man's elevation and refinement, in this country. But, alas for them!—the very means which they employ for their own aggrandizement and advantage, only serve to put us more on the alert, and make us the more vigilant and active in our own elevation and improvement. So far from their persecutions of the colored man having a tendency to make him the willing instrument, in the hands of his oppressors, for his own expatriation, they only serve to increase our attachment to our *native country,* (which, though she has wronged, cruelly wronged us, we love fondly still)—and act as stimulants for us, to resist every attempt which may be made to exile us from the land of our birth and the home of our fathers, so long as we are conscious of the consistency and justice of that resistance. And surely we have the approving smile of a righteous Providence, to sustain us in the assertion and maintenance of our rights, as men and as citizens.

That Colonizationists, in their operations and designs, are actuated by sheer prejudice and hatred towards the colored man, is sufficiently evident. It needs no comment. It is the general and unbiased opinion of all. If they regarded us in the light of brethren and equals—as they certainly ought to do, consistently with their high professions of christianity, and in obedience to the divine injunction, "Whatsoever ye would that men should do unto you, do ye even so to them,"—would they be so very anxious to have us removed from their sight, and colonized in a strange and inhospitable country, entirely remote from the haunts of civilized men, in a region unexplored and almost unknown—with a wide ocean intervening between us and our own country—encompassed on the one hand by impassable deserts of burning sand, and on the other by hordes of untamed and ferocious barbarians? Certainly not. Then it is evident that they hate and despise us so much, that they wish us out of their sight; and, so long as that is accomplished, they care not whether we be starved, massacred, or (what, if possible, is still worse) kidnapped and sold into perpetual slavery. Is *this* their boasted philanthropy and benevolence? Is *this* their zeal, and patriotism, and love of the colored man? Shame, shame upon them!!

> Then what is man—and what man seeing this,
> And having human feelings, does not blush
> And hang his head, to think himself a man?

If Gurley, Fisk, Bethune,* and all such philanthropists, in our country, wish to consummate their wishes, let them first set the example, by emigrating to their African paradise—and, if they are satisfied with the place and its attractions, and resolve to make it their permanent place of residence, *then,* and not till then, will we begin to entertain thoughts of emigrating. But, meanwhile, all the persuasions, entreaties, falsehoods and persecutions of these

* Ralph Randolph Gurley, secretary of the American Colonization Society; Wilbur Fisk, president of Wesleyan University; and Divie Bethune, a prominent New Yorker, were supporters of the Colonization movement—Ed.

dough-faced philanthropists, to induce us to remove to their modern Golgotha, will be fruitless and unavailing.

Cushing

Abolitionism

90. Providence Anti-Slavery Society

They are no more Africans than we are Europeans

Abolition societies sprang up throughout the Northern states in the early 1830s. As the following report indicates, they arose in part in order to oppose the colonizationists' claim that Negroes were inferior beings who would never be assimilated into American society. The report also conveys the religious fervor animating most antislavery groups in this country.

First annual report
of the
Providence Anti-Slavery Society

The Providence Anti-Slavery Society was organized on the 7th of June last [1833]. It was then determined that the annual meetings should be held on the second Friday of November. That time has arrived; and although only five months have elapsed since our formation, many events have transpired to encourage us greatly in the work we then began. We associated that we might co-operate together, and with others, in the use of all Christian means for the Abolition of Slavery in our land. The glad tidings have since reached us, that, by the persevering use of such means, the philanthropists of Great Britain have at length achieved the overthrow of the same abomination, so long upheld by that government. And we rejoice this day in being able to report that

From *Report and Proceedings of the First Annual Meeting of the Providence Anti-Slavery Society* (Providence: H. H. Brown, 1833), 3–10.

hundreds in our country have espoused the same righteous cause, since the date of our Association. Within the past five months, an Anti-Slavery Society has been formed in Andover, Mass.; another by the Young Men in Boston; a *third* in Portland, Maine; a *fourth* in New Haven; a *fifth* in Plainfield, Conn.; a *sixth* at Hudson, in the Western Reserve, Ohio; a *seventh* in Paint Valley, Ohio; an *eighth* in New York City, and a *ninth* in Pittsburgh, Penn. We have moreover every reason to believe that a National Anti-Slavery Society will be instituted ere long. Numerous excellent tracts and larger works, on Slavery, have been issued during the brief term of which we have been speaking; and every where throughout our country the newspapers and other periodicals have ventured to broach this hitherto interdicted subject. Well may these things animate us! They do indeed strengthen our hands and encourage our hearts to go on and labor more abundantly in the cause we have espoused.

Are there any here who would damp our ardor by reminding us that every where the project, in which we have engaged, is opposed—the very name we bear cast out as evil, and our sentiments denounced as fanatical, incendiary and treasonable? Let them tell us, if they can, what great moral reformation was ever undertaken, which did not arouse opposition, violent in proportion to the inveteracy of the wickedness to be overborne, and the determination with which its strong holds were assailed! It is indeed the best proof we can have, that the proper means to reform a public vice have been devised, when those who are implicated in that vice are disturbed. How patient and uncomplaining were the votaries and abettors of Intemperance, under the discourses which were from time to time delivered from the pulpit, and the essays which occasionally appeared in our periodicals, upon the sin of drunkenness *in the abstract.* But when the Temperance Association was formed, then was heard the voice of angry opposition—and why? Because, forsooth, that Association struck at the root of the vice, and the blow was felt through all its branches.

When Clarkson and Wilberforce commenced their labors for the suppression of the Slave Trade, they were reviled and execrated. The life even of CLARKSON was repeatedly threatened, and several times in imminent peril, from the malice of his foes, who were the men engaged directly or indirectly in the atrocious traffic he had determined to suppress.

We might adduce several other striking illustrations, but we need mention only the signal example in the history of our Lord Jesus Christ. Though now he is acknowledged by all to have been the Sun of Righteousness, the Anointed of God, the Savior of the world, yet was he despised and rejected of men, and persecuted even unto death, because he preached the truth, exposed wickedness wherever it existed, and labored to redeem men from all their sins.

Let it not then be thought that the opposition which is shown to our project, and the opprobrious epithets that are so liberally bestowed upon those who are engaged in it, are any evidence that the Anti-Slavery cause is unworthy of the patronage of the wisest and best. No. All history shows that the opposite inference ought rather to be drawn.

The only points, upon which rational and moral men can consistently require to be satisfied, are, *first*, whether the principles of the Anti-Slavery Societies are correct and accordant with the Christian religion. *Secondly*, whether the means they propose to use are lawful, worthy and judicious. Every one, whom we call upon to unite with us to abolish Slavery, may very properly demand of us to satisfy them that we are not laboring to disseminate erroneous sentiments, and unnecessarily stirring up strife. What then, let it now be explicitly stated, are our sentiments?

We believe, and would do all in our power to convince others, that "God hath made of *one blood* all nations of men for to dwell on all the face of the earth." The numerous physical, intellectual and moral diversities, which are found to subsist in the human race, we believe to be incidental, not originally inherent. We do not and cannot know what was the complexion, or the stature, or the precise form, of the first parents of mankind; and therefore we cannot know which of all their descendants have departed most, and which least, from a resemblance to them.

We believe, and would disseminate as widely as possible the belief, that "God is no respecter of persons, but that in every nation he that feareth him and worketh righteousness, is accepted with him." We cannot persuade ourselves that anything else is of so much value in the sight of God, or that anything else should be so highly valued among men as *righteousness*. Incalculable mischief is done to the cause of human happiness, no less than to human virtue, by the undue estimation which is so generally placed upon the possession of wealth, of beauty, of elegant accomplishments, and upon the color of the skin.

We believe, and would do all in our power to persuade our countrymen to believe, that "all men are created free and equal, and are endowed by their Creator with certain *inalienable rights*, among which are life, liberty and the pursuit of happiness." This momentous doctrine is indeed very solemnly announced in our Declaration of Independence; and our nation vaunts itself as the champion of this doctrine; yet there is not a nation in the world that has so grossly violated the rights of man as we have done, and are doing this moment! More than two millions of our fellow beings, more than one sixth of the inhabitants of this land, are held in the most abject bondage!

We believe, yes, we peremptorily declare, and shall resolutely maintain that no man can have a right of property in *human creatures*. No individual or community can have a good title to the liberty of men, excepting only where liberty has been forfeited to society by crime. This follows as an unavoidable inference, if the previous doctrine be true. If one is self-evident, the other is equally so.

We therefore do not think it enough to call Slavery in the United States a national evil—we denounce it as *an atrocious national sin*—a sin for which we can offer less excuse than any people on earth—a sin which is bringing upon us the contempt of the world, the high displeasure of Heaven, and, if it be persisted in, must ere long cause our ruin.

We believe that men cannot leave off sinning too soon—that it cannot be dangerous to cease from doing evil at any moment.

We insist that the colored inhabitants of our land have as good a right to the privileges and immunities of American citizens, as any other class of our inhabitants. Those who were born here, i. e. a large proportion of the colored people, are Americans by birth. They are no more Africans, than we are Europeans. The United States is their home, as much as ours. It is heinous wickedness, it is cruel persecution, in us so to treat them as to make them wish to flee from their country. And to insist, that their removal from the land of their birth should be the condition of their emancipation from Slavery, is an outrageous violation of our most sacred civil as well as religious principles. All the colored people who possess the qualifications which are demanded of others, ought to be admitted forthwith to the enjoyment of the same privileges, and the exercise of the same prerogatives as others. And all of them who do not possess such qualifications, ought to have every facility afforded for attaining them as soon as possible. They ought not to be held as property, and treated as brutes a moment longer. All laws derogatory to them as rational and moral beings, ought to be repealed. They should no longer be left at the mercy of their petty tyrants—liable to be bought and sold like cattle—denied the protection of public justice—withheld from the lights of knowledge and of religion. They should be in subjection only to the civil arm—and that arm ought to hold over them and their white brethren *the equal scale of justice.* The life and liberty of colored men should be as sacred as our own; and they ought to be fitted as soon as they may be to exercise and enjoy all the prerogatives of freemen. These changes in their condition surely cannot be effected too soon. Let therefore such measures only be adopted, as will tend *directly* to produce them. Let us not temporize about the highest interests—the inalienable rights of more than two millions of the inhabitants of our land!!

Such are our principles. Is there one of them which any rational man, especially if he be a Christian, will venture to controvert?

We now proceed to the inquiry of those, who demand of us by what *means* we propose to accomplish our purposes? We answer, by means precisely like those which have been employed with so much effect towards the subversion of Intemperance. We propose to circulate Tracts urging upon the consciences of our fellow-citizens the heinous wickedness of Slavery—exposing the perpetual injustice, and the occasional cruelties which are tolerated and enforced by the laws of our land—exhibiting also without a veil the loathsome vices which are prevalent wherever the Institution of Slavery is upheld.

We intend, so soon as we may be able, to send out living agents to cry aloud and spare not, to lift up their voices like trumpets, and show this people their great transgressions, and the fearful calamities which impend over them.

Respecting Slavery in the District of Columbia, and other portions of our territory, which are under the immediate government of Congress, we mean to petition Congress, and reiterate our petitions year after year, until at least the place where our national legislators convene, is purified. We shall labor, in co-operation with others, so to correct public opinion, and arouse public feeling in New England, that she will utter herself in the cause of the oppressed, as it would become her to do; and instruct her Representatives in Congress on all occasions to announce her sentiments, and urge her wishes in opposition to Slavery.

Thus it will be seen that we rely wholly on *moral power*—the *power of the truth.* Who is there that will dare say this is not a proper, legitimate, Christian-like, republican mode of proceeding? Is not this the mode provided in the very Constitution of the United States, by which we are to correct the evils, that may exist under the government, of which that Constitution is the basis; or even to amend the defects of that instrument itself? Is not the freedom of speech and of the press secured to us in that charter of our liberties? Is it not acknowledged by all, who understand the genius of a republican government, that the right of thinking for ourselves, and of speaking, writing and printing our opinions, is fundamental? Without this, the evils, which are incident to this form of society, cannot be corrected; no—nor our freedom long preserved.

The Anti-Slavery Societies wish for no other means than these. We have hitherto used only these; nor can we ever have need to resort to any other.

Our numbers, in this Providence Society, are comparatively,

few; but we have not therefore been idle nor timid in our appropriate sphere of duty. Assured of the justice of our cause, we have labored in it as we were able. Our first public meeting was held on the 4th of July, when an Address was delivered in the afternoon in this city, by Rev. Thomas Williams, and repeated in the evening of the same day, at Pawtucket. The audiences assembled at both places were highly respectable; and a collection of about twenty dollars was taken in aid of our funds.

The next quarterly meeting of the Society was held on the 13th of September, when a public address was delivered by Rev. Samuel J. May, of Brooklyn.

We have purchased and distributed one hundred copies of Stuart's "West India Question," a pamphlet published in England, showing in the most conclusive manner, the duty, safety and good economy of the Immediate Emancipation of Slaves. Also, one hundred copies of "Prejudice Vincible," a letter from James Cropper of Liverpool to the venerable Clarkson, showing that the prejudices against our colored brethren may be and ought to be overcome. Also, one hundred and sixty-eight copies of Rankin's Letters, exposing some of the abominations of Slavery in our own country. Besides these, we have distributed several hundreds of other tracts, which have been given us by benevolent individuals; and we have lately ordered four hundred copies of J. G. Whittier's excellent pamphlet entitled "Justice and Expediency."

Such, friends and fellow-citizens, is our Report. In conclusion, we beg of you to examine thoroughly the Tracts we have issued—and, scrutinize, as closely as you may, every sentiment contained in them. We shrink not from the investigation of our opinions. If they are erroneous, let it be made to appear as soon as possible.

We intreat those of you who are thoroughly convinced of the correctness of our views and sentiments, to come without delay and unite with us to deliver more than *two millions* of our countrymen from Slavery and degradation; and redeem our beloved country from her greatest iniquity.

Public Education

91. Thomas Cooper

Diffuse useful information as widely as possible

Educational reform came close to being the universal American panacea. Labor radicals hoped that the working classes might become educated to their own true worth and reshape society accordingly. Conservatives, such as Thomas Cooper, President of the University of South Carolina, would also educate the working classes but with an altogether different end in view: to instill in them respect for the established order. Reformers who rejected an environmental explanation of human misbehavior hoped that a liberal education would purify men from within. Moderates hoped that an expanded educational system would enhance the market value of its beneficiaries and thus promote social harmony by narrowing the gulf between the classes. Supported as they were by so diverse a coalition, it is not surprising that significant educational reforms were approved during the era. Public schools lost much of their stigma as educational taxes were substantially increased.

I am the more inclined to recommend such a system of national education as here proposed—free in every part of it, and open to every citizen who is desirous of benefitting by the use of it—because if the ultra democratic doctrines now in vogue, of universal suffrage, and instructed representatives, are destined to prevail among us, I know no means of remedying their defects in practice, but to diffuse useful information as widely as possible.

Many years did I obstinately refuse to acknowledge that there was any truth in the observation, that the people are too often ignorant of, and too often false and traitorous to their own best interests; and that in many cases, their worst enemies are themselves; but melancholy experience, has forced this truth upon my conviction; and however unpalatable to myself or to others, to entertain or to express it, I find it impossible to escape from its

From Thomas Cooper, *Lectures on the Elements of Political Economy* (Columbia, S.C.: M'Morris and Wilson, 1831), 332–335.

pressure. But the evil is the result of ignorance, and the only cure for it, the extension of education and of knowledge.

For all this, I know no cure but a comprehensive system of education, and information of every kind widely diffused, and sedulously pressed upon the people. I am not afraid of a well educated, well informed community; but I already see enough, to dread and to deplore the careless, unfeeling despotism of ignorance.

When I was young, I was desirous, like Mr. Bentham and his followers, of deducing the maxims of civil government, from what seemed to be the prevailing tendencies of human nature; and I took for granted, that every man, and every body of men, would act uniformly on the obvious motive of self-interest. I was mistaken. The fact is otherwise; not in a few, but in the majority of cases. Neither individuals or bodies of men, are generally guided by just considerations of their own good. They act as often from present temptations, from caprice, from prejudice, from flattery, from temporary excitements, from unfounded likings and dislikings, from imperfect apprehension of the question before them, from unavoidable want of information, from sudden impulse, from want of reflection and consideration—as they do from deliberate and enlightened views of what will ultimately prove to be their real and permanent interest. The maxims of civil government therefore, ought not to be founded on any theory of abstract rights, or any a priori claims or positions, but on *public utility*, as pointed out by experience; on the result of past facts, accurately observed and well considered. Abstract theories of political rights, will then only prove useful in their application and operation, when they have been brought to the test of history—compared with the known conduct of men in communities—and subjected to the limitations which want of information in the great mass of the people, may reasonably suggest, at any assigned period, or state of society. Would a republican form of government be expedient at Constantinople or Tombuctoo? What these limitations reasonably may be, it is not my province here to discuss. One general position alone I will venture upon, viz: that no right whatever, can exist, that will not bear the test of utility—that does not, in the present state of our knowledge of past facts and present probabilities, appear to be really coincident with the public good. Those maxims of government for instance, that on a fair appeal to experience, can be shewn to be best calculated to promote and preserve equal protection, peace, good order, and moral conduct throughout the community, are the only maxims really obligatory; and any supposed right which in its exercise, would interfere with these great objects ought to be rejected. The man who would throw experience out of the discussion, in favour of any à priori theory, is not a real friend to the cause he professes to advocate; for any theory not founded on facts, is worthless. I shall have occasion in the chapter on the Distribution of Wealth, to touch again upon the doctrine of abstract rights.

Education universally extended throughout the community, will tend moreover to disabuse the working class of people, in respect of a notion that has crept into the minds of our mechanics, and gradually prevailing, that manual labour is the only source of wealth; that it is at present, very inadequately rewarded, owing to combinations of the rich against the poor; that mere mental labour is comparatively worthless; that property or wealth, ought not to be accumulated or transmitted; that to take interest on money lent, or profit on capital employed, is unjust. These are notions that tend strongly toward an equal division of property, and the right of the poor to plunder the rich. The mistaken and ignorant people who entertain these fallacies as truths, will learn, when they have the opportunity of learning, that the institution of political society originated in the protection of property; and this has ever continued to be its main end and design; that equality to-day, would be inequality to-morrow; that labour is, of itself, nearly useless, and can never be brought into action but by means of wealth or capital; that the rich are as necessary to the poor, as the poor are to the rich; and that there is no injustice in giving RAPHAEL a little higher wages per day, than his colour-grinder received; or a better recompense to CANOVA, than to the man who quarried the marble. James Watt and Robert Fulton were worth more to society, than 500,000 hedgers or ditchers. If the mechanics should seriously continue to press such silly notions, they will justly make enemies of those who would otherwise be their reasonable friends; and they are much mistaken if they suppose the wealthy will not find the means as well as the inclination, to defend their property against the attacks of ignorance and injustice.

All that a good government can do, is to give to every man an equal chance of acquiring useful knowledge; to lighten as much as possible the burthens of taxation in favour of the poor; to grant no artificial privileges to the rich; and to throw no impediment in the way of industry or talent. But nature has ordained great and permanent differences as to strength of body and strength of mind, such as no human institution can hope to equalize; circumstances around us, furnishing the motives and stimuli to action or to indolence, to useful or useless pursuits, to profitable or unprofitable industry and occupation, and even the mere chapter of accidents, create still more numerous differences, over which society has no controul. Who would labour for the benefit of those with whom he has no connexion? What stimulus would there be to industry and frugality, if a man were deprived of the right of bequeathing his earnings and his savings to his family? What regulation of wages *can* there be in practice, but the voluntary contract of the hirer and the hired? Nature, and the unavoidable circumstances of society, have created inequalities that are also unavoidable. Each of us in our station, therefore, must submit patiently to that which cannot be avoided; nor would the poor be benefitted by obtaining full command over the wealth of the rich, for the same quarrels would ensue about distribution of wealth the week after, that would take place at the hour of successful plunder.

A Mr. L. Byllesby published "Observations on the Sources and Effects of Unequal Wealth," New-York, 1826. This is an attempt in fact, to shew, that he who possesses more strength and talent, or has acquired more knowledge and skill, or used more industry and frugality, or exercised more temperance and self denial than another, has no right to accumulate or dispose of the resulting advantages, or to bequeath them to his widow or children. This book will do no injury, and the author has a right to his own opinions, and to propose them; but they are too manifestly the effusions of ignorance and rapacity to need formal confutation.

For all these errors of opinion, I know of no remedy but the diffusion of knowledge, as fully and as widely as possible. I am therefore, strongly impressed, not merely with the great expedience, but the urgent necessity of a real, substantial system of education, open to all. The citizens who neglect to use it, will have themselves only to accuse, should they be ignorant; and the force of society will be very properly exerted in compelling those to be patient and peaceable, who are inclined to be turbulent. Our creator has not thought fit to make every man six feet high, or to distribute brain and intellect in precise and equal proportions; while therefore bodily strength, mental talent and energy, bodily health, fertility of soil, and lucrative employment, are distributed by nature in all possible portions and varieties, it is neither just or profitable, for those who have less, to quarrel on that account with those who have more. It is not society, but nature that is in fault.

92. HORACE MANN

Education gives the humblest person an open field for competition

The following passage illustrates the breadth of view of the nation's best known educational reformer. Horace Mann was indubitably a democrat, an optimist, a humanitarian. He was also a pragmatist with a vengeance. One would be hard put to find clearer expressions of the belief that additional formal education for the working man increases his earning power, promotes productivity, and is good for the economy. Obviously, many business men agreed with him, as the selection makes clear.

So where there are different kinds of labor, some simple, others complicated, and, of course, requiring different degrees of intelli-

From Horace Mann, *Annual Report of the Secretary of the Board of Education of Massachusetts*, 1841 (Boston: Lee and Shepard, 1891), 96–109.

gence and skill, it is easy to observe what class of persons rise from a lower to a higher grade of employment.

This, too, is not to be forgotten,—that in a manufacturing or mechanical establishment, or among a set of hands engaged in filling up a valley or cutting down a hill, where scores of people are working together, the absurd and adventitious distinctions of society do not intrude. The capitalist and his agents are looking for the greatest amount of labor, or the largest income in money from their investments; and they do not promote a dunce to a station where he will destroy raw material, or slacken industry, because of his name or birth or family connections. The obscurest and humblest person has an open and fair field for competition. That he proves himself capable of earning more money for his employer is a testimonial better than a diploma from all the colleges.

Now, many of the most intelligent and valuable men in our community, in compliance with my request,—for which I tender them my public and grateful acknowledgments,—have examined their books for a series of years, and have ascertained both the quality and the amount of work performed by persons in their employment; and the result of the investigation is a most astonishing superiority, in productive power, on the part of the educated over the uneducated laborer. The hand is found to be another hand when guided by an intelligent mind. Processes are performed, not only more rapidly, but better, when faculties which have been exercised in early life furnish their assistance. Individuals who, without the aid of knowledge, would have been condemned to perpetual inferiority of condition, and subjected to all the evils of want and poverty, rise to competence and independence by the uplifting power of education. In great establishments, and among large bodies of laboring men, where all services are rated according to their pecuniary value; where there are no extrinsic circumstances to bind a man down to a fixed position, after he has shown a capacity to rise above it; where, indeed, men pass by each other, ascending or descending in their grades of labor, just as easily and certainly as particles of water of different degrees of temperature glide by each other,—there it is found as an almost invariable fact, other things being equal, that those who have been blessed with a good common-school education rise to a higher and a higher point in the kinds of labor performed, and also in the rate of wages paid, while the ignorant sink like dregs, and are always found at the bottom.

I now proceed to lay before the Board some portions of the evidence I have obtained, first inserting my Circular Letter, in answer to which, communications have been made.

Circular Letter

To———.

Dear Sir,—My best and only apology for taking the liberty to address you will be found in the object I have in view, which, therefore, I proceed to state without further preface.

In fulfilling the duties with which I have been intrusted by the Board of Education, I am led into frequent conversation and correspondence, not only with persons in every part of the State, but more or less with every class and description of persons in the whole community.

I regret to say, that among these I occasionally meet with individuals, who, although very differently circumstanced in life, cordially agree in their indifference towards the cause of common education; and some of whom even profess to be alarmed at possible mischiefs that may come in its train, and therefore stand in its path, and obstruct its advancement.

The individuals who thus maintain an attitude of neutrality, or assume one of active opposition, are either persons who, in their worldly circumstances, are deemed the favorites of fortune, or they are persons who are alike strangers to mental cultivation, and to all the outward and ordinary signs of temporal prosperity. In a word, they are found, in regard to their worldly condition, at the two extremes of the social scale. I would by no means be understood to say, that any considerable proportion of the men of wealth amongst us look with an unfriendly eye on the general diffusion of the means of knowledge. On the contrary, some of the best friends of education are to be found amongst this class, who, uniting abundance of means with benevolence of disposition, are truly efficient in advancing the work. Nor, on this subject, are the lines of demarcation between parties broadly drawn; but they shade off, by imperceptible degrees, from friends to opponents.

But this I do mean to say, that there are men of wealth and leisure, too numerous to be overlooked in a calculation of friendly and of adverse agencies, who profess to fear that a more thorough and comprehensive education for the whole people will destroy contentment, loosen habits of industry, engender a false ambition, and prompt to an incursion into their own favored sphere, by which great loss will accrue to themselves, without any corresponding benefit to the invaders.

The other class are those who, suffering from a neglected or a perverted education in themselves, seem incapable of appreciating either the temporal and material well-being, or the mental elevation and enjoyment, which it is the prerogative of a good education to confer. These two parties, though alien from each other in all other respects, are allies here; and although, with the exception of a very few towns in the Commonwealth, they are not numerically strong, yet, by adroitly implicating other questions with that of the Public Schools, they are able in many cases to baffle all efforts at reform and improvement.

The views of these parties I believe to be radically wrong, anti-social, anti-Republican, anti-Christian; and I believe that all action in pursuance of them will impair the best interests of society, and originate a train of calamities, in which not only their advocates, but all portions of the community, will be involved. Convinced that such is the inevitable and accelerating tendency of such views, it seems to me to be the duty of the friends of mankind to meet them with fairness and a conciliatory spirit indeed, but with earnestness and energy, and to confute them by the production of evidence and the exposition of principles.

It is for this reason that I address you, and solicit a reply, founded upon your personal knowledge, to the following questions:—

First,—Have you had large numbers of persons in your employment or under your superintendence? If so, will you please to state how many? Within what period of time? In what department of business? Whether at different places? Whether natives or foreigners?

Second,—Have you observed differences among the persons you have employed, growing out of differences in their education, *and independent of their natural abilities;* that is, whether, as a class, those who from early life have been accustomed to exercise their minds by reading and studying have greater docility and quickness in applying themselves to work? and, after the simplest details are mastered, have they greater aptitude, dexterity, or ingenuity in comprehending ordinary processes, or in originating new ones? Do they more readily or frequently devise new modes by which the same amount of work can be better done, or by which more work can be done in the same time, or by which raw material or motive-power can be economized? In short, do you obtain more work and better work, with less waste, from those who have received what, in Massachusetts, we call a good common-school education, or from those who have grown up in neglect and ignorance? Is there any difference in the earnings of these two classes, and consequently in their wages?

Third,—What, within your knowledge, has been the effect of higher degrees of mental application and culture upon the domestic and social habits of persons in your employment? Is this class more cleanly in their persons, their dress, and their households? and do they enjoy a greater immunity from those diseases which originate in a want of personal neatness and purity? Are they more exemplary in their deportment and conversation, devoting more time to intellectual pursuits or to the refining art of music, and spending their evenings and leisure hours more with their families, and less at places of resort for idle and dissipated men? Is a smaller portion of them addicted to intemperance? Are their houses kept in a superior condition? Does a more economical and judicious mode of living purchase greater comforts at the same expense, or equal comforts with less means? Are their families better brought up, more respectably dressed, more regularly attendant upon the school and the church? and do their children, when arrived at years of maturity, enter upon the active scenes of life with better prospects of success?

Fourth,—In regard to standing and respectability among co-laborers, neighbors, and fellow-citizens generally, how do those who have enjoyed and improved the privilege of good common schools compare with the neglected and the illiterate? Do the former exercise greater influence among their associates? Are they more often applied to for advice and counsel in cases of difficulty, or selected as umpires or arbitrators for the decision of minor controversies? Are higher and more intelligent circles for acquaintance open to them, from conversation and intercourse with which their own minds can be constantly improved? Are they more likely to rise from grade to grade in the scale of labor, until they enter departments where greater skill, judgment, and responsibility are required, and which therefore command a larger remuneration? Are they more likely to rise from the condition of employés, and to establish themselves in business on their own account?

Fifth,—Have you observed any difference in the classes above named (I speak of them as classes, for there will, of course, be individual exceptions) in regard to punctuality and fidelity in the performance of duties? Which class is most regardful of the rights of others, and most intelligent and successful in securing their own? You will, of course, perceive that this question involves a more general one; viz., from which of the above-described classes have those who possess property, and who hope to transmit it to their children, most to fear from secret aggression, or from such public degeneracy as will loosen the bands of society, corrupt the testimony of witnesses, violate the sanctity of the juror's oath, and substitute, as a rule of right, the power of a numerical majority for the unvarying principles of justice?

Sixth,—Finally, in regard to those who possess the largest shares in the stock of worldly goods, could there, in your opinion, be any police so vigilant and effective, for the protection of all the rights of person, property, and character, as such a sound and comprehensive education and training as our system of common schools could be made to impart? and would not the payment of a sufficient tax to make such education and training universal be the cheapest means of self-protection and insurance? And in regard to that class which, from the accident of birth and parentage, are subjected to the privations and the temptations of poverty, would not such an education open to them new resources in habits of industry and economy, in increased skill, and the awakening of inventive power, which would yield returns a thousand-fold greater than can ever be hoped for from the most successful clandestine depredations, or open invasion of the property of others?

I am aware, my dear sir, that, to every intelligent and reflecting man, these inquiries will seem superfluous and nugatory; and your first impulse may be to put some such interrogatory to me in reply, as whether the sun has any influence on vegetable growth, or whether it is expedient to have windows in our houses for the admission of light. I acknowledge the close analogy of the cases in point of self-evidence; but my reply is, that while we have influential persons, who dwell with us in the same common mansion of society, and who, having secured for themselves a few well-lighted apartments, now insist that total darkness is better for a portion of the occupants born and dwelling under the same roof; and while, unfortunately, a portion of these benighted occupants, from never having seen more than the feeblest glimmerings of the light of day, insist that it is better for them and their children to remain blind; while these opinions continue to exist, I hold that it is necessary to adduce facts and arguments, and to present motives, which shall prove, both to the blinded and those who would keep them so, the value and beauty of light.

HORACE MANN,
Secretary of the Board of Education

LETTER FROM J. CLARK, ESQ.

Lowell, Dec. 3, 1841

Dear Sir,—I owe you an apology for not having made an earlier reply to your inquiries respecting the influences of education upon the character and conduct of our operatives. I have to plead in excuse for my neglect an unusual press of business, which has almost literally occupied every moment of my time; and, while I was seeking a leisure hour to devote to this purpose, my friend, Mr. Bartlett, has kindly allowed me to read the very full and particular answers prepared by him to your several interrogatories.

. . . We have in our mills about one hundred and fifty females who have, at some time, been engaged in *teaching schools.* Many of them teach during the summer months, and work in the mills in winter. The average wages of these ex-teachers I find to be seventeen and three-fourths per cent *above the general average of our mills, and about forty per cent above the wages of the twenty-six who cannot write their names.* It may be said that they are generally employed in the higher departments, where the pay is better. This is true; but this again may be, in most cases, fairly attributed to their better education, which brings us to the same result. If I had included in my calculations the remaining fourteen of the forty, who are mostly sweepers and scrubbers, and who are paid by the day, the contrasts would have been still more striking; but having no well-educated females engaged in this department with whom to compare them, I have omitted them altogether. In arriving at the above results, I have considered the *net wages* merely,—the price of board being in all cases the same. I do not consider these results as either extraordinary or surprising, but as a part only of the legitimate and proper fruits of a better cultivation and fuller development of the intellectual and moral powers.

Yours very respectfully,
JOHN CLARK,
Superintendent of Merrimack Mills

HON. HORACE MANN, BOSTON.

EXTRACTS FROM A LETTER OF JONATHAN CRANE, ESQ., FOR SEVERAL YEARS A LARGE CONTRACTOR ON THE RAILROADS IN MASSACHUSETTS

My principal business, for about ten years past, has been grading railroads. During that time, the number of men employed has varied from fifty to three hundred and fifty, nearly all Irishmen, with the exception of superintendents. Some facts have been so apparent, that my superintendents and myself could not but notice them: these I will freely give you. I should say that not less than three thousand different men have been, more or less, in my employment during the before-mentioned period, and that the number that could read and write intelligibly was about one to eight. Independently of their natural endowments, those who could read and write, and had some knowledge of the first principles of arithmetic, have almost invariably manifested a readiness to apprehend what was required of them, and skill in performing it, and have more readily and frequently devised new modes by which the same amount of work could be better done. Some of these men we have selected for superintendents, and they are now contractors. With regard to the morals of the two classes, we have seen very little difference; but the better-educated class are more cleanly in their persons and their households, and generally discover more refinement in their manners, and practise a more economical mode in their living. Their families are better brought up, and they are more anxious to send their children to school. In regard to their standing and respectability among co-laborers, neighbors, and fellow-citizens, the more educated are much more respected; and in settling minor controversies, they are more commonly applied to as arbitrators. With

> regard to the morals of the two classes before mentioned, permit me to remark, that it furnishes an illustration of the truth of a common saying, that merely cultivating the understanding, without improving the heart, does not make a man better. The more extensively knowledge and virtue prevail in our country, the greater security have we that our institutions will not be overthrown. Our common-school system, connected as it is, or ought to be, with the inculcation of sound and practical morality, is the most vigilant and efficient police for the protection of persons, property, and character, that could be devised; and is it not gratifying that men of wealth are beginning to see, that, if they would protect their property and persons, a portion of that property should be expended for the education of the poorer classes? Merely selfish considerations would lead any man of wealth to do this, if he would only view the subject in its true light. Nowhere is this subject better understood than in Massachusetts; and the free discussions which have of late been held, in county and town meetings, have had the effect to call the attention of the public to it; and I trust the time is not far distant, when, at least in Massachusetts, the *common-school system* will accomplish all the good which it is capable of producing. Why do we not in these United States have a revolution, almost annually, as in the republics of South America? Ignorance and vice always have invited, and always will invite, such characters as Shakespeare's Jack Cade to rule over them. And may we not feel an assurance, that in proportion as the nation shall recover from the baneful influence of intemperance, so will its attention be directed pre-eminently to the promotion of virtue and knowledge, and nowhere in our country will an incompetent or intemperate common-school teacher be intrusted with the education of our children?

These are a fair specimen, and no more than a fair specimen, of a mass of facts which I have obtained from the most authentic sources. They seem to prove incontestably that education is not only a moral renovator, and a multiplier of intellectual power, but that it is also the most prolific parent of material riches. It has a right, therefore, not only to be included in the grand inventory of a nation's resources, but to be placed at the very head of that inventory. It is not only the most honest and honorable, but the surest means of amassing property. A trespasser or a knave may forcibly or fraudulently appropriate the earnings of others to himself; but education has the prerogative of originating or generating property more certainly and more rapidly than it was ever accumulated by force or fraud.

93. Charles Haddock
Nothing is more worthy than the education of children

Charles Haddock, a Dartmouth professor, became the commissioner of New Hampshire's common schools in the 1840s. His two circulars, one addressed to the young "scholars" and the other to their teachers, illustrate the high-mindedness, the optimism, the sense of morality, the faith in discipline and sensible regulations, the paternalism and the religious spirit pervading much educational thought during the era. These documents offer a clue to the mind of the little-known yet significant educational administrators who bore the burden of translating into reality the ideas of celebrated educational theorists.

Circular, Addressed to the schools in New-Hampshire

My young friends,

It would give me true happiness to see you all, and to converse with you upon the subject of your education. The State expends a very large sum of money, every year, for the instruction of youth; many of its most intelligent and virtuous citizens are engaged in the business of teaching; and the parents and friends of the young all over the State are feeling a lively interest in their improvement. The Newspapers now speak of the subject oftener and with a more hearty zeal than ever before. And all good men and true

Charles B. Haddock, *Circulars Addressed to the Schools and to the Teachers of the Common Schools in New-Hampshire* (Hanover, New Hampshire, December 25, 1846).

patriots begin to see, that nothing is more worthy of the general attention and encouragement of our people, than the education of their own children.

I am employed, you know, as Commissioner of Common Schools. My object, in this office, is to do what I can to make these schools better than they have ever been, and to induce all children to attend them.

I am, this winter, calling Common School Conventions in the most convenient places in the State, and addressing the friends of the young upon the subject of the Schools. I have lately sent a letter to every School-master and School-mistress, which, perhaps, your teacher has read to you. I send this letter to you; and I hope that every member of the school, as he hears it read, will consider it addressed directly to him. The members of this school are part of the children and youth of New Hampshire, for whose benefit so much money is spent and so much anxious care endured.

My object is to give you some advice; to induce you to do what you can, yourselves, to make the instruction given you, this winter, of important and lasting use to you all.

Do not forget, that something depends on you. The best master in the world, and the best books and the best School-house will not, all together, FORCE you to be wise and good. If you choose to be ignorant and vicious, in spite of instruction, not much can be done for you. If you intend to learn, and really wish and strive to improve, you may help to keep a first-rate school. It depends as much, upon the scholars as it does upon the teacher, whether the school shall be good or bad. And every boy and every girl should go to school every morning with the feeling that they have, each, a part to perform, a duty to do, that day, *in keeping the school;* and that, if it is not a quiet, useful, happy day to all, the fault may be partly their own.

Did you ever think that you have DUTIES? That your duties are just as binding, and just as important to you, as the duties of a man are to him? That, within your sphere, as a child, even the youngest of you, is as really responsible to God, as you ever will be? He does not, indeed, require you to fill the place of a man or a woman; but He does require you to fill the place of a child—to do every thing that belongs to a child, as perfectly and as conscientiously, as you should do the duties of manhood, when you grow up. It is a great mistake to suppose that the faults of the young are of little consequence, because they do not much affect the world. And grownup people sometimes very unwisely talk of the follies and even the vices of their childhood—their mean tricks, their sly, mischievous, wicked practices, as "harmless sport," "innocent fun," "sowing their wildoats;" or at worst, as indiscretions, which time has corrected. It may be, that time will correct the worst faults of youth; but it does not always; it does not often; it more frequently confirms and increases them. They that sow wild oats, must expect to reap wild oats. The only promise you can give to your parents and to society, that you will be true and right to-morrow, is that you are so to-day. "The child is father of the man." This being always *about* to live as we should is a great delusion; he that is actually doing wrong NOW has no reason to expect that he ever will do right. The idle, vulgar, false, cruel, wicked boy is on the way to a useless, vicious manhood, and a miserable age. How can you hope to escape ruin, when you follow a path that leads nowhere else?

A virtuous boy! a faultless child! of gentle manners, of pure words, of a soft voice, of a sweet spirit, studious to know, and faithful to do, open, generous, just—is any thing so beautiful? so full of promise? the very bud and flower—the fragrant spring of life.

To the older scholars let me say, Place your mark high. Do not doubt, that a substantial, thorough education, sufficient for all the ordinary pursuits of life, may be acquired in the District school. You need not be all winter in getting to the Rule of Three, and then go over the same ground again another year. You may finish Arithmetic, and obtain a respectable knowledge of Geography, Grammar, Algebra, Geometry and Physiology, without leaving the Common School; may become good readers, writers, and accountants, and may acquaint yourselves with the Constitution of your country, and the Laws of your moral being.

The love of study can be created; it will come, infallibly, with diligence and patience. And then how easy, how natural, how delightful it becomes to learn.

But there are some things, which you must not do, if you mean to be true scholars. You must not spend your leisure hours about taverns, or stores, or shops; you must not waste the long, and fruitful evening in noisy, vulgar plays in the streets, with the profane, the dissolute, the reckless, calling after strangers, and annoying peaceable citizens.

You must not be ashamed to be polite. A coarse, gross, rude address never expresses a delicate, thoughtful, regulated mind. You must not be afraid to be right. Boys are, often, tempted to show their courage by ridiculing merit. They sometimes think it mean to be afraid of offending their parents, or their teacher, or God Himself. Remember that true spirit, consists in following the dictates of a noble nature; and that he is the real coward, who can be shamed out of his principles.

You must not find your best pleasures away from your own homes. I am always afraid of a boy, who begins to be uneasy at home. When the presence of your parents and your sisters puts a restraint upon you and you feel shy of them, be sure all is not right. An uncorrupted, unperverted child is no where so happy as at home. Never suffer yourself to lose, never allow any body to taint in your bosom, the fond and kindly affections, that grow up and shed their odors round the family fireside.

You must not take pleasure in inflicting pain. It is the spirit of the Devil.

You must not imagine, that you and your teacher have different interests. He labors for you; he lives for you. His interest is in your welfare. His honor is in your progress; his happiness in your highest good. If you could disturb his plans and hinder his success, you would triumph in your own defeat.

You must not tempt others to do wrong. It is enough to lose advantages for oneself; to fail of the great ends of all education. To be the occasion of misleading and injuring another—to set about corrupting an innocent mind—to lure a guileless, confiding child from the path of purity—to estrange an affectionate nature from the love of truth and the sacred endearments of home—

there is deep, deep guilt in this unnatural, malignant influence.

To you all let me say, Be punctual. If a scholar is late, the whole school is disturbed; his own progress is interrupted; the order of the day is interfered with; and, what is worst of all, a habit of punctuality is not formed, a habit essential to the success and happiness of life. A LITTLE TOO LATE is a fit motto to be inscribed upon the tombstones of half the unfortunate in the business of this world, and of more than half who fail of the happiness of the future.

Take pains to comply exactly with the regulations of the school. Do not take for granted, that what is required is unreasonable. Confide in the teacher; respect the opinions he has deliberately formed; suffer him to rule within the sphere of his duty.

Be not in haste to advance. Cultivate carefully the ground you go over; be sure you obtain distinct, clear ideas; and dwell upon a thing till you master it. Then, and not till then, you may safely advance. Let others be in this class or that, upon this or the other study, using such and such books, it matters not to you; if you are not prepared for them, they are not the class, or the study, or the books for you; to be put into them would only embarrass, or confuse you, and tend to defeat the best objects of a good education. For, next to not knowing any thing, and, I have thought, sometimes, worse than not knowing any thing, is the crude half-knowledge of persons, who have been urged forward faster than they are qualified to go. Carrying a burden too big for one's legs may make him a cripple all his days.

Dont whisper; dont whisper. One thoughtless boy, one careless girl, may, by this one mischievous habit, disturb a whole school. Learn to study without *buzzing;* to think without moving the lips. It is easy, after a little practice. Indeed, to be able to be STILL is almost a virtue; it is so necessary to order. Certainly, it is one of the *graces.* A boy who can sit still, and stand still, without twisting and wriggling, or fumbling in his pockets, or drumming with his feet or his fingers, has made a good deal of an acquisition. He can move with ease, and speak with composure. He can appear in a room full of company without feeling embarrassed, and rise, or sit down, without awkwardness.

Never make light of a serious subject, nor trifle with the misfortunes of a fellow creature.

Never sneer at a tender conscience, nor laugh at the scruples or the weaknesses of a pious heart. Contempt for principle is an affectation; nobody really feels it; and simple goodness is too rare not to be prized and cherished wherever it appears.

Do not think, that, in this long letter, I am trying to persuade you to put on the soberness and gravity of age, while you are yet children. I know all about the vivacity, the sprightliness, the buoyancy of youth; and I love them. I would not have "*a child,*

> Whose blood is warm within,
> Sit like his grandsire,
> Cut in Alabaster."

But spirit, gayety even, is not vice; freedom is not folly; your presence may be all cheerfulness, your life all sunshine; and yet not an impure or unkind word may escape your lips, not an ungentle action mar your example, nor a guilty passion corrode your bosom.

In a few years you will all be men and women. It may seem to you many years; but they will be few and short, very, very short. And then you will look back, as we do now, to your school days. Many pleasant thoughts will these days bring with them. I should be pleased to know, that any thing I am now saying to you will be remembered then; and still more pleased to know that any thing I say is to make one of you wiser, happier, better. It will be worth a great deal of labor, if that labor only renders the children of New Hampshire better sons and daughters, kinder brothers and sisters, truer friends, nobler patriots, more virtuous, more devoted, more faithful servants of our blessed Savior.

Your friend, &c.,

CHARLES B. HADDOCK,
Commissioner of Common Schools

N. B. Teachers are requested to read this Letter to their schools.

CIRCULAR,
TO THE TEACHERS OF COMMON SCHOOLS IN NEW-HAMPSHIRE

Dear Sir,

The relation which I sustain to the schools of this State renders it unnecessary for me to offer an apology for addressing you. Indeed, I trust, that you have assumed the office of an Instructer of youth with such a sense of the responsibilities and difficulties of that trust, as would incline you to welcome a useful hint, or an encouraging word, from any quarter.

The nature of my duties does not allow me the satisfaction of a personal interview; a visit to the schools of the State would be impracticable, even were my term of service much longer than it is. I regret this the less because in every town the Law provides for a Superintending Committee, who will, in most cases, be found fully competent to the general inspection and regulation of the schools.

I therefore, take this mode of suggesting to you a few of the many things which I should be still happier to address to you in person.

And, in the first place, permit me to say, my dear Sir, that you can hardly estimate too highly the importance of the work in which you are engaged. It is true your intercourse is with children; your business is with the elements of learning; the period of your connection with the school will, probably, be short; you will attract no public attention, will gratify no feverish thirst for notoriety. The winter will pass quietly away; your round of daily duties will be patiently run through; and you will take your leave of the little group of girls and boys, whose minds you have endeavored to open to the light of knowledge, whose hearts you have sought to imbue with virtuous principles; and nothing extraordinary will seem to have been done. An agreeable school will have been kept among an agreeable people—a pleasant passage of three months only in their life and your own. And yet, who fully estimates the latent influences of that three months? Who duly weighs the remote results upon the circle of conscious, social, spiritual, immortal beings, to whom you will have been an authority in learning and a model of character for so much of life? How shall we over-estimate the possible effects of a single winter's school upon the personal life, the domestic relations, the public character of those future men and women of the district and citizens of the State? Thought is vital; it never dies in the soil of the young heart; it may lie covered up and dormant for years, but the sun and the rains will reach it, and it will vegetate and grow and bear fruit. Every time you put your finger on the springs of moral life, you do something to form an imperishable character, in a son or a daughter, a father or a mother, a member of society and a probationer for eternity. You are a worker, not in brass, or marble, or gold, but in MIND; and your workmanship is to endure, when all the devices of Art are worn out of the Ruby and the Diamond, and the precious stones themselves have grown old and vanished away.

Suffer me, in the next place, to recommend to you certain Rules, not unsuitable to be observed in your conduct of the school, which, however obvious when once suggested, might, possibly, not all occur to you with sufficient distinctness to be at once reduced to practice.

1. Adopt, at the outset, a PLAN of operation; survey the field before you, and form for yourself a distinct system of instruction and discipline. Avail yourself, if practicable, of some work of reputation, upon the subject of School-keeping, as "the School and School-master," the "Lectures before the American Institute of Instruction," the "Massachusetts School Reports," or other similar publications. I need hardly intimate, that he must have great resources, and great confidence, in himself, who, at this day, presumes that nothing better is to be learned than we have practiced from the beginning, in the management of a public school. The *Literature* of school-keeping is already considerable; and the subjects of reflection contained in it, not unworthy of the maturest and ablest minds.

2. Study to excite the *attention* and to awaken *thought* and moral *sensibility* in your pupils. Little is done, in education, till mind is called into active, earnest exercise. It is of more

importance to teach a child to *think* for himself than to burden him with other men's ideas. To induce him to *feel* right and to *do* right, while yet a boy, is the best means of ensuring right feelings and right action, when he becomes a man. A present duty done is the proper and only certain promise of future fidelity.

Attention is excited and interest created very much in proportion to the skill of the teacher in presenting *one thing at a time*, and entering himself with his whole heart into it. It is found a useful exercise to practice the *voices* of the pupils upon the elementary sounds of their native language. It is wonderful how little the ordinary careless reading of the schools does in developing the human voice, the sweetest, richest, noblest instrument of sound in the world. No power so equally possessed by nature, is so sadly neglected in education. Go through the sounds of the language daily, in all their variety of inflection, emphasis and tone; it will not fail to amuse and relieve the pupil, at the same time that it gives him new command over a power, whose insinuating, fascinating influence contributes so much to the force of eloquence and the charm of society.

Make it a point to cultivate in the scholars an accurate and natural style of conversation—oral composition. Insist on a full, clear, correct expression, whenever a question is proposed or answered. Allow no clipped, imperfect, clumsy phraseology. It will be found very useful for this purpose, and a great assistance to the student in after life, in writing letters of business or friendship, and in keeping records of events, or drawing a Will, a Deed, or a Contract, to accustom him to translate passages of poetry, or prose, which he has just read, into his own language.

If possible, introduce some simple music among the exercises of the day. It will serve the double purpose of interrupting the monotony of school hours, and of soothing and humanizing the spirit. Gentle music is a moral teacher.

Make frequent use of the Maps and the Black-board. If a subscription could be got up in the district to purchase a set of Mitchell's Outline Maps, (costing about $10) they would last as long as they would be sufficiently correct for use.

3. In discipline appeal always to the best motives first. Insist on

the *right*, the *proper*, the *becoming*, till grosser reasons are found to be indispensable; but maintain ORDER.

And be sure, whatever system of government you may resolve to adopt, first of all to *govern yourself*. A clear-thinking, fair-minded, composed, quiet, dignified man is rarely insulted, or long disobeyed. There is no sphere of life, in which the silent influence of thought and goodness is more certain or more valuable than in the discipline of the young.

The utility of formal Rules is reasonably questioned. The general laws of propriety are obvious enough even to children. And it is not well to treat them as if they had either just done something wrong, or were just going to do so.

4. Make MORAL instruction a prominent object. Not by formal lectures, but by interweaving with the whole system of discipline those moral and religious sentiments, in which all Christians agree, and without which learning and talent are doubtful blessings, and life itself bleak, barren and desolate.

It is most desirable, and, properly done, would be rarely objected to, to open the daily exercises with a short, simple, pertinent prayer, or at least, with a portion of Scripture. And, in some form, it is, I think, the nearly unanimous opinion of experienced teachers, that a portion of the Scriptures should always be read. In many schools the day is opened with a reading from the Bible, and closed with a simple Hymn of Praise. The peculiar sentiments of particular sects of christians are forbidden by law to be taught in the public schools. But the same law enjoins upon all teachers "to impress upon the minds of the young the principles of piety and justice; a sacred regard to truth, love of country, humanity and benevolence; sobriety, industry and frugality; chastity, moderation and temperance; and all other virtues, which are the support and ornament of society; and to endeavor to lead them into a particular understanding of the tendency of all such virtues to preserve and perfect a republican government, to secure the blessings of liberty and to promote their future happiness, and the tendency of the opposite vices to degradation, ruin and misery."

5. Cultivate an acquaintance with the youth under your care,

and with the families of the district. The children will often best be reached through the parents. And the general tone of feeling toward the master out of school, has much to do with his influence in school. You will be at liberty to assume, that the highest families, in their own esteem, or in the esteem of others, are accessible to the teacher of their children; and you must not consider the lowest, that has a child under your care, unworthy to be consulted by you. You will find intelligence without outward show, and meet, oftentimes, with sensibilities the most delicate, where the world sees least to wonder at or talk of—the sweetest clusters of the vine are not always open to the glare of day.

6. Do not forget, that among your own pupils, or in the circle to which they belong, there may be minds of the highest order—diamonds—ingots of virgin gold. Look for them; delight in them; rejoice to bring them out from their dark bed, and to hold them up to the sun. In yourself, it is not unlikely, such a mind may see realized, for the first time, its idea of an educated man—a scholar. Let it not fail to find, in this model—so certain to give direction to its ambition and to form, in some degree, its ultimate character—a simple, earnest lover of truth, and an example of gentleness, courtesy, purity, integrity and piety.

CHS. B. HADDOCK,
Commissioner of Common Schools

N. B. It is of great importance, that a School Register should be kept—Mason's is recommended. The Report is to be made to the Superintending Committee at the close of the school, "of the number of scholars, male and female, that have attended, the branches of learning taught, and the progress made." No teacher is entitled to pay for his services until this provision has been complied with.

94. Stephen Simpson

The ignorance of working people degrades and improverishes them

Labor spokesmen anticipated gains from educational reform that were not dreamed of by its middle-class supporters. Among other things, the working class was expected to achieve a truer perception of its own worth and importance. The following selection is drawn from a volume that earned for its author, Stephen Simpson, a reputation as labor's most articulate voice on the issue of education.

In relation to the productive faculties of a nation, popular education assumes an importance, not suspected even by its best friends. By implanting the principles of science in the mass of intellect, *invention* is provided with materials for the production of improvements, that may change the whole face of society into one radiant smile of content and enjoyment. The invention of *machinery* is the fruit of an educated age, and the more we diffuse that education, the more we advance the arts and sciences, manufactures and agriculture, to perfection. Not one seed of knowledge dropped into the common mind is lost. On some occasion it will germinate to a profit, and recompense society ten fold for the gift; nor do I mean a merely intellectual reward, but a substantial one of labour, of an increase of the means of sustaining and enjoying life, at the least expenditure of time and toil.

Ignorance and inferiority of mind are the only causes of human degradation; except that of poverty, which is the general concomitant of ignorance—as ignorance is its invariable cause. In the progress of nations, civilized people are generally found to vanquish barbarians, either by the force of superior skill, or the charms of science, literature, and knowledge. Nations, like individuals, hold one another in contempt, or look up with respect and admiration, as they rise or fall in the scale of intelligence and

From Stephen Simpson, *The Working Man's Manual: A New Theory of Political Economy* (Philadelphia: Thomas L. Bonsal, 1831), 210–216. Footnote is in the original.

wisdom, refinement and civilization. It is only, however, when we come to scrutinize more closely the elements of a single nation, that we can obtain an accurate and full perception of the debasing effects of ignorance. This becomes obvious, the moment we penetrate into the manners, and non-intercourse of different classes of society, which we may distinguish into the ignorant, or the enlightened. Between these two classes, one of whom labours, and the other remains in idleness, there exists so great a separation in all the social duties and associations, as almost to constitute them different species. The enlightened and educated look down upon the ignorant as a debased order of beings, and treat them, as matter of course, with contempt; and the ignorant on their part, look up to the refined with a sensation approaching to hatred. It is found, that where vigorous intellect bursts the bonds of its ignorance, in this contemned class, that it is immediately merged into the higher and cultivated class; and, notwithstanding the stigma of labour, comes at length to excite respect. Thus the proof is afforded that it is the *ignorance,* not the *occupation* of the working people, that degrades them on the one hand, and empoverishes them on the other. Owing to this ignorance and degradation, it is, that the educated and enlightened, taking advantage of their contemned condition, have oppressed and bound them in the fetters of servile subjection. It is not ignorance that can make laws, organize governments, or administer justice. Education, therefore, is the key to government—it opens the path of power. In vain will you boast of equal rights, and a form of government that secures power to the most humble, when qualified for the task; the blessing will only be nominal whilst the *mass of people* remain ignorant, and incapable of performing those functions that belong to the great civil machine of society. The educated will still occupy the high posts of honour, and devise the system of law and justice; and law and justice thus devised will forever partake of the sentiments peculiar to wisdom and refinement. Hence the maxim that "those who think must govern those who toil"; a maxim, however, that is predicated on the *ignorance* of those who toil, as a necessary property of their condition. But educate those who toil—teach them *to think;* and they take the place of those who govern. This has been strenuously opposed by the great body of the enlightened, because they were fearful of losing their *exclusive privileges,* by imparting knowledge to the mass of the people.

A system of *general education,* one would hardly imagine, could meet with an opponent in an age so enlightened and so philanthropic—an age so distinguished for the *march of mind,* the diffusion of knowledge, and a severe scrutiny into all the principles that combine in the structure of society. And yet, wonderful to say, *public education for the people* has met with gothic adversaries, and illiberal, narrow-minded traducers. The extension of the lights of knowledge, *by popular education,* to all the people of the republic, has ever been the avowed object of all of our most illustrious statesmen. It teems from the lips of the venerated Washington—it glows in the pen of the immortal Jefferson—it formed the daily toil and the midnight study of the lamented and great Clinton. The text of the friends of liberty was—*to enlighten the people is to promote and cement the public virtue!* The soundness of this text was never questioned *anterior* to the organization of a party, whose object it was to obtain it from the legislature, *as a right,* unjustly withheld. When public instruction was bestowed as the *boon of charity,* it found numerous advocates, and met with no opponents; but now, when we justly demand it as a *right*—and under our constitution it must be a *right* and not a charity—it is not only refused by some, but to our utter amazement, its consequences are painted as baneful to the people, and deprecated as having a fatal tendency upon the good order of government! We seem to have resuscitated from the tomb of time the very spirit of the *feudal ages,* in the breasts of certain bigots, intolerants, aristocrats, and narrow-minded *monopolists of knowledge,* who seem as averse to giving the people LIGHT, as they are to paying them for their labour in *hard money.* Actuated by this spirit of an era long past, it is pretended to have been suddenly discovered that *ignorance* is necessary to obedience, and that *public education* is incompatible with public virtue and public order! Sophistry like this is too flimsy to call for confutation; but it reveals a fact that may be useful to us: that although we live under a free constitution, much of the leaven of despotism still remains among us, and that our *theoretical* freedom demands eternal vigilance to preserve it in practice. It is said, that a tax to support common schools would be an *Agrarian Law*, an unjust taking away from the wealth of the rich, for the benefit of the common people. On this principle ALL laws are Agrarian laws; for the rich pay more than the poor individually, though not collectively, for the support of government.

Objections to popular education, however, at the present day, come too late to command attention, or require arguments to show their fallacy. The age has happily outrun those who would keep it stationary in ignorance, or arrest its progress towards general knowledge. The cloud of absolute power in governments has passed away from the firmament of the mind; and left it clear and unspecked by one of the fetters of passive submission, non-resistance, and blind credulity. In time long past, the sovereign power was in the king—now it is in the people; positions being thus reversed, it is incumbent on the people to conform their knowledge to their power.

The influence of education on the manners, is not less important than its operation on the mind; between which there exists so close an intimacy—so powerful a sympathy. Civility, politeness, deference, and all the amiable and softer virtues, are generally found to be residents of minds refined and educated; while ignorance assumes manners of corresponding rudeness, and imperious insolence. As it is the tendency of knowledge to inspire diffidence, the more the mind imbibes, the less it presumes to trespass upon the feelings or challenge the opinions of others. Besides that, in educated people there exists a natural assimilation, the general result of which is good breeding; hence one of the most salutary consequences of popular instruction—that those who labour, and have heretofore been rude and insolent, will gradually become polite and civil; and thus remove one of the most serious difficulties that prevents the working people emerging from that debasing condition in which they are now held by the customs of intellect and power. It is to *education*, therefore, that we must mainly look for a redress of that perverted system of society, which dooms the producer to ignorance, to toil, and to penury,* to moral degradation, physical want, and social barbarism.

The power of the ballot boxes will do little, without the auxiliary help of our moral and intellectual energies. How can it be a marvel, that wealth practises oppression, when it holds as its allies, all the riches of knowledge, and the exterior semblances of virtue and truth? Moving in the high orbit of science, government and laws; ordaining justice and morality after their own images, how shall we ever counteract the principles of vassalage that now prevail, unless we procure EDUCATION for our offspring, and diffuse SCIENCE among our brethren? It is through this door that we must at last enter into the temple of justice, to consecrate on the altar of reason the true rights of man. Knowledge is *power*, in respect to the procurement of equity to the great mass of the sons of labour. It is the light of intelligence that abashes despotism—it is the fire of intellect that dissolves and melts the chains that enthral seven eighths of mankind to the caprice and luxury of the other few. *"In what way shall this evil be attacked and removed?"* I have answered, by giving our children equal or superior knowledge, virtue and intelligence, to the rich—by EDUCATION to direct and qualify us for government and laws; and by concentrating our SUFFRAGE to enable us to reach that point of influence, at which we shall be able to make the laws conform to the spirit of justice, and the government congenial to the equality of human rights.

* A great writer observes—"According to ancient practice, *all checks were on the inferior,* to restrain him to the duty of submission; none on the superior, to engage him to the reciprocal duties of gentleness and humanity. In modern times, a bad servant finds not easily a good master, nor a bad master a good servant; and the checks are mutual, *suitably to the inviolable and eternal laws of reason and equity.*" The principle admitted in the last sentence, is the pith of this quotation; and this principle it is, that we desire to extend, by the diffusion of education. The ancient practice is still too prevalent; notwithstanding theories of freedom which denounce and supersede it. The checks *ought* to be mutual, but they are not; and where *rights are equal,* the failure becomes an oppression. It is EDUCATION only that can bring this theory of *reciprocal checks* into practice.

Prison Reform

95. Samuel Gridley Howe

A minority view on how to reform the criminal

It is hard for our jaded era to fathom the interest high-minded men one hundred and thirty years ago had in prison reform. The teachings of the Enlightenment were then still fresh. Man, the *philosophes* had taught, was perfectible. The prison, organized along sound rational lines, could be an instrument for human regeneration. In America a lively dispute broke out as to how the process could best be organized. On one side were those who favored isolation of prisoners, simultaneously separating them from moral infection and compelling them to meditate on their lapse from decency. This regime obtained in Philadelphia and parts of Pennsylvania. The opposing view, while urging the rule of silence, would permit men to work together, as they did in Auburn prison, New York. A dispute broke out among Boston reformers over the proper system to follow. In the following minority report, the eminent reformer Samuel Gridley Howe argued vehemently in favor of isolation or the "separate" system over the "congregate" system, despite the much greater costs of the former.

But, finally, it will be asked, If the Separate system is really so much superior to the Congregate system, why has the latter obtained such general favor? This question will, however, no longer be asked by those who know the real state of the case in the most enlightened countries of Europe. There, as we shall show presently, the Separate system has found favor, and is rapidly gaining ground. If the question is asked with respect to the United States, we answer, that the causes of the greater prevalence of the Congregate system are these:—first, it is supposed to be cheaper; second, it has been advocated by the only Society in the country which has funds, and an agent of zeal and ability, namely, this

From Samuel Gridley Howe, *Report of a Minority of the Boston Prison Discipline Society,* May 27, 1845 (Boston: William D. Ticknor, 1846), 78–81, 82–87. Footnotes are in the original.

Society; and, third, because it really is such an immense improvement on the old prison system which it superseded.

First, as to the expense. The original outlay of capital for the edifice must be greater in the Separate system; that cannot be denied. The mechanical operations can be carried on to more profit where the men work in common. The officers and overseers and instructers may be less numerous and less expensive in the Congregate system; less numerous, because they oversee companies, and deal with masses; less expensive, because, having little moral relation with their men, they need not be persons of so high character. On the other hand, if, as we believe, the Separate system inflicts a more severe punishment,—if it operates more quickly to deter from crime and persuade to virtue, then a very material diminution of the length of sentences may be made, and this would turn the tables at once in its favor.

But we are not inclined to press this point far, because the whole tendency of the discussion about the comparative economy of the two systems has had, among its other evil effects, that of tempting legislatures to decide in favor of the Congregate system, on the ground that it is cheaper. Such a motive is an unworthy one, and our Society should not appeal to it. Grant that the Separate system is more expensive; nay, that the Congregate system may, and does, prove a source of income to the State! What then? One great object of prison discipline is to reform convicts; and what should we say, if the directors of a hospital refused to give to patients the medicine most likely to save their lives, because it costs more than poorer drugs?—and is the soul of less import than the body? If a musket or cannon, or any warlike implement of a novel and more destructive quality, be adopted by one government, do not the others straightway throw aside the old one, and take up the new?—and is it of more importance to destroy than to save?

Shame upon such sordid arguments! Thousands of convicts are made so in consequence of a faulty organization of society,—in consequence of ignorance and temptation; many are made so in consequence of almost inevitable hereditary propensities, too strong for their control; some ought, doubtless, to be considered as victims, and moral patients, rather than responsible beings; they are thrown upon society as a sacred charge; and that society is false to its trust, if it neglects any means for their reformation, especially if it refuses the necessary funds, while it has money to throw away on any pomp or pride, be it of peace or war.

We hold that the moment the earnings of a prison come up to its expense, then the severity of labor should be diminished, and more time be given to the convicts for intellectual and moral instruction, for which extra teachers should be provided, until there be one for every ten or twelve men, if the funds will allow it; and if the profits still increase, they should then be appropriated in some other way to the convict's improvement, and not tempt the cupidity of the State, and excite the prisoner's distrust of the motives of his imprisonment, by making his earnings seem a *bonus* upon legal convictions and the prolonged sentences.

Some may maintain that the State has a right to require of the convict to pay back, as far as possible, the expense to which he has put it by his depredations and by his trial. As a matter of abstract right, this may be so; but it should be considered, that to require entire repayment would be to exact the pound of flesh which would draw with it every drop of blood from the body; for, were a convict to live to the age of Methuselah, he could not pay back his full proportion of the cost of the vast machinery of justice. If this principle be acted upon at all, it should be administered in the spirit of the new dispensation, which forgives seventy times seven, and not in that of the old, which requires an eye for an eye and a tooth for a tooth. The convict should, at any rate, be able to lay up something for the day of his departure from the prison.

But to return to the subject,—the preference in this country for Congregate prisons. When a new prison is to be established, the edifice and the system of discipline are to be discussed and selected by a body of men who, however unfitted they may be for understanding any other merit of a system, can all appreciate that of economy. When, therefore, it is proved, as it can be, that a prison upon the Congregate system will pay its own way, the strongest argument has been urged in its favor; and when it is added, as it may be with truth, that some State prisons pay several thousand dollars *per annum* net gain into the State treasury, what chance is there for the adoption of another system, which, however favorable it may be to the reformation of the prisoners, may require a tax for its support?

The next reason why the Congregate system has found favor in this country is, that this Society has strenuously advocated it, and by its pecuniary resources, and by the whole moral influence of the names of its members, been instrumental in its propagation. When it is considered that this Society is the only one of its kind in the country that has the disposal of any considerable funds,—that its Reports have been the only regular publication upon the subject of Prison Discipline, until quite recently,—that those Reports have been prepared and the whole power of the Society directed by its agent, who has zealously advocated the Congregate system, and as zealously decried the Separate system,—it will be evident that we do not underrate the effect upon the public, some of whom know little, and many of whom care less, about the whole subject.

Far be it from us to disparage the merits of that officer. He has been a most important agent in a great work of reformation and improvement. He has helped to introduce the order, the sobriety, and the industry of the Congregate system into prisons which were once foul dens of corruption. But while we recognize the importance of his labors and the honesty of his purpose, we are constrained to say that he has been led by zeal for a favorite system to underrate and decry a rival one, which, in our view, is vastly superior. Like all of us, he is liable to err; and, having once engaged in a partisan strife (for such has become the contest among the advocates of the two systems), his very zeal for the side which he espoused has made him blind to the merits of the other. It must be apparent to any impartial person who reads the Reports of our Society, that, instead of discussing the merits of the two systems upon the high ground of principle, they have harped upon the imperfections and short-comings of the penitentiaries of Pennsylvania, as though failures in their administration were decisive of the great question at issue. . . .

However we may dislike the principle of concentration of the whole power of a people in the hands of a few, we must confess, that, when that power is brought to bear upon great questions of science or humanity, its effects are as brilliant and satisfactory as they are rapid. When we reflect how much has been done towards collecting facts by this Society, with an income of $3,000, and the agency of one man, who devoted his whole time to it, we can conceive what a great government, with immense funds at its disposal, can do, with the agency of scores of men of talents, learning, and zeal, whom it sets to work in every country. It is scarcely ten years since the governments of France and Great Britain began to bestow close attention to the subject of Prison Discipline. They selected as their agents men already distinguished for talent and learning, and, giving them ample means, bade them visit all the countries where any knowledge could be gained upon the subject, and, in their own time, give the result of their personal observations, with whatever valuable knowledge they could collect from the experience of others.

In Central Europe, the Prussian government, and some of the smaller German States, and even some of the Swiss Cantons, took measures to collect information upon the subject. In the North, Sweden began to demand light upon a subject which had long been discussed in Holland, and her king himself compiled a work upon it; and the young kingdom of Belgium has already discussed it thoroughly. Several of these governments sent commissioners to this country, to examine closely all our prisons; all of them obtained the most minute information that could be had, and it is undoubtedly true that at this moment there are more men in Europe who have a thorough knowledge of the condition and merits of the various prisons in the United States, than there are in this country. As an instance of the attention of the government of France to the subject, it caused the question to be put to the Academy of Medicine, whether there was any thing in the Separate-system discipline that would be peculiarly injurious to the bodily or mental health of the prisoners. That body, perhaps the most learned and scientific in the world, employed some of its ablest heads in the solution of the question, and they (as we have said), after mature examination, pronounced that there was not.

After the return of the various commissioners from this country to Europe, the subject of their mission was taken up in England, France, and Belgium, and made the topic of animated and prolonged discussion, especially in the French Chamber of Deputies.

Now, it is very remarkable, that, while this Society has been resting in the assurance that the system which it advocated was the best, all the foreign commissioners who have been sent here reported it to be very defective, and far inferior to its rival. While we were reading pages upon the superiority of the Congregate system, the people of the five most enlightened countries in Europe were reading the conclusions of their impartial, scientific men, upon its inferiority; and while we were rejoicing in the erection of two or three new prisons upon the Congregate system, as a proof of its final triumph and prevalence, the people of Europe were witnessing the erection of scores of prisons upon the Separate system.

The history of this revolution of opinion is well worthy of notice. The first French commissioners, Messieurs Beaumont and De Tocqueville, after careful comparison of the prisons in the United States, pronounced decidedly in favor of the Separate system, as administered in Philadelphia, and against the Auburn system. In the recent debate in the Chamber of Deputies, M. De Tocqueville expressed himself thus, in answer to the assertion, that the preference manifested in France for the Separate system was owing to his exertions:—"I defy any one to name a single subject which has been so long studied, by so many different persons, in so persevering and practical a manner, as the question before us. Did the government, after having sent us to the United States, in 1831, rest there? Did it not, two years afterwards, send two other commissioners upon the same errand? Did not the British government, likewise, send commissioners with this object? Has not the Prussian government done the same thing? Is it not true, that all these commissioners, without exception, even those who left Europe opponents to the Separate system, after having examined the different systems upon the spot, brought home to their governments views precisely similar to ours? Have not the governments since then entered upon this course with all the knowledge they possessed, with all the experience they have gained, with all the light which could be furnished from every quarter?"

Again, this eminent statesman, who has such a rare combination of clear insight into principles, and practical knowledge of facts, who, without party feeling, and with a view only to truth, studied so long and intimately our prisons, says,—"Most of those who have gone to the United States to study prisons upon the spot have returned warm advocates of the Separate system, although before their departure they had conceived and even expressed opinions unfavorable to it; all have acknowledged its powerful effect upon the prisoners."

De Tocqueville alludes to a second commission. It seems, that, to make sure that all was right, the government sent M. De Metz, a few years later, and on his return he reported in these words:—"We declare that our preferences and our sympathies are for the system of Pennsylvania. In this system there are positive advantages for society, and positive advantages for the convict. Under it corruption is impossible; amendment is probable, and, in a great number of cases, certain." He goes on to enumerate many other advantages, and closes with these words:— "Such are the principal motives which have inclined us to the system of Pennsylvania, which now has the sanction of time and experience." [1]

The Report of the Prussian commissioner is still more remarkable, for he had been an advocate of the Congregate system. He says of the Philadelphia Penitentiary:—"I declare frankly, that, after the knowledge which I have gained of the different prisons of Europe and America, none appears to me to allow so much equity and justice in the infliction of punishment, none presents so many chances of amendment of the criminal, as the Separate system, combined with the regular visits of the keepers, inspectors, preachers, teachers, and physicians. I say *chances of amendment*,—for all human efforts are limited, and ought as much

1. Rapport sur les Penitencières des États Unis, p. 41, et suiv.

as possible to ward off obstacles that may prevent the action of divine grace, which can alone effect a complete reform of the guilty. This opinion is the result of my observations during my sojourn in America, as well as of my studies and reflections since my return, although I went to America entertaining a preference for the Auburn system." [2]

The British commissioner, Mr. Crawford, made a most valuable Report, in which he advocates the Separate system. He says of the Eastern Penitentiary of Pennsylvania:—"Upon a careful review of every part of it, after seeing the whole, and examining a considerable number of the individuals confined in it, I have no hesitation in declaring my conviction, that its discipline is a safe and efficacious mode of prison management; THAT IT HAS NO UNFAVORABLE EFFECT UPON MIND OR HEALTH," &c.[3] Again, he says,—"In America, the opponents of this system have produced very erroneous impressions by the publication of certain experiments, made a few years since, of solitude without labor; statements which have been widely circulated in England, to the great prejudice of solitary imprisonment of every description."

Another official Report may be cited,—that of the Commissioners appointed by the government of Lower Canada, who, after visiting our prisons, became convinced of the superiority of the Separate system, and close their Report by saying,—"Such are the considerations which have determined us to give the preference to the Pennsylvania system, although it is not so economical, and may even require considerable outlay in the beginning." [4]

These, we believe, are all the official Reports that have been made, except one to the government of Upper Canada, which we have not yet been able to procure. Now, when we consider that the commissioners of four governments, without any concert of action, some of them even opposed to the Separate system, have all come to the conclusion that it is superior to the Congregate system, we cannot help considering it most remarkable and

2. Die Amerikanischen Besserunge Systeme. Leipzig, Brockhaus, 1837.

3. Crawford's Report, pp. 14, 15.

4. Not having the original document, we retranslate it from the French translation.

important evidence upon the great subject for the consideration of which our Society was formed; and we cannot help regretting that it has not been spread upon the pages of our Reports.

Is it fair in our Society to assume, as it has done, that the Separate system is in every respect so inferior to the Congregate system, that it will not even consider the arguments in its favor? Is it modest to do so, when that system is advocated by another Society in this country, much older than ours, and comprehending among its active members many more men practically acquainted with the subject of prisons than does ours, and whose experience leads them to opposite conclusions? Is it wise to do so, when enlightened and disinterested foreigners, who are lifted above the *disturbing forces of sectional or party feelings,* all pronounce us wrong, and others right?

Besides the mass of evidence furnished in favor of the Separate system by the special commissioners of the European governments, there is a vast amount of testimony in its favor given by unofficial travellers, and by authors who have written on the subject. Should we cite all the philosophical and practical writers upon the subject, who give their testimony in favor of the Separate system, we should frame a long catalogue; but, after naming Professor Mittemair, of Germany, and Lucas, of France, we should not know where to find another author of note who has written in favor of the Congregate system. We will not even give a list of the names of the first; but there is one circumstance so significant of the importance in which the subject is held, so honorable too to humanity, that we must allude to it. The young king of Prussia, an absolute monarch of immense power, has paid great personal attention to the subject. He closely examined the model prison upon the Separate system, in England, and other prisons, and was so impressed with the superiority of the first, that, after consultation, he ordered four prisons upon the Separate system to be erected in his dominions. The king of Sweden, too, a man of clear head and kind heart, gave very close personal attention to the subject; collected all the evidence he could from this country, and finally himself wrote a book upon it,—a book breathing a beautiful spirit of humanity, full of sound wisdom, and which warmly advocates the Separate system. But Europe furnishes other and stronger evidence in favor of the Separate system, than the written opinions of philosophers, practical men, and monarchs;—there are, and have for years been, many prisons in full operation upon both systems; those upon the Congregate system have been tried, and found wanting; those upon the other have had great success.

Abolition of Capital Punishment

96. Rhode Island Committee

Capital punishments ought to be abolished, in TOC because they are irremediable

The reforms championed in the 1830s and 1840s ran a wide gamut. As the following "minority report" to the Rhode Island legislature indicates, many of the most popular arguments used today against capital punishment were anticipated one hundred and thirty-five years ago.

To the Honorable The General Assembly: [R.J.]

January Session, A. D. 1838

The subscribers, two of the Commiteee appointed to revise the Penal Code,

Respectfully Represent,

That it will appear by the Report of said Committee, which accompanies the bill presented by them, that they were divided equally on the abolition of capital punishments, and that it was agreed to report a bill that should not provide for their infliction in any case, that the point might be brought directly before the Legislature. In the report afore refered to, the committee have given their reasons for many of the alterations which they propose, in the laws now in force, but it does not and could not

W. R. Staples and Samuel Y. Atwell, *[Minority] Report of the Committee on the Abolition of Capital Punishments*, Rhode Island, January, 1839.

rightfully contain a single word for or against the abolition of capital punishment. Hence, the subscribers, in this separate report, propose to lay before the Assembly some of the reasons why they think such punishments ought to be abolished in this State.

The severity of such punishments favors the escape of the guilty. There are many persons in our community who will not complain or prosecute for a crime punishable with death. No man willingly takes a part in a capital trial against the prisoner. Many men summoned as jurors in such cases refuse to appear, and some who do appear, resort to unwarrantable expedients to create a bias in their minds for or against the prisoner, that they may be challenged for cause. When a jury is empanelled in such a case, how often is it, that having reference to the consequences of a verdict of guilty, they adopt a bare, naked possibility of innocence as the legal reasonable doubt of guilt, and so acquit the prisoner. But if a verdict of guilty be rendered, and judgment of death passed, it is the settled practice to postpone the day of execution until after one, if not two sessions of the Assembly, that the convict may petition for pardon or commutation of sentence. How readily such petitions are granted, the records of the Assembly will show. When the life of any individual rests solely on the votes of the members of this Assembly, they can tell with what reluctance they pronounce the irrevocable doom, and how readily and gladly they seize upon every circumstance which seems to justify them in showing mercy. He who proposes to commit a capital crime is as well aware of these circumstances as we are. They enter into his calculation of chances of escape. He takes every means to escape detection. If detected he leans on the mercy of a jury, and if convicted relies with almost perfect security on the exercise of the pardoning power in his favor. The severity of the punishment which the law has affixed to his crime, is outweighed in his mind by the greater chances of escape from that punishment which that very severity creates. It is not the severity, but the certainty of punishment which deters men from the commission of crime.

Such punishments are unequal. The crimes punishable with death by our law are murder, rape, robbery, arson, burglary and petit treason. Some of these remotely affect property, some endanger life, and some are the destruction of life. Yet the same punishment awaits them all. He who willfully and maliciously poisons a whole family or assassinates his father, and he who raises a window in a dwelling-house in the night and puts in a finger with intent to steal, though he steal nothing, are hung on the same gallows. They are also unequal as regards the criminals themselves. Can it be pretended that he to whom life has become a burden, who has outlived friends and connections, and even hope itself, suffers equally with him who is surrounded with every thing to make life desirable? Does he who looks on death as the end of his existence, or as the end of all suffering, and he who has learned from reason and revelation a future existence of rewards and punishments, suffer equally? But the inequality of such punishments is conclusively shown from the fact, that they are frequently remitted, from the peculiar circumstances that attend either the crime or the criminal, or both. Nothing but a sense of their injustice, in certain cases, can justify the granting of a pardon, or even commutation of punishment.

Such punishments are considered peculiarly appropriate for murder and petit treason. This we apprehend arises from a mistaken idea of the design of punishments. Society has no revenge to seek against its delinquent members. The State deals out no vengeance to those who offend against its laws. Penal laws always look to the future.

The State requires obedience to its laws by the sanction of punishments for the good of the whole. The end in view is the prevention of crime. The sole object of punishment is to deter others from offending against the laws. Admit that death is the appropriate and the only appropriate punishment for murder; that life should be taken for life, and the law of retaliation ought to be re-established. An eye for an eye, and a tooth for a tooth, would constitute our whole penal code.

Capital punishments ought to be abolished, because they are irremediable. By false witnesses, and by wrong conclusions from testimony that is true, the innocent have been oftentimes condemned; nor will this cease to be the case, so long as man possesses such limited, finite means of ascertaining truth. Until he can unerringly decide, he should inflict no punishment that is in its nature irremediable.

Murder, with which we include petit treason, is readily admitted to be the most heinous offence that can be committed. All savage as well as civilized nations have so considered it. It is placed at the head of all penal codes, because it inflicts an irreparable injury on man. The life of a man is taken. Society is deprived of his services. His wife, his children, his parents, are deprived of a companion, a guide, and a support. The image of the Almighty is defaced, and the scene of his probation closed, by a fellow-being. Capital punishment produces the same results, and inflicts the same irreparable injury. The services of the most depraved may be useful to society. The most abandoned profligate cannot alienate the affections of a wife—a mother's heart still owns the felon for a son—a child regards him with reverence as a father. He stands the image of his God; though debased and dishonored, the object of the mercy of the indulgent Father of all men.

But it will be said, in the one case the evil is maliciously inflicted, in the other necessarily for the safety of society. We deny that necessity. We ask, we demand that it be proved. He who claims the right thus to trample under foot the holy ties of nature—to set a bound to human life—to send unbidden his fellow-man to the presence of his Maker—to arraign the long-suffering of Heaven—and to impugn the justice of God, ought to be ready to show that he acts from necessity. Have capital punishments been demonstrated to be necessary? If it could be shown that they had eradicated crime, that would not prove them necessary. Other means might have produced the same result. It will not follow that imprisonment or some other punishment would not also have done it. This result not only would not prove the necessity of capital punishments, it would not even raise a probability of such a necessity. But such has not been the result. They have formed a part of the penal code of every nation under heaven, yet the golden age has existed only in the imagination of poets. Crimes have ever existed, and history bears witness that in those nations whose codes have been the most bloody, there, crimes have more increased and multiplied. They have been fully tried and found insufficient to produce the desired result. When once a milder system has been fairly and fully tried, and found equally insufficient, then may the advocates of capital punishments contend that they have proved such punishments to be probably necessary.

The strongest argument against the abolition of such punishment, and the one most frequently resorted to is, that it is a great innovation in criminal jurisprudence. To this it might be answered, if those punishments have been in use ever since society has been formed, and have not been found sufficient to repress crime, it is time some other system was tried. What possible evil can result from trying the experiment in this State? It will always be in the power of the General Assembly to repeal it, and it ill becomes a Rhode-Island man to yield to an argument of innovation. Up to the settlement of this colony, civil government had ever claimed the right to regulate the religious faith of its citizens. Only a single voice had been raised against it, in the whole human family. That was the voice of the founder of this State. The cry of innovation was raised against him. Dreadful scenes of anarchy and confusion, irreligion and immorality, were conjured up as the inevitable consequences of religious liberty. Yet, being convinced that "a most flourishing civil state may stand and best be maintained with a full liberty in religious concernments," against the concurrent practice of the whole world, the experiment was commenced. Two hundred years have passed and the experiment has succeeded—gloriously succeeded.

We appeal now to the Legislature of Rhode-Island to try another experiment—one which is approved by the philosophy of a Franklin, the philanthropy of a Rush, and the research of a Livingston. By adopting it before any of her sister States, Rhode-Island will show that she still possesses that independence of feeling, sentiment, and action, which characterized her first settlers, and will regain that proud pre-eminence among them, which she only lost by their imitating her example.

W. R. Staples
Samuel Y. Atwell.

Abolition of Imprisonment for Debt

97. Citizens of New York

Imprisonment for debt is cruel and useless to the creditor

Imprisonment for debt hurt poor, small debtors above all, but as Joseph Dorfman has shown, it was resented too by prosperous men of affairs as an outworn relic inimical to the spirit of enterprise. The accompanying memorial was drawn up in 1830 by prominent men in New York City and it bore fruit the following year with the passage of a law abolishing the institution. Antimasonic leaders were later to charge that Van Buren's machine was secretly hostile to enactment of the great reform. The evidence indicates that the appeal of abolition cut across party lines.

Memorial
To the Legislature of the State of New-York

The Memorial

Of the Subscribers, Citizens of the City of New-York,

Respectfully Sheweth:
That your Memorialists deem the Law of Imprisonment for Debt a great grievance to the people of this State, and that it ought to be entirely *abolished.*

Though a detailed history of the origin of that *evil,* the iniquity which has been practised under it, and the miseries which have constituted its black and numerous train, is not necessary on this occasion; yet we beg leave to state, that the law in question emanated from the tyranny of the darker ages, when the power of kings was nearly absolute, when the mass of mankind were regarded as but little better than *live-stock,* attached to the soil of Lords and Barons—when the true principles of free political government were not generally known, or but partially understood;—when the Rights of Man were but little respected, and the

Memorial of Citizens of the City of New-York to the Legislature of the State of New-York (New York, December 29, 1830), 2–7.

complaints of the People seldom heeded, when their resentments were not feared;—and when the powers of Church and State were united, and Kings, Priests, and Temporal Lords, were joined in *"holy alliance,"* to violate the MAGNA CHARTA of Civil Liberty, and to oppress the people by laws, from the operation and evils of which, those who made them were exempted.

That the American people have so long preserved that relic of the rubbish of exploded British laws—so quietly submitted to sustain that offspring of despotism in the bosom of the body politic of their free government, would be matter of much wonder, had we not reason to believe that the law in question has not heretofore been examined and scrutinized in the manner necessary to a correct understanding of the subject by the people.

That the law of imprisonment for debt is radically wrong in moral principle, a violation of the unalienable rights of man, adverse to the express provisions of the constitution of this state, which have been placed as guards against the invasion and abridgment of personal liberty; that it is cruel and oppressive to the debtor, useless to the creditor, demoralizing to *both,* and fertile of mischief to society, are *truths* which can be established by irrefragible proofs too voluminous to be comprised within the limits of this Memorial. We shall therefore confine ourselves to such remarks as will be necessary to prove that our objections to the law in question are neither incorrect in point of *fact,* nor too highly coloured.

We hold these truths to be too evident to require proof on this occasion. That to *molest* any person, to *punish* him, to *"deprive him of his liberty,"* or of any other *"right or privilege,"* who has done no wilful wrong, committed no *criminal offence,* would be an act of cruelty, and a violation of moral principle. That he who would treat a fellow being *thus,* would be justly deemed a cruel, unrighteous and immoral man. That the law which authorises such an act, influences the disposition to commit it, and hence is identified in character with the mischievous effects it produces, and the cruelty and immorality which it authorises and justifies. Such is the law by which an honest, unfortunate insolvent debtor is "deprived of his liberty," and cast into a loathsome prison; the most natural and most certain effects of which are, to add oppression to misfortune—to increase the debtor's inability to pay, and hence his imprisonment is useless to his creditor, and injurious to *both*.

As the *involuntary* non-payment of a debt—the *inability* occasioned by misfortune, to fulfil a civil contract, is not a *criminal offence*, imprisonment for such cause, is punishment without *crime*—oppressive to the sufferer—*unjust* on the part of the oppressor,—iniquitous in the law which occasions it, and a reproach to the intelligence and benevolent character of the people who permit and approve it. That all our insolvent laws, so called, *admit those truths*. Those laws were enacted for the relief of the honest insolvent debtor. Relief!—from what?—not from the tender mercies of his creditors, nor the injustice of the law by which he was *"deprived of his liberty"*; but from the unrighteous conduct of the one, and the unjust provisions and the evil operation of the other. If it is right to release honest unfortunate debtors from imprisonment, the law must be wrong which *"deprived them of their liberty."*

That the law of imprisonment for debt violates the principles of humanity and justice, is also proved by the facts that it treats the honest unfortunate debtor, worse in some respects than any *criminal*, and the *fraudulent* debtor worse than any *other* criminal. Besides imprisoning them in violation of the provisions of the constitution, which were intended to protect the innocent, and to secure to the guilty the right of trial, and other privileges, to which all criminals are entitled; all imprisoned debtors are subjected to a degree of rigour and privation, beyond that with which murderers and other felons are treated.

All persons imprisoned for *crime*, are humanely furnished with the means to sustain life and health. Not so in the case of an imprisoned debtor, honest or fraudulent. They can be imprisoned an indefinite length of time, without trial, proof, or even the allegation of *crime* against them, and are left without the necessaries of life, to perish for want, unless the hand of voluntary charity should be interposed to avert the murderous tendency, and the horrible consequences of the law of imprisonment for debt.

The character of men is made and ascertained by their conduct—the character of a law by the actions which it induces, enjoins or authorises. When the action itself is immoral, he who commits it is no less so—the law which authorises it partakes of the same character, and those who approve and support it, are voluntary participators in the merited animadversion.

Were a man to confine his *dog* for some real or pretended offence, without meat or drink, and leave him to live or die as chance might happen, would not his neighbors justly deem such conduct cruel, cry out shame, and throw the dog a *bone*, or let him loose to procure his own subsistence? Is there a man in this community whose moral sense would not revolt at the bare relation of such an instance of moral depravity, and condemn such cruel treatment of a *dog* by his owner? And were the master to plead a law of the state in justification of his conduct, would he not be told, that however *legal*, no legislative statute, nor judiciary decision, could establish the righteousness or morality of such an action?

How strange—how inconsistent—how lamentable, that in a free and enlightened nation, where the moral sense of the community would condemn the above mentioned treatment of a *dog*, as an act of moral depravity, and where the law regards cruelty to dumb beasts, as a criminal and indictable offence, other laws also exist, which leaves the rights of human beings less protected than those of the *brute creation!* Yes, we repeat the disgraceful truth, that in this free, enlightened, moral, and religious community, human beings—debtors, whether honest or dishonest, may by law be imprisoned, unprovided *except by charity*, even with bread or water, and left to live or die, as either event may happen; while similar treatment practised on a *dumb brute*, would be condemned as an act of unjustifiable cruelty, and its perpetrator punished for such a criminal offence against the common and the moral law!!!

According to the best estimates which the Prison Discipline Society, in Boston, has been enabled to make, "75,000 debtors are imprisoned annually in the United States—more than one-half of whom are imprisoned for sums less than $20, while the costs are more than one-half the original debts, and in many cases quadruple the debts." By information derived within a few days past, from the books in the office of the Sheriff of this city and county, there were imprisoned in the debtors' jail in the year 1829, one thousand and twenty-seven debtors.

We will now, with a view further to illustrate the evil of the law, by virtue of which such facts exist, ascertain the true character of the *action* it enjoins or justifies, abstractly from the law which induces and authorises it.

Were a single individual creditor to incarcerate 1027 debtors, without respect to age, character, condition, or ability, more than half of whom being poor, honest, and unable to pay, and leave them to live as they list, or to suffer or die for want of subsistence, would not the moral feelings of a virtuous community regard such conduct as evidence of extreme depravity? Would not the good sense of an intelligent people, correctly view and duly deprecate the iniquity of such proceeding? Would not the indignation of an honest and benevolent public, rise in judgment against such hardened inhumanity? And would not public opinion protest against such gross injustice, and condemn the individual acting thus, to the merited scorn of a just, humane, & enlightened people? Is there a man in the community who would be willing to incur such responsibility, or encounter such consequences, or who would not regard the imputation of such conduct to him as a foul stain on all that is valuable of human character? And if two or more individuals should participate in the above mentioned measure, would not its character be the same, and alike obnoxious to merited censure? And if a whole people "go and do likewise," is the action more just, or animadversion less merited? Does not the multiplication of evil doers increase, rather than diminish the mischief of evil doing? And is it not truly astonishing to hear sane and serious men gravely contend that *all* the people have a right to do or participate in an action, which if done by a single individual, the whole community would unite in condemning as immoral, cruel and oppressive? And yet as incongruous as it may seem, and lamentable as it certainly is, there are in this enlightened community, men who ought to know better, but who are so deficent in correct information, as to regard the law of imprisonment for debt, as salutary and righteous in itself, and who are opposed to its abolishment as a violation of the *rights,* and an infringement of the *privileges* of *creditors!!*

By a report of the Society in this city, for the relief of debtors confined for small debts, it appears that they have recently procured the liberation of fifteen prisoners, the whole of whose debts together, amounted to $132, which debts were increased by the addition of more than *sixty dollars* costs! And though the sorrowing supplications of oppressed poverty, which are constantly issuing from the debtors' prison in this city, are sometimes mingled with grateful acknowledgments for some scanty relief dispensed by the hand of charity; those who have the best opportunity to know the whole amount of suffering within the walls of the debtors' prison, know that but a very small portion of the distress occasioned by imprisonment for debt, can be relieved by aid thus afforded by the benevolence of humane individuals.

Here let us ask—were those debtors destitute when first imprisoned? Then have we in this enlightened age and nation, a law authorising the imprisonment of *objects of charity,* to compel them to pay their debts and to punish them for not being able to do so!! Were they not *objects of charity* when first "deprived of their liberty?" Then their imprisonment has made them so; and in either case, the law of imprisonment for debt holds paupers in confinement, to compel them, able or unable, to pay their debts, and to punish indiscriminately, the *honest* and the *fraudulent,* for the non-fulfilment of their contracts!!

"This law," says a learned American jurist, "by virtue of which 'such deeds be done,' is so unrighteous—so inconsistent, and drags so many evils and so much suffering in its train, is often indignantly denounced as *barbarous.* But such an imputation is a libel on *barbarous* nations. They never incurred the disgrace of such a practice. Neither Goths, Vandals, nor Hottentots, ever had a law to imprison debtors, for not doing exactly what they could not do." It is one of the *refinements* of the *arts* and *science* of *civil* government, by which the innocent are punished least the guilty should escape. It was left for civilized nations to discover and enjoy the "benefit of the *act*" of imprisonment for debt. Unenlightened and *uncivilized savages* never thought of shutting a man up in prison, and depriving him of the ability to earn subsistence for himself or family, to compel him to pay his debts: and they never laid claim to the discovery of any utility, expediency, humanity, justice, or moral influence, in such an institution.

But it is alleged, as a cardinal objection to the abolishment of imprisonment for debt, "that there are many *fraudulent* as well as honest and unfortunate debtors—that it is generally very difficult to detect, and frequently impossible to prove fraud on the part of the debtor; and were the law in question abolished, many *fraudulent* debtors would escape punishment." This is doubtless true; but shall all debtors be involved in one common fate, and the innocent punished lest the guilty should escape? Shall all the guilty be punished without *legal proof*, lest *proof* should be wanting against a *portion* of them? Shall the innocent and guilty indiscriminately be "deprived of their liberty," because it is difficult or impossible to make a correct discrimination? Behold, then, the absurdity which is involved in the above quoted objections—all debtors must be punished by imprisonment—not on *proof* of any fraud, but because no proof of fraud can be obtained against any of them!

Fraudulent debtors even now escape punishment, and it is owing to the indiscriminate imprisonment of the innocent and the guilty, under existing laws, that so few of the latter class are ever brought to merited justice. Repeal the law of imprisonment *for debt*, and the injured creditor will be obliged to resort to the only legitimate means recognized by the constitution for the *punishment* of criminals. Indictment for fraud and punishment of fraudulent debtors, would then be events of more frequent occurrence than now or heretofore. In truth, the present law of imprisonment for debt has been the principal cause of the almost uniform escape of the fraudulent debtors from merited punishment. The evils of the law in question have been so multiform and so great, and so many legislative attempts have been made to obviate them, that when the law opened the prison door, to release the honest debtor from unjust imprisonment, the fraudulent debtor has slipped out with full pockets, and with such facility, that his creditors, seeing the inefficiency of imprisonment, to coerce the payment of debts, have deemed it most advisable to accept whatever sum a dishonest debtor may choose to offer, and are thus constrained, rather than to lose *all*, to accept from a dishonest, less than they would from an honest debtor, in discharge of his debt. And thus does the immoral influence of the present laws, induce, if not oblige creditors, to treat fraudulent debtors with more lenity and forbearance, than they would those whose integrity is more apparent, or less suspected.

But the law of imprisonment for debt, as it operates on *fraudulent debtors*, is subject to other great and tenable objections than those we have before mentioned. We would have the fraudulent debtor punished. We regard him as worse than a highway robber. The latter can take no more property than his victim happens to have about his person. The *fraudulent debtor*, besides committing a breach of *contract* and *confidence*, can, and too often does beggar a whole family at a single operation. We would therefore have him punished; not for *owing a debt*, but for the *fraud* he commits. But though a criminal, he has rights which are secured by the constitution, to *all* criminals; those charged with *treason* and *murder*, not excepted; and of which rights no legislative law, nor righteous exercise of legislative power can deprive them. And that the imprisonment *for debt* of a fraudulent debtor, at the will and pleasure of his creditor, without the intervention of the *"due process of law,"* in criminal cases is *unconstitutional*, we will now proceed to prove.

The constitution is the supreme *"law of the land"*; and by that instrument it is enacted that *"no person shall be deprived of life,* LIBERTY, *or property, without due process of law."* It has already been proved and admitted, that no person can righteously or *constitutionally* be *"deprived of his liberty,"* who is guiltless of any *criminal act:* and the constitution declares that *"no person shall be held to answer for any infamous crime, unless on presentment or indictment of a grand jury.*" It follows then, irresistibly, that by the constitution—the supreme *"law of the land," "presentment or indictment of a grand jury"* is the *"due process of law"*—without which, *"no person can be held to answer for any criminal offence."* Fraud being a *criminal offence,* he who commits it, is a *criminal;* and cannot, according to the constitution, the paramount "law of the land," be "deprived of his liberty," *"unless by presentment or indictment of a grand jury,"* and *"the judgment of his peers,"* or petit jury, as in other criminal cases. The law, therefore, by which fraudulent debtors, as such, are "deprived of their liberty," at the will of their creditors, is a direct violation of the above mentioned provisions of the constitution.

No discreet man will give credit to *one* in whose *honesty,* or in whose ability to pay, he has *no confidence.* If the *honesty,* or the *ability* of the *creditee* should be doubted, no prudent man would become his *creditor,* because of his power to *imprison,* in the event of an attempted fraud by the *debtor.* It follows then, that *character* and *property* are the basis of mercantile *credit,* and that the power to imprison either the *honest* or the fraudulent debtor, constitutes no part of the *consideration* of the contract between the parties.

The misfortune of the debtor, is a common hazard to both the contracting parties. The *ability* of the insolvent is the amount of the property he may happen to possess: which when given up to his creditors, he fulfils his original undertaking to the full extent of its meaning; and the deficiency of the debtor's property to pay all his debts, is the measure of the misfortunes of the debtor, which by the original understanding of the parties, falls to the share of the creditors.

The *moral turpitude* of the debtor *begins* where his honesty ends; and it is only then that he justly becomes obnoxious to punishment. If he attempts to withhold his property from his creditors, or to secrete it in order to evade the payment of his debts, he ceases to be an honest unfortunate debtor—becomes a *criminal,* and ought to be prosecuted and punished "by due process of law in *criminal cases.*"

That your memorialists beg leave further to remark, that any law would contravene the constitution which would allow an individual whose property had been taken by a *thief*, to *imprison the offender* "without presentment or indictment of a grand jury" without *trial* for the alleged *crime*—without "the judgment of his peers"—but barely at the will of the injured party, and during the pleasure of the prosecutor: and that the provisions of the constitution which guard the *rights* and *liberty* of a *thief*, ought equally to protect those of a *criminal* charged with committing *fraud* against his creditor.

"Nothing," says a learned English writer, can be a stronger proof of the inexpediency of *imprisonment for debt*, than the introduction of those occasional insolvent laws which have originated merely from the humanity and compassion of the legislature, for the sufferings of miserable and helpless debtors." If the evils arising from that law are equal in number to the statutes intended to counteract them, they may well be considered as almost incalculable. "Those laws in England, originated in the reign of Elizabeth. From Charles II. to George III. *one* such act was passed (on an average) every four and a half years"; and were all the insolvent laws which have been made in the several States of the Union, collected and compiled, they would probably exceed in bulk all the volumes of the late revised laws of this State.

What more conclusively can prove the existence and the magnitude of the evils of imprisonment for debt, than those repeated legislative efforts to counteract them? What more fully illustrates the futility of those attempts, than the present existing evil effects of the law in question? What more than centuries of unavailing legislative labor, can expose the fallacy of the hope to obviate *effects* while the *cause* from which they proceed is permitted to survive? And what, more than the failure of all tried means, can emphatically indicate the propriety of "laying the axe at the root of the tree of evil," as the only untried and most certain means to destroy its fruit.

Your memorialists are fully and firmly convinced, that the total abolishment of imprisonment for debt, is the only measure by which its numerous train of wrongs and miseries can be destroyed; and for the reasons we have assigned, and others which we could state, we beg leave respectfully and unequivocally to declare, that the law of imprisonment for debt, violates the unalienable rights of your constituents—contravenes the provisions of the constitution, "the supreme law of the land"—is inefficient as a coercive measure—useless to the creditor—oppressive to the debtor—injurious to both, and has been productive of a demoralizing influence on the people of every country in which its existence has been permitted, and ought therefore to be entirely abolished.

That both houses of the Legislature have expressed the like opinion, we know; but the reasons why such a law has been permitted to be in force, so long after the Legislature have declared that it ought to be repealed, we do not know. Yet so the facts are. In the year 1818, so much of Governor Clinton's message as related to imprisonment for debt, was referred to a joint committee of the Senate and Assembly. That committee reported, and brought in a bill to abolish imprisonment for debt, and to punish fraudulent debtors: which bill passed the Senate by an *unanimous vote*—the reason why it was not acted on in the Assembly does not appear. The subject however was permitted to rest until the last session of the Legislature, when the Assembly declared by a large vote, "that imprisonment for debt ought to be abolished."

Your memorialists therefore confidently hope, and earnestly and respectfully pray, that the said law may be *entirely abolished.*

Signed by order of the Meeting,
JOHN STEARNS, *President.*
M. M. NOAH,
BARNABAS BATES,
Vice-Presidents
JAMES RYAN,
J. M. BROWN,
Secretaries

98. Benjamin Rodman

One hundred days in prison have confirmed my views on imprisonment for debt

The following passage was written by a man who was imprisoned in the New Bedford, Massachusetts, jail in 1840 for a debt to a local bank. The author, Benjamin Rodman, described himself as a substantial property owner. It is likely that most imprisoned debtors were men too poor and lacking in the necessary resources to take up pen and ink either to describe or to protest their situation.

There remain in this jail very few poor debtors. How it happens I cannot tell; but of those that come, some find help to bail them out, though poor as need be; and some intend to stay and pay their debts with their liberty. The story of almost all is instructive. One, still here, could give a lesson to legislators, and show them they arm the basest of men against the friendless. He owed something for house rent in the country. His landlord removed to town and opened a Rum House in spite of the law, for he has no license. As an apology for a tavern, he has a stable. The poor man offered to live with him, and leave half his wages in payment of his debt. It was agreed to;—but what shall be your wages?—I will work for $15 a month.—I will not give it, you shall work for $13.—I cannot afford it; I have a family.—If you will not work at my price, I will put you in jail for the old debt.—You may do it!—It was done. He has been here a month or more. His wife is out at service, and is an industrious, worthy woman. Being a farmer and laborer, it is hard for him to earn anything here. Still necessity is the mother of invention. He has now contrived a way by which he thinks he can earn a dollar a week, and pay the board of his child!

It is a mercy for this poor man to be here; for I can scarcely

From B[enjamin] Rodman, *A Voice from the Prison of the New Bedford Jail* (New Bedford: Benjamin Lindsey, 1840), 48, 58, 59.

recollect a single rum-seller in town, but he bears the evidence in his face or elsewhere of being his own customer; verifying the proverb, "Curses like chickens come home to roost." Those whom they employ frequently follow their example; and the jail is a more enviable abode than an unlicensed rum-selling tavern.

Strange to say, some of the *owners* of these nuisances are men of wealth; I mean owners of the buildings. But their day also is at hand. "I have seen the foolish taking root; but suddenly I cursed his habitation,"—is the language of the Scriptures. . . .

Conclusion

Reader, I have detained you long. Little did I think that my leaves would run to their present number. But as the occurrences of the day fastened themselves on my mind, I could only throw them off again through the aid of my pen. And I have selected for publication those only, which I think have a bearing on the subjects that are closely connected with the happiness of our community. And though my life has been, as it were, in a cell, yet it has been neither inactive nor solitary. If I have written much, it is because I have thought much and seen much; and what I have learned here seems to be a part of all life, and a portion of all the evils which blight the prosperity even of a republic. No place so small as to escape them, none so large as not to be overshadowed by them. One hundred days' residence in the prison has confirmed all the views, which I had at my entrance, on the subject of imprisonment for debt. It is the cause of more villainy, more bankruptcy, more poverty, more drunkenness, and more misery than any other institution in the commonwealth; and simply because it is the rod of tyrants, and its fruits are oppression, corruption, fraud, and fear, which grow only in the soil that tyranny waters.

The prison has been to me a link between the bright and the dark side of human life. Few have the courage to embrace it; all, or nearly all, fly from it. Could the educated, the refined, the elegant make free to enter, they would learn what makes the darkness within it. They would then see it is but the reflected or *absorbed* darkness from without. And from the window that places the iron between them and the world, they would see all the vices which are *represented* within. They would see the arts and the power by which the little oppress the *less.* They would learn how mighty is the arm of the law, and how unequal is the scale of justice. They would see how the public good is prostituted to individual gain, and how the public peace is bartered for *private* pay. And then they would *apply themselves* to the task of correcting the evils, that weigh like an incubus upon the bosom of society. Not because there is not a power of virtue in the system, but because technicality and form and ceremony have so clogged the vital current, that truth and freedom appear only as dreams.

Could they but see things as they exist in the unvarnished coloring, in which all things are seen *here,* there is not a class in the community but what would be aroused to more exertion than they had before imagined themselves capable of. They would join as a band of brothers, regardless of all party differences, aye, *as one man* they would go forth and *uproot* the evils, which are darkening our land. I charge them upon no particular class, for the very age seems to be marked with forgetfulness of duty, and we are all involved. And there is no way to promote the public welfare so effectually, as to pass and put in force laws of wisdom and mercy, and let honest men execute them.

Aid to Paupers

99. Baltimore House of Refuge

We do not war against the severest safeguards of person and property

A bewildering variety of voluntary associations, dedicated to ameliorating the lot of deserving paupers of all ages and ethnic background, flourished in the nation's cities during the second quarter of the nineteenth century.

From the *First Annual Report of the Managers of the [Baltimore] House of Refuge* (Baltimore: James Lucas, 1852), 6–17.

These organizations were typically led by benevolent, strongly religious gentlemen of the propertied classes. As the following document indicates, such men blamed social distress on individual fault rather than on society. Characteristically they dispensed modest material benefits supplemented by the social message that the poor were the authors of their own misery.

In the name of the God of the poor—the light and the balm of the erring—we have laid this corner-stone of a temple of humanity. From this summit, that looks down on our city's thrift and cares, and urgent race of life, we offer on an altar of pity the incense of anxious duty, of guardian charity. Here under this free firmament and the attesting heavens, we bow in a dedication that shames not these skies. We come bearing at heart the young and misguided and endangered, without shelter from harshness and wretchedness, unshielded against ruin. We come in worship of the holy tenet that every human being is the shrine of a soul and the material for celebrating an immortal destiny. We gather to this field of hope, listening to the Supreme dictate, *that we live not for ourselves alone.*

On such a height as this, uplifted to a calm that blended with the divine office of the hour, the delegate of God wreathed the sceptre of a Savior's majesty with the moral glory of the sermon of the Mount—the perfect message of Deity—the digest of all christianity's wisdom for solace and warning and guidance. There a heart was opened for the humble and defenceless. There the tender economy of Heaven enfolds earth's thwarted wayfarer—not those most whose path prosperity lights, and whose career is luxurious ease, and whose wealth would win to wealth's usurping idolatry. There spoke he who claimed the young spirits for his moulding, and their wants for his care, in the fond accents, "Suffer little children to come unto me." In that faith we move. The melodies of that Divinity wake us to action. Here we plant our trust for a beneficent fruit, and all around gives type and token of a rich attainment. This quiet, this genial, eminence—so crowned by nature with favor to our purpose, and where she seems to have set her seal to give us assurance of success—would beckon us to effort and kindle us to zeal. How goodly this prospect that is bound on its brow! Not a perspective of towering fastness or of martial terror, but of the towers of sacred temples and industrial structures—an array of a city's illustrated toil—in graceful architecture or substantial homes, the triumph and embodiment of taste and utility. Here before the subjects of our patronage is an ever fresh painting of a moral lesson—the picture of all that is promised to labor and order and peaceful zeal—from this lodgment of our enterprise ever to greet their eyes and stir their ambition—the happy plain of the future inviting them in contrast with the fearful waste their steps have left! All, indeed, promises well to our cordial intent, and we will cherish the good omens.

What philanthropists among us have yearned for, and what in misery and peril has in startling characters been defined as the great social need, now dawns on us—we salute it at least in the horizon. We have gone thus far up the arduous height of our task, and Baltimore at least begins to vindicate her wisdom and her humanity, mingling the soundest policy with redeeming charity. She will cherish a House of Refuge, as an appendage of christian civilization—a resource defensive and beneficent, a conservatory, belonging to the very religion of the social state. Late as we are to reach this sphere of duty, we shall yet win the honors, as we assuredly shall achieve the kindly fruits, of this circumspect benevolence.

Let our purpose be understood. We do not war against punishment, nor against the severest safeguards of person and property. But we would forestall crime by intercepting the growth of the criminal nature, and by averting and estranging the criminal purpose. We would take the pliant spirit of youth, and gain it to virtue through conscious capability of virtue, and infused or re-animated self-respect. By kind concern we would make the froward young, communicants of our common humanity. We would install denizens of the kingdom of good-will and charity those thrown outside of the wall of a close and callous polity—who are caste as squalid refuse on the strand of life to drift on dark seas of bitterness, to coasts of a dreary destiny. We bring into our communion of humanity all who are daringly rebels to parental authority, or are made vagrants by parental worthlessness.

Such is the fold of this benevolence. So would we seek the fountains of guilt and combat with the evil spirits that hover upon the career of the young. We wish to prevent waywardness being nurtured into profligacy; we would save the youthful heart from hardening into the rigid and miserable bias of crime. We would not that those should be labelled for ignominy and reckless infamy on whom have come the first blemish of guilt, nor let the first and slight invading taint be aggravated by chafing and crushing sternness into a leprous ruin. In such a range and culture as this, control and restraint may reform, proving more than coercive and vindictive—to mitigate and exalt, not to scourge—to conquer by benignant persuasion, not to deaden by the soreness of suffering and the chill horrors of privation.

Not only does this policy of our self-protection demand this generous discipline, but it is pressed upon us by every view of duty that religion enlightens. In such views, it is not enough that we have an armament of social strength against wrong, nor keep up a bristling front of criminal appliances, but we have to remember that we are here militant for good, to prevent evil, and not merely to hunt it down with the vengeful spear of power or daunt and revolt it by the terrors of torture. Charity which hopes all things for amendment is the firmament of christianity; charity which proclaims capacity for amendment is the light of that firmament, brightning and adorning the avenue to a joyous, restorative eternity. It is the sweetest tone of the Savior's harp of promise. That charity is a sovereign duty.

We mourn over the pangs of that night of suffocating frenzy which, in the "Black Hole of Calcutta," cut off its victims from Heaven's vital air and left them to die in panting, maddened, agony. We dwell with horror upon that feat of summary chivalry of the French which history has given to the chapters of infamy—by which the hunted Arab foe was stifled in the refuge of their cave. The packed hold of the slave-ship revolts us where fiends, in guise and sacrilege of the human form, range as in beastly piles the reeking rows of human breathing flesh, in foul and stinted air, to be tortured each moment to the verge of death, and then to breathe again to suffer tortures over—all this the heart sickens at and fancy faints in picturing, and all this pillage of human right is a theme too black with demon savageness to be treated with aught but riving vengeance. But what to all this—where cruelty wreaks itself on the harmless—is the wrong of sovereign society, which dooms to eternal death, after a foreground of reprobation and infamy, spirits whom that very wrong first depraves? What is all the suffocation of this passing physical frame to the stifling of the spirit by moral contamination, the infusion of the deadly plague—by crushing the nerve, and by tramping down every bounding impulse, of self-respect—of hopeful elasticity? Yet such is the deep horror, the transcendent sin, of the penitentiary system, which blends the young in guilt with the veteran offender, the cankered profligate—levels all grades of criminality and obliquity—stamps all with the like damning stigma, and alike brings all into debasement, deeply desperate debasement.

Can such methodical poisoning be less than heinous wrong? What is it but dire outrage under seal of State; and ferocity authenticated by power? Is it worthy of a christian civilization? Can society be less than torpid not to rouse itself to such transgression, and on its social honor feel the rank offence of such pollution? Lighted then by these humanities do these wrongs thus define themselves in hideous lineaments—thus does our imminent duty glare upon us.

But treat the evil and the exigency on the narrow computation of grudging, pecuniary, expediency. Count the multiplying perils, the increased outlays, from thus making penitentiaries recruiting grounds for crime and endowments for villainy, and seminaries for headlong pupils in all daring and lasting rebellion against person and substance—for keeping supplied the bands of youthful auxiliaries and tenders to the old and practised criminals. What then shall we, as selfish tremblers, or as sordid calculators, conclude for our due and urgent action?

Punishment rarely does much with the trained and habitual offender of years, to better his taste, or give sway to his conscience, for a virtuous change. Seldom there is reformation more than a merely abstract purpose—to serve as a charm for theory, and to give a Corinthian finish to the philosophy of retributive justice—no matter how that punishment be graced and tempered with every proffered resource for the mind's recreation, and for rectifying the heart.

Here, and only here, in this our sphere of effort, is the home for a system of reformation. We invest the very germ of crime. We touch with enervating discipline the tendency to delinquency. We insinuate mitigated and gradually better temperaments by raising into government, and enduing with attractions, new tastes, through changed pursuits and engaging forms of industry. We baffle crime and extinguish it. We save men for society—souls for eternity. Is not this a mission worthy of our christian nobility? With less than not only an aspiration, but a struggle, for such consummations are we unstained of guilt before a compassionate, all-encompassing, Heaven? We have but to eye and measure the ruthlessness of our neglect, to hasten with atoning speed, and with an alacrity that must be thrice blessed, to the rescue and the purification.

Stern as may be the walls that are to grow to their frowning stature upon this hill, they will shut in no harsh nor penal area. Our restraints do not punish. We are the guardians, the friendly instructors, of these captives to our sympathy. Our monarchy, though absolute, is cordial—all our dispensations speak that spirit and signify a present care for our wards, and a happy future for their improved natures.

To our Institution, as an adjunct to the criminal executive, the Maryland Legislature has accorded an office as comprehensive as gracious. In the governors of this Institution is inaugurated and embodied a new organic grace of the Maryland sovereignty, by their being thus made allies of the judicial power. The acts of the Legislature under which we are now embarked in our ministry, are of 8th February, 1831, and 7th March, 1850. They will be found to bring under our control, with powers of apprenticing at the time the stay in the Refuge is over:

1. Children convicted of criminal offences.

2. Those who are committed as street beggars or vagrants.

3. Children whose parents ask their admission for incorrigible habits or vicious conduct.

4. Those with parents, from moral depravity or otherwise, incapable or unwilling to take care of them.

Wide and varied is the charge thus appointed to us! What misery, what infirmities, what sad necessities, are to make their appeal to us and claim the nurture and safeguard of our retreat! Who has not been pained as his eye has rested on the children who stroll in vagrancy and beggary along our streets, abandoned to wild neglect, lounging listless and reckless through the rounds of a mere animal existence, pinched and subdued by want, embedded in ragged and filthy degradation, encrusting them too deeply, it would seem, for a hope that any persuasion, however kind, or exhortation, the most thrilling, could penetrate to the soul that may yet twinkle under that whelming obstruction.

But, look at the detected and conquered child—shrinking and trembling at the bar of Criminal Justice—startled at his guilt, as first seen in its imposing features, symbolled in the grave array and peremptory machinery of judicature. But however guilt's aspect may now appal him, even to hate of it, the law dedicates him to permanent and systematic guilt—for he is to wear the brand of the felonious herd—the only fit signet and career by the State assessed for debasement by the State enjoined! No longer shall such assassinations of the young soul be tolerated! Here, in blessed Providence, is shelter for the neglected and disdained; here is disciplinary kindness to dissolve the torpor that was technically cursed as impracticable profligacy—here is assiduous care to touch the chords of scarred and lacerated nature—to vivify the moral sense, foully enveloped, almost buried under misery, and almost dead in the obtuseness to which want and contumely break down the outcast child of neglect and sorrow! No! the eye shall again brighten with the energy and the vision of Hope—moisten to the dirge of memory as it pours from the recess of the past, or shed the tear of gratitude for a home to him who never knew a home before. His young heart shall again have its native tides, and beat to the harmonies of the social world, as their echoes visit his retired nook. The redeemed child shall feel the justice that reigns around him in vigilance, and encompasses him with support; and his spirit shall recline on the protective sympathy that anoints his griefs and anticipates his wants, and is balmy strength to his intelligence!

The virtue and consequent social order of a community are not to be achieved by interdicts or terrors of the law. That process gives but a frail tenure to civil security—*the end and the glory of all government.* Intercept vice, and do so by checking and by forestalling vicious habits. Infuse inclinations and tastes whose current tends to good, and, for that, invite to occupations that wean and lure from mischievous plots and yearnings. The ranks of marauders and of the licentious will then have no material to fill or to keep them up—and society will know a peace pledged and fortified for its best safeguard upon the love, or the habit, of virtue.

Our sister States are daily rallying to these truths, and enroll these refuges as primary and commanding muniments of the public order—not dealing with them as benignant experiments, or play-grounds of philanthropy, to gratify humane humors—but as essential resources, and as dedications and structures of sacred duty.

The city of New York opened its refuge in 1825, and since that epoch up to the 1st of January 1851, five thousand and fifteen inmates have been under its care—371 leaving it for employ, as apprentices or otherwise, in 1850, and 411 now remaining. The last year's expenses for the institution are $26,000. Its endowment from the State and city is munificent, only one item of resource being yielded by the institution, the labor of the boys, amounting to $8,700. But the patronage of the State supplied means for purchases of land to the amount of nearly $13,500.

The city of Philadelphia opened its refuge in 1828, and as far as the close of 1849 had had under charge 2,500 youth. The annual expense is nearly at the rates of the New York refuge outlay; Philadelphia county giving yearly to it $13,000, the State $6,000, and the labor of inmates yielding about $7,000; and it had, for 1849, 355 inmates. But a larger endowment of a yearly sum of

$40,000 from the State, and $20,000 from the city, is agitated and expected, and a new refuge is contemplated, with an appropriation of $220,000.

Cincinnati has, however, crowned herself with a pre-eminent lustre, for she, from her county resources alone, yearly supplies a tribute of $60,000—and Ohio, in her wise support of her social defences, is liberally the patron of this great cause.

Massachusetts is equally signalized as the friend of the youthful delinquent—and Boston had in the State Reform School, at the end of 1850, 440 youth; their average age being 12¾ years, which corresponds very nearly to the average in that particular of the other refuges. The larger number in most refuges are orphans, and in Philadelphia at least one-half are intractable children, committed by the parents.

The period of stay in these institutions is generally eighteen months, when the inmates are either returned to parents or bound as apprentices. From the data I have given we may decide how many yearly are discharged upon the walks of social life, and gain the freedom of the world's privileges and emulous toils. The statistics show that at least three-fourths are redeemed, and become permanently respectable members of society—and when we learn that the same statistics show that the larger number of criminals fall within the period between the ages of 15 and 20 years, we may estimate the glorious beneficence that is wrought. And we count this host of trophies and triumphs with a more anxious intentness when we deduce from the black arithmetic of crime in the city of New York, filling up the period between 1835 and 1844 (including both years,) that while population increased 35½, crime outstripped it and increased 354–1000 per cent.

All these States have in their judicial and moral economy lit up these stars over the dark fate of youthful delinquency; and so they have honored and advanced the supreme purpose of government, and have done what its most illustrious care embraces. In the institutions thus consecrated by them, the pupils of their charge (as is our purpose) are classed by sex, and by grades of conduct and of disposition. Their time is divided between education in plain and useful branches, religious instruction, recreation by physical exercise, and by books cheering and engaging, and learning trades and occupations of light and easy toil—so chosen that no undue portion of time shall be absorbed in mere drudgery, and that they shall not feel a slavery, while in fact they are but under a parental sway and friendly guardianship. Their minds and natures are the predominant concern in the control they experience.

We have attained much in procuring these grounds and commanding the construction of a building, as the home of our charity, large enough for *immediate* wants, as we now estimate them. But the building must exceed these first limits, and that, perhaps, at a very early day. For that, and immediately for the ample and sure *support* of our institution, we need means: and we *must* have them. We use this imperative language pointedly—and because society *must* have the protection we would here build up for it. Government must, in unison with our aims and meeting our requirements, work out in our adventure its prominent and evident duty. Even in the closest view of expediency, by the lessening of the numbers and the costly punishments of matured offenders, there is the clearest inducement for the readiest and most liberal appropriation in aid of our enterprise.

The thickening evil of crime throughout our land summons the public solicitude to weigh all devices, and to ponder every pertinent philosophy, for reducing it. The stock of recurring crime is, of the native growth, large enough to be coped with; but we have it extraneously increased. We invite the stranger to our free hemisphere, and many of welcome worth plant their fortunes under our skies. But in the swarms of immigrants, the mass of whom visit our shores for happier days and secure and bounteous industry, there are necessarily many who prowl here for the chances of luckier idleness and easier prey; and who leave in our cities a needy and vicious sediment. Whether worthless or improvident, the paupers multiply, of such qualities, their squalid forces upon us, prone to glide into criminals; and thus we have a new and fertile nuisance to overcome. This incumbrance is to be aggravated to us by the European despotism, now more watchful and potent than ever; since, where the local tyranny falters it is reinforced from adjacent tyrannies, whether it be the ruffian majesty of Russia, or the stubborn and growling absoluteness of Austria. This despotism scourges to desperation, and then drives its subjects from want to crime.

The evil thus swells daily, and becomes more threatening, in this foreign direction; for in the torrent of the opened sluice, all species of humanity are drifted with the miscellaneous influx into our borders. The statistics of the Refuge of New York, for 1849, show the vastly predominant proportion of foreign inmates for that year (169 out of 208). That feature is explained by the view that I now have taken. In all this and our intrinsic increase of crime, is there not a most ominous intimation of darkening peril, and an urgent warning for measures of relief? We need show no enhanced reason for having a liberal endowment from our State, and from our citizens.

Do not the highest duty and sanctions—does not holy religion —command the tribute? In the thrifty chase of life and its golden triumphs, we forget to look *above* the earthly level of our eager track, and forget that that track is in the bounds of our probation and in the territory of a Divine superintendency. We mean to utter no homilies. But, where such profound humane interests are staked, the plain truth of duty and of default must be canvassed and proclaimed—sternly and unreservedly proclaimed. Let all awake from sordid and callous reveries. Let us rend the film of arrogant and thoughtless prosperity, and interpret the disparity of heaven's dispensations, as they figure in men's contrasted fortunes.

The rich are not rich because they are favorites of Deity. The code of the throne of Deity announces the reverse, but it proclaims *duties parallel with the prosperity and commensurate with the wealth; and tremendous is the rich man's responsibleness under the delegated agency that comes with riches.* The abundance of prosperity is designed in the councils above for good and diffusion, and that destination is inscribed on it by the signet of Providence as distinctly as an invoice appropriates the merchandize it describes, or as the marks and superscription of bales and boxes govern their delivery. The prosperous were not meant to be mere receptacles of inert treasure, animated purses and gorgeous exchequers of Providence for earthly exhibition. *Charity, beneficence, is a strict and inexorable duty*—not an optional grace nor discretional action—for in the great province of the code of God there are *no imperfect obligations*. They are relative to the laws of men, and to their positive enforcements.

We *owe* aid to our fellow-men; and, owing it to them under Heaven's dictate, *we owe the debt to God;* and Heaven takes note not only of what is thus rendered "to the least of its creatures," but a fearful note, too, of what is omitted to be paid. God, in writing on every man's heart, defines his mandates of benevolence; which social law is forced to put to the title of imperfect obligations. In every soul he has set a tissue of chords that are moved by his breath and vibrate to his descended will. That nervous and responsive frame is conscience—and that breath the voice of conscience, the whisper of God—*the only moral sense*—the only instructor and sanction for the right and the wrong, under natural religion. Here, then, in the blended dominion of sympathy, and of this inspired suggestion of right, in the very and direct communion with Divinity, our sense of duty in all the charities springs into being and power.

Be honest, then, to God, as to man—that honesty which expands for the whole heart's wide province—which alone is coordinate with the reign of "peace and good will on earth"—which concedes no dispensation, and is tender to no lagging tribute, and endures no compromise. Every unheeded tear that gives signal of misery falls on the record of the eternal account. Every slighted sigh of the torn heart lingers in the vaults above to be a groan of remorse to the hard of heart.

Let wealth bless in its issues of benevolence, and in cheerful buoyancy the blessing will be reflected on the man of wealth. With such secretion of happiness to others, the plethora of success will not oppress—no surfeit of good fortune will sicken. The tedium of opulent ease will pass away—no distempered fancy will haunt with shadowy dread—and here is the specific for all corroding solicitudes that wait on the rich man's hours. Let the rich be the purveyors—the financial ministry to God's economy—

and then, but absolutely *then only,* is their credential sealed for joy on earth, and their "hard entry into Heaven," God's favor widens with eternity's welcome.

What is individual duty is no less *the obligation of State.* "They judge not the cause of the fatherless, yet they prosper; *the right of the needy* they do not judge. Shall not my soul be avenged on *such a nation* as this?" And does not the slight of the duties we are now commending load every hour with the avenging scourge, and in our midst verify the Prophet's retributive words? Crime, rife, abounding, and exulting, raises its demon crest and over-awes every moment of social existence, affrighting all sense of security. And all this because a *grovelling economy* counts the present cost of duty and security; and, to future and gradual and consolidated safety, prefers war with the fiend in the very core of society and in the very sanctuary of social law.

Shall these things longer be? Let Maryland come up into line with the civilized—the christian—march of our sisters of the Union. Let her not longer lag in darkness—middle-age darkness—in sordid hesitancy—as if money were the pearl of the soul, or could prove a treasure while theft and murder are invited to challenge it. Such things shall not longer be. All omens tell us so. The scene that animates us proclaims the end of such evil—the air around us is instinct with the wish of all angels for our triumph. Charity, in vestments of Redemption, blessed of God himself, opens our temple of humanity—and on its altars shall ever bloom and brighten the true, *because the practical,* "beauty of holiness."

Radical Social Reform

100. Stephen Simpson

Profits of labour accruing to the idle capitalist

On July 1, 1828, a Working Men's party was organized by trade unionists in Philadelphia. Over the next five years this development was duplicated

From Stephen Simpson's reply to the Philadelphia Working Men's Party, in the Boston *Working Man's Advocate,* October 9, 1830.

in large cities and small in most states of the Union. Not all the new party's members were workers, by any means, while the candidates it selected for office were as often as not of the middle class. In view of the fact too that the party fell into the hands of transparent opportunists in a number of cities, it is not surprising that questions have been raised about its authenticity. The circumstances surrounding the following selection provide a classic illustration of the issue. The document is a letter by Stephen Simpson accepting nomination as congressional candidate of the Philadelphia Working Men in 1830. Simpson had become well known for his publication the previous year of *The Working Man's Manual*, a sharp critique of American capitalistic society.

> *Mr. S. Simpson, formerly Editor of the Columbian Observer, has been selected as one of the candidates for Congress, from Philadelphia. On being apprized of his nomination, by a Committee of the Workingmen, he addressed the following letter to the Committee. Mr. Simpson has come out boldly and decidedly, and we cannot too highly express our admiration of his frankness and sincerity. The letter contains a luminous and accurate view of all the great objects for which the "Workingmen" are contending. We recommend it to the careful perusal of our readers.*

MR. SIMPSON'S REPLY
To the Working Men's committee of correspondence

TO MESSRS. GEO. GILES AND WM. J. YOUNG,
On behalf of the delegation of Working Men, for the 1st Congressional District

Gentlemen,—It is with pleasure that I acknowledge the receipt of your letter of the 13th instant, apprizing me of having been nominated to represent the first district in the 22d congress; requesting to know, whether it is my intention to comply with the wishes of the delegation, and expressing a desire to have my opinions upon such questions as may appear of most interest to the working men. I will answer you in that spirit of frankness, which has ever induced me to shun concealment of what I thought, or to fain what I did not think, or could not feel.

It is with sincere gratification, and a pride founded on the noblest of human principles, that I reciprocate the views and motives which have actuated you on this occasion, in favour of the purity of the elective right, and the unrestricted freedom of the popular suffrage. To be deemed worthy to represent, in the national legislature, a large portion of the people who have publicly renounced all factious distinctions, and merged all party animosities, for the sake of general principles of sound practical utility, as conducive to the benefit of society as to themselves, is an honour *in itself*, detached from all considerations of success. It forms an additional source of gratification to me, however, to receive this as the spontaneous and pure offering of your confidence and good will; unsolicited by me, and free from all taint of intrigue, bargain, and management. As such, I need not say I receive it with pleasure, and accept it with pride. These emotions, however, are distinct from any participation of success, which could scarcely be indulged, in a first canvass by a new party; and that too, in a district *originally cut out to serve the purpose of my opponent;* and whose subservency to the *system* of *trading politics*, threatens to procure it the opprobius appellation of a "rottenborough"; to avert the disgrace of which, you have so meritoriously exerted yourselves.

The hope, however, of giving a gradual extension to your principles, and procuring a consummation of your views, is amply sufficient to induce me to peril, what many may term a hopeless canvass, against the management and machinations of an old and expert *trader in votes.* Whether represented, or not, in the councils of the nation, your votes ought to be counted in the ballot boxes, as dissentients from a system of corruption, if it is only to vindicate the honest portion of our district from the vices imputed to it, and to show the world that there is still within it a redeeming spirit that may finally exalt it in the scale of public virtue. Besides, what becomes of the freedom of suffrage, if there exists no plurality of candidates? To take it for granted, that our district is totally abandoned to profligate politics, would be as unjust, as it is romantic to imagine it susceptible of an *instantaneous reform.* I conceive our path to be a plain and open one, with no windings to perplex us,—*to do our duty to* OUR CONSCIENCES and OUR

COUNTRY, regardless of the consequences, and only solicitous of success, so far as success may benefit our country.

Let us proceed, therefore, as if the incumbent had *no life-estate* in the district of his own cutting out—as if the system of *trading politics* and the *license power* had no existence. Let us proceed on the exploded and old fashioned assumption, the POLITICAL MORALITY is absolutely necessary to the liberty of a free people, and the duration of a noble republic, now rioting in the lustful vigor of its youth, quivering on the precipiece of experiment, and hourly falling a prey to the flattery of parasites, and the temptations and vices of demagogues. We shall at least have the co-operation of the virtuous and the wise; we shall have the assistence of the patriot, and the sympathy of the philanthropist; and if we fail, our conscience and our country, (no mean consolation,) will sanction and approve the effort. Considerations of this character have influenced me to accept your nomination, with little expectation that our ticket will prevail; yet under a full conviction that such a cause deserves to succeed, and that time and perseverance will bring a reward.

Coinciding with you, that the electors have a right to be thoroughly apprized of the views of their candidates, I most freely yield to such a development of mine, as the limits of this communication admit; confining myself to those questions of predominating interest, which now engross the public mind. These I apprehended to be.

1. The profits of labour accruing to the *idle* capitalist, instead of the industrious working man.

2. The subtraction from the profits of labour, by the PAPER CURRENCY SYSTEM.

3. The reduction of TAXES, indirect, covert, and unseen, but not the less oppressive to the working man.

4. The *abolishment of imprisonment for debt,* as proposed by RICHARD M. JOHNSON, in the Senate of the United States.

5. A system of GENERAL EDUCATION.

6. A well organized MILITIA SYSTEM.

Upon these points permit me to touch briefly. How is it that the sons of industry are the children of sorrow? Ought this to be, in a land so free and so fertile, and so profusely blessed by the gracious hand of a beautiful God?

That society is at present constituted on an unjust and erroneous basis, and that its original principles have suffered perversion, from causes inimical to the general happiness, may be seen by the narrow streets, noxious alleys and fetid courts, as impervious to the winds of heaven as to the feelings of humanity, which make up so large a portion of our *great cities*—where, in space too small for health, and too dismal for happiness, are cooped up in narrow boxes that immense population, *which produces all the wealth*—who build palaces for the rich, frigates for the nation, and ships for our merchants—who produce at least *one half* of the national wealth, and pay one half of the public taxes—and yet are doomed, by the perversion of a good government, to drag out life, beset by all the evils that flow from penury, disease and incessant labour; without the intervening enjoyment of one of those pleasures, which the product of their toil procures to the opulent.

When I contrast this condition of the working men with those who *never labour,* who *produce nothing,* and yet *consume all*—who live in castles, roll in carriages, and monopolize all the goods of life—how can the conclusion be avoided, that the working people labour under oppression, that their rights have been wrested from them, and that *industry,* instead of being the *basis of wealth,* as in the olden time, and under just principles, has now become the source of poverty. That *extortion,* combined with *speculation,* are the agents that operate to strip labour of three-fourths of its earnings. That CAPITAL has unsurped the place of labour,—and that *bank credits,* drawn at sight, upon the industry, and wages, and wealth of the people, are the radical causes of that misery in society, which results from squalid poverty on the one hand, and exorbitant fortunes on the other.

Nor are these evils confined to those classes of *Working men,* who preside within the borders of our cities: they are shared largely by our *farmers* and *gardeners;* who toil to make the *bank capitalists* rich, and to keep themselves poor. The agriculturalist works for a *living,* but he makes fortunes for the speculator, the banker, and the capitalist for those, who, either from the force of law, or the influence of wealth, can indulge in the offensive exercise of *monopoly*. Without, therefore, aiming at doing wrong unto others, as our adversaries have alleged against us, we have certainly just grounds for drawing a *party line*, that will enable you, through your representatives, to procure a restoration of those rights that have been taken from you by the creation of *privileged incorporations*, or otherwise; and give to you, and your children, their proper enjoyments in life, under the sanction of a constitution that guarantees *equality*, on the basis of justice, to all her citizens.

In producing this state of things, no doubt exists, that the PAPER CURRENCY SYSTEM, has been chiefly instrumental. It unsettles the standard of value; and by the power of contraction and expansion on the monied world, keeps property fluctuating, so as to plunder the working man, and profit the capitalist. It affects *prices* injuriously—it imposes a *tax* on the labour of all; and while it builds palaces, it causes a thousand hovels to rise where one mansion of content and competency springs up as its fruit. On another occasion, I shall be more diffuse on this subject.

The reduction of taxes, I should say their *abolishment*, upon all the NECESSARIES of LIFE, or those comforts which habit has made *necessaries*, is an important object of the Workingmen. The duty on *salt, molasses, tea, sugar, wine, coffee*, and other commodities of domestic comfort, ought now to be repealed by Congress, while the treasury is overflowing, the republic at peace, and the states wrangling about the division of a spoil, that ought never to have been gathered from the hard earnings of an industrious people.

The *abolishment* of IMPRISONMENT FOR DEBT, is another important question that ought to rouse the combined energies of every American, who venerates the principles of liberty, on which our government is founded; or looks back with humiliation and sorrow to the iron despotism of the feudal ages, in which this barbarous custom had its origin. Colonel Johnson has won the gratitude of freemen, for his labours to procure this great and desirable object. A law that makes poverty a crime, and a poor man a felon, after those very laws have made poverty inevitable, is not only cruel and oppressive, but absurd and revolting.

A system of *general education,* one would hardly imagine, could meet with an opponent in an age so enlightened and so philanthropic—an age so distinguished for the *march of mind,* the diffusion of knowledge, and a severe scrutiny into all the principles that combine in the structure of society. And yet, wonderful to say, *public education for the people* has met with gothic adversaries, and illiberal, narrow minded traducers. Yet the extension of the lights of knowledge, *by popular education,* to all the people of the republic, has ever been the avowed object of all our most illustrious statesmen. It teems from the lips of the venerated Washington—it glows in the pen of the immortal Jefferson—it formed the daily toil and the midnight study of the lamented and great Clinton. The text of the friends of liberty was—*to enlighten the people is to promote and cement the public virtue!* The soundness of this text was never questioned *anterior* to the organization of your party. When public instruction was bestowed as the *boon of charity,* it found numerous advocates, and met with no opponents; but now, when you justly demand it as a *right*—and under our constitution it must be a *right* and not a charity—it is not only refused by some, but to our utter amazement its consequences are painted as baneful to the people, and depreciated as having a fatal tendency upon the good order of government! !

We seem to have resuscitated from the tomb of time the very spirit of the *feudal ages,* in the breasts of certain bigots, intolerants, aristocrats, and narrow minded *monopolists of knowledge,* who seem as adverse to giving the people LIGHT, as they are to paying them for their labour, in *hard money.* Actuated by this spirit of an era long past, it is pretended to have been suddenly discovered that *ignorance* is necessary to obedience, and that *public education* is incompatible with public virtue and public order! Sophistry like this, is too flimsy to call for confutation; but it reveals a fact that may be useful to us; that although we live under a free constitution, much of the leaven of despotism still remains among us, and that our *theoretical* freedom demands eternal vigilance to preserve it in practice. It is said, that a tax to support common schools would be an *Agrarian Law*, an unjust taking away from the wealth of the rich, for the benefit of the common people. On this principle, ALL laws are Agrarian laws; for the rich pay more than the poor individually, though not collectively. In particular, the *Southern Review*, which mixes up *rebellion and legitimacy* very strangely together; and is, at the same time, a champion for *anarchy and despotism*—has gone so far in its insidious misrepresentations, as to warn *men of property* against our views, as depredatory and unjust!

We must smile upon this false gloss upon our principles, even accompanied as it is, by an affection of solemn conviction; and an attempt to defeat our rights, by the pretext of wrong committed upon them, by imputing to us robbery and pillage. But we must learn to endure slander when conscious of *right*, and to go on in the straight path of reform, heedless of the solemn mummery of aristocrats, who would charge the people with plunder, when they crave the means of education; and *yet are themselves employed in lighting up the flames of a* CIVIL WAR; thus putting in jeopardy the *power of an entire people*, together with their lives and happiness. Such is the consistency of our opponents; such the logic of those who fear the people may become too enlightened to succumb to their deceptions.

A well organized militia system is a very important object to be attained by our united exertion.—The present one concentrates oppression upon the *Working Men*, without producing an iota of benefit to the commonwealth; but, on the contrary, is fertile in mischief, crime, and confusion. Acknowledged on all hands to be a disgrace to our state, we may hope that on this point, our views will be crowned with success by the next legislature of the state, or from an intelligent congress of our own choosing. Unanimity on this point can hardly be doubted.

In conclusion, permit me to remark, that one *object alone* of our united exertions ought to ensure veneration to your party, and success to your principles and your candidates,—that is, the restoration of a SOUND CURRENCY TO THE NATION, in place of that depreciated and rotten machine of exchange which now impoverishes the *productive classes*, and throws the reward of their labour into the pockets of the capitalist.

This accomplished, the Republic will soon be redeemed from the canker of luxury and the perils of profligate politics.

With much respect, I am, gentlemen,

Your friend and fellow citizen,
STEPHEN SIMPSON

Edge-Hill Cottage, Philadelphia County
September 15, 1830

101. THOMAS SKIDMORE AND ROBERT DALE OWEN
The world is not now overpeopled

The situation of the laboring poor was not on the agenda either of Democrats or Whigs. That fact may account for the prevalent tendency to discount as the ravings of fanatics contemporary exhortations to redress the social balance. Thomas Skidmore and Robert Dale Owen, leaders of the New York Working Men, were considered zealots. They had little use for each other, Owen feeling a profound distaste for Skidmore, who in his turn felt scorn for Owen. Skidmore was an uncompromising radical who would never forgive Owen his wealth, his "false views," and his role in reading Skidmore out of their party. Their argument over birth-control anticipates the modern dispute over the same issue between Marxists and liberals. Skidmore, like present-day radicals, regarded birth control as a spurious means of ameliorating the condition of the poor. Owen's *Moral Physiology* appears in regular print at the top of the page, while Skidmore's criticisms are at the bottom of the page, in numbered footnotes.

[You who believe] that violence and vice are inherent in human nature, and that nothing but laws and ceremonies prevent the

From Thomas Skidmore, *Moral Physiology Exposed and Refuted* (New York: Skidmore and Jacobus, 1831), 8, 9, 15–17, 44, 52, 53. Footnotes have been re-numbered for the convenience of the reader.

world from becoming a vast slaughter-house or a universal brothel. You judge your own sex and the other by the specimens you have met with in wretched haunts of mercenary profligacy; and, with such a standard in your minds, I marvel not that you remain incorrigible unbelievers in any virtue, but that which is forced, on the prudish hot-bed of ceremonious orthodoxy. I wonder not, that you will not trust the natural soil, watered from the free skies and warmed by the life-bringing sun. How should you? you have never seen it produce but weeds and poisons. Libertines and debauchees! cast my book aside! You will find in it nothing to gratify a licentious curiosity; and, if you read it, you will probably only give me credit for motives and impulses like your own.

And you, prudes and hypocrites! you who strain at a gnat and swallow a camel; you whom Jesus likened to whited sepulchres, which without indeed are beautiful, but within are full of all uncleanness; you who affect to blush if the ancle is incidentally mentioned in conversation, or displayed in crossing a style, but will read indecencies enough, without scruple, in your closets; you who, at dinner, ask to be helped to the bosom of a duck, lest, by mention of the word breast, you call up improper associations; you who have nothing but a head and feet and fingers; you who look demure by daylight, and make appointments only in the dark—you, prudes and hypocrites! I do not address. Even if honest in your prudery, your ideas of right and wrong are too artificial and confused to profit by the present discussion; if dishonest, I desire to have no communication with you.

Reader! if you belong to the class of prudes or of libertines, I pray you, follow my argument no farther. Stop here, and believe that my heresies will not suit you. As a prude, you would find them too honest; as a libertine, too temperate. In the former case, you might call me a very shocking person; in the latter, a quiz or a bore.

But if you be honest, upright, pure-minded; if you be unconscious of unworthy motive or selfish passion; if truth be your ambition, and the welfare of our race your object—then approach with me a subject the most important to man's well-being; and approach it, as I do, in a spirit of dispassionate, disinterested, free enquiry. Approach it, resolving to prove all things, and hold fast that which is good. The discussion is one to which it is every man's and every woman's *duty*, (and ought to be every one's *business*,) to attend.[1] The welfare of the present generation, and—yet far more—of the next, requires it. Common sense sanctions it. And the national motto of my former country, "Honi soit qui mal y pense," [2] may explain the spirit in which it is undertaken, and in which it ought to be received.

Reader! it ought to concern you nothing who or what I am, who now address you. Truth is truth, if it fall from Satan's lips; and error ought to be rejected, though preached by an angel from heaven. Even as an anonymous work, therefore, this treatise ought

1. By no means. The world is not now overpeopled, nor is it likely to be in hundreds of generations, even if the art of raising food should never receive any further improvement. How then is it the *duty* or the *business* of every man and woman to attend to a discussion, the object of which is to repress the increase of population? To me it seems that Robert Dale Owen's time as well as that of any other man, is badly employed in devising means to diminish the number of mouths. Better, far better, it seems to me, it would be, to seek the means of *filling* them, and of increasing their number, and thus to make the great aggregate of human enjoyment as great as possible. Better, far better, it appears to me, it would be, to set about discovering the means of preventing the existence of enormous incomes, derived from the labor of others, such as that of half a million or a million dollars annually, whereby half a million or a million of bushels of wheat for example are or can be annually monopolized by a single person; and the laborers, who produce it, along with their children are made to hunger and perish. It is *this* power of thus monopolizing immense quantities of the results of the annual labor, no matter whether it be thro' rents of lands or houses, thro' interest on money, thro' profits on speculations or thro' inadequate compensations for labor, that fills society with the evils of scarcity and famine. Destroy this, and it will be a long time before Robert Dale Owen, or any other man will have any cause to complain of the number of mouths. So far then as he succeeds in turning public attention from the object of discovering the means of destroying these unequal and enormous incomes thus derived from the labor of others, he effectually serves the cause of oppression, injuring those for whose benefit he affects to write.

2. One of the English kings, Edward III., in the year 1344, picked up from the floor of a ball-room, an embroidered garter belonging to a lady of rank. In returning it to her, he checked the rising smile of his courtiers with the words, "Honi soit que mal y pense!" or, paraphrased in English, "Shame on him who invidiously interprets it!" The sentiment was so greatly approved that it has become the motto of the English national arms. It is one which might be not inaptly nor unfrequently applied in rebuking the mawkish, skin-deep, and intolerant morality of this hypocritical and profligate age.

to obtain a full and candid examination from you. But, that you may not imagine I am ashamed of honestly discussing a subject so useful and important, I have given you my name on the title page.

Upon this distinction of the instinct into its two-fold character, hinges the chief point in the present discussion. It sometimes happens, nay, it happens every day and hour, that mankind obey its impulses, not from any calculation of consequences, but simply from animal impulse. Thus many children that are brought into the world owe their existence, not to deliberate conviction in their parents that their birth was really desirable, but simply to an unreasoning instinct, which men in the mass, have not learnt either to resist or control.

It is a serious question—and surely an exceedingly proper and important one—whether man can obtain, and whether he is benefitted by obtaining, control over this instinct. IS IT DESIRABLE, THAT IT SHOULD NEVER BE GRATIFIED WITHOUT AN INCREASE TO POPULATION? OR, IS IT DESIRABLE, THAT, IN GRATIFYING IT, MAN SHALL BE ABLE TO SAY WHETHER OFFSPRING SHALL BE THE RESULT OR NOT?[3]

3. I say, population ought not to be repressed. It ought to be increased; because society will be the happier; or if not so, at least, the less miserable for it. I repeat, that an increase of population, in any and every country on the globe and under any and every form of government, would be beneficial, even to the great mass of those who now labor and suffer most. This I am aware, is taking the bull by the horns; but this I mean to do, and if I can, drive Robert Dale Owen from his position that it is *now* desirable, in a general point of view, for men to repress the increase of population, by showing, even as society is now, that their evils will be less and their enjoyments greater by adding to their numbers. If I show this, I show of course that all time spent in discussing the means of repressing the production of human beings is misemployed, and I show also, so far as those means may be attended with any practical effects, that they injure the mass of nations, by preventing their situation from being as comfortable as an augmentation of their numbers would make it. I proceed thus.—If tomorrow, for instance, the population of the United States were increased to ten times their number of to-day, is it not a fair presumption that ten times the number of copies of this or any other work would be sold, even at the present price? But if so great an increase would happen in the sale of it, could it not, and would it not most probably be afforded at a reduced price? In this case not only would each purchaser obtain a copy for less money, and the number of purchasers be increased by this reduction, but the vender of the work, if he did not reduce the price too low, would obtain a greater amount as the reward of his genius, labor and enterprise. Prevent,

To answer the questions satisfactorily, it would be necessary to substantiate, that such control may be obtained without the slightest injury to the physical health, or violence to the moral feelings; and also, that it should be obtained without any real sacrifice of enjoyment; or, if that cannot be, with as little as possible.

---

however, by any means whatever, it matters not what, this or a similar augmentation of the population, and you compel each individual purchaser of the work referred to, to pay more for it than he otherwise need; and you prevent the proprietor from receiving as much for his aggregate returns, as he would otherwise command.

Again.—People this country with ten times its present number, and from the mere operation of this increase, men for example, will be carried in our steam-boats from New York to Albany at a cheaper rate than now, and for the obvious reason, if there were no other, that the steam-boats would then much more seldom than they do now, make their trips with fewer passengers than they can accommodate. If any one doubts that such would be the operation, let him ask himself, if steam-boat passage is not uniformly cheaper, under the same circumstances, in thickly peopled sections of our country, than in those of a contrary description?

Once more.—No truth is better established among men than that a division of labor is that by which a community can perform more than can be done in any other manner. Yet it must be obvious to the plainest understanding that the more numerous a community is, the more this principle can be brought into operation. And every where in human society is it found to prevail to a greater or less extent—So that the greater the amount of the annual toil, accomplished by the division and subdivision of labor, the greater will be the abundance of good things to be shared, more or less equally among all.

But I shall be told perhaps that so soon as this augmentation in the number of the people takes place, the price of labor will be so much the less; and that as a consequence, the poor cannot reap the advantage I have supposed. The supposition I made was, of course, predicated on the idea that if we multiplied the number of the rich ten-fold we should do the same for the poor. They would then bear the same proportion to one another in both cases. Now let it be remembered that the rate of wages of the laborer, of whatever kind he may be, depends not upon the absolute number of the people of any nation, but *upon the number of rich, or employers, compared with the number of poor or employed.* Thus, if one fourth be employers or men of wealth—and three fourths be the poor, or employed, the wages of the latter will be less than if *half* were employers and *half* employed. And when *all* shall have wealth so as to be able to be employers—and of course employing only themselves, jointly with others or, singly and on their own materials, then will the rate of wages become the greatest possible—for then will men obtain all that they earn.

But how is Robert Dale Owen's theory to tend to raise the rate of wages, if my reasoning is correct? I cannot discover, unless indeed he means that rich men may have large families say six, eight or ten children, and poor men only one or two.

Thus have I plainly stated the subject. It resolves itself, as my readers may observe, into two distinct heads: first, the *desirability* of such control; and, secondly, its *possibility*.

That chastity which is worth preserving is not the chastity that owes its birth to fear and to ignorance. If to enlighten a woman

---

But this, lately, he has thought it prudent to disavow, and seemingly to say that the poor *may* increase their numbers as fast as do the rich. Yet if they do, but do it no faster, it is certain their wages would not be less; and it is equally certain that they could purchase more of the comforts of life with its avails, when the population of a nation, for example, was one hundred millions, than when it was ten millions. If such be the case, then it is surely an injury done to the laborer to persuade him that the nation ought not to increase in numbers. We arrive thus at the conclusion, if the laborer of all countries is suffering and perishing it is because he is *poor,* and not because his fellows are numerous, except it be in relation to the number of the rich. Their absolute number has nothing to do with the question. It has therefore been a work of futility to invite public attention, to discuss that as a remedy which I think I have shown could not fail to aggravate the disease.

I know indeed I shall be told, if the laborer by the adoption of the advice of our "Moral Physiologist" were to have a family of, say, only one or two children, that, receiving the same wages, he could live more comfortably. But my reply is, that when *all* the laborers or a great majority shall have only one or two children instead of five, six or more; they will soon labor for so much the less. Their own competition among themselves will bring about this result. Robert Dale Owen's remedy would therefore accomplish nothing save that of making things worse. If any one doubts the truth of this, I beg him to tell me, and I particularly desire R. D. Owen to show, why are not the laborers, that is every description of working people of Great Britain, for example, at least two hundred times better off, than they were some 70 or 80 years ago. According to his reasoning they ought certainly to be; for it is a fact that the same population now, by means of scientific power in every *branch* of science, are able to perform at least two hundred times as much as could be performed by them in the middle of the last century. If improvements, in the present state of society, went to the benefit, equally, of all classes, the present population ought to be able to support *two hundred times* as many children, for instance as formerly, and still have as much of enjoyment as they had then. But every one knows that this is by no means the fact. Yet it is precisely the same thing, whether our children remain the same in number to each family as formerly and our power of producing the good things of this life *be augmented;* or the children be diminished in number, the processes of labor remaining *without improvement.* In neither case is there aught of benefit or blessing to the poor man. He is doomed to be chained to the wheel of Sysiphus—and it is some better and honester logic than that of R. D. Owen's, if it is ever to be done, that shall break the chain.

Never in the whole course of my life, in the midst of the most inflated conceptions of himself as a master of the science of political economy, have I met with so egregious a blunderer as R. D. Owen. In strict connection with the subject of this note, it is not amiss perhaps to mention, as another instance, how great a regarding a simple physiological fact will make her a prostitute, she must be especially predisposed to profligacy. But it is a libel on the sex. Few, indeed, there are, who would continue so miserable and degrading a calling, could they but escape from it.[4]

wiseacre may come from the schools of Switzerland as well as from other seminaries to teach a people whom he is perpetually reproaching for their ignorance and want of common sense. This gentleman is the author of a system of education, such that the children bro't up under it, are to support themselves, from a very tender age up to maturity, by their own co-operative labor, without assistance from any one, except it be about five dollars a year from each parent. And as an inducement to poor fathers and mothers to consent to part with their children and place them in these establishments of co-operative labor, he displays before them the advantages which they, the parents as he says, will obtain, in not having their children to support. He forgets that competition, always active, always energetic to bring down everything to the lowest possible price, will bring down the reward of the labor of the working classes to exactly one half, for example, when the family expenses are only one half what they previously were. Let then a system of education be adopted such as I have alluded to—and the speedy result will be, that the rich, or employers will then obtain the poor man's labor for much less money. The children will then be compelled, to use a homely phrase, *to bring themselves up*, and the rich will be as much richer than they are now, as the children shall do more than they do now to defray the expenses of their own maintenance. Such are the just, the generous, the judicious plans of the honest, the intelligent, the educated reformer Owen. Look, laboring men, into his reasonings, and see whether they do not tend to swell the purses of the wealthy at the expense of an augmentation of the labor of the poor. I think they do; and, if it be your opinion, it well becomes you to consider how you give him your political confidence in any shape whatever.

4. *None*, Mr. Owen. I wonder, then, that you are so unwilling to use your talents, so far as they may avail, to bring about such a change in government that the condition of all shall be equal and comfortable and this without postponing it for one, two, or three hundred years. When first you came to this city, and for some time afterwards, you and your coadjutors preached the equality of man, you advocated the cause of the poor; you seemed to identify your own existence with the promotion of their happiness—but when I, as one of these, proposed that you should give me one of your tables, load it with a share of your provisions, give me one of your houses and divide with me and others your acres of land, reducing yourself precisely to our level, and thus beyond all dispute, if you had accepted the proposition, or rather had consented to advocate it *proved* yourself the friend of equality, in a regular, rational and perpetual system extending its blessings thro' all future generations, you turned your heel upon it, and proclaimed to the world in a voice not to be mistaken, your hollow-hearted insincerity. You discovered then, perhaps to your own surprize, and the public discovered it too, that you did not possess one real feeling in favor of equal rights. True, if men could be equal, while you should possess a million of dollars or two or three counties of land—and they possessed nothing—*you were willing:*—and as a matter of excessive liberality on your part you *were willing also*, that they should know—*as much as yourself.* But

For one prostitute that is made by inclination, ten are made by necessity. Reform the laws—equalize the comforts of society, and you need withhold no knowledge from your wives and daughters. It is want, not knowledge, that leads to prostitution.[5]

And now, let my readers pause. Let them review the various arguments I have placed before them. Let them reflect how intimately the instinct of which I treat is connected with the social welfare of society. Let them bear in mind, that just in proportion to its social influence, is it important that we should know how to control and govern it; that, when we obtain such control, we may save ourselves—and, what we ought to prize much more highly, may save our companions and our offspring, from suffering or misery; that, by such knowledge, the young may form virtuous connexions, instead of becoming profligates or ascetics; that, by it, early marriage is deprived of its heaviest consequences, and seduction of its sharpest sting; that, by it, man may be saved from moral ruin, and woman from desolating dishonour; that by it the first pure affections may be soothed and satisfied, instead of being thwarted or destroyed—let them call to mind all this, and then let them say, whether the possession of such control be not a blessing to man.[6]

---

while you were willing to grant this mighty concession, you secretly knew, no doubt, and might have openly declared it to others had you been honestly so disposed, that where all should have been educated equally, the educated poor must still be the slaves and prostitutes of the educated rich! Slavery would still exist, but with this aggravation that an enlightened understanding would make its evils more acutely felt. Look then upon yourself, as I think you may, at least in treachery to equal rights however it be in talents, as the Edmund Burke of America.

Beyond all question there would be no prostitutes among women if their condition was as it ought to be; and I hold it as a consequence from which you cannot escape, that you assist to perpetuate the existence of this wretched description of females, so long as you refrain from doing all in your power forthwith to change the present structure of government, which with-holds from them a competent and equal share of property and which is alone the cause of it.

5. Why not then advocate an equal division of property? I ask again. There would then be no want.

6. At the end of this chapter it may not be amiss to exhibit a few more of the absurdities of Mr. Owen in order that the reader may be aware of them with less trouble of research than otherwise might be necessary.

"To such causes as these, [monopolies, taxes, and commercial rivalry,] and *not to over-population*, at the time being, is the actual distress (felt more or less over the civilized world) to be attributed." p. 28.

Does Mr. Owen then mean to attribute the distress of the Kentucky lady for example, to another cause than that of her having a fine family of little children? If so he ought to teach her, that the use of the *sponge* can do her no good, and that nothing can remove her distress, and the distress of millions like herself but an entire renovation of society; for it is an axiom not now to be questioned that the evil will exist so long as the cause which produces it remains unremoved.

"They, [the foes of reform] *force* it [the population question] upon us," p. 28.

And why talk of having this question *forced* upon you, Mr. Owen, when every where throughout your book you are saying all you can to recommend its importance particularly to the humble in life? Are you so reluctant to do good, that it is necessary to *drive* you to it? This does not argue well in favour of your philanthropy; this does not speak advantageously of your superiority, in point of *independence* over the "celebrated and talented Mill."

Few men complain of their enemies more than does Mr. Owen. But can these enemies force him to be inconsistent? How then came he to say? p. 28,—"If the enemies of reform would but let us alone, we might *safely postpone* to other important practical discussions this population question." Has it really then been of no consequence that the sufferings and miseries, great as he has represented them to be, of the great mass of the poor, should be mitigated, as he pretends it is possible they can be, by his anti-population specifics? Has he been willing that they should still *suffer on*, and that what he calls, in some measure at least, a remedy for their distresses, should be, and may be *safely postponed?*

If so, and if also, these specifics are *really* of any value to any body, it is well indeed that Mr. Owen *is* surrounded with enemies—for they alone it seems, have the power to force him to speak out his benefactions to mankind; otherwise, it appears, they would never possess them. He would be as barren of utility as he would have our women to be of children.

O! for a world of such highly cultivated, talented and *educated* philosophers as Mr. Owen! Every thing no doubt, would then go smoothly on—and let me add if the world do not *now* become convinced thro' the personal exhibition of the example of Mr. Owen himself, of the mighty advantages of education, and *superior* education, too, even *I* shall certainly be disposed to think them a set of boobies quite as incorrigible indeed as he seems to consider them in most of his writings.

But in sober seriousness, does Mr. Owen expect the public to consider a man who pursues such a zig-zag course as being both intelligent and honest? If he does, he will find himself most sadly mistaken. Thomas Paine observed to a friend of mine that truth was like a straight line. The same is true also of honesty. Either then Mr. Owen is not clear sighted as it regards his understanding; or he is a knave. Let him take the alternative that pleases him best. Let his friends do the same; for one or the other of these is all that remains to him and to them out of which to take their choice. And in either case, what a pilot reformer is he? Can a cause prosper that has such an inefficient advocate as regards his understanding; or such a corrupt one as regards his heart? Working men! Working Men! Either error or vice in your system of reform, or in your prominent champions, will only, *can* only lead you to defeat. It is for you to look to it.

Socialism

102. Robert Dale Owen

A common stock into which each producer puts articles of wealth

A number of the trades' union and Working Men's party leaders of the 1820s and 1830s advocated one or another form of socialist society. Although their proposals differed in details, they agreed that the system of private inheritance and profit had to be discarded for one based on cooperative labor. In this passage Owen, son of the famous Scottish humanitarian, urges a federative or "common storehouse" system, which would reward individuals according to their needs. Although the article appeared in the journal of the utopian community at New Harmony, Indiana, it is of interest that in it the younger Owen conceived his proposals not as a blueprint for isolated perfectionist communities but rather as a guide to "the world"—which *"must sooner or later, adopt some system of distribution, that, like the federative system, can bear abundance and prosperity."*

The world, in its progressive movement towards knowledge and happiness, is rapidly approaching a point when commercial competition must cease. Nations are becoming too wealthy and prosperous to be commercial. A system of distribution which requires *scarcity* to support it, becomes worse than useless at a time of plenty. Wealth is already beginning to be, like water, too easy of production to remain an article of commerce.

Water, though one of the most valuable articles of wealth, is so abundant in most countries that it cannot be distributed through the medium of commerce. If any one attempted to sell water, it is evident, *that he could not obtain for it any monied representative* in the market, because every one has already a full supply of it. But because this *commercial* method of distributing a most

From Robert Dale Owen, "Wealth and Misery," *The New Harmony Gazette*, New Harmony, Indiana, November 29, 1826.

valuable article of wealth is impracticable, must mankind, therefore, die of thirst? No; the matter was so glaringly obvious that men could not avoid seeing the possibility and practicability of using water freely, *even though it could neither be bought nor sold.*

One article of wealth then, and a most valuable one too, *cannot* become an article of commerce, *solely because it is so easily obtained.* Hence it is evident, that if the aids of science render it gradually more and more easy to obtain each article of desire, we shall at last arrive at a point when no article of wealth can possibly become an article of commerce. Hence, too, it follows, that science is rendering commerce every day less and less adapted to the gradually advancing state of society; and the gradually increasing means of wealth and comfort.

Now, if we are to merit the character of wisdom or avoid the imputation of improvidence, we must not cling to an antiquated and injurious system of distribution, until necessity shall force us to abandon it. Commerce is beneficial or it is injurious.—I have proved it, as I believe, to be injurious. Am I wrong? let my arguments be examined and disproved. Am I right? let not careless supineness put off the evil day, nor say, "To-morrow will take thought for the things of itself." Indifference cannot avert the coming crisis, no more than she can neutralize any of the other great effects produced by the world's progressive improvement. But prudence may foresee, and wisdom prevent the evils that would be produced on the one hand by a pertinacious adherence to long established though destructive and tottering institutions, and, on the other, by a forced and sudden change to a new and untried system.

We are a prosperous nation. Riches are increasing on our hands. We possess the means, or we are rapidly acquiring them, to produce forty times as much wealth as our ancestors did. But embarked as we are with all this abundant wealth on the ocean of commerce, whither is our course? The very gale of plenty that fills our sails is bearing us along to hidden shoals and engulphing breakers—England's vessel is aground amongst them already. If we would escape her fate, let us put about the helm while we may.

To speak without a metaphor—let us enquire what system of distribution adapted to the present state of science and civilization, may beneficially supersede the distribution of commerce.

It appears that we are wealthy; that, as a nation, we possess abundantly the means of continuing and increasing our wealth; and that the only real difficulty before us in our progress to permanent affluence is removed, so soon as the problem is solved: how to distribute wealth in such a manner, that the surplus produce of one producer may always procure him a just share of the surplus of his neighbors.

Let us see whether we shall derive, in the solution of this great problem, any assistance from considering the effects produced in a large family, acting on the second plan we supposed possible, (namely, the *federative* system)—by a gradual increase of productive power.

This system presupposes a common stock into which each producer puts the articles of wealth he creates, so soon as they are created; and from which he draws articles of necessity and comfort, as he requires them. So long, therefore, as this industrial magazine is kept fully supplied, there *can* be no want or distress among the producers.

Now there might possibly have been some difficulty in obtaining supplies during a period of comparative *adversity;* that is, while production was difficult, and the demand was, therefore, beyond the supply. But in a period of *prosperity,* that is, when the world's powers of production are increasing to forty-fold, at least, what they were formerly, there can be no possible difficulty in supplying most abundantly the family storehouse; seeing that one fortieth part of the labor our ancestors must have expended to obtain this object, will suffice in our days. It appears, then, at first sight, that the *federative* system of distribution is excellently adapted to a family producing all the articles of wealth and abundance.

We have traced the results produced by the introduction of scientific power in aid of a family whose produce was distributed under the commercial system. Let us examine what effects follow this same gradual increase of powers of production under the *federative* system.

The first effect is to over-stock the common storehouses. Well, no one need starve surely on that account: on the contrary, there is an opportunity of increasing the supply of comforts to each producer, if such increase be desired; or to lay up an extra stock in case of the failure of crops and other unforeseen accidents; or to exchange the useless surplus for foreign articles of wealth, if the family desire them. It is true that men cannot use more than a certain quantity of wealth, domestic and foreign, with benefit to themselves, nor accumulate beyond a certain quantity of produce with advantage, or indeed, with any possibility of preserving it from decay: and therefore it must be admitted that without any additional exertion on the part of the family, the increase of mechanical power would at last fairly over-supply their warehouses, so that they know not what to do with so abundant a surplus, as in England at present. And what then? Why, the remedy for this mighty evil is self-evident, and most easy and pleasant of practice, a remedy to which no one probably will object. *Let the family relax its exertions and shorten its hours of labor.* This is the only *natural* result produced by superabundance.

Can such a remedy be applied under the individual commercial system? Evidently not: each man must push on to increase his production, regardless of the consequences to society, or else competition will leave him behind to starve.

Now scientific power *must* continue and must increase; to desire that it should not, would be to wish for a gradual sinking back into ignorance and barbarism. The supply must continue to exceed the demand: to desire that it should not, would be to wish for a relapse into adversity and indigence.

But if productive powers must increase, and the supply must exceed the demand, *then the world must sooner or later, adopt some system of distribution, that, like the federative system, can bear abundance and prosperity.* At present, the greatest misfortune that can befall a commercial nation, is to attain to wealth and plenty.

The United States are rapidly approaching to both. "And yet at the present moment," it will be said, "we are truly prosperous. Our condition resembles not that of Britain: no one need starve here who desires to be industrious. Our present situation, therefore, is proof of the benefits *we* derive from commerce."

True: but, is it possible that our present resources should remain stationary? No, nor do we desire it: they will increase, and fortunately so. What then? We shall soon rival Great Britain in all her productions. And then?—Then we shall be able to supply all our own wants, and become perfectly independent, if we choose to be so, of all foreign supplies.—And afterwards?—Afterwards we may proceed to supply other nations, and spread the products of our country over all the civilized world. What then?—Must we stop here? Is there no analogy to light our steps further into futurity? There is: Britain has passed on before us, and already obtained what we anticipate. She was over-supplied herself and all her neighbors, and sent the produce of her industry to the farthest countries on the globe. And what then? She has become a national Tantalus, tormented by the display of abundance she may not use, and expiring beside streams of plenty she cannot enjoy.

If a fate like this be our object, let us proceed in our present course. We have all the advantages Great Britain ever had, and many more too: we have a liberal government, light taxes, security at home, increasing markets abroad—every thing in our favor; and we shall soon attain this envied situation—then to reflect that we have been toiling in vain—and to discover that the same commerce which *once* raised us from indigence and adversity, *now* ruins us in prosperity and amidst abundance.

Associationism

103. Albert Brisbane

Political reforms operate merely on the surface of society

A variety of "utopian socialist" theories were promulgated by European thinkers in the second quarter of the nineteenth century, against the backdrop of a crude industrialism that threatened to widen the gulf between the classes, despite its seeming potential of achieving abundance for all. One of the most influential of these doctrines was put forward by the Frenchman Charles Fourier, calling for the establishment of separate "phalanxes" in the countryside. In the aftermath of the panics of 1837 and 1839, as unemployment and social distress spread over the United States, Fourier's ideas took root among an increasing number of Americans, particularly with a circle of cultivated men in the Northeast. Albert Brisbane, friend to Horace Greeley, James Russell Lowell, and John Greenleaf Whittier, became the foremost disciple of Fourier and the chief theorist of the "Associationist" movement in the United States.

Association

Association is the social destiny of Man—is the true and natural system of Society, predestined for him by the Creator, and will, when established upon earth, secure to him that happiness for which he has so long sought in vain, and the elements of which exist in and around him—in the beautiful creations of material Nature, and in the noble faculties and sentiments with which God has endowed him.

This true and natural System of Society cannot be established at once; it must be a gradual work, and before it can become universal, the truth and goodness of its Principles must be demonstrated practically and upon a small scale. For that reason a commencement must be made with a single Association, which will show its immense advantages—show the happiness and

From Albert Brisbane, *A Concise Exposition of the Doctrine of Association or Plan for a Re-organization of Society* (New York: J. S. Redfield, 1844), 3–6.

prosperity which it will secure to man, and lead to a general adoption.

We shall explain the laws and mechanism of this single Association, which is the germ or primary element of the System of Society which we advocate, as the village or township is the germ or primary element of the present System of Society. A county, as we know, is composed of townships, a state of counties, and the United States of states; thus, the United States is but a repetition of townships. Now, if the township be falsely organized—that is, if the families composing it, live according to a false system; if there be conflicts of interests, opposition, discord, waste and poverty among them, then the whole body politic, composed of these falsely organized townships, will contain all their defects, and discord, injustice, poverty, and the numerous evils which they engender, will exist universally. But if we can organize the townships rightly, so that unity of interests, concert of action, vast economies and general riches will be attained, then, in spreading these rightly organized townships, and rendering them general, a Social Order will be gradually established, in which peace, prosperity and happiness will be secured to all.

The great and primary object which we have in view is, consequently, *to effect the establishment of one Association*, which will exhibit practically the great economies, the riches, the order and unity of the system, and serve as a model for, and lead to the founding of others.

We shall explain the laws and mechanism of this one Association, and we will remark that in so doing, we shall explain the whole System of Society which we seek to establish, the same as in explaining the physiological laws of one Individual, we explain those of the whole Human Race.

The system of Association which we propose to the world, is not the plan or scheme of an individual; it is not the invention of mere human reason, like so many political systems which have been established, from the Republic of Lycurgus down to our modern Democracies. It is deduced from and based upon universal Principles, and is the application to the social relations of Mankind of the laws of Order and Unity, which govern the Universe.

Fourier discovered the laws of UNIVERSAL UNITY, or the laws which govern Creation in its five grand Spheres or Movements, which are: 1st, the MATERIAL MOVEMENT, or the laws which govern the movements of the heavenly bodies, or universal Matter; 2d, the AROMAL, or the laws which regulate the distribution and influences of the imponderable fluids on the kingdoms of Creation—animal, vegetable and mineral; 3d, the ORGANIC, or the laws according to which God distributes forms, properties, colors, flavors, etc. to all created things; 4th, the INSTINCTUAL, or the laws according to which God distributes instincts and passions; and lastly, the SOCIAL, or the laws which govern the succession and mechanisms of the societies of intelligent Beings throughout the Universe.

From a knowledge of these laws of Universal Unity, Fourier deduced the true and natural system of society, destined for Man, and which, when realized in practice, will produce social Order and Harmony upon the globe—a reflex of the Harmony which reigns in the Universe. Throughout his works, he declares that he gives no system or plan of his own; he claims the merit only of having discovered the system of Nature, which will secure to Mankind as many blessings as the false social Institutions, set up by human reason, have entailed upon them miseries and misfortunes.

"The Social Order," says the LONDON PHALANX, (a Magazine devoted to the cause of Association,) "deduced from the Science of Universal Unity, is based on the three primary Unities which compose the

UNIVERSAL UNITY
Unity of Man with God
in true Religion
Unity of Man with Man
in true Society
Unity of Man with Nature
in creative Art
and Industry

"In practice, it resolves itself into the Moral, the Artistic, and the Scientific spheres of action.

"In *Morals*, friendly unity, conjugal unity, family unity, and hierarchal unity.

"In *Art*, scenic beauty, musical harmony, nutritive excellence, fragrant purity, and comfortable homes.

"In *Science*, critical understanding and well-founded hope, inventive energy and genuine faith, variety of information, liberty of conscience, toleration of opinion, and true charity in action.

"This is what we wish to realize in Unitary Combination; and both Faith and Science say, 'It can be done; and shall! and soon!' "

Before concluding these general remarks, let us particularly request the reader not to confound the system of Association, discovered by Fourier, with the trials made by the Shakers, Rappites and others, nor with the system devised by Mr. Owen. The views of the latter have excited in the public mind the strongest prepossessions against the magnificent problem of Association, and raised up most serious obstacles to its impartial examination. The errors of individuals, however, should be carefully separated from so grand and important a subject, and to condemn Association because Mr. Owen has advocated a community of property or attacked religion, shows a want of impartiality and discrimination which no reflecting mind, we hope, will be guilty of.

NECESSITY OF A SOCIAL REFORM

When new views and principles are put forth, they invariably meet with the opposition and condemnation of the great majority of men, no matter how good or true they may be, or how important the results which they promise to realize. Against this procedure we protest, and, in behalf of suffering Humanity, we ask that preconceived notions and prejudices as well as hasty criticism be for a time laid aside, and an impartial and conscientious investigation of the system, which we advocate, be entered into.

If we look around us, we see numerous Parties, laboring isolatedly to carry out various reforms—political, administrative, currency, abolition, temperance, moral, &c. &c.—which proves,

First, the depth and extent of the evil that preys upon Society, and *Second*, the necessity of a fundamental Reform, which will attack that evil at its root and eradicate it effectually, instead of lopping off a few branches. If the plan of such a reform has really been discovered, how worthy of the candid examination of every being, whose Soul burns with a desire to see poverty and misery banished from the earth, and who feels a sacred pride for the happiness and elevation of his Race!

To meet and disarm fears and suspicions which may arise in the conservative Mind, we will hasten to state that the reform we contemplate, although fundamental in its character, is not destructive, but constructive; it will not tear down, but build up; it will respect what is true and good in Society, and will change quietly and by substitution, what is false and defective; it will violate no rights, injure no class; it will not impoverish the Rich to enrich slightly the Poor; it will not change the victims of poverty and misery, but will improve and elevate the condition of all, without taking from any. It can moreover be tried on a small scale, and it will only spread, when practice has shown its superiority over the present system. Unlike political reforms, which, to effect the smallest change of policy, agitate and often convulse a whole country, and array one half of the People against the other half, it will not affect a space as large as a township and but a few hundred persons, and will not extend beyond these narrow limits unless its advantages—*practically demonstrated*—excite a strong and general approbation in its favor.

To show the necessity of a Social Reform, we will glance at the misery which exists upon earth; its extent, depth, and intensity prove that political and other partial reforms can effect but little permanent good, and that recourse must be had to new and thorough measures.

HUMAN MISERY

If we look abroad over the earth and examine the condition of the Human Race upon it, what do we see? A spectacle at which the soul shudders. A large majority of our fellow-creatures are slaves, serfs or poor hired laborers, toiling from fear of the lash or fear of want to obtain a miserable subsistence, or to produce the means of supporting a favored few in luxury and idle ease. Discords and hatreds are rife among them, and the darkest selfishness benumbs their hearts and renders them indifferent to each other's misery. There are millions upon millions of beings, who are now suffering every variety of physical wretchedness and moral wo; there are hearts that are torn with care and anxiety—bodies that are worn out with overburthening toil; there are multitudes of miserable wretches immured in gloomy prisons and dungeons, expiating by suffering and ignominy, crimes into which they were plunged by poverty, ignorance and other circumstances over which they had no control—far less culpable in many cases than the false Society which exposed them to become outcasts and criminals; there are other multitudes of beings buried in dismal and suffocating mines, toiling in the bowels of the earth with the dim lamp, the pick-axe and the wheelbarrow for their only companions; there are members of the human family, who, at this moment, are mounting the bloody scaffold, where the soul, amidst awful horror and despair, is to be torn by violence asunder from the body, and launched into an unknown future. All these varied woes and miseries exist, and there are *living, feeling Souls that must undergo them!*

The affections and sympathies of the heart are also outraged and violated; there are parents who see their offspring exposed to privations which they cannot alleviate, or led astray by the temptations, vices and crimes of a false Society, and ingulfed in ruin. There are broken friendships, disappointed loves, thwarted ambitions, and other mental sufferings which tongue cannot tell and language cannot depict.

The surface of the Earth is in as miserable a condition as the Race upon it. Vast deserts and marshes, which generate pestilential winds and miasmatic exhalations—the source of the most frightful diseases, such as the plague, the cholera, the yellow fever, &c., and wild forests and plains, inhabited by noxious reptiles, and savage beasts cover at least three-fourths of it. The portion which has been brought under cultivation is but miserably cultivated, and parts are devoted to the worst of purposes; here we see regions exhausted in the production of noxious plants, like the poppy and tobacco, which are grown to furnish mental vacuity and idleness with the means of a momentary occupation and excitement: there districts planted with grain—not to sustain life—but to be converted into a poisonous liquid, which may afford to degraded masses a brutal exhilaration with its attendants, folly, disease and death. Besides, whole regions have been devastated by fire and sword, and remain in a neglected state—testaments of the folly and madness of nations.

Such is the spectacle which a general view of the condition of the Earth and the Race upon it, presents! Does it not call for some great Reforms?

It will be declared perhaps that our remarks are exaggerated, but it is not so; they are in fact far below the truth. If the extent and depth of human Misery are not felt and heeded, it is because men are so occupied with their own little projects and interests that they cannot lend a thought to the higher concerns and interests of Humanity, and because in our societies of selfish Individualism and narrow Nationality, no universal and generous sympathies for Mankind, no sentiment for their collective welfare —a sentiment which Christ so strongly inculcated—are aroused and cherished in their hearts. . . . If we had space to enter fully into a description of the condition of European populations, we could present statistical facts that would reveal a depth and intensity of misery that is appalling to contemplate.

. . . Political reforms operate merely on the surface of society; they cannot go to the root of social Evil, and eradicate those deeply seated Miseries, which result from repugnant and ill-requited labor, from an unjust distribution of profits, from false and anarchical competition in trade and industry, and from social institutions, which violate and outrage in every way human nature.

Let Politicians be called upon to say whether their wisest measures, their plans the best matured, would, if fully and faithfully carried out, remedy a tithe of the manifold and complicated Evils which exist, and which blight the existence of so many of our fellow-creatures.

104. The Harbinger

Why are you Associationists so busy with the outward

In this passage the editors of *The Harbinger*, the journal published by George Ripley, Brisbane, and diverse friends of Ralph Waldo Emerson and Henry David Thoreau, attempted to deal with the criticisms of Associationism raised by religious and moralistic critics. To the latter, society could not be made over until men had first become good. Social justice, they held, awaited the spiritual regeneration of individuals. Socialists of a materialistic persuasion in effect held that men as they were could create the good society, in the process changing themselves for the better. The Associationists, as the following selection indicates, took a halfway position.

The ins and the outs

S. Why are you Associationists so busy always and only with the outward. You seem to be a humane and generous set of people, but you are always scratching on the surface. What can you accomplish in this way? Have the central life right, and all will be right. Make men to *be* good, they will then *do* good.

A. I bathe my whole body every morning, because I find that when the skin is in healthy action, all the organs are aided in the vigorous discharge of their functions. Industry and enjoyment are the skin, so to speak, of Society. In them all social and spiritual affections ultimate. And if you will pardon the allusion, Society just now seems suffering from cutaneous disease.

S. Yes! But you think outward arrangements come first in order, and are all important. Now external order must follow and be derived from internal order. And the former is important only as related to the latter.

A. Most true. But let me answer by another illustration. I gathered a ripe apple just now, beautiful to the eye, and savory to the taste and smell. It derived its juice of course, from the central

From *The Harbinger*, July 19, 1845, p. 81.

vessels entering from the tree; but meanwhile it had been working up this juice with sunlight and warmth by marvellous processes of its own. And again this fruit was only a seed vessel. And yet the very sweetness of the juices, as made over again in that ripe fruit, had aided the full development of the virtues of the seed. More than that, the fruit had a virtue and beauty for itself. So I say, *Society is a seed vessel of souls;* its life is from God's spirit; but under the sun of Divine Providence in nature it moulds this love into sweet and beautiful forms; and according to the perfection of the social relations, will be the fitness of the souls inclosed in it to be planted in heaven. And I doubt not also, that a perfect Society is delightful to God for its own worth, as ripe fruit is to us.

S. Very well: But you do not yet answer my objections. You still make the outward precede the inward, reversing God's law of progress.

A. Pardon another illustration. The Spiritual life of a man doubtless precedes the animal life; and the animal life is but accessory to the spiritual life. Yet do but observe the process of Nature. Slowly from a minute germ developes the embryo, the child, till it is born; slowly it is nourished and grows; and proportionately to its mature symmetric vigor unfold the affections and faculties. Derange the circulations, paralyze the limbs, obstruct in any way or degree the functions, and just so far you check the growth of the Spirit. The social relations of the Race, of a Nation, of a Community are the Body, of which the Faith and Character are the Spirit. Slowly with every improvement in customs, inventions, and arts, legislation unfolds to consciousness the idea and love of a People until suddenly it is born as a Nation. It grows up to maturity. And just in the degree in which social order in all interests of life expresses the intrinsic Spirit of that People, does that spirit itself unfold.

S. Still, according to your own admission, the Love and Idea of a Nation must precede the industry and laws of that People, and the Spirit is the cause and condition of the growth of the body.

A. Unquestionably! Did you suppose, that we Associationists are so stupid as to expect an *effect* without a *cause*, an *ex*-istence without a *sub*-stance. Your oversight is Love. You on your side do not perceive that the *mode of the Spirit's development is by expressing itself outwardly;* and that just in the degree of the fulness of that outward expression does the Spirit gain *experience*, or *find itself out*, and learn to confirm its own principles if good, or reform them if bad, and so grow. The Spirit cannot grow alone. It grows by Re-Action.

S. Yet you seem very mechanical in your processes of groups and series, &c.

A. Very mechanical is the growth of a tree branching into boughs, with angular points, and the leaves raying off from their stems, and the fibres of the wood and the arrangement of the sap-vessels. Very mechanical, the arrangement of the bones of the head and trunk and limbs of a man, of the overlaying muscles and the permeating blood-vessels. How very like a machine is a wax automaton; is not man's body a yet more perfect machine?

S. Ah! ha! my friend. You have caught yourself. The difference between the wax automaton and the man is, that one is a mere putting together of dead matter, the other is the growth of living matter. One is mechanism, the other organization. The difference between them is *Life.* How full of untold wonders is the living body, which no Mannikin can represent.

A. And ah! ha! again my friend. I answer *Society is always living*, and you cannot get it to *seem* dead even, much less to *keep* dead, in order to try mechanical experiments with it. Its life is the Love of God in Man, is Humanity. And the question between two forms of Society is only this, will you, like the Indians, make it flat headed, or like the Chinese, make it club-footed by compression, or let it grow in symmetry? Depend upon it, brother, justice, and charity, and self-love even, in all their varied forms are not cog-wheels and gearing, but living Spirit. And there are infinite wonders even in the most deformed Societies: how infinite in a divinely formed Society.

105. Ohio and Illinois Phalanxes

Thriving phalanxes in the western states

The following selections by George Sampson, secretary of the Clermont, Ohio Phalanx, and the secretary of the Integral Phalanx, Illinois, are perhaps longer on glowing descriptions of future prospects than on accurate descriptions of past performance. Yet embedded in the optimistic, sentimental, romantic rhetoric so typical of the era's reform utterances are accounts of the concrete problems faced by Associationists and the measures they took in dealing with them.

To the friends of Association

The members of the Clermont (Ohio) Phalanx have the satisfaction of announcing that they have just paid off this year's instalment due for their Domain, amounting to four thousand five hundred and five dollars, and have also advanced nearly one thousand dollars on their next year's payment. With increased zeal and confidence we now look forward to certain success. To accomplish this, it is desirable that we have further accessions of labor, skill and capital. We therefore invite the friends of industrial Association, (to whom it is not convenient to become Resident Members), to subscribe for Stock, the shares of which are $25.00 each. Mechanics and Manufacturers, as well as Framers, are likewise wanted on the Domain as Resident Members.

To become a Resident Member, it is necessary that the applicant should subscribe and pay for as large an amount of stock as convenient, and the amount should be proportioned to the number of the applicant's family. Persons should direct their applications (post paid) to the Secretary, stating,

1. How many shares of stock they are willing to subscribe and pay for, either in cash or such other property at a fair cash valuation, as may prove available to the Association.
2. Their age, occupation, and general health.

From *The Harbinger*, June 16, 1845, p. 16, December 6, 1845, pp. 406–408.

3. The number, age, &c., of their family, (if they have any).
4. At what time they wish to come upon the Domain.

If the Council like the terms offered, they will admit them conditionally, say from four to six months; if at the expiration of that time the parties are mutually agreed, the applicant subscribes to the constitution, and is admitted to all the privileges of full membership; if not agreed, the applicant retires, he holding, as a Non-Resident Member, the stock subscribed and paid for, unless in debt to the Phalanx.

We will add here that our Domain is situated in Clermont county, on the Ohio River, about forty miles above Cincinnati. The situation is beautiful and healthy, entirely free from fever and ague, or any endemic diseases. The soil is rich, a part of it bottom land, cleared and sowed with crops of wheat, oats, corn, potatoes, hemp, vegetable gardens, &c. We have also a fine orchard coming on, comprising 1,000 fruit trees, presented by A. H. Ernst, of Cincinnati. There is also on the Domain a moderate stock of cattle, hogs, sheep and teams, with agricultural implements; a steam saw, and grist mill, is in operation; also, shoe, brush, tin, and tailor's shops. We wish to start, also, as soon as possible, a blacksmith's, cooper's, and wagon maker's shops, and to organize as many other kinds of manufactures as can be prosecuted to advantage, and to diversify labor as much as possible. A perfectly equitable system of compensation for labor is established, by which every man is graded according to his skill or tact, and every hour's labor is passed to his credit.

We last season made a dividend on our stock, of seven per cent, for seven months, being at the rate of twelve per cent per annum. There is reason to think the dividend will not be much less for some years, the amount paid to capital being one-fourth of the product.

Persons wishing to join the Association, are requested to visit us personally, if convenient; or to write to the subscriber, post paid, at the Cincinnati Post Office, giving full replies to the queries proposed above, in regard to the qualifications for membership.

Geo. Sampson, Sec'y.

Clermont Phalanx, May 12, 1845.

ASSOCIATION

This movement for the reorganization of society according to the principles discovered and proposed by CHARLES FOURIER, appears to be on the increase. An association of citizens of Ohio, calling themselves *"The Integral Phalanx"* have recently purchased the valuable property of Mr. Abner Enoch, near Middletown, Butler County, in this State [Ohio], known by the name of Manchester Mills, twenty-three miles north of Cincinnati, on the Miami Canal. This property embraces about 900 acres of the most fertile land in Ohio, or perhaps in the world; 600 acres of which lies in one body, and is now in the highest state of cultivation, according to the usual mode of farming; 300 acres in wood and timber land. There are now in operation on the place a large flouring mill, saw mill, lath factory and shingle cutter, propelled by water power, which is abundantly sufficient to propel every necessary machinery that the company may choose to put in operation. The property is estimated to be worth $75,000, but was sold to the Phalanx for $45,000. As Mr. Enoch is himself an Associationist, and a devoted friend of the cause, the terms of sale were made still more favorable to the Phalanx, by the subscription, on the part of Mr. Enoch, of $25,000 of purchase money, as capital stock of the Phalanx. Entire possession of the Domain is to be given to the Phalanx, as soon as existing contracts of the proprietor are completed.

Arrangements are already made for the vigorous prosecution of the plans of the Phalanx. A press is to be established on the Domain, devoted to the science of Industrial Association generally, and the interests of the Integral Phalanx particularly. Competent agents are appointed to lecture on the science and receive subscriptions of stock and membership; and it is contemplated to erect, as soon as possible, one wing of a unitary edifice, large enough to accommodate sixty-four families, more than one-half of which number are already in the Association. . . .

ASSOCIATION IN ILLINOIS

HOME OF THE INTEGRAL PHALANX

Sangamon Co., Ill., Oct. 20th

To the Editor of the N. Y. Tribune.

We wish to apprise the friends of Association that the INTEGRAL PHALANX, having for the space of one year, wandered like Noah's dove, finding no resting place for the sole of its foot, has at length found a habitation. A Union was formed on the 16th October inst., between it and the Sangamon Association; or rather the Sangamon Association was merged into the Integral Phalanx; its members having abandoned its name and constitution and become members of the Integral Phalanx by placing their signatures to its pledges and rules; the Phalanx adopting their Domain as its Home. We were defeated, and we now believe very fortunately for us, in securing a location in Ohio. We have, during the time of our wanderings, gained some experience, which we could not otherwise have gained, and without which we were not prepared to settle down upon a location. Our members have been tried. We now know what kind of stuff they are made of. Those who have abandoned us in consequence of our difficulties, were "with us but not of us," and would have been a hindrance to our efforts. They, who are continually hankering after "the fleshpots of Egypt," and are ready to abandon the cause upon the first appearance of difficulties, had better stay out of Association. If they *will* embark in the cause, every Association should pray for difficulties sufficient to drive them out. We need not only clear heads, but also true hearts. We are by no means sorry for the difficulties which we have encountered and all we fear is that we have not yet had sufficient difficulties to try our souls, and show the principles by which we are actuated.

We have now a home, embracing 508 acres of as good land as can be found within the limits of "Uncle Sam's" dominions, fourteen miles Southwest from Springfield, the Capital of the State [of Illinois], and in what is considered the best county and wealthiest portion of the State. Our Domain can be extended to any distance, embracing three miles square, at an average of from five to seven dollars per acre, as we wish to make additions. We have, however, at present, sufficient land for our purposes. It consists of high rolling prairie and woodlands adjoining, which cannot be excelled in the State for beauty of scenery and richness of soil, covered with a luxuriant growth of timber, of almost every description,—Oak, Hickory, Sugar-Maple, Walnut, &c. &c. The land is well watered, lying upon Lick Creek, with springs in abundance, and excellent well-water at the depth of twenty feet. The land under proper cultivation, will produce one hundred bushels of corn to the acre, and every thing else in proportion. There are five or six comfortable buildings upon the property, and a temporary frame building, commenced by the Sangamon Association, intended, when finished, to be 360 feet by 24 feet, (124 feet of it to be two stories high) is now being erected for the accommodation of families.

The whole Domain is, in every particular, admirably adapted to the industrial development of a Phalanx. The railroad connecting Springfield with the Illinois river runs within two miles of the Domain. There is a steam saw and flouring mill within a few yards of our present East boundary, which we can secure on fair terms and shall purchase, as we will need it immediately.

But we will not occupy more time with a description, as those who feel sufficiently interested, will visit us and examine for themselves. . . .

Objections have been made to "Pledge 2," in which the members pledge themselves to remain three and one half years in order to test the system. It was supposed that those who thus pledged themselves would remain until the system was fairly tested; but we attempt to hold no one who is disposed to violate his pledge; and every dissatisfied member has had and ever shall have the privilege of withdrawing from us, as by remaining he would only be a dead weight upon our efforts. Conscious that our position so far is safe, and that by using the necessary precaution and energy we will gradually move forward until we have realized all the blessings of health, individual liberty and permanent happiness, proceeding from combined action as their pivot; we persuade no one either to remain with us or join us, unless he can do so in perfect accordance with his own feelings and wishes: but we are at the same time ready to extend the right hand of fellowship to all those who by a union with us, can think they are doing justice to themselves and advancing the great work of Man's Social Regeneration. We want those who have a clear perception of the dire curses of Civilization and who are animated by a true love for Associative principles. We do not believe that men associated together and actuated by no other motive than a love for money can ever carry out the principles or realize the blessings of Association.

With regard to religious sentiments our Rules guarantee perfect freedom in opinion and action. We want those who are willing to "do unto others as they would have others do unto them" but we wish them at the same time to be free from partisan feeling and sectarian prejudice. If they are not, they had better remain in a state of society better suited and more congenial to their feelings and principles until they learn that "sectarianism" is not religion.

We are ready at all times to give information of our situation and progress, and we pledge ourselves to give a *true* and correct statement of the actual situation of the Phalanx. We pledge ourselves that there shall not be found a variance between our written and published statements and the statements appearing upon our records. Those of our members now upon the ground are composed principally of the former members of the Sangamon Association. We expect a number of our members from Ohio this Fall, and many more of them in the Spring. We have applications for information and membership from different directions, and expect large accession in numbers and capital during the coming year. We can extend our domain to suit our own convenience, as, in this land of prairies and pure atmosphere, we are not hemmed in by Civilization to the same extent that exists in other States. We have elbow-room, and there is no danger of trampling upon each others' toes and then fighting about it.

The citizens of this State are well prepared for Association. They are, to a great extent, free from the prejudices and bigotry which pervade every nook and corner of the older States. There is here a feeling of liberality, a spirit of inquiry, before which spurious Civilization cannot long make headway. We say to all friends of Association, come West; to the land of 'suckers' and liberal opinions. But we say, at the same time, don't come until you are convinced it is for your interest and the interest of the cause of Association that you should come. If you are not yet tired of paying onerous interests and rents and thus expending all your energies to afford food for the horse leech appetites of the land-sharks of Civilization; for the sake of your own satisfaction, remain and pay interest and rents until you are tired of it. Then come, and if we don't suit you, form Phalanxes under rules to suit yourselves. If you can go into an organism of Groups and Series in twenty-four hours, you can do so here as quick as any other place, and if you do progress thus rapidly and succeed, we will not only extend to you our best wishes, but will also acknowledge that you are not only ahead of us in a knowledge of the Science of Association, but that you are also ahead of Nature herself in her most minute and in her vastest operations. But seriously, if you have had difficulties which have operated against you, we ask you, for the sake of the great cause in which we are all laboring, to search for the cause of these difficulties, and, if they are found to originate in an improper organization, or in attempting to organize too hastily, we ask you to examine, correct and extend the benefit of your experience to others. We have not yet made our experiment, and will at all times be thankful for the experience of others, and will try to profit by it. We do not claim that our Rules are perfect, but we wish to make them so; being firmly convinced that the Science taught by Fourier will ultimately lead us into true Association, if we follow it as a science, and that we must have some correct rules of progress to govern us during the transition period from Civilization to Association. We would urge all the friends of Association to exert themselves with unwearied and unwavering energy in the great cause. Whatever feeling of indifference may exist, whatever opposition they may meet with from ignorance, bigotry, and scoffs and sneers of the "would be witty," the great principles of Combined Action, Attractive Industry, the grand social law that governs universal movement, are silently and gradually gaining ground and sooner or later must and will be crowned with universal and triumphant success. The night is passed, and, although darkness still prevails, the dawn is breaking.

The Ploughshare and Pruninghook will be continued from its second number and published from the Home of the Integral Phalanx in a few weeks, as soon as a press can be procured.

The Secretary of the Integral Phalanx

Index